A PRACTICAL GUIDE TO FINANCIAL SERVICES

Financial services are an ever increasing part of the infrastructure of everyday life. From banking to credit, insurance to investment and mortgages to advice, we all consume financial services, and many millions globally work in the sector. Moreover, the way we consume them is changing with the growing dominance of fintech and Big Data. Yet, the part of financial services that we engage with as consumers is just the tip of a vast network of markets, institutions and regulators – and fraudsters too.

Many books about financial services are designed to serve corporate finance education, focusing on capital structures, maximising shareholder value, regulatory compliance and other business-oriented topics. *A Practical Guide to Financial Services: Knowledge, Opportunities and Inclusion* is different: it swings the perspective towards the end-user, the customer, the essential but often overlooked participant without whom retail financial services markets would not exist. While still introducing all the key areas of financial services, it explores how the sector serves or sometimes fails to serve consumers, why consumers need protection in some areas and what form that protection takes, and how consumers can best navigate the risks and uncertainties that are inherent in financial products and services.

For consumers, a greater understanding of how the financial system works is a prerequisite of ensuring that the system works for their benefit. For students of financial services – those aspiring to or those already working in the sector – understanding the consumer perspective is an essential part of becoming an effective, holistically informed and ethical member of the financial services community. *A Practical Guide to Financial Services: Knowledge, Opportunities and Inclusion* will equip you for both these roles.

The editors and authors of *A Practical Guide to Financial Services: Knowledge, Opportunities and Inclusion* combine a wealth of financial services, educational and consumer-oriented practitioner experience.

Lien Luu is an associate professor in finance, Coventry Business School, Coventry University, UK.

Jonquil Lowe is a senior lecturer in economics and personal finance at the Open University, UK.

Patrick John Ring is a reader in financial services in the Glasgow School for Business and Society at Glasgow Caledonian University, UK.

Amandeep Sahota is a lecturer in finance at Coventry Business School, Coventry University, UK.

A PRACTICAL GUIDE TO FINANCIAL SERVICES

Knowledge, Opportunities and Inclusion

Edited by Lien Luu, Jonquil Lowe,
Patrick John Ring and Amandeep Sahota

Routledge
Taylor & Francis Group

LONDON AND NEW YORK

Cover image: Nikada/Getty Images

First published 2022
by Routledge
4 Park Square, Milton Park, Abingdon, Oxon OX14 4RN

and by Routledge
605 Third Avenue, New York, NY 10158

Routledge is an imprint of the Taylor & Francis Group, an informa business

© 2022 selection and editorial matter, Lien Luu, Jonquil Lowe, Patrick John Ring and Amandeep Sahota; individual chapters, the contributors

The right of Lien Luu, Jonquil Lowe, Patrick John Ring and Amandeep Sahota to be identified as the authors of the editorial material, and of the authors for their individual chapters, has been asserted in accordance with sections 77 and 78 of the Copyright, Designs and Patents Act 1988.

All rights reserved. No part of this book may be reprinted or reproduced or utilised in any form or by any electronic, mechanical, or other means, now known or hereafter invented, including photocopying and recording, or in any information storage or retrieval system, without permission in writing from the publishers.

Trademark notice: Product or corporate names may be trademarks or registered trademarks, and are used only for identification and explanation without intent to infringe.

British Library Cataloguing-in-Publication Data
A catalogue record for this book is available from the British Library

Library of Congress Cataloging-in-Publication Data
Names: Luu, Liên, 1967– editor. | Lowe, Jonquil, editor. |
Ring, Patrick, editor.
Title: A practical guide to financial services : knowledge, opportunities and inclusion / edited by Lien Luu, Jonquil Lowe, Patrick Ring and Amandeep Sahota.
Description: 1 Edition. | New York, NY: Routledge, 2022. |
Includes bibliographical references and index.
Identifiers: LCCN 2021033718 (print) | LCCN 2021033719 (ebook) |
ISBN 9781032130996 (paperback) | ISBN 9781032131016 (hardback) |
ISBN 9781003227663 (ebook)
Subjects: LCSH: Financial services industry. | Financial services industry—Great Britain. | Financial services industry—Law and legislation. | Financial services industry—Technological innovations. |
Financial institutions, International—Law and legislation.
Classification: LCC HG173 .P73 2022 (print) | LCC HG173 (ebook) |
DDC 332.1—dc23
LC record available at https://lccn.loc.gov/2021033718
LC ebook record available at https://lccn.loc.gov/2021033719

ISBN: 978-1-032-13101-6 (hbk)
ISBN: 978-1-032-13099-6 (pbk)
ISBN: 978-1-003-22766-3 (ebk)

DOI: 10.4324/9781003227663

Typeset in Bembo
by codeMantra

Access the Support Material: www.routledge.com/9781032130996

CONTENTS

ABOUT THE AUTHORS

Dr. Gbenga Adamolekun is a lecturer in finance at Edinburgh Napier University (previously at Coventry University). He is a member of the Chartered Institute for Securities and Investment (CISI). His research interest lies in the intersection of fintech and corporate outcomes. Other areas of interest are pension funds, corporate finance and behavioural finance.

Dr. Tinashe C. Bvirindi is currently a lecturer in finance at Coventry University with more than 6 years of experience in the banking and financial services industry. He earned his PhD in finance from The University of Manchester and is a fully certified FRM (financial risk manager) and a member of the Chartered Institute for Securities and Investment. His Ph.D. examines the impact of unconventional monetary policy on UK corporates, and his research interest covers a broad range of areas in banking including macro-finance, financial stability, macroprudential policy, corporate finance, monetary policy, financial inclusion and SME financing.

Dr. Viet Le is currently teaching finance at Coventry University. Viet has been teaching and researching a wide range of finance areas including fintech, corporate finance and investment. Prior to Coventry University, he was teaching at Newcastle University (London) and Middlesex University.

Jonquil Lowe, B.SC. (Econ), M.Sc. (Social Research Methods), SFHEA, ACSI, is a senior lecturer in economics and personal finance at The Open University. She has a background as an investment analyst and subsequently head of money research at the consumer organisation, 'Which?', and now combines being an academic with running her own personal finance consultancy. She has worked extensively with regulators, consumer organisations and financial firms to promote wider access to and understanding of financial services, written numerous books and specialises particularly in the areas of retirement provision, investment, taxation and financial capability. She serves as an independent consumer representative with the Finance and Leasing Association and the Open Banking Implementation Entity Consumer Forum.

Dr Lien Luu is an associate professor in finance at Coventry University, where she enjoys teaching and researching about financial planning, retirement planning, personal finance and investments. She has a Ph.D. in history and taught history for 10 years at university before changing her career to become a financial planner and mortgage adviser. Lien is a chartered financial planner and a fellow of the Chartered Insurance Institute, a CFP (certified financial planner) professional, and a registered life planner with the Kinder Institute.

Dr Thang Nguyen is currently an assistant professor in finance in the Centre for Financial and Corporate Integrity at Coventry University. His expertise is in the research areas of fintech and crowdfunding. His research has been published in top-quality journals such as *British Journal of Management* and *Journal of Corporate Finance*. As a recognised scholar in the field, Dr Nguyen was sponsored by the British Council – 'Newton Fund Research Links Scheme' – to participate and present at 'Developing an agenda for fintech research in emerging economies' international workshop in November 2017 in Kuala Lumpur, Malaysia.

Dr Pythagoras N. Petratos is a lecturer in finance at Coventry University. Earlier he was doing research at the Blavatnik School of Government, University of Oxford, and he was a Departmental Lecturer in Finance at Saïd Business School, University of Oxford. He has also taught at numerous universities in the UK and abroad, including ESCP and the University of London. He earned his Ph.D. from the University of London, and his research included examining corporate finance, entrepreneurial finance and valuation of new technologies. In addition, he is interested in cybersecurity, risk management and investment and fintech.

Dr Patrick John Ring is a reader in financial services in the Glasgow School for Business and Society at Glasgow Caledonian University. He is a qualified solicitor and a member of the Chartered Institute of Securities and Investment and Chartered Insurance Institute, as well as an Associate of the Pensions Management Institute. His teaching and research interests include financial regulation and compliance; operational risk management and culture in financial services; trust in financial services; and pension policy and reform.

Dr Amandeep Sahota is a lecturer in finance at Coventry University. Amandeep teaches corporate finance and financial services at undergraduate and postgraduate levels. His research focuses on the financing, investment and governance issues faced by businesses. He has published in the area of mergers and acquisitions, and current research focuses on the management turnover and its impact on internal capital markets, corporate restructuring and governance. He completed his Ph.D. from Loughborough University.

Dr Nikhil Sapre is a lecturer in finance at Coventry University (UK), with over six years of banking, financial services and other industry experience. His Ph.D. research focused on financial inclusion and its association with financial stability and economic growth. His other research interests include financial intermediation, banking and related topics in development studies.

Jordan Wong is an Independent financial planner in the UK, currently working for Chesterton House Financial Planning Ltd., providing a holistic financial planning service to many high-net-worth individuals. He is a member of the Personal Finance Society and has previously undertaken projects for the Chartered Institute for Securities and Investments (CISI). He has obtained the Diploma for Regulated Financial Planning and is close to completing his Advanced Diploma to become a Chartered Financial Planner.

ACKNOWLEDGEMENTS

We have received a lot of help and support with the publication of this book. We would like to thank Kristina Abbotts, our commissioning editor, for her inexorable enthusiasm, encouragement and support for the project, as these greatly inspire and motivate us.

We are also grateful to the editorial board, the anonymous reviewers and the production team for their invaluable support.

We are also lucky to receive help from the editorial assistant, Christiana Mandizha, who has done a great job preparing the manuscript for publication. We also would like to thank Alan Marchant for his help with proof reading.

We have enjoyed writing this book and hope you will be pleased with the result.

Terms in **bold** throughout the book are defined in the Glossary.

1

OVERVIEW OF FINANCIAL SERVICES

Jonquil Lowe

Key points summary

- 'Financial services' is an umbrella term for a wide range of different products and services, including day-to-day money management, saving and borrowing, insurance and investing for the future.
- Globally financial services have been growing and are concentrated in geographical centres, including, for example, New York, London and several Asian cities.
- This development of financial services markets may contribute to economic growth and shapes the way that individuals and households manage their financial affairs.
- The nature and level of household engagement with financial services is also shaped by major contextual factors, such as income growth and distribution, migration, ageing populations and climate change.

Most student texts about financial services use a corporate finance lens, while most books about personal finance focus on financial planning and products. There are very few books that aim to help both students and consumers understand from a personal finance perspective the implications of how the financial services sector works. This book aims to fill that gap. It unfolds the workings of financial services to illuminate how consumers can navigate the system better and turn it to their best advantage.

DOI: 10.4324/9781003227663-1

Learning outcomes

The learning outcomes for this chapter are to:

- Appreciate the scale of financial services both globally and in the UK.
- Understand key events that have shaped the current financial services system.
- Begin to see the implications of the financial system for the well-being of individuals and households and how they manage their financial affairs.

1.1 The financial services sector

Historically, many financial services were seen as facilitating productive economic activity rather than directly creating value themselves – a debate that continues today (see, for example, Mazzucato, 2019). However, the international system, which countries use to measure the size of their **gross domestic product (GDP)**, started to more comprehensively identify the financial sector contribution from 1993 onwards (Harrison, 2005). As the statisticians wrangled back then, before the scale of financial services sector can be measured, it is necessary first to define what it includes.

Figure 1.1 shows the main categories of financial services today, including, for example, banking, insurance, **securities** markets, asset management and mortgages. From a corporate perspective, these are large global markets that generate billions in profit, and the central importance of financial markets will be discussed in Chapter 2. From a consumer perspective, the categories in Figure 1.1 are the source of essential products and services needed to manage everyday living and planning for the future.

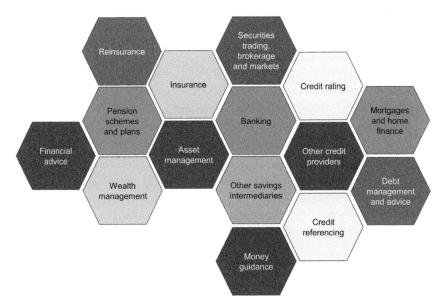

FIGURE 1.1 Key financial services.
Source: author's diagram.

1.1.1 The size of the financial sector

While individuals and households deal mainly with financial services firms located in their own country, the products they buy or invest in are the tip of a vast global network of markets.

The overall size of the global financial services market is estimated to be around $22.5 trillion (The Business Research Company, 2021). Putting the scale into context, that's slightly larger than the whole US economy or nearly ten times the size of the UK economy, at $21.4 trillion and $2.8 trillion, respectively (World Bank, 2021a).

Financial markets function best when expertise and liquidity come together and so activity tends to concentrate in specific financial centres. Z/Yen, a commercial think tank, publishes twice a year a ranking of financial centres based on five 'areas of competitiveness': business environment, human capital, infrastructure, financial sector development and reputation. Figure 1.2 shows the ten most highly ranked financial centres from their spring 2021 survey. New York and London, which may be considered the historical cradles of financial services, retain their top spots, but there is an increasing growth of financial centres in Asia, particularly in China. While the traditional financial centres in the US and Europe have an advantage in terms of well-established regulatory regimes, Asian centres are already becoming dominant in some areas such as insurance and fintech (Z/Yen and CDI, 2021, Table 5).

However, the importance of financial services to individual countries varies, as shown in Figure 1.3. While New York and London are globally important financial centres, financial services account for only 8% and 7% of the US and UK economies, respectively, because other sectors, such as agriculture and industry,

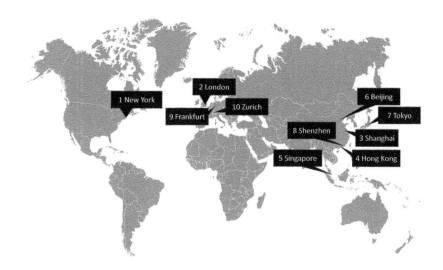

FIGURE 1.2 The world's top 10 financial centres, 2021.
Source: author's diagram based on data from Z/Yen and CDI (2021).

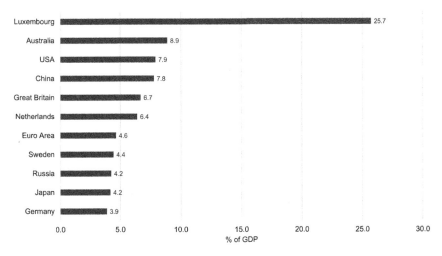

FIGURE 1.3 Financial services sector as a percentage of GDP, selected countries, most recent data (2018 to 2020).

Source: author's chart based on OECD Data (2021).

are larger (OECD Data, 2021). On the other hand, the tiny state of Luxembourg (population 0.6 million, GDP $0.07 trillion) specialises in investment fund services, with the result that financial services account for over a quarter of its GDP (OECD 2019; OECD Data, 2021).

Yet, even at 7% of GDP, UK financial services are sizeable – it is the eighth largest sector of the economy, contributes around £130 billion a year and employs over 1.1 million people, albeit with a hefty skew towards London (Hutton and Shalchi, 2021). However, in 2021, London has given ground to some European Union (EU) financial centres - for example, Amsterdam (ranked 28th in the Z/Yen survey) - following the end of the '**Brexit**' (Britain leaving the EU) transition period (Stafford, 2021). It is possible that more financial firms and jobs will relocate from the UK to the EU over time.

1.1.2 Why financial services matter to consumers

Thinking about economies as a whole, while the evidence is not conclusive, it suggests that well-developed financial systems contribute to the growth of a country's GDP, particularly by enabling more efficient and cheaper access to finance for firms which ultimately are the engines of growth (Levine, 2004). However, access to the financial system is not necessarily equal and, especially in developing countries, may be skewed towards a privileged minority rather than benefitting the population as a whole (Claessens and Perotti, 2007). This can leave poorer segments of the population without access to the most basic financial products and services that are taken for granted in higher-income countries, where financial services are for most people part of the warp and weft of modern life. One of the most essential is banking, described in Chapter 3. It provides the means for individuals to receive income and pay their expenses, and it is the major provider of saving and borrowing products. In addition, in more developed countries having a bank account is the gateway to other financial services, acting as a first line of information about a person's identity, creditworthiness and financial stability.

Living is an uncertain venture, and, beyond savings, insurance (Chapter 4) offers another way for households to increase their resilience against possible future adverse events, such as redundancy, illness or death. Other financial events, for example, the costs associated with bringing up children and eventual retirement, can be anticipated and planned for. The cornerstone of long-term planning is investment (the topic of Chapter 5).

In all areas of personal financial management and planning, consumers may seek financial advice, which is described in Chapter 6.

1.2 Growth and deregulation

The scale of the financial services industry has increased enormously in recent decades – in the UK alone doubling in **real** terms (see Figure 1.4). This section explores the drivers of growth and the implications for how the sector has developed in the UK.

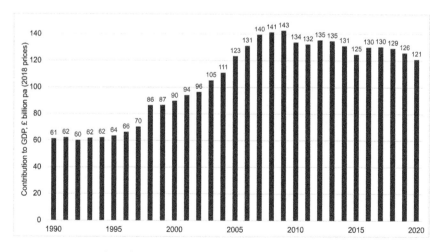

FIGURE 1.4 Growth in the contribution of financial services to UK GDP, 1990–2020. *Source*: author's chart based on data from ONS (2021).

1.2.1 The drivers of growth

A key stimulus to this growth was **financial deregulation** during the 1980s. However, the factors that brought about deregulation go back much further.

After the 1939–1945 World War, economies across Europe were ravaged and trade between them was severely constrained. Initially, many countries accepted only US dollars as a trusted form of payment for trade with their neighbours. A major breakthrough came in 1958 when the European Monetary Agreement (EMA) brought in a system for coordinating direct convertibility between different currencies. This created an opportunity for banks to take deposits and lend in a multiplicity of currencies and stimulated markets where banks traded in different currencies with each other. London, already established as an international financial centre, became the hub for these new eurocurrency and **Eurobond** markets. These markets were given a further boost in 1973 when most developed countries gave up trying to align their currencies and, instead, adopted freely **floating exchange rates** (Versluysen, 1988).

The international markets were lightly regulated, and hence attractive to savers and borrowers who, at the time, often faced restrictions in their home markets, such as caps on the amount they could borrow or the interest rates they could earn. As the markets grew, they became magnets for countries with surplus funds, such as the oil-producing nations of the Middle East and for the newly developing multinational organisations looking to fund their global operations. At the same time, the technologies surrounding data processing and communications were advancing rapidly, allowing market prices to instantly respond to changing events and for trading to take place cheaply and efficiently, with opportunities to profit from **arbitrage** as well as trade-related transactions. This resulted in an increase in new offshore centres, for example, in Hong Kong, Singapore and Dubai, often with the promise of light regulation and low taxes to attract participants (Versluysen, 1988).

National financial markets risked being bypassed if they did not respond to this international competition, and by the late 1970s there was the political will in the US, UK and subsequently many European countries to cut government intervention in financial markets so that they were free to respond to market forces. Deregulatory legislation came into force over the next decade, and the growth of financial services was unleashed.

You will discover more about the main financial markets and how they operate in Chapter 2.

1.2.2 Deregulation in the UK

The conservative governments of 1979–1987 passed financial deregulation measures that rapidly changed the UK financial landscape:

- breaking down barriers that had kept financial firms specialising in niche areas
- breaking up industry-wide agreements that had set the level of commissions that could be charged

- opening up UK financial firms to foreign takeovers and competitors, fostering the growth of multinational banking conglomerates
- privatising previously state-owned **natural monopolies** in industries such as telecoms, water, electricity and gas, encouraging ordinary people to become shareholders
- challenging paternalistic company-run pension schemes by launching new markets for individualised, but more risky, personal pension plans.

The convergence of this switch to free markets with continuing technological innovation marked a shift in financial services away from the largely personalised relationships that consumers had previously had with financial institutions. Instead, new business models were adopted where potential customers could be assessed remotely using algorithms and a proportion of 'failures' (such as loan defaults) built in to calculating the expected profit margin. Financial technological (**fintech**) advances continue, though, as Chapter 7 explores, the impetus and benefits these days are often focused on meeting perceived consumer needs rather than simply streamlining business processes.

The mantra of free markets is that they are more efficient and, as such, result in better outcomes for all. However, this depends on some fairly stringent assumptions. One is that all the players in the market – firms and consumers alike – are equipped to make informed decisions and have access to these markets. Chapter 8 considers how consumers may be excluded from financial services markets or be unable to fully participate, its consequence and how financial inclusion can be improved.

The solutions do not all lie in the hands of consumers and firms. Chapter 9 looks at the role of government in setting the wider economic context for personal financial decisions and in the extent to which it may need to step in to moderate or replace market forces.

Despite this, consumers face considerable challenges navigating financial services markets and are vulnerable to many types of scams (Chapter 10). Paradoxically then, deregulated free markets in fact require a substantial amount of regulation to ensure that providers are honest and professional and that there are routes for redress where the system falls short.

In the UK, initial regulation of the newly liberated financial sector was placed in the hands of several self-regulatory organisations (SROs) – non-government bodies with statutory power to set and enforce rules and standards for their sector. Each SRO focused on a different area of financial services, such as securities and investments, life insurance and investment funds, and financial advice and wealth management. It soon became apparent that this model was inadequate in a world where financial institutions were rapidly expanding, merging, morphing into organisations offering multiple types of services and innovating to create new financial instruments, products and services. This led first to a couple of the SROs merging but ultimately to the replacement of the SRO structure with a new overarching regulator, the Financial Services Authority (FSA), from 2001. However, the near collapse of the banking system during the **Global Financial**

Crisis (GFC) – see Box 1.1 – called into question the effectiveness of the FSA and led to its own replacement in 2013 by the Financial Conduct Authority (FCA). This heralded a different approach to regulation, which you will read about in Chapter 11.

Even with these safeguards and even where individuals and households make sound judgements and take suitable actions, the outcomes are not assured, because financial services markets are at their heart dealing with risk – always estimating a probable but not guaranteed course that future events may take. This theme of risk runs through all the chapters in the book but is brought into sharp focus in Chapter 12, before you reflect in the Conclusion on how the future of financial services may unfold next.

BOX 1.1 THE GLOBAL FINANCIAL CRISIS

While the world in the early 2020s grappled with the coronavirus pandemic, it was still absorbing the aftermath of a previous crisis: the GFC that started in 2007.

Deregulation fostered innovation in financial markets. Two areas of particular growth were **securitisation** and **derivatives**.

Securitisation became a standard feature of the home-finance industry. Previously, mortgage lenders had been in the business of holding long-term loans made to their customers. Securitisation enabled profits to be realised more quickly by packaging the loans together and selling them to investors in the form of securities that would pay out an income related to the mortgage repayments. **Credit rating agencies** assessed the risk inherent in the various securities which fed into how they were priced.

Not only was there a market trading in these **mortgage-backed securities** themselves, there were also markets in a wide range of derivatives, for example speculations that the price of the underlying security would rise or fall by more or less than a given amount over a specified time period (see Chapter 2 for more information about derivatives). A feature of many derivatives is that only a small portion of the money involved has to be paid upfront (the capital) so that gains – but also losses – can be many times greater than the capital (an example of **leverage**).

The main investors in mortgage-backed securities and their derivatives were financial institutions, including many banks, both household names and more specialist investment banks. It has been estimated that some of the institutions were so heavily leveraged that they stood to lose up to 40 times the amount invested if the mortgage-backed securities turned sour (Lewis, 2011).

In 2007, they did turn sour. It turned out that the mortgages on which the edifice was based were riskier than the credit rating agencies had suggested, and a downturn in US house prices caused many homeowners to default on their loans (see Box 10.4 in Chapter 10). As a result, the value of the mort-gage-backed securities and derivatives in the balance sheets of the banks and other institutions tumbled. Many banks were technically insolvent, and nota-bly Lehman Brothers went bankrupt. The normal functioning of the financial markets and day-to-day banking dried up as banks became reluctant to lend to each other, even overnight, for fear of which bank would fold next, and customers started to queue outside some banks (such as Northern Rock in the UK) to withdraw all their money.

To save the worldwide banking system from collapse, governments stepped in. They pumped money into the banks to prevent them from col-lapsing, funding this with massive public borrowing. This was widely ac-cepted as justified because the alternative for individuals and businesses would be their bills going unpaid, no access to cash, loss of savings (with the exception of amounts covered by any national **deposit insurance** scheme) and inability to borrow.

However, saving the banks came at a cost. Some governments, includ-ing the UK, took the decision that high levels of public debt would have to brought down to more normal levels by imposing **austerity meas-ures**. In the UK, over the period 2010–2020, these included freezing state benefits (except for pensioners), freezing the pay of public-sector work-ers and cutting back on public services either directly or by slashing the funding for local councils that provide services such as children's centres, social care, transport and libraries. As a result, by 2019–2020, spending on public services was around 9% lower per person than in 2010–2011 and welfare spending around £39 billion lower (Crawford and Zaranko, 2019). Even excluding the cuts to public services (used more heavily by lower-income households), the measures were deemed **regressive**, with, for example, single-parent households losing around 15% of their net in-come (EHRC, 2017).

1.3 The wider context

You have seen how, over the decades, deregulation and technology have changed the *nature* of individuals' relationships with financial services. However, this has taken place against the context of other important changes that have increased the *level* of engagement that most households and individuals must have with the financial services sector, which is the focus of this section. Moreover, financial services are now so embedded in the way that economies function and are so interconnected that they have the potential to trigger significant and long-last-ing impacts on households regardless of their own use of financial services, as demonstrated by the GFC (see Box 1.1).

1.3.1 Income, wealth and work

In general, as people become better off, they are more likely to use financial services, particularly if they start to have surplus income that can buy insurance, be put down as a deposit on a home or saved to provide a safety net for emergencies and resources for retirement. Meanwhile, poorer households may have little choice but to take out loans, though these may include informal ones from family and friends, through community schemes, such as **rotating credit and savings associations (ROSCAs)** or from illegal money lenders, and not just though engagement with the financial services sector.

The world as a whole has been getting richer. World Bank data (2021b) show that real GDP per head has increased nearly threefold over the period 1960–2019 and now stands at just over $11,000 per person. However, GDP per head is a crude measure of prosperity because it says nothing about the way that GDP is distributed across different people. While down from 43% in 1981, over 9% of the world's population still live below the official poverty line of $1.90 a day (World Bank, 2021c). At the other extreme, the world now has over 2,800 billionaires (Statista, 2021a). Moreover, in two-thirds of countries, income inequality is increasing, particularly in developed countries like the US and UK and in some middle-income countries, including China (UN, 2020). Nevertheless, before the coronavirus pandemic caused living standards worldwide to fall, China, India and some other Asia-Pacific countries had been experiencing a growing 'middle class' (Kochhar, 2021) with an increasing ability to purchase consumer goods and, particularly in China, a high adoption of fintech and a high rate of saving to fund healthcare and education (IMA Ltd, 2013; Kharas and Dooley, 2020).

One of key factors driving income inequality is low-paid and precarious work. Firms have an incentive to pay wages that are as low as possible because this increases their profit; the workers, on the other hand, want wages that are as high as possible and at least enough to live on. In cases where there is an ample supply of workers, the ability to replace labour with technology and/or low trade union membership, individuals have little or no power over their wages. Governments may step in by setting a statutory minimum wage, though firms may be able to bypass this by engaging casual or **gig economy** labour instead of formal employees (see, for example, Moen, 2017) or outsourcing production to low-wage economies abroad. In developed countries, there has been a declining trend in the share of GDP going to workers, but a mixed picture presents for middle-income countries such as India and China, as shown in Figure 1.5.

In addition to the labour share of GDP falling, there has been increasing inequality *among* wage earners due to both an increased number of people in low-income work and a disproportionate amount of earnings flowing to higher-skilled workers and managers (OECD, 2015). Income inequality is one of the factors

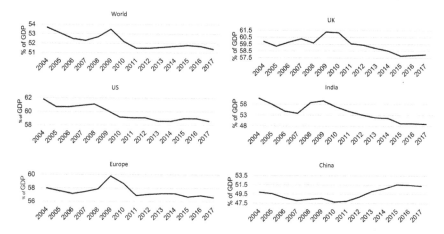

FIGURE 1.5   Labour share of GDP.
Source: author's chart based on ILO cited in UN (2021a).

contributing to high levels of household debt, particularly among low-income households (IMF, 2017).

1.3.2 Migration and travel

Related to income inequality between countries, there is a steady stream of workers migrating from lower-income to higher-income countries in search of job opportunities and better paid work, for example, from Mexico to the US, from the Philippines to Dubai, from Africa to Europe, and (prior to Brexit) from Eastern Europe to the UK. Many migrant workers leave their families behind and send money back to them. Thus, a key financial service for migrant workers is **remittances**. Although traditional banks can convert payments from domestic accounts into another currency and send them to a receiving account abroad, charges are generally high. Therefore, specialist remittance firms, such as Western Union and newer fintech entrants, tend to dominate this field. The World Bank (2021d) estimates that remittance flows to middle- and lower-income countries amounted to $540 billion in 2020.

Migration from developed countries is on a smaller scale and includes those seeking to retire abroad. The main issue for this group is to ensure cross-border payment or transfer of pensions.

Although disrupted by the coronavirus pandemic, tourism is also a substantial sector, which is estimated to have contributed approximately $2.9 trillion to global GDP in 2019 (Statista, 2021b). Tourists must use financial services for example to acquire payment methods and travel insurance.

What links all of these activities is the need for participants to engage with foreign exchange markets (see Chapter 2) and thus a degree of uncertainty over the buying power of their money once it is converted to another currency.

1.3.3 Demographic change

A third factor driving increased engagement with financial services over the past few decades is ageing populations. In 1990, worldwide just one person in 16 was over age 65; by 2019, this figure was 1 in 11; and by 2050 it is forecast to rise to one in six (UN, 2019). Many countries experienced a baby boom during the period 1946–1965 (following the Second World War), and, as countries get wealthier, women are tending to choose to have fewer children. Moreover, medical advances mean that people are tending to live longer than in the past. As a result, many countries around the world are experiencing a rising number of citizens in retirement but a shrinking workforce to generate the GDP needed to support everyone. Table 1.1 shows the **dependency ratio** (which can be measured in various ways but is defined here as the number of people aged 65 and more as a percentage of people aged 20 to 64) for selected countries. For example, 27.0 means that there are 27 people aged 65 and more for every 100 people of working age.

Table 1.1 reveals that ageing population is a worldwide phenomenon but most pronounced in high-income countries, such as Japan, Germany, the UK and the US. However, even middle-income countries are on the same path, especially China. Nevertheless, there are parts of the world, such as African states like Nigeria, that have relatively young populations and are forecast to stay that way.

Ageing populations are typically portrayed as a problem and a challenge to pension, healthcare and social care systems. However, it is important to keep this problem in perspective:

- Firstly, people living longer is good news, especially if medical advances mean that many of those extra years can be spent in relatively good health.
- Not everyone aged 65 and more is retired. Many countries have been increasing the age at which pensions normally start and passing legislation to

TABLE 1.1 Old-age dependency ratio (%) for selected countries and years

Country	1960 actual	1980 actual	2000 actual	2020 forecast	2040 forecast	2060 forecast
China	7.6	9.6	11.3	18.5	41.8	58.3
Germany	19.1	27.3	26.5	36.5	55.7	60.3
India	6.4	7.7	8.6	11.3	17.6	28.8
Japan	10.4	14.7	27.3	52.0	70.7	83.3
Nigeria	6.2	6.5	6.6	6.3	6.9	8.6
UK	20.2	26.9	27.0	32.0	43.5	51.5
United Arab Emirates (UAE)	8.1	2.2	1.6	1.6	17.3	24.5
US	17.3	20.4	20.9	28.4	39.0	44.5
World	10.1	12.1	12.8	16.3	25.0	32.3

Source: author's table using data from UN DESA (2019).

outlaw age discrimination in the workplace in an effort to keep people in the workforce for longer.
- A relatively smaller workforce does not mean that a country's GDP is necessarily smaller. Technology can increase output per worker (productivity), and increasingly automation means that some work can be carried out by technology alone.

The main question then is how should GDP be shared among retired people and workers? As you've seen above, workers gain GDP through their wages. State pensions are typically financed by using the tax system to collect part of workers' share of GDP and transferring it direct to pensioners. When people save for retirement, the assets they hold in effect become claims on future GDP, although investors can seldom be sure how much GDP they will eventually get. Some fear that automation will eliminate many jobs; thus, a fairer system might be for people of working age to receive a universal basic income (UBI) rather than being reliant on wages that may be low, precarious or non-existent. State pensions are in effect UBI for older people. Whether looking at mechanisms for sharing GDP among working-age people, older people or both, the issues are similar and there are no objective answers, only decisions for society that are ideological and political.

1.3.4 Climate change

The final major contextual issue that may affect individual and household engagement with financial services is climate change. It is now widely accepted that the actions of humans, particularly the use of fossil fuels which emit 'greenhouse gases', are causing global warming and climate change, triggering events that are affecting human affairs and other life on Earth. Even in countries such as the UK, where the effects so far have been relatively benign, flooding is becoming a more regular event and has triggered the setting up of a special scheme to ensure households can continue to access affordable flood cover as part of their home insurance (see Flood Re, 2021).

Under the auspices of the United Nations, 196 countries have signed the Paris Agreement which binds them to adopt measures to limit the rise in global temperatures to no more than 2 degrees Celsius, and preferable only 1.5 degrees compared with pre-industrial levels (UN, 2021b). Increasingly, those financial services firms and institutions (such as pension schemes) that manage assets are expected to report their approach to environmental and other issues that are deemed socially desirable – collectively called **Environmental Social and Governance (ESG)** issues. By the same token, firms are increasingly being required to report their ESG policies as a guide to investors. Some governments have started to issue 'green' securities where the proceeds are used to finance projects such as alternative energy and carbon capture schemes. Thus, private investors more than ever before have environmental and ethical information on which to base their judgements about where to invest.

1.4 Conclusion

The global markets where professionals trade currencies, bonds and other assets may at first seem remote from the everyday experience of individuals and households. Yet, increasingly, we are all part of a complex web of financial connections.

As the chapters that follow will demonstrate, the way households manage their finances is inevitably shaped by the global financial industry and the way governments and regulators choose to intervene or stand back to let markets take their course.

Understanding how personal finance is connected to the wider forces of the financial system, and the bigger picture of the social and political context, you will be better equipped to adapt your financial planning to weather the ups and downs of the system and pursue the best outcomes.

Self-test questions

1   Describe two factors that have led to the growth of financial services in recent decades.
2   Explain the paradox of why deregulated markets need to be regulated.
3   Based on your own experience or that of someone you know (maybe someone from a different generation), reflect on whether any of the factors described in Section 1.3 (growing incomes and wealth, inequality, job insecurity, migration, travel, ageing population or climate change) have affected your or their engagement with financial services.

Further reading

McKinsey & Co, Insights on financial services: https://www.mckinsey.com/industries/financial-services/our-insights

New Economics Foundation, Banking and Finance topics: https://neweconomics.org/section/all/banking-and-finance/p5

References

The Business Research Company (2021) *Financial Services Global Market Report 2021: COVID-19 impact and recovery to 2030*, News release, 31 March. Available at: https://www.globenewswire.com/news-release/2021/03/31/2202641/0/en/Financial-Services-Global-Market-Report-2021-COVID-19-Impact-And-Recovery-To-2030.html (Accessed: 4 May 2021).

Claessens, S. and Perotti, E. (2007) 'Finance and inequality' in *Journal of Comparative Economics*, 35 (2007), pp.748–773.

Crawford, R. and Zaranko, B. (2019) *Tax revenues and spending on social security benefits and public services since the crisis*. Available at: https://www.ifs.org.uk/uploads/BN261-Tax-revenues-and-spending-on-social-security-benefits-and-public-services-since-the-crisis.pdf (Accessed: 1 June 2021).

Equality and Human Rights Commission (EHRC) (2017) *Distributional results or the impact of tax and welfare reforms between 2010–17, modelled in the 2021/22 tax year*, Interim findings. Available at: https://www.equalityhumanrights.com/sites/default/files/

impact-of-tax-and-welfare-reforms-2010-2017-interim-report_0.pdf (Accessed: 1 June 2021).

Flood Re (2021) *Flood Re*. Available at: https://www.floodre.co.uk/ (Accessed: 2 June 2021).

Harrison, A. (2005) *The background to the 1993 revision of the System of National Accounts (SNA)*. Available at: https://unstats.un.org/unsd/sna1993/history/backgrd.pdf (Accessed: 4 May 2021).

Hutton, G. and Shalchi, A. (2021) *Financial services: contribution to the UK economy*, House of Commons Briefing Paper No. 6193. Available at: https://commonslibrary.parliament.uk/research-briefings/sn06193/ (Accessed: 3 May 2021).

IMA Ltd (2013) *China's middle-income consumers*. Available at: http://www.2ndedition-china.doingbusinessguide.co.uk/the-guide/chinas-middle-income-consumers/ (Accessed: 2 June 2021).

International Monetary Fund (IMF) (2017) *Global financial stability report: Is growth at risk?* Available at: https://www.imf.org/en/Publications/GFSR/Issues/2017/09/27/global-al-financial-stability-report-october-2017 (Accessed: 2 June 2021).

Lewis, M. (2011) *The big short. A true story* London: Penguin Books.

Kharas, H. and Dooley, M. (2020) *China's influence on the global middle class*. Available at: https://www.brookings.edu/wp-content/uploads/2020/10/FP_20201012_china_middle_class_kharas_dooley.pdf (Accessed: 2 June 2021).

Kochhar, R. (2021) *The pandemic stalls growth in the global middle class, pushes poverty up sharply*. Available at: https://www.pewresearch.org/global/2021/03/18/the-pandemic-stalls-growth-in-the-global-middle-class-pushes-poverty-up-sharply/#:~:text=-From%202011%20to%202019%2C%20the, unchanged%20from%202019%20to%20 2020 (Accessed: 1 June 2021).

Levine, R. (2004) *Finance and growth: theory and evidence*, National Bureau of Economic Research (NBER) working paper 10766. Available at: https://www.nber.org/system/files/working_papers/w10766/w10766.pdf (Accessed: 8 June 2021).

Mazzucato, M. (2019) *The value of everything*, London: Penguin Books.

Moen, E. (2017) 'Weakening trade union power: new forms of employment relations. The case of Norwegian Air Shuttle' in *Transfer: European Review of Labour and Research*, 23 (4), pp.425–439.

Office for National Statistics (ONS) (2021) *GDP output approach – low-level aggregates*. Available at: https://www.ons.gov.uk/economy/grossdomesticproductgdp/datasets/ukgdpolowlevelaggregates (Accessed: 4 May 2021).

Organisation for Economic Cooperation and Development (OECD) Data (2021) 'Finance and insurance' in *Value added by activity*. Available at: https://data.oecd.org/natincome/value-added-by-activity.htm (Accessed: 4 May 2021).

Organisation for Economic Cooperation and Development (OECD) (2019) OECD *Economic Surveys: Luxembourg*. Available at: https://read.oecd-ilibrary.org/economics/oecd-economic-surveys-luxembourg-2019_424839c1-en#page1 (Accessed: 4 May 2021).

Organisation for Economic Cooperation and Development (OECD) (2015) Why is income inequality rising? OECD Insights. Available at: https://www.oecd-ilibrary.org/docserver/9789264246010-5-en.pdf?expires=1622618820&id=id&accname=guest&checksum=32D0979BA6095AE8B60AAF0E4EA28002 (Accessed: 2 June 2021).

Stafford, P. (2021) 'Amsterdam ousts London as Europe's top share trading hub' in *Financial Times*, 10 February. Available at: https://www-ft-com.libezproxy.open.ac.uk/content/3dad4ef3-59e8-437e-8f63-f629a5b7d0aa (Accessed: 4 May 2021).

Statista (2021a) *Number of billionaires worldwide in 2019, by region.* Available at: https://www. statista.com/statistics/620926/global-billionaire-population-by-region/ (Accessed: 1 June 2021).

Statista (2021b) *Global tourism industry – statistics and facts.* Available at: https://www.stati-sta.com/topics/962/global-tourism/ (Accessed: 2 June 2021).

United Nations (2021a) 'Indicator 10.4.1 Labour share of GDP' in *SDG Indicators.* Available at: https://unstats.un.org/sdgs/indicators/database/ (Accessed: 2 June 2021).

United Nations (2021b) *The Paris Agreement.* Available at: https://unfccc.int/pro-cess-and-meetings/the-paris-agreement/the-paris-agreement (Accessed: 2 June 2021).

United Nations (2020) *World Social Report 2020: Inequality in a rapidly changing world.* Available at: https://www.un.org/development/desa/dspd/wp-content/uploads/sites/22/2020/02/World-Social-Report2020-FullReport.pdf. (Accessed: 1 June 2020).

United Nations (2019) *World population ageing 2019.* Available at: https://www.un.org/en/development/desa/population/publications/pdf/ageing/WorldPopulationAge-ing2019-Highlights.pdf (Accessed 2 June 2021).

United Nations Department of Economic and Social Affairs, Population Division (UN DESA) (2019) *World population prospects 2019.* Available at: https://population.un.org/wpp/DataQuery/ (Accessed: 2 June 2021).

Versluysen, E.L. (1988) *Financial deregulation and globalisation of capital markets.* Available at: https://documents.worldbank.org/en/publication/documents-reports/document-detail/235201468764398871/financial-deregulation-and-the-globalization-of-capi-tal-markets (Accessed: 4 May 2021).

World Bank (2021a) 'GDP (current US$)' in *Data.* Available at: https://data.worldbank. org/indicator/NY.GDP.MKTP.CD (Accessed: 4 May 2021).

World Bank (2021b) 'GDP per capital (constant 2010 US$)' in *Data.* Available at: https:// data.worldbank.org/indicator/NY.GDP.PCAP.KD (Accessed: 1 June 2021).

World Bank (2021c) *Poverty headcount ratio at $1.90 a day (2011 PPP) (% of population).* Available at: https://data.worldbank.org/indicator/SI.POV.DDAY (Accessed: 1 June 2021).

World Bank (2021d) *Migration and remittances,* Migration and development brief 34. Avail-able at: https://www.knomad.org/sites/default/files/2021-05/Migration%20and%20Development%20Brief%2034_1.pdf (Accessed: 2 June 2021).

Z/Yen and China Development Institute (CDI) (2021) *The global financial centres index 29.* Available at: https://www.longfinance.net/media/documents/GFCI_29_Full_Re-port_2021.03.17_v1.1.pdf (Accessed: 4 May 2021).

2

FINANCIAL MARKETS

Amandeep Sahota

Key points summary

- Financial markets are marketplaces where financial securities such as equities, bonds, futures and options are traded.
- Companies and governments use financial markets for many reasons, such as raising capital, hedging risk and managing the economy.
- Both large and small investors participate in financial markets to take advantage of variety of investment opportunities and access the potential to earn higher returns than available on cash savings.

Financial markets are the venues – typically dematerialised – where participants can shift resources and risk from one to another and/or from one point in time to another. The reasons for doing so may pertain to providing liquidity and finance for ongoing business, funding new investment, managing risks or simply generating profit from the markets themselves. Transactions involves buying or selling financial securities such as **equities**, **bonds** and derivatives.

As Figure 2.1 demonstrates, financial markets are huge - collectively dwarfing the value of global GDP which was estimated to be $88 trillion in 2019 (World Bank, 2021). Financial markets may seem exotic and remote from the everyday life of the average consumer, with only a minority engaging in them directly. However, while it is true that the majority of direct participants are typically institutions, like banks, and professional traders, the retail products that consumers use – including debt products, insurance contracts, pension schemes and other savings and investments – are all underpinned by these vast, global markets (Valdez and Molyneux, 2016). For an investor - retail or institutional - to make sound financial judgements and decisions, it is important to understand the types

DOI: 10.4324/9781003227663-2

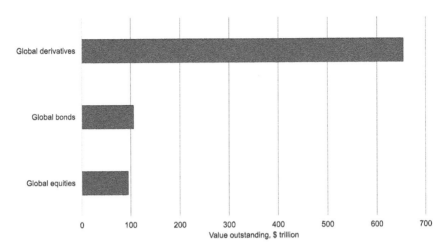

FIGURE 2.1   Value of assets outstanding in some of the main global financial markets, 2019.

Source: author's chart based on data from SIMFA (2020).

of securities available in these markets and the risk-reward trade-off they offer, which are the topics you will consider in this chapter.

Learning outcomes

The learning outcomes for this chapter are to:

- Understand the role of financial markets and their relevance to retail investors.
- Be able to describe the difference between equity and debt, who are the players and their motivations for participating in these markets.
- Be able to compare the risk-reward trade-off for investors implicit in the different markets.

2.1 Markets, functions and players

Financial markets enable the issue and trading of securities such as equities, bonds and derivatives. These assets or securities may be listed on formal exchanges like the London Stock Exchange or traded **over-the-counter (OTC)**. Participants in these markets are investors, corporations and governments who come to the market for diverse reasons, such as:

- **Raising capital**: This is done, for example, to finance growth or investment in new opportunities or infrastructure. It can be through issuing bonds to investors (who are thus lenders), or through equity which means investors in effect become part-owners and share more directly in the risks of the company issuing the equities.

- **Managing the economy (fiscal policy)**: Governments may issue bonds to raise capital for, say, infrastructure projects, but also as a way of stimulating the economy by running a **fiscal deficit**, as discussed in Chapter 9.
- **Exit**: 'Going public' by issuing equities on a stock exchange enables founders and early investors to exit (in other words, cash in by selling their business or a stake in it).
- **Investing**: Investment in bonds and equities provides an opportunity to earn a return. As their market price changes, there is a chance of making a gain (but a loss if price falls). In addition, investors may receive an income in the form of **dividends** to shareholders, while bonds typically pay **interest**.
- **Managing liquidity**: Banks and companies can temporarily park excess funds in short-term financial markets and borrow on a short-term basis.
- **Risk management**: Companies issuing securities and investors buying them may have a primary objective of reducing risk, for example, offsetting adverse price fluctuations in an underlying asset. A common way to accomplish this is through derivatives, such as **futures**, **options** and **swaps**.
- **Arbitrage**: This is done by buying and selling securities simultaneously in two different markets to take advantage of variations in price of the same or a very similar asset and so make a profit.

Through buyer and seller interactions, financial markets determine the **spot price** of an asset. These prices are not only important to those buying and selling but are a reference point for a wide range of users who need to calculate asset valuations. If markets operate efficiently, the security prices they generate may be good estimates of the **intrinsic value** of the assets being traded. Financial markets are more likely to be efficient if they have the characteristics shown in Figure 2.2.

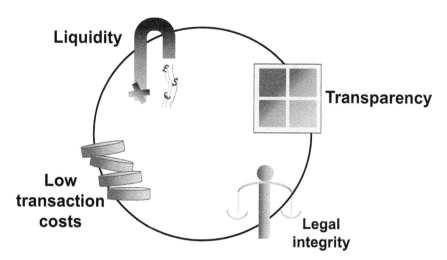

FIGURE 2.2 Characteristics of efficient financial markets.
Source: author's diagram.

Liquidity refers to buyers and sellers being readily able to find other participants willing to sell to them or to buy from them. When investors can sell their shares, bonds or other assets quickly, this makes the securities more attractive, which, in turn, draws more participants to the market, thus further increasing liquidity. Transparency – the availability of published market prices, financial accounts of traded firms, and so on – can increase investor confidence and could mean more people are willing to trade these securities. Legal integrity is necessary to ensure investors have suitable protection and regulation. Excessive regulation can stifle a market. However, if investors do not have confidence in the information that is available or in the legal system to settle disputes and enforce contracts, then it could have a significantly negative impact on financial markets. Transaction costs are the expenses incurred when buying or selling assets on the financial markets, and they are a friction that can build inefficiencies into the system. It follows that market inefficiencies are lower in larger, well-developed financial markets.

Investors can be divided broadly into two categories:

- **Retail (or non-institutional)**: These investors invest with their own capital rather than investing on someone's behalf. They usually buy and sell bonds, equities or other securities through an intermediary, such as a broker or a bank, often via an online platform or mobile app. They may have many motivations such as long-term saving for the future, shorter-term, more speculative trading to make a profit or simply a desire to store any surplus capital.
- **Institutional investors**: Institutional investors are large financial firms such as money managers, asset managers, banks, pension funds, mutual funds, hedge funds and insurance companies who manage and invest assets on other people's behalf, and in some cases on their own account as well. They usually buy or sell large blocks of shares, bonds or other securities and can have a large impact on the market price.

The financial markets that are most likely to be directly familiar to retail investors are those where government and corporate bonds (called **fixed income securities**) are traded, and the markets for equities. In their capacity as travellers rather than investors, individuals also engage in a limited way in foreign exchange trading. Indirectly, many individuals are exposed to these and other financial markets through their pension savings and holdings of investment funds.

2.2 Fixed income markets

Fixed income securities, also called bonds, are one of the most common ways firms and governments raise capital globally (Adams and Smith, 2013). The largest issuer of bonds is the US (with a total of $47.2 trillion outstanding in 2020), followed by China ($18.6 trillion); the UK had $7.2 trillion of bonds outstanding in 2020, of which about half ($3.6 trillion) were government bonds (Bank of International Settlements, no date).

2.2.1 Bond basics

A bond is a contractual agreement between the issuer (for example, a company or a government) and the investor/lender. Bonds have the following characteristics:

- Features of the bond determine the regular payments to bondholders (called **coupons**) and amount paid on maturity, the currency in which they will be paid and the time period (term) over which they will be made, as illustrated in Figure 2.3. Note that the contractual payments are specified in relation to the **par value** (also known as the nominal value), which is simply a standard unit of account (e.g. £100), although bonds can be traded in smaller or larger and fractional amounts.
- Legal and tax implications that apply.
- Any contingency provisions affecting the rights of the issuer or bondholder, for example the option of the issuer to buy back the bonds before the original maturity date.

Bonds typically pay coupons on an annual basis, but it is common to have bonds paying coupons on a semi-annual basis (i.e. six-monthly basis). Note that the coupon is expressed as a percentage of par value (not market price). For example, a bond with an annual 5% coupon and a par value of £100 will pay a fixed sum of £5 every year until maturity. The term of a bond at issue can range anywhere

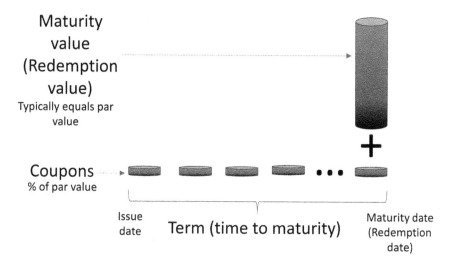

FIGURE 2.3   Main features of a bond.
Source: author's diagram.

TABLE 2.1 Common types of bond

Type of bond	Main characteristics
Ordinary bonds*	• Pre-agreed coupons and maturity payment. • Pre-set maturity date. • Likelihood of payments being paid as promised depends on financial strength of the issuer.
Index-linked bonds	• As ordinary bonds, except coupons and maturity payment, increase in line with **inflation** measured by changes in a specified price index.
Perpetual bonds	• Pre-agreed coupons. • But no maturity date and so no maturity payment. • Investors who want to cash in have to sell in the market.
Zero-coupon bonds	• As ordinary bonds but they pay no coupons, only the maturity value.
STRIPS	• Full name: Separate Trading of Registered Interest and Principle of Securities (STRIPS). • An ordinary bond divided into a series of separate bonds, with each one paying just one coupon payment or just the maturity value. • In effect a series of zero-coupon bonds.

Bonds with contingency provisions

Callable bonds	• The issuer the right but not the obligation to redeem all or part of the bond before its maturity date.
Putable bonds	• The bondholder has the right to sell the bonds back to the issuer at designated price before the maturity date.
Convertible bonds	• The bondholder has the right but not the obligation to convert the bond into a specified number of shares in the issuing company.

Source: author's table.

* Ordinary bonds are called debentures in the US. However, in the UK, 'debenture' typically means a bond secured against some asset (and in the US, these secured bonds are called 'mortgage bonds').

from a month to 30 years or longer. Fixed income securities that have an original term of less than a year are known as **money market** securities (see Section 2.5). Securities that have no maturity date are known as perpetual bonds (or 'irredeemables'). Table 2.1 summarises these and some other common types of bonds.

2.2.2 Why do firms issue bonds rather than equities?

Bonds are just one way that corporations can raise capital from retail and institutional investors. However, there are several reasons why a firm might opt to issue bonds rather than equities:

- **Financing costs**: Equities are riskier for investors, who therefore expect a higher return from them than from bonds. This means bonds are generally a cheaper form of finance from the firm's perspective (unless their total borrowing reaches very high levels). Also, tax systems tend to favour bonds as interest costs are often tax-deductible, whereas dividends paid to share-holders are not.

- **Leverage**: Unlike equities, the cost of debt is fixed, so returns on whatever project is being financed do not have to be shared with investors.
- **Risk**: Issuing debt legally binds the issuer to the agreed payments to bondholders at the pre-agreed dates even if the firm loses money on the projects financed by the bond issue. However, issuing bonds that are tied to a particular project through a **special purpose vehicle (SPV)** can insulate the parent company from the most severe risks should the project fail.
- **Financial constraints**: Fixed-income securities can be easier and faster to arrange than issuing new shares to the public in the event that compa-nies or governments are strapped for cash or have an immediate need for capital.
- **Matching revenue and expenses**: Infrastructure, such as roads, hospitals and similar projects can take years before they begin generating any revenue. Issuers can customise features of the bond to align the pay-outs to bondhold-ers with the time when the project starts making revenue.

2.2.3 Issuing and trading bonds

Issuers sell new bonds in the 'primary bond market' to investors to raise capital; on the other hand, the trading of existing bonds among investors is called the 'secondary market'. The process of issuing new bonds can be different depend-ing on the method chosen. The three main methods are underwritten offering, best-efforts offering and auctions. In an underwritten offering, an investment bank guarantees the sale of the bonds, thus taking on the risk of the sale being unsuccessful in exchange for a fee. With a best-efforts offering, the investment bank will simply serve as a broker, thus taking on less risk. In an auction, inves-tors are asked to bid by submitting their best offers. A common misconception is that bonds are issued at par, whereas the issue price under any of the three methods is typically at a discount or premium that aligns the rate of return with prevailing market rates. The purchase of new issues tends to be dominated by institutional investors.

In the UK, retail investors can buy and sell existing bonds, including those issued by the UK government (often called **gilts**) through the London Stock Exchange, which has a dedicated retail bonds sector designed to make corporate bond trading more accessible for smaller investors. Typically, retail investors will trade through a broker often via an online platform. Brokers sometimes offer retail investors the opportunity to participate in buying newly issued corpo-rate bonds. Primary purchases and secondary trading in gilts are alternatively available through a government-organised purchase and sale service (UK DMO, no date).

2.2.4 Bond pricing

A key question when buying newly issued or existing bonds is as follows: How much is it worth paying for them? Suppose you can invest £1,000 today at a 1% interest rate per year. after one year you would expect to get back £1,000 plus £10 interest, making a total of £1,010. It follows that the maximum amount you would be willing to pay today for a bond that would pay you £1,010 in a year's time would be £1,000; in other words, £1,010 reduced ('discounted') by the amount of interest that you could get if you invested your money elsewhere. This is the general principle that can be applied to pricing an ordinary bond. Since a bond typically offers investors a flow of many payments rather than just one, the technique is called **discounted cash flow (DCF)** analysis.

A basic example is given in Box 2.1. Valuing bonds becomes more complex once variations in bond features (such as contingency provisions) are taken into account. However, for all types of valuation, a decision has to be made about the most appropriate discount rate (Tuckman and Serrat, 2012).

BOX 2.1 BOND VALUATION USING DCF ANALYSIS

Orange is a (fictitious) online insurance provider and has been operating for almost five years. It is looking to raise capital by issuing a bond with a term of three years offering a 2% coupon rate, with interest paid annually. If investors can get a 4% annual return on competing bonds, how should Orange's bond be valued?

The value of the bond can be seen as the sum of all the payments it will make over the three-year term discounted by the return the investor could have got elsewhere. The sum of the discounted payments is called the **present value (PV)** of the bond. Mathematically, the DCF equation looks like this:

$$PV = \frac{C}{(1+r)} + \frac{C}{(1+r)^2} + \frac{C+P}{(1+r)^3}$$

Where:
PV is the present value of the bond today
C is the coupon payment
r is the discount rate
t is the time to maturity
P is the par value

Using this equation and setting the discount rate equal to 4% that investors could get elsewhere, you can calculate the present value of Orange's bond as:

$$PV = \frac{2}{(1+0.04)} + \frac{2}{(1+0.04)^2} + \frac{2+100}{(1+0.04)^3}$$

$$= 94.45 \ (\text{rounded to 2 decimal places})$$

This tells the investor that they can get an annual return of 4% or more if they are able to buy the bond at 94.45 or less. If they have to pay more, the bond will be too expensive given that they can already get 4% by investing elsewhere.

The DCF equation introduced in Box 2.1 can also be used in reverse to calculate the return from the bond (the discount rate) if the present value is set equal to the bond's market price. This is called the **yield-to-maturity (YTM)** or redemption yield, since it takes into account both the coupon payments and the final payment on maturity.

Investors may simply be interested in looking at the income the bond produces and can do this by looking at the current yield, also called running yield. This is the bond's annual coupon divided by its market price. For example, a bond with 5% coupon rate, a par value of £100 and current market price of £105 would have a current yield of 4.76% (£5/£105 x 100).

2.2.5 Bond risks

You may have deduced already that bond prices and their interest rates are inversely related – a higher price means the yield from a bond is reduced. Similarly, bond prices decline when interest rates generally increase. A major risk factor for investors is that the price of bonds they hold will fall (creating a capital loss on paper that crystallises into an actual loss if they have to sell), and so a key question for bond investors is as follows: How much might the price of their bonds fall if general interest rates rise?

The sensitivity of a bond's price to changes in general interest rates can be expressed using a measure called **duration**. There are two different ways to calculate duration: 'Macaulay duration' measures how long, in terms of years, it takes the investor to be repaid their investment by the bond's cash flows; 'modified duration' shows the percentage fall in price that will result from a 1% increase in interest rates (or vice versa). Time to maturity and coupon rate can affect a bond's duration, as summarised in Figure 2.4. For example, the longer the time to maturity, the higher the duration, and the higher the coupon rate of a bond, the lower the duration.

The other main types of risks for bond investors, discussed in more detail in Chapter 12, are credit risk (the borrower may not be able to repay), market risk (prices declining in value due to economic developments including a change in general interest rates as discussed above), liquidity risk (not being able to sell the investment immediately at a fair price) and inflation risk (loss in purchasing power).

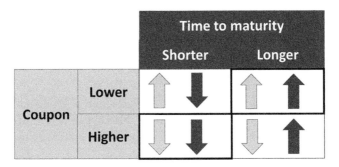

FIGURE 2.4 How duration is affected by coupon and time to maturity.
Source: author's chart.

Credit risk will vary with the financial standing and resources of the issuer. The bonds of governments in large, developed economies are generally highly rated and deemed to be virtually free of credit risk because, as a last resort, governments can always raise more tax to meet their obligations or, more controversially, may be able to create new money to pay their debts (see Chapter 9). The credit rating of bonds issued by other government offices such as states, regions and cities (called non-sovereign bonds) can vary, but historically they have low default rates. Similarly, large companies tend to be at low risk of default, while smaller and newer companies are generally deemed higher risk. Credit rating agencies, such as Fitch and Moody's, provide debt ratings for corporate and government bonds. The rating can range from AA or AAA to D, with the former representing a high-quality rating with little risk of default and the latter implying the opposite. Investors or lenders can use this information when considering investment in the sale of new securities or buying an existing security on a secondary exchange. In general, investors will require a higher return from higher risk bonds, and so, when working out what price it is worth paying for such bonds, it will be appropriate to use a higher discount rate.

2.2.6 Why invest in bonds?

The fixed income that bonds offer can be particularly attractive to retail investors who are seeking a regular income. Similarly, institutional investors such as pension funds need income-generating securities to match the funds' liability to pay out regular pension payments.

Bonds, especially government bonds, are usually classed as being less risky for investors than equities. In fact, an investor who buys a bond and holds it until maturity will know in advance exactly what payments they will receive and so is promised a fixed return. However, an investor who sells before maturity does not know what total return they will get because that will depend on the market price at the time of sale. Nevertheless, bond prices tend to be less volatile than equity prices, and therefore investors frequently combine bonds, equities and other assets as a way of tailoring their portfolio as a whole to their risk preferences (see Chapter 5 for more information on this).

Although mixing bonds with other assets can reduce an investor's exposure to risk in terms of fluctuations in income or losses due to price falls, the income from bonds is normally fixed only in **nominal** terms, so the buying power of the income is eroded by price inflation. However, governments and occasionally firms do sometimes issue index-linked bonds, where both the coupon and maturity value are increased throughout the term in line with inflation. These can be useful for investors seeking protection against rising prices.

2.3 Equity markets

Equities, also called shares, are securities that give holders a direct stake in the company that issued them, potentially sharing in its ups and downs. It is estimated that in 2019 the global value of all shares outstanding was $95 trillion, with the largest players being the US at £37.5 trillion and China at $8.5 trillion (SIMFA, 2020).

2.3.1 Equity basics

Equities, in the simplest terms, represent an ownership claim on the issuing firm's assets. So, if you are an investor with shares in a listed company like Tesco PLC, then you own a percentage of that company and, in the event of company being wound up, you have a claim on the company's assets but only after all other liabilities have been paid.

Companies can issue different types of equities that are different in terms of their payoffs and other conditions. The most common type is ordinary shares. These represent an ownership in the issuing company and the most popular type of equity security issued to investors. They will usually carry the following rights:

- **Voting rights**: Shareholders are entitled to vote at the annual general meeting (AGM) of shareholders. Usually one share carries one vote unless specified by the company; for example, there are more than one type of ordinary shares such as Class A and Class B shares.
- **Dividends**: Shareholders are entitled to dividends when the issuing company announces to make a dividend payment, but ordinary shares rank behind preference shares (see below). Companies are under no obligation to make dividend payments, and as such the decision to pay out is at the discretion of the board.
- **Liquidation rights**: In the event of liquidation, ordinary shareholders receive distributions but only after all other creditors and stockholders have been paid. In practice, this means that ordinary shareholders may get nothing back.

Preference shareholders, as the name suggests, receive preferential treatment compared with ordinary shareholders. They rank ahead of ordinary shares when it comes to dividend payments and distributing the company's assets upon liquidation, but still behind bondholders and other creditors. Preference shares have some characteristics of both debt and ordinary shares. For example, preference shareholders receive fixed dividends from the issuing company just like bondholders receive coupon payments. However, the company is not obliged to make these dividend payments (unlike coupons payments). Hence, unpaid dividends on 'cumulative preference shares' accrue, so if the company does decide to pay dividends in the future it must pay dividend arrears to preference shareholders before it pays out to ordinary shareholders.

Some companies also issue warrants. A warrant is an option, but not the obligation, to buy or sell the underlying stock at a specified price before the expiration date. Unlike the options discussed in Section 2.5, exercising a warrant means receiving newly issued shares and hence diluting the share in the company held by the existing shareholders.

2.3.2 Issuing and trading shares

Raising capital by issuing equity is a popular method for corporations around the world. Issuing equity that is traded on exchanges like the New York Stock Exchange (NYSE) or the London Stock Exchange (LSE) not only brings in capital that the firm needs but also a number of other benefits such as liquidity, reputation and transparency.

When firms issue stock to the public for the first time, they must go through a process known as an initial public offering (IPO). Some companies offer their shares only to institutional investors, while others offer a percentage of the issue directly to retail investors, who then gain access to the IPO through a broker. Once shares are issued on the primary market, they can be bought and sold by investors on the secondary market. Buyers and sellers come together via the formal exchanges, such as the New York Stock Exchange (NYSE) and London Stock Exchange (LSE). Some offer markets specialising in particular types of equity, such as the Alternative Investment Market (AIM) which is part of the LSE and offers trading in newer, smaller ventures. Other markets can become places where certain types of company tend to list; for example, NASDAQ is a US exchange that is particularly popular with tech companies.

2.3.3 Share pricing

The fundamental value (or intrinsic value) of equity is based on an analysis of the characteristics of the investment (Beisland, 2014). There are three common methods for equity valuation.

- **Discounted cash flow (DCF) models**: These, when applied to equity, are also called **dividend discount models (DDM)**. It is the method you looked at in Box 2.1, but in contrast to valuing bonds, the present value of equity is based on the *estimated* future cash flows, such as dividends and capital gains. This approach can look at the free-cash-flow-to-the-firm (FCFF) which is available for all stakeholders or free-cash-flow-to-equity (FCFE) that looks at only the cash available to shareholders (after all other liabilities have been paid). It can incorporate how dividends are expected to grow over time at a steady rate (Gordon growth models – see the example in Box 2.2) and look at when dividend payments are different (two-step dividend discount models).

• **Multiplier models**: This method looks at the equity or enterprise multiples of companies that are publicly listed or that have been recently sold.

BOX 2.2 EQUITY VALUATION USING DDM

The Gordon growth model is a dividend discount model (DDM) commonly used for estimating a company's share price which is based on the present value of all future dividend payments.

Price per share =

$$\frac{D_1 \left(Dividend\ next\ year \right)}{\left(r \left(company's\ cost\ of\ equity \right) - g \left(growth\ rate\ for\ dividends,\ in\ perpetuity \right) \right)}$$

For example, consider a fictitious company Blue Global, which paid dividends per share of $1.56 this year, and dividends are expected to grow 1.5% a year forever. Blue's cost of equity (in other words, the return its shareholders expect in order to be persuaded to buy the shares, taking into account the company's prospects and level of risk) is 11.3%. The key question for investors is as follows: What price would accurately reflect the value of the shares? Using the equation above:

$$Value\ per\ share = \frac{1.56 \times 1.015}{\left(0.1130 - 0.015 \right)}$$

$$= \$16.16$$

Conversely, given the current market price of the shares, say $20, the above model can be used to find the rate at which dividends would have to grow to justify that price. First, rearranging the equation to solve for g, it becomes:

$$Growth\ rate\ (g) = \frac{\left(r \times Price \right) - Current\ dividend}{Current\ dividend + Price}$$

$$= \frac{\left(0.1130 \times 20 \right) - 1.56}{1.56 + 20}$$

$$= 3.25\%$$

Essentially, it looks at the price of some fundamental variable such as earnings, revenue or assets.

- **Asset-based valuation**: The idea behind this method is that the value of the firm is the value of its assets. Therefore, the value of firm is based on the value of the assets of firm minus its liabilities.

For multiplier models, an important metric for investors is earnings per share (EPS), which is the ratio of earnings available to common shareholders divided by the number of shares outstanding. It is usually reported as both basic EPS and diluted EPS. Unlike the basic EPS that takes into the account the reported earnings and the weighted average number of shares, the diluted EPS takes into account the outstanding shares if all convertible instruments (such as the convertible bonds mentioned in Section 2.2.1) were converted to ordinary shares. Dividing price per share by EPS gives a widely used metric called the price-earnings ratio (PER). Comparing the PERs of firms within similar industrial sectors can indicate which ones are overpriced or which are underpriced.

2.3.4 Equity risks

The main risks from investing in equities are income risk and capital risk. Unlike bonds, the income from shares is not guaranteed. If a company has a poor year or if it prefers to reinvest its profits, it can decide to pay no dividends at all or, except with preference shares, reduce the amount it will pay out to shareholders.

Capital risk is the chance, due to a fall in share price, that an investor will lose some of the money they originally invested or gains that had previously accrued. In the worst-case scenario, if the company goes out of business, investors could lose the full amount they had invested. This risk is highest if the investor holds the shares of just one company or of companies that are all in the same sector. One way of reducing and managing capital risk is to invest in a range of different companies, across different sectors and different countries, and also to balance equity holdings with other assets such as bonds (see Chapter 5 for more information).

2.3.5 Why invest in equities?

The GDP of a country is the value of everything it produces. Investing in shares means investing in the producers who contribute to GDP, and therefore, all being well, equity investors can expect returns that broadly follow the growth of nominal GDP, reflecting both increasing output and rising prices. So, while equities expose investors to the risk of making capital losses, they also expose them to the chance of making returns that are likely, as a minimum, to keep pace with inflation. Moreover, these returns tend on average to be substantially higher than those available from bonds; for example, based on data from 1900 to 2019, Credit Suisse (2020) estimates that globally the return on equities has exceeded bonds

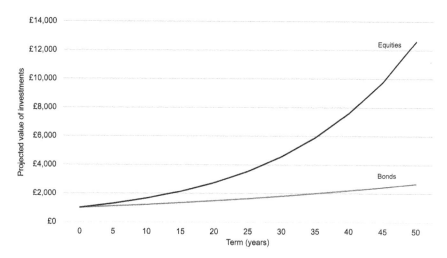

FIGURE 2.5 Projected value of investments using historic global real growth rates★.
Source: author's chart using assumptions based on data from Credit Suisse (2020).

★ *Average annual real growth rates 1900–2019*: equities 5.2%; bonds 2%. Assumes £1,000 lump
sum invested at start.

by an average of 3.2% a year. Figure 2.5 shows the substantial difference that this
growth differential could make over time. This makes equities the mainstay of
investing for growth.

However, share prices are usually more volatile than those of bonds; this can be
measured based on past data using a statistical measure called standard deviation.
The higher the deviation, the more volatile the prices. Data from Credit Suisse
(2020) show that the volatility of global equities over the period 1900–2019 measured 17.4 compared with 10.9 for bonds. Therefore, equities are not recommended
for savings that might need to be cashed in at short notice or in the short-term,
when share prices could be in a downturn. Equities are typically suggested only
for growth-oriented goals over the longer term - say, periods of ten years or more.

2.4 Foreign exchange market

Foreign exchange (FX) markets play a critical role and have significant importance in the world economy. When nations trade, lend or borrow with each
other, payment has to made in a mutually agreed currency which will require
one or both parties converting their home currency to or from the currency
used for trade or other transaction. You saw in Chapter 1 how, in the 1940s and
1950s, weak European countries were reluctant to trust each other's currencies,
preferring instead to settle their trades in US dollars (USDs). The USD continues
to be the world's dominant **reserve currency**; others include the euro (EUR),
Japanese yen, pound sterling (GBP) and Chinese yuan. FX markets are also popular with arbitrageurs and speculators.

The bulk of FX trading does not take place in formal exchanges, but as OTC transactions with each deal pairing the purchasers and sellers of the currencies involved. For example, currencies are traded in pairs when you convert your pound sterling into euros ahead of a holiday on the continent. According to the Bank for International Settlements (no date), the turnover of OTC FX instruments globally in 2019 was $8.3 trillion, of which the largest share of $3.6 trillion went through the UK's international FX market. In all, 90% of the trades through the UK market involved the US dollar, and the USD/EUR was the most traded currency pair globally, accounting for just under 25% of all FX business (Goodacre and Razak, 2019). The FX market is an OTC marketplace that is one of the largest markets in the world, and it trades 24 hours a day around the globe (Weithers, 2006).

2.4.1 The spot market

The exchange rate between currencies is driven by market forces when they are free-float currencies, as is the case with, say, the USD and the pound sterling. For example, suppose the exchange rate starts with £1 buying $1.39, but there is a surge in demand for dollars. This will cause the price of dollars to go up, which means that £1 will buy fewer of these now more expensive dollars, say only $1.20 for each £1.

Currencies can also be fixed-float, meaning that they are pegged to another currency such as the USD. The Chinese yuan and the Indian rupee are examples of fixed-float currencies.

The spot rate is the rate at which a currency can be purchased or sold in an immediate transaction. In the example above, $1.39 was the spot rate for USDs against the pound sterling. However, banks, brokers and traders will usually quote two rates: a bid and offer rate. The former is the price at which they will buy a particular currency, and the latter is the price at which they will sell a particular currency. The spread is how they generate profit (though retail customers are often charged a fee or commission as well). The spot rate or exchange rate is usually the mid-point of the bid-offer spread. Once a buyer and seller enter into an agreement to trade at the spot rate, it is common for the 'delivery' (or the settlement date) to take place one or two business days after the agreement. However, it can take even longer for hard-to-source currencies. A forward FX contract (see Section 2.5) means buyer and seller agree to transact at a date in the future at the pre-specified rate.

2.4.2 The players

Participants in the FX markets can be grouped into three main categories: exporters and importers, banks and speculators (also see Chaboud et al., 2014).

Exporters and importers are typically multinational companies that use FX markets to hedge currency risk to foreign transactions. For example, a UK-based company with major clients in the US and it expects to receive payments for goods or services supplied in USD. Companies may have suppliers in other countries that prefer to receive payments in local currency. In both situations, the company is exposed to currency risk – the markets could move in unfavourable direction, which means the company may receive less in GBP from their US clients or costs more to buy foreign currency in order to make supplier payments. So forward markets are particularly important as a way of reducing that risk.

Many banks, commercial and investment, will conduct FX trades either for clients or from their own trading accounts. Banks make money on the bid-offer spread offered to customers. As the settlement date is unusually not immediate, banks don't necessarily need to have the currency to be sold on hand (but should be able to source it in time for settlement) at the time they enter into an agreement with a customer.

Central Banks play a key role in the FX market. As a representative of the nation's government, they will set the exchange rate regime by which the currency will trade in the open market. The regime can include whether the currency is free-float or fixed-float. Central banks can purchase and sell currency in the open market just like other players in the market. They may do this to appreciate or depreciate the price at which their currency is trading by decreasing or increasing the supply of currency.

Speculators are usually sophisticated investors who buy and sell currencies solely to profit from anticipated changes in exchange rates. Unlike companies that have a need to hedge risk, speculative traders take on the risk of FX rates fluctuating and in the hope that their bets will pay off. Speculators can combine short-term financial instruments, such as treasury bills, with FX positions. The biggest speculators include leading banks and investment banks, almost all of which engage in proprietary trading using their own (as opposed to their customers') money, as well as hedge funds and other investment funds.

2.4.3 Consumers and the FX market

Allegedly during the coronavirus, retail investors confined to home during 'lockdowns' and with time on their hands turned to playing the FX market through online platforms like eToro (Insights Success, 2021). However, most individuals are more likely to engage directly with the FX market when changing money for foreign trips, buying a home or other assets abroad, or remitting earnings or transferring pensions while living overseas.

It is also important to be aware that if a retail investor holds shares or bonds issued in another country, these will commonly be denominated in another currency, which means that the investor may be exposed to the risk of the value of their investment changing because of shifts in the exchange rate. Most retail investors holding foreign investments do so through an investment fund. Fund managers have varying approaches to exchange rate risk: some take no action and allow the value of the assets in the fund to vary with exchange rate changes; others make compensating trades in FX futures market to offset the effect of exchange rate fluctuations. Investors should check which approach their funds take.

2.5 Other financial markets

There are other financial markets with which individuals usually have little direct contact but to which they may be exposed to through investment funds.

2.5.1 Money markets

Money markets, as you have already seen in Section 2.2, are a section of the fixed-interest markets that deals with the buying and selling of short-term financial securities (with terms less than one year). Banks are at the centre of money markets as both users and suppliers of capital, since short-term transfers of liquidity to each other is central to their payments business. Companies also regularly come to the money markets when they need to raise capital for short term, for example, to cover unexpected payments and working capital needs.

In essence, money markets provide governments, banks and firms with short-term liquidity, much as the bank current accounts and savings accounts that you'll study in Chapter 3 do for retail investors. However, the rates of interest payable in money markets are typically higher than those available on bank and savings accounts. Retail investors can tap into these better returns through **money market funds** which are mutual funds that pool the money of many retail investors and place it on the money markets. While money market funds are treated as safe investments, unlike a bank account, it is possible – although unusual – to lose money (if issuers default on some of the underlying short-term debts) and there is no deposit insurance for money market funds.

Investors tend to increase the amount they put into money market funds during times of uncertainty, for example during the coronavirus pandemic when equity markets became more volatile and households wanted to have ready access to their money in case of job loss (Pound, 2020). Money market funds are particularly popular with retail investors in the US where the total sum invested was $4.6 trillion in 2021 (ICI, 2021).

2.5.2 Derivatives

Derivatives are contracts the value of which depends on (in other words, is derived from) the price or value of some underlying asset or measure, such as price of a company's shares, a commodity price, the value of a stock market index, an exchange rate and an interest rate. Derivatives markets are some of the most innovative areas of financial services, and there are numerous types of contract,

TABLE 2.2 Some common types of derivative contract

Type of derivative	Main characteristics
Forward contracts	• OTC agreements between two parties. • Terms customised to the particular contract. • Binding agreement to buy or sell an underlying asset at a specified price on a specified future date. • A party who does not want to take delivery of, or sell, the underlying asset can buy an opposite forward contract to offset the deal.
Futures contracts	As for forward contracts except that contract: • has standardised terms, and • can be traded on a futures exchange, such as the Chicago Mercantile Exchange (CME).
Traded options	• Contract giving the buyer the right but not the obligation to buy or sell an underlying asset at a specified price on (or sometimes on or before) a specified future date. • The seller (writer) of the contract is obliged to deliver or buy the asset if the option is exercised. • Standardised terms. • Can be traded on an exchange.
Swaps	• OTC agreements between two parties. • Terms customised to the particular contract. • Parties agree to exchange the values or cash flows from one asset for another, for example swapping a variable-interest cash flow for a fixed-interest cash flow and vice versa, or one exchange rate for another.

Source: author's table.

some highly exotic. Table 2.2 summarises some of the more mainstream types of derivative in common use.

Derivative markets facilitate the trading of derivative contracts such as futures, options and swaps (Chance and Brooks, 2015), but by far the largest volume of these contracts is traded on the OTC market. In 2019, the value of outstanding exchange-traded derivatives was $95 trillion compared with $558 trillion OTC (SIMFA, 2021).

There are various reasons why companies and investors trade derivatives:

• **Risk management**: Companies enter derivatives contracts to reduce the risk of changes in the price of a commodity or fluctuations in interest rates. For example, a company worried about a rise in oil prices may enter an options contract enabling it to buy oil at a future date at the current price. The company may benefit if the oil price declines but will lose the fee it paid for the derivative contract. On the other hand, the company will gain from a derivative contract if the oil price does rise.

- **Speculation**: Speculators aim to make a profit from fluctuations in prices or rates. For example, a speculator may enter a derivative to buy the underlying asset at a specified price sometime in the future. If the price of the underlying asset increases, the speculator can purchase the asset at a lower price stated in the derivative contract and immediately sell it in the market for a higher price. They will make a loss if the prices move in the opposite direction.
- **Transaction costs**: Derivative contracts can allow investors to achieve the same effect as if the underlying asset or security had been brought or sold. For example, rather than buying and selling a basket of assets or securities which would incur costs for each transaction, a single derivate contract based on the collective price of the basket can be created to achieve the net effect.
- **Retention of rights**: An investor who owns shares and wants to benefit from a change in their price may enter into a derivative without selling the shares, and, by so doing, still retain certain rights, for example voting rights, attached to the shares.

While a minority of retail investors directly trade derivatives, many are exposed to them indirectly through investment funds. For example, **passive funds** (also called tracker funds) that aim to perform in line with a specified market index can be designed in one of two ways. In the first, the fund holds all the shares or other assets that make up the index. In the second, the fund holds derivatives that aim to replicate the performance of the index using the technique described under 'Transaction costs'. Another example is an 'absolute return fund' that aims consistently to produce a stated minimum return in each time period and typically uses derivatives to do this.

2.6 Conclusion

Financial markets play a key role in resource allocation enabling companies, governments and other organisations to raise capital for investment in projects, growth opportunities or day-to-day operations. This in turn may help to create jobs and boost economic growth. These markets operate most efficiently when there are many players, which increases liquidity, transparency to foster trust and access to information, sufficient regulation to ensure legal integrity and low transaction costs.

Investors, both small and large, access financial markets to take advantage of the opportunity to preserve liquidity (money markets), generate income (bond markets) and target higher returns for growth (equity markets).

Understanding the types of securities traded in these markets, their risk-reward trade-off and how these markets feed into the management of investment funds can help potential investors to better plan and take advantage of investment opportunities.

Self-test questions

1   Thinking about your investment goals and risk appetite, which of the above financial markets would you consider investing in and why?
2   Describe the difference in risks and returns faced by an investor choosing between ordinary and preference shares of a company.
3   How might the foreign exchange market and derivatives be relevant to an individual who holds foreign equities either directly or through an investment fund?

Further reading

For more information about the theory, operation and regulation of financial markets:
Bank of England: https://www.bankofengland.co.uk/knowledgebank/what-are-financial-markets-and-why-are-they-important
Buckle, M. and Thompson, J. (2016) *The UK financial system: Theory and practice.* Manchester: Manchester University Press.

To keep up to date with developments in financial markets:
Bloomberg: https://www.bloomberg.com/markets
Financial Times: https://www.ft.com/markets
Organisation for Economic Cooperation and Development (OECD): https://www.oecd.org/finance/financial-markets/

References

Adams, J.F. and Smith, D.J. (2013) 'Chapter 3 Introduction to fixed-income valuation'. *Fixed Income Analysis* (3rd edition). CFA Institute Investment Series.
Bank for International Settlements (BIS) (no date) *Turnover of OTC foreign exchange instruments by currency.* Available at: https://stats.bis.org/statx/srs/table/d11.2 (Accessed: 25 June 2021).
Beisland, L.A. (2014) 'Equity valuation in practice: The influence of net financial expenses' in *Accounting Forum*, 38(2), pp. 122–131.
Chaboud, A.P., Chiquoine, B., Hjalmarsson, E. and Vega, C. (2014) 'Rise of the machines: Algorithmic trading in the foreign exchange market' in *The Journal of Finance*, 69(5), pp. 2045–2084.
Chance, D.M. and Brooks, R. (2015) *Introduction to derivatives and risk management.* Boston: Cengage Learning.
Credit Suisse Research Institute. (2020). *Summary edition credit suisse global investment returns yearbook 2020.* Available at: https://www.credit-suisse.com/media/assets/corporate/docs/about-us/research/publications/credit-suisse-global-investment-returns-yearbook-2020-summary-edition.pdf (Accessed: 26 June 2020).
Goodacre, H. and Razak, E. (2019) 'The foreign exchange and over-the-counter interest rate derivatives market in the UK' in *Bank of England Quarterly Bulletin 2019 Q4.* Available at: https://www.bankofengland.co.uk/quarterly-bulletin/2019/2019-q4/the-foreign-exchange-and-over-the-counter-interest-rate-derivatives-market-in-the-uk (Accessed: 26 June 2021).

Insights Success (2021) *How the forex market has done in 2020.* Available at: https://www. insightssuccess.com/how-the-forex-market-has-done-in-2020/ (Accessed: 26 June 2021).

Investment Company Institute (ICI) (2021) *Release: money market fund assets.* Available at: https://www.ici.org/research/stats/mmf (Accessed: 26 June 2021).

Pound, J. (2020) 'There's nearly $5 trillion parked in money markets as many investors are still afraid of stocks' in *CNBC.* Available at: https://www.cnbc.com/2020/06/22/ theres-nearly-5-trillion-parked-in-money-markets-as-many-investors-are-still-afraid-of-stocks.html (Accessed: 26 June 2021).

Securities Industry and Financial Markets Association (SIMFA) (2020) 'Data tables' in *Capital markets factbook, 2020.* Available at: https://www.sifma.org/resources/re-search/fact-book/ (Accessed: 26 June 2021).

Tuckman, B. and Serrat, A. (2012) *Fixed income securities: tools for today's markets* (Vol. 626). Hoboken: John Wiley & Sons.

UK Debt Management Office (UK DMO) (no date) *Gilt market.* Available at: https:// www.dmo.gov.uk/responsibilities/gilt-market/buying-selling/purchase-sale-service/ (Accessed: 26 June 2021).

Valdez, S. and Molyneux, P. (2016) *An introduction to global financial* markets (8th edition). London: Macmillan International Higher Education.

Weithers, T. (2006) *Foreign exchange: a practical guide to the FX markets* (Vol. 309). Hoboken: John Wiley & Sons.

World Bank (2021) 'GDP (current US$)' in *Data.* Available at: https://data.worldbank. org/indicator/NY.GDP.MKTP.CD (Accessed: 4 May 2021).

3

BANKING

Tinashe C. Bvirindi

Key points summary

- Banks play a key role in the economy through financial intermediation, enabling the efficient allocation of resources between savers and borrowers.
- Banking institutions provide a wide variety of financial products and services and take different forms depending on the markets in which they specialise.
- The banking sector in the UK has traditionally suffered from a lack of competition, although changes in technology are beginning to have an impact on the market.

Banks play a key role in most economies as vehicles both for mobilising savings and for financing investment to support economic growth and development. In most economies, banks are the primary providers of savings products and the suppliers of external finance (capital) to both individuals and firms. In developing economies, where capital markets are relatively underdeveloped, banks dominate in the supply of both short-term and long-term capital. In developed economies, where capital markets play a dominant role in the financing of business enterprises, banks are the dominant suppliers of capital to individuals and to a large subset of SMEs that have no access to capital markets.

In this chapter, we define a bank, explore the role of banks and discuss the different types of banks, as well as the different products and services they offer. In addition, we discuss some of the recent developments in banking such as open banking and digital banking (although see Chapter 7 for more detailed discussion

DOI: 10.4324/9781003227663-3

in digital and fintech developments). Lastly, we consider the factors that have been driving change in the banking sector, as well as some of the regulatory changes that have been implemented in the aftermath of the global financial crisis of 2008.

Learning outcomes

The learning outcomes for this chapter are to:

—   Define a bank.
—   Explain the role and functions of a bank.
—   Describe the different types of banking institutions and how they benefit consumers.
—   Examine the different banking products and services available to consumers.
—   Discuss the recent regulatory changes in banking in the UK and how they benefit consumers.
—   Explain the factors driving change in the banking sector.
—   Explain the recent developments in banking.

3.1 What is a bank?

A bank can be defined as an institution whose core and current operations consist of the granting of loans and receiving of deposits from the public as well as providing payment services. This legal definition distinguishes banks from other financial institutions and is used by regulators to decide whether a financial institution should be subjected to **prudential regulations** (which you will look at in Chapter 11). However, nowadays the modern bank also offers a wide range of other services in addition to these core functions.

One element that makes banks unique is the nature of their balance sheets and the differences in the characteristics of their main assets and liabilities. Banks carry deposits and loans on their balance sheets. Deposits are the main liability for the bank and represent what the bank owes to the general public. Deposits function as money, are generally short term in nature and can be repaid when a customer demands to make a withdrawal from their deposit account or gives notice to the bank of their intention to do so (demand deposits). To the businesses and general public which the bank serves, deposits can be seen as savings instruments as they earn an interest as well as being a means for conducting economic transactions (money). The interest rate paid on deposits varies depending on general interest rate levels in the economy, the level of competition in the banking sector and demand and supply factors in the markets for loans and deposits. Contemporary economic theory also asserts that demand deposits act as a commitment mechanism that forces banks to behave prudently when taking risks. This is because the demand and supply of demand deposits influences the cost of funding for the bank, and when depositors withdraw their money en-masse a bank may be forced to sell assets at a loss to pay depositors. As a result, deposits also serve to discipline bank behaviour.

Loans, on the other hand, represent the assets that the bank creates through lending and are one channel through which the bank generates profits. When a bank lends money, it charges interest on the principal. The interest that the bank charges is often higher than the rate it pays on deposits and its other sources of funding. Traditionally, the difference between the interest earned on loans and the interest paid on deposits and other funding sources makes up the bank's profit. This difference is termed the net interest margin. A bank earns profits through lending when interest is paid and when the principal that has been loaned out is returned. Failure to return the principal will result in the bank making losses as defaulted loans must be written off against the bank's own capital.

However, it is worth noting that the traditional role of generating profits through the granting of loans has shifted as banks have found ways to diversify their income sources, for example through trading activities, payment services, advisory services among other products and services. Banks manage their assets and liabilities in order to maximise profit. This means a bank will screen its customers so that it can lend primarily to those borrowers that are likely to repay their loans. In doing so, banks assess the borrower's credit risk in order to limit the chances that the bank will lose money.

Generally, the numbers of depositors and loan holders are large and fragmented, which allows some level of diversification on both sides of the bank's balance sheet. This diversification on the asset and liability sides of a bank's balance sheet provides a natural way for the bank to reduce the risk of loans and deposits being concentrated in a few individuals or companies, which may cause problems for the bank if large borrowers fail or large depositors withdraw all of their money from the bank.

3.2 Banks and financial intermediation

In order to understand how banks operate and why we need banks, it is important to understand the process of **financial intermediation**. There are primarily two ways in which financial resources can be transferred from surplus units (savers) to deficit units (borrowers). The surplus units can provide lending directly to deficit units through financial markets or indirectly through the use of financial intermediaries such as banks (see Figure 3.1). The provision of finance through the market is referred to as direct finance and the provision of the same through intermediaries is termed indirect finance.

In the absence of market imperfections, such as information disparities between borrowers and lenders, the ultimate savers within the economy can lend directly to ultimate borrowers at no cost and without any risk of losing money. However, once market imperfections are factored in, lending directly would require that the ultimate lenders continuously monitor the activities of the

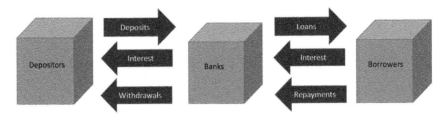

FIGURE 3.1 Banks as financial intermediaries.

borrower to ensure that the borrower is not misusing the borrowed funds and that he or she is exerting the necessary managerial effort to ensure that the project succeeds to allow loans to be repaid. In a market where the ultimate lenders (savers) are fragmented and often widely dispersed, this would require that each lender monitors the borrower and incurs costs in setting up contracts with the borrower.

This results in substantial inefficiencies as monitoring effort and transaction costs are unnecessarily duplicated. Moreover, since the benefits of monitoring are not exclusive to only those that monitor the activities of the borrower but are enjoyed by all who lend directly to the borrower, the incentive to continue monitoring the borrower deteriorates, which may result in suboptimal outcomes. In the extreme, it may lead to an outcome where monitoring does not occur. As a result, direct finance is often a privilege of firms that are large and have low **asymmetric information** costs. However, the development of new technologies which reduce monitoring costs, transaction costs and information asymmetries between borrowers and lenders has resulted in the growth of a number of direct finance platforms, for example, crowdfunding, peer-to-peer lending and direct lending (particularly in private debt markets).

When an intermediary exists, surplus units (ultimate savers/ lenders) may delegate the monitoring responsibility to the intermediary. This will allow the intermediary to monitor the borrowers on the ultimate lenders' behalf (**delegated monitoring**). The costs of monitoring the borrowers are then spread across a large depositor base, which lowers the average cost of monitoring for each individual lender (the depositor or ultimate saver). In addition, the information obtained by the intermediary during the monitoring process becomes its property and can be reused in future lending, resulting in intermediaries having information monopolies. Thus, the existence of information asymmetries (both moral hazard and adverse selection problems) and transaction costs necessitate the existence of financial intermediaries (see Figure 3.2).

3.2.1 The role of banks

Banks therefore occupy an important space in economies. Banks mediate the flow of savings and investments within the economy. At the most basic level, banks mobilise resources from the 'surplus units' (savers) and efficiently allocate

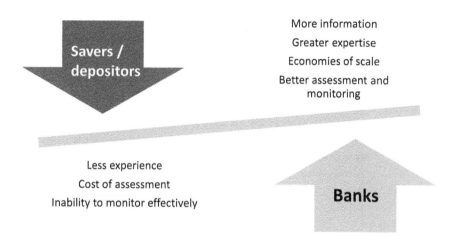

FIGURE 3.2 The benefits of banks as financial intermediaries.

them towards 'deficit units' (borrowers), who, in most cases, offer productive investment opportunities or require short-term finance in order to bridge timing differences in cash outflows and cash inflows. This process is known as financial intermediation. In the process of intermediation, banks face a number of costs when seeking to ascertain the credit-worthiness of the borrower and to minimise the risk of loss from lending money. These costs include search costs, verification costs, monitoring costs, enforcement costs, administration costs, among others. Since banks have a wider base of depositors (ultimate savers), they enjoy **economies of scale** over savers and are able to spread their costs among a wide base of savers, which lowers the average cost of financial intermediation to depositors.

In theory, the provision of credit by banking institutions allows the financial system and the economy to operate efficiently and smoothly. In the absence of banking institutions, it is hard for savers to assess whether borrowers have the capacity to repay their loans with interest. Savers generally lack information about the borrowers' credit standing, credit quality or their true intentions (asymmetric information). As a result, bad borrowers who are unlikely to repay a loan are often first in line to aggressively seek a loan (**adverse selection**). Alternatively, once borrowers obtain a loan, they may undertake activities other than those for which they obtained the loan, potentially increasing the likelihood that the lender will lose both the principal and the interest (**moral hazard**). For example, an individual obtains a business loan but uses it to go on holiday. In the presence of these information asymmetry problems, savers may decide to not lend money, resulting in a **credit crunch**. Banks have the advantage that they specialise in lending and have appropriate technologies to circumvent challenges posed by adverse selection and moral hazard problems.

Banks have advantages in the production of private information about borrowers. They have screening technologies (e.g. credit risk assessments) which can help reveal the credit quality of the borrower and thus narrow potential adverse selection problems. Moreover, they have better monitoring incentives since they can fully capture the benefits arising from information production and monitoring, and are also able to use this information in future lending decisions. As a result, **free rider problems** concerning the benefits of monitoring do not arise and monitoring efforts are not unnecessarily duplicated. This also makes it possible for bank loans to be renegotiated should the financial circumstances of the borrower change (James, 1996). In addition, banks can impose loan covenants and require collateral in lending, both of which help reduce moral hazard problems. In some countries, for example Germany, banks may also impose their officials as executives in the business of the borrower. Such practices place banks in a better position to resolve both the moral hazard and adverse selection problems that might otherwise exclude most borrowers from obtaining finance from capital markets.

Generally, savers or depositors like to lend very small amounts, which may not meet the needs of the borrowers or ultimate users. In addition, when they lend, they prefer that the lending contract to be convertible into readily usable fund (liquidity), whereas borrowers prefer loans to be long term. For example, the amount required for a mortgage is, on average, many multiples greater than the funds available in an average savings account. Banks collect the small-size deposits from a very large depositor base and cumulate these savings into larger-sized loans which they then provide to the ultimate borrowers. This process is known as size transformation, and it is made possible by exploiting the bank's scale economies.

In order to provide loans, the bank must borrow resources through deposits and other funding sources. Banks generally borrow short term in order for them to lend long term. This process is called **maturity transformation** and is one of the defining functions of a bank. Borrowers also prefer that the amount they borrow be for longer tenures, and not be available on demand, whereas lenders prefer that their claims be safe, short term and as liquid as possible. Banks resolve this mismatch in the liquidity preferences of borrowers and lenders by converting short-term liquid claims into long-term assets that cannot be easily resold (although the development of securitisation and other transacting technologies has improved the liquidity of loans and other long-term assets in banks' asset portfolios). Using our mortgage example above, banks collect short-term deposits that can be withdrawn on demand and use them to create long-term mortgage that can be repaid in 30 years. The bank's liabilities (i.e. deposits) are largely short term and in most cases can be withdrawn on demand. Bank assets on the other hand are often of a longer maturity and are generally less liquid. This mismatch in the maturity and liquidity profile of bank assets and liabilities makes banks inherently unstable and fragile (Gu et al., 2020), and is one of the reasons why banks are subjected to prudential regulations and why risk management is a fundamental part of their business (see Chapters 11 and 12).

Savers often seek to minimise risk and prefer that their money be held in safe assets. Borrowers on the other hand are willing to take more risk and as a result may default on the loans that they obtain or on their interest obligations. Banks can minimise the risk of individual loans defaulting by diversifying the loan portfolio and investments, pooling the risks together (insurance principle), screening and monitoring borrowers, holding reserves and capital buffers as well as insuring depositors' funds (see the discussion of the Financial Services Compensation Scheme in Chapter 11). This process is known as risk transformation and is one of the key roles of a bank.

At the level of the individual borrower, banks provide **liquidity insurance** by giving credit when the financial conditions of otherwise credit-worthy individuals and firms deteriorate – for example, by using overdraft facilities and credit lines to cover the period between a business supplying a product or service and receiving payment. Banks also facilitate intertemporal **consumption smoothing** by allowing deficit units to borrow against future incomes in order to fund their consumption schedules or investments and hence reduce the fluctuation of consumption or investment over time by disconnecting present-day consumption from present-day income. This means that consumers will be able to enjoy a relatively smooth consumption plan over their lifetime.

As already indicated, lenders prefer the securities they hold (deposits) to be liquid (i.e. short term and low risk), while borrowers prefer the securities that they issue (loans) to be of a longer maturity and capable of absorbing more risk (i.e. less liquid). These differences in the liquidity preferences of borrowers and lenders make the provision of liquidity another core function of banks. Banks are able to pool a large number of borrowers and lenders together and in turn produce a deposit contract that is more liquid and less risky than ultimate lenders would obtain through direct financing. At the same time, they can provide loan contracts that suit the time preferences of the borrower. Unlike other non-bank and near-bank financial institutions, banks can also provide liquidity on demand should a client's liquidity preferences change. Although banks charge a penalty for early withdrawals for time deposits or other contractual deposits, they cannot deny a client from liquidating their financial claim or from repaying their loans early. At the level of the firm, banks can also provide liquidity by, for example, backing commercial paper issuance through use of loan commitments or standby letters of credit (Gorton and Whinton, 2002).

In theory, banks enjoy information **economies of scope** in lending decisions because they have access to privileged information about current and potential borrowers with accounts at the bank, which they can use for making evaluations of borrower credit-worthiness across the bank's different product categories. For example, the same information that is used for providing a customer with a mortgage can be used by the bank when deciding whether to grant the customer an overdraft or car loan. Therefore, banks can produce and use private information to improve their lending portfolio, and hence maximise bank profitability. In the event of financial distress or potential bankruptcy, a bank may make use of its private information to make optimal decisions with regards to liquidating a business or continuing to finance its operations in the face of distress. In the same way, it can use this information to decide whether it can renegotiate initial terms of lending when circumstances change. It is worth noting that although relationship banking has continued to yield value for the banks, the development of credit reference bureaus and credit rating companies has reduced the returns that banks can reap from their internally generated private information.

Although other financial institutions may also provide credit and payment services, it is the process of taking deposits from the public and granting it as loans that makes banks unique. The creation of credit by banking institutions increases the level of money supply in the economy and has a significant impact on economic outcomes, for example, employment, asset prices, inflation and economic growth. This creation of money supply, which is regarded as a public good, is also one of the reasons banks are subjected to prudential regulations (Mishkin, 2019). Banks also serve as the conduits through which monetary policy is transmitted to the real economy. Different transmission channels of monetary policy occur with the help of the banking sector, for example the broad credit channel, interest rate/money view channel, bank lending channel and bank balance sheet channel all require the involvement of the banking sector. In addition, banks also facilitate the flow of financial transactions through payment and clearing systems.

3.3 Banks in market-based versus bank-based financial systems

In many bank-based financial systems (e.g. Japan and Germany), banks are the primary sources of finance for funding productive investments. The primary financial assets and liabilities in these bank-based financial systems are, respectively, bank loans and bank deposits. For example, in Japan and Germany, the banking system accounts for more than 60% of total financial system assets. To the average individual, the majority of savings and investment products in bank-based financial systems are provided by banking institutions in the form of deposit accounts and savings and investment accounts. In bank-based financial systems, banks engage in financial intermediation and carry risks on their balance sheet, generally because of the close relationships they maintain with their customers (Bats and Houben, 2020).

In market-based financial systems, markets channel resources directly from savers to borrowers and serve as platforms where debt and equity securities are priced, traded and distributed. In market-based financial systems, securities that are tradeable in the financial markets are the main sources of financial assets held by the public. A common example of a market-based financial institution is the US where banking institutions account for less than 25% of total financial system assets. To a lesser extent, the UK is also regarded as a market-based financial system, where banks and markets contribute fairly equal shares in corporate funding. For a basic contrast of the two systems, see Figure 3.3.

In both bank-based and market-based financial systems, banks play a crucial role in providing capital to a large subset of firms that cannot obtain finance

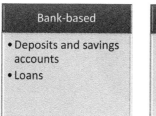

FIGURE 3.3 Basic contrast between bank-based and market-based financing.

from the market because they either lack the necessary scale economies to cover the fixed costs of market financing or carry substantial information asymmetry problems that exclude them from capital markets and make it uneconomical to raise capital through the market. Moreover, banks as delegated monitors (see Diamond, 1984) play a role in the corporate governance of the firm, particularly during episodes of financial distress.

3.4 Types of banks

The type of a bank depends on its areas of specialisation or expertise. The most common banking classifications are commercial banks, investment banks, retail banks, building societies or mortgage banks, universal banks, cooperative banks, credit unions, savings and loans corporations, among other classifications. In this section, we explore some of these classifications (see Figure 3.4).

3.4.1 Building societies or Mortgage banks

These are licensed financial institutions that specialise in providing financing for the purchase of real estate. Unlike banks, building societies are not owned by external shareholders. Mortgage holders, savers and current account holders are the members of the society and can vote on matters that affect the society. Building societies are heavily engaged in originating and servicing mortgages. Investments financed by mortgage banks can include commercial real estate, residential real estate, timberland and farmland. Mortgage banks make loans directly to their customers and generally use the purchased property as the security for the loan. Building societies operate much like credit unions in the US. Since building societies do not need to pay dividends, profits from lending are reinvested as reserves in the society which allows them to offer better rates of interests on savings and mortgages. Up until the reforms of the 1980s, the provision of mortgages was the sole responsibility of building societies, who were also barred from offering some traditional banking products such as current account. However, since then building societies have been allowed to offer traditional banking products and were even allowed to demutualise into banks.

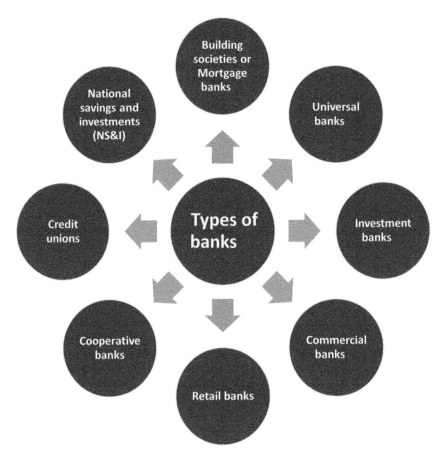

FIGURE 3.4 Main classifications of banks in the UK.

3.4.2 Universal banks

These banks offer a full range of banking services and a number of non-banking financial services under one legal entity. Universal banks provide services that include insurance, deposits and loans, trading of financial instruments (bonds, equity, currency, derivatives, commodities), advisory services, mergers and ac-quisitions, broking services and other investment banking activities.

3.4.3 Investment banks

Modern investment banks are a specialised set of financial institutions whose fundamental function is to help finance the long-term capital needs of corporates and governments. They often intermediate between the issuers of, and investors in, financial securities such as stocks and bonds. Typically, the modern invest-ment bank is engaged in providing advisory services; raising capital for large corporate entities and governments and underwriting the issuance of private and public securities; trading in equities, fixed income, commodities, derivatives and proprietary products on behalf of its customers and on its own behalf; consultancy; fund management; and custodial services. Although investment banks are generally referred to as banks, they differ significantly from traditional banks. They do not offer liquidity services in the same way that a standard bank does. However, they do offer traditional deposits, cheque and loan facilities to high-net-worth clients. In most countries, investment banks report to both the bank and securities regulators.

3.4.4 Commercial banks

Commercial banks are the largest financial intermediaries in any economy. They are involved in the provision of payment mechanisms, deposit accounts and loans to the general public and to business. These institutions play a crucial role in ensuring sustainable economic growth and ensuring social and economic stability. In the UK, at present, the largest five commercial banks –HSBC, Lloyds Bank, Barclays Bank, Royal Bank of Scotland and Standard Chartered Bank – control more than 75% of UK current accounts and 85% of UK business accounts. They employ more than 560,000 people and have more than £5 trillion in total assets. Commercial banks provide a number of services that include mortgages, car loans, business loans, personal loans, international payments, safe custody arrangements and overdrafts. However, commercial banks are not permitted to underwrite securities except for municipal bonds, government bonds and private placements. These banks are run on behalf of their shareholders and are often listed on the stock exchange.

3.4.5 Retail banks

Retail banks provide banking services to the general public and small to medium enterprises rather than to large corporations and other financial institutions. Retail banks are also known as consumer banks and focus mainly on the mass market. They often operate as a division with the banking business that deals specifically with individual customers. They offer products and services that are similar to those of commercial banks but cater only to retail customers. Retail banks offer personal current accounts and savings accounts, savings and mortgage products, credit cards and payment services such as point of sale infrastructure. In the UK, as in June 2019, there were about 77.4 million personal current accounts (96% of UK adults), and interest-bearing deposit accounts were valued at £1,208 billion (FCA, 2020: 10).

3.4.6 Cooperative banks

Cooperative banks are retail and commercial banks that are established on a cooperative basis. They are owned by their customers and are regulated under both banking and cooperative legislation. Traditionally, cooperative banks were exclusive to small villages and played a role in community development and in supporting local business. Most of the cooperative banks are now traded on the equities market and partly owned by non-members. Local branches of cooperative banks select their own board of directors and manage their own operations. However, any strategic decisions of the local branches will still require approval from the central management of the bank. Cooperative banks operate just like retail and commercial banks and provide a variety of deposit accounts and lending products to their customers.

3.4.7 Credit unions

Credit unions operate much like cooperative banks. They offer savings products, affordable lending and other financial services to their members. They are membership-based, and each member has a say in how the credit union is run. To be a member of a credit union, one must have a common connection or bond with the other members in the union commonly known as the 'field of membership'. This may include living in the same area, working in the same profession or in the same company, doing a similar kind of job, being a family member or sharing membership in a group such as a church. Savings from members are used to create a common pool of funds that is used to lend to members on fair terms that are often more favourable compared to the market. For example, interest rates made on loans are capped by the regulator, and repayment terms are flexible and do not carry penalties or hidden costs.

The funds in a credit union are generally managed and controlled for the common good of all the union members, and lending is designed to benefit the local community and offers members access to fair and manageable loans. Typically credit unions are not-for-profit institutions. Any surplus generated from their operations is either ploughed back into the union as a reserve or distributed to members as a dividend. In the UK, savings placed in a credit union are protected by the Financial Services Compensation Scheme (FSCS) (see Chapter 11). Credit unions are increasing in popularity in the UK. Currently, there are more than 500 credit unions with more than 2 million members.

3.4.8 National savings and investments

National savings and investments (NS&I) is a state-owned savings bank in the UK. Deposits in NS&I are guaranteed in full by the government. The bank offers premium bonds and a range of other savings and investments, including direct saver. It is both a non-ministerial department and an executive agency of the UK Treasury, which offers government-backed savings and investment products. It offers tax-free savings products to the UK residents.

3.5 Services provided by banking institutions

Banking institutions provide a range of financial services and products to their customers. These products and services allow consumers to meet their various financial needs. The range of products available for the customer range from payment services, savings and loan products to risk management products and safe custody services. In this section, we look at some of these products (see Figure 3.5).

3.5.1 Payment services

Banks provide a number of payments services enabling consumers to conduct economic transactions and transfer funds from one to another. These services allow consumers to buy assets and to settle liabilities, whether locally or internationally, using the financial resources that are available to them. Some of the most common payment services provided by banks include current or checking accounts, credit transfers, direct debits, card payments and mobile and online payments. Checking accounts or current accounts are transaction accounts and allow the consumer to withdraw money through writing cheques, ATM cards, withdrawal slips, direct debits or online. Until recently, money in current

FIGURE 3.5 Main savings products provided by banks in the UK.

accounts did not earn interest. Current accounts carry the lowest rate of interest among all deposit accounts. For consumers, current accounts are mainly useful for holding funds which one wishes to transact. It is more profitable for consumers with funds that are not immediately required but which they wish to keep safe, secure and liquid, to place them in higher-interest-earning savings accounts.

3.5.2 Basic bank accounts

Basic bank accounts are fee-free accounts designed for people that do not have, or do not qualify, for standard current accounts. They are suitable for people who do not have sufficient credit history to open a standard current account. Basic bank accounts offer fewer services than a standard current account, for example, they generally do not have overdraft facilities However, the accounts allow the holder to set up direct debits, withdraw money over the counter, pay online and use a debit card for payments.

3.5.3 Savings products

Savings products, as the title suggests, provide users of financial services a channel through which they can save money for future consumption. Savings products earn an interest rate and are meant to hold a customer's funds for a predetermined period of time. Banks offer a number of safe savings options that allow consumers to earn interest on their money while at the same time retaining the liquidity they desire. There are a different number of savings products, and the main ones are set out below.

3.5.3.1 Savings accounts

Savings accounts offer consumers interest on their deposits. With savings accounts, a customer is expected to keep a certain minimum amount in the account. Failure to meet this minimum requirement may result in the consumer incurring a fee. In recent times the distinction between savings accounts and current accounts has been blurred; a number of customers can now withdraw money from the account over the counter and with ATM cards and can also settle transactions with these accounts. Approximately 56% of the UK population owned a savings account in 2019, and the aggregate amount of deposits held in interest-bearing accounts amounted to £1.2 trillion.

3.5.3.2 Money market accounts

Money market accounts are often offered by banks and credit unions. They are deposit accounts that earn interest based on prevailing rates in the **money market**. The interest earned on money market accounts is higher than on savings accounts, although customers may be required to deposit a certain amount of money to set up the account and keep their account balance above a pre-specified minimum amount.

These accounts include checking and debit card privileges, but they are less flexible than regular current accounts and may carry restrictions on their use. Often these accounts charge fees, which may increase if the account balance falls below the minimum threshold. These accounts may be appropriate for savers who are risk-averse but would wish to earn higher rates of interest than obtained on savings accounts, whilst still also desiring the ability to transact on the account from time to time.

3.5.3.3 Savings bonds

Savings bonds are interest-paying deposit products offered by banks and building societies. They pay interest for a set period of time. Investing in a savings bond is similar to giving a fixed-term loan to the issuer of the bond in return of a higher rate of interest than obtained on traditional deposit accounts. The interest rate applicable varies depending on the term of the savings bond. These instruments offer capital protection to the saver whilst providing an opportunity to earn interest on capital. Minimum investments on savings bond vary from as low as £1, and maximum investments are typically set at £500,000. There are two common types of savings bonds in the UK, namely fixed-term savings bonds and tracker bonds.

I Fixed-term savings bonds usually range from six months to five years. Once money is deposited, it cannot be withdrawn until the agreed time has passed. In exchange for this inflexibility, the bonds pay a higher rate of interest than obtainable on other savings accounts that offer greater flexibility. These bonds are suitable for investing surplus funds that are not required for meeting day-to-day needs or emergencies. The longer the term that is chosen on a fixed rate bond, the higher the interest rate that is paid to the customer. However, if the customer withdraws their money before the end of the term, they will usually pay a penalty and may end up losing a portion of their capital.

II Tracker bonds are savings bonds designed to track the performance of a given index or rate – usually the inflation rate or the Bank of England base rate – over the term of the bond.

3.5.3.4 Call accounts

Call accounts combine the features of current accounts and savings accounts to give the customer some flexibility in accessing their money while also earning interest on their balances.

3.5.3.5 Individual Savings Accounts

Individual Savings Accounts (ISAs) are a creation of the UK government designed to encourage people to develop savings habits. They are a form of savings account where returns on the amount placed in the account are not taxed. However, the amount that you can save in an ISA that is shielded from taxation is limited to £20,000 per year (the 'annual allowance'). ISAs are a form of a tax wrapper and come in different types such as cash ISA and stock and shares ISA. These products are suitable when seeking to minimise tax obligations and when saving for retirement.

3.5.3.6 Lifetime ISAs (LISAs)

Lifetime ISAs (LISAs) are also a creation of the UK government to encourage saving for retirement or for the purchase of a first home. These accounts can be opened by anyone aged from 18 to 39. With LISAs one can save up to a maximum of £4,000 per annum and get a 25% bonus of up to £1,000 per year from the state until age 50. However, money invested in a LISA can only be withdrawn when buying a first home or when one reaches the age of 60 years. LISAs are also another form of tax wrapper

3.5.3.7 Direct saver

Direct saver is a savings account offered by NS&I that provides access to saving for individuals with low income. Savings in these accounts can be as low as £1 up to a maximum of £2 million. Holders of the accounts can manage their savings online and by phone.

In the UK, money held by consumers in accounts at banking institutions authorised by the Prudential Regulatory Authority (PRA) is protected by the FSCS. By contrast, sums deposited with the NS&I are backed by the government. For more detail, see Chapter 11.

3.5.4 Loan products

Banks offer a number of loan products to both individuals and firms. Loan products can be thought of as an 'I owe you' issued by the customer to the bank. Loan products offered by banks differ in terms of their characteristics, terms, flexibility and target markets. Generally, loans offer customers access to lump sum amounts to enable them to fund purchases or expenditure that they would otherwise could not afford based on their current level of savings. In return, customers will pay interest to the lender as well as the principal upon maturity. Depending on the terms of the loan, the borrower can pay regular amounts at a predetermined frequency that cover both interest and principal over the life of the loan or can pay **bullet payments** that exhaust both interest and principal. The main loan products offered by banks are discussed in the following sections.

3.5.4.1 Overdraft facilities

Overdraft facilities are a form of credit given by a bank to a customer when the customer's account has a zero balance. They allow the customer to continue withdrawing funds or transacting in excess of what they have in their account up to a pre-agreed limit in exchange for a fee. Overdrafts are often useful when a customer faces temporary fluctuations in expenditures or temporary timing differences which require them to borrow on a very short-term basis to cover outgoings before receiving payments. Generally, interest rates on overdrafts are compounded on a daily basis which makes them a very expensive source of funds. As a result, it is usually advisable only to use overdrafts in emergencies. However, in the UK, the FCA introduced overdraft simplification rules in April 2020 which forced banks to only charge simple interest on overdrafts and scrapped other fees and charges on overdraft facilities. It was envisaged that this new rule could lower costs for at least 70% of customers with overdraft facilities.

3.5.4.2 Credit cards

Credit cards are payment cards issued by banks that allow cardholders to borrow funds, up to an agreed pre-set limit, with which to pay for goods and services with merchants. Credit cards impose the condition that cardholders pay back the borrowed money, plus any applicable interest, as well as any additional agreed-upon charges, either in full by the billing date or over time. Interest on credit cards is charged on the unpaid balance, and interest rates are generally higher than those on other consumer loans. By law, the bank must allow 21 days before interest on purchases begins to accrue. Most credit cards offer incentives to customers such as cash-back on purchases, gift vouchers, airline miles and discounts, and other rewards which make them attractive to customers. Credit cards are often useful for building credit history through making low-value discretionary expenditures which a consumer wishes to repay in the very short term.

3.5.4.3 Personal loans

Personal loans are lump sum loans by banking institutions to their customers and cover a variety of needs. Personal loans can be provided on a secured (with collateral) or non-secured (without collateral) basis. Usually the maximum lump sum loan amount is a multiple of the borrower's current earnings. The money borrowed must be repaid over time, typically with interest. Interest rates charged on the loans are generally a function of the loan tenure, customer's credit standing and available collateral. Personal loans may be used for a variety of reasons such as home renovations, debt consolidation, funeral costs, vacation costs, planning a wedding, medical bills and moving costs. Personal loans are different from other loans such as car loans and mortgages that are used to fund specific expenditures. When considering a personal loan, it is important for the consumer to check whether they meet the minimum requirements for lending; determine how much it will cost (interest rates plus fees); and understand the repayment terms, collateral requirements and borrowing limits (the minimum and maximum amounts that can be borrowed).

3.5.4.4 Business loans

Business loans are, as the name suggests, loans that are provided to finance business activities. Like every other loan, they are repaid with interest and can be on a secured or unsecured basis. Unsecured loans allow the business to borrow without using any of its assets as collateral. Interest rates paid on unsecured loans tend to be higher than those that apply to secured loans, which require the borrower to use assets on the business balance sheet as collateral. Where assets are insufficient, personal guarantees may also be required from the borrower, giving assurances that they will repay the loan if the business fails to pay.

3.5.4.5 Mortgage loans

Mortgage loans are provided by banks and building societies for the purposes of buying property or land. The loan is secured by the value of the property or the land purchased until the loan is repaid. The repayment periods for mortgage loans vary from 10 years to 30 years. Mortgages generally fall into two broad categories: fixed rate mortgages and variable rate mortgages. For fixed rate mortgages, the interest rate you are charged on the mortgage stays unchanged for a pre-specified period of time, typically two to five years. Interest rates on variable rate mortgages vary, depending on the movement of the base rate. Fixed rate mortgages account for more than 75% of UK mortgages. These mortgages are popular because they offer the consumer some predictability. Knowing what the interest and principal payments will be for the duration of the loan allows the borrower to plan. With a conventional fixed rate mortgage, once the interest rate is set at the start of the mortgage it remains unchanged for the duration of the mortgage.

Another type of mortgage is the interest-only mortgage or balloon mortgage. These mortgages allow the homeowner to pay only the interest component during the life of the mortgage and then a lump sum or bullet payment of the principal on the terminal date of the mortgage. Interest-only mortgages are appropriate for customers whose intention is to dispose of the property before the mortgage expires (repaying the principal with the proceeds) or who intend accumulating sufficient savings during the period of the mortgage so as to pay the lump sum payment at the terminal date. Generally, interest-only mortgages are appropriate when property prices are rising. However, these mortgages can be risky if the borrower cannot afford the lump sum payment at the terminal date. If the homeowner fails to service their loan or to repay the loan, the property may be foreclosed and repossessed. The bank will then sell the property in order to recover the loan. Any residual amount after meeting the costs of the repossession and the disposal of the property is then paid to the borrower.

3.6 The banking sector in the UK

The UK banking sector is the largest in Europe and the fourth largest in the world. It includes over 320 banks – of which about 156 banks are incorporated in the UK – and 43 building societies (Bank of England, 2021). There are approximately 9,000 bank branches and 70,000 ATMs available in the United Kingdom. In 2019, the size of the UK banking sector was roughly 378% of nominal GDP, a significant increase from around 100% in 1975 (Norrestad, 2021). Relative to nominal GDP, the UK has the largest banking sector, compared to the US, Japan and the ten largest EU countries (Bush, Knott and Peacock, 2014). The UK as a financial centre is responsible for nearly a fifth of global banking activity. The UK hosts more than 150 deposit-taking foreign branches and 98 deposit-taking foreign subsidiaries from 56 different countries. The UK financial services sector contributes approximately 7% of total UK output and creates approximately 1.1 million jobs in the UK, accounting for almost 1.6% of all UK jobs (Hutton and Shalchi, 2021). The Big Four (HSBC, Barclays, Royal Bank of Scotland and Lloyds Banking Group) banks manage over 75% of UK current accounts and 85% of business accounts.

Although the UK banking sector is very big, its oligopolistic structure means that big banks do not face substantial competition and hence have bargaining power over their customers.

The Competition and Markets Authority (CMA) 2016 reported that customers faced barriers to switching from one bank to another and in accessing and assessing information on charges and service quality for banking products; hence, they were reluctant to switch from one bank to another, and thus older and more mature banks enjoyed first-mover advantage in the banking sector. These factors were identified as having had adverse effects on competition in the UK banking sector. In particular, the CMA report documents that large banks that enjoy more market share charge higher fees and interest rates for their products and services. The CMA report states that '... *older and larger banks do not have to work hard enough to win and retain customers, so it's difficult for new and smaller banks to grow'* (CMA, 2016). However, there have been a number of developments in the banking sector which seek to change the situation and stimulate greater competition from challenger banks. Some of the recently introduced changes to promote greater competition include open banking and overdraft simplification rules.

Bank customer behaviour has also been changing. The growing shift towards banking through digital channels for transactional purposes and increasing pressure to reduce costs has driven branch closures in the UK. The FCA reported that between 2012 and 2016, more than 8930 bank and building society branches were closed in the UK (FCA, 2018). Moreover, the recently introduced measures to increase competition in the UK banking sectors are likely to accelerate this drive towards branch closures as innovations from challenger banks and fintech (see Chapter 7) are pushing more and more customers towards digital platforms.

3.7 Recent developments in UK banking

In the aftermath of the global financial crisis of 2008, there has been an increase in the financial innovations that are changing the face of the banking industry by promoting competition and seeking to reduce costs. In this section we consider some of these developments, although it should be noted that these are only some of the key changes taking place in the banking sector.

3.7.1 Digital banking

The Bank for International Settlements (BIS, 2020) defines digital banks as

> deposit-taking institutions that are members of a deposit insurance scheme and deliver banking services primarily through electronic channels instead of physical branches. While they engage in risk transformation like traditional banks, digital banks have a technology-enabled business model and provide their services remotely with limited or no branch infrastructure. Alternative terms used by market participants and regulators are virtual banks, internet-only banks, neo banks, challenger banks and fintech banks. In contrast, online banking is often used to refer to a service provided by traditional banking institutions that allows their customers to conduct financial transactions over the internet.

Since 2011, European entities engaged in digital banking have attracted more than 15 million customers. It is envisaged that the number could exceed one-fifth of the population above the age of 14 by 2023 (Ehrentraud, Ocampo and Vega, 2020). In the UK, digital banks nearly tripled their customer base between 2018 and 2019. The Bank for International Settlements (BIS, 2020) claims that the Covid-19 pandemic may have slowed down the growth of digital banks but expects that the trend will continue once the pandemic is over.

3.7.2 Open banking and open finance

Open banking, enabled in Europe by the second Payment Services Directive, means banks can be required to release their customer data to third parties. This requires the explicit consent of the account holder, who can then enable third parties to use their financial data to provide, amongst other things, money management and payment services. Open banking gives fintech companies the opportunity to access the infrastructure behind financial services, and provides consumers with the ability to coordinate and organise all of their financial records and transactions through one single medium. For more details about open banking and its potential, see Box 3.1. Although open banking will increase competitive pressure on the traditional banking institutions and force them to innovate, the technology exposes consumers to potential risks relating to data security and data sharing.

In 2019, the FCA consulted the UK's financial services industry about the extension of the concept of open banking to other products and services (FCA, 2019). This is commonly referred to as 'Open Finance'. It found that open finance could:

BOX 3.1 OPEN BANKING IN THE UK

In 2014, the UK's competition regulator, the Competition and Markets Authority (CMA), announced an investigation into the market for bank current accounts (CMA, 2014). The concern was that there was too little competition in the sector, which was dominated by four large banks, mainly because consumers were not shopping around and switching between accounts and as a result found it hard to compare what different banks offered.

The investigation culminated in the 'open banking remedy' (CMA, 2017, Part 2) whereby the eight largest banks and the UK's largest building society (dubbed 'the CMA9') would have to develop the technology to enable a customer's current account data to be shared using a standard, secure, electronic method with third parties if the customer chooses to do this. This would open the way for price comparison sites to help consumers to compare and switch accounts by making comparisons tailored to the consumer's own specific account usage (such as volume and nature of transactions and use of overdraft).

From this modest aim, a whole new open banking ecosystem has developed. Open banking went live in the UK (the first country in world to adopt open banking) on 13 January 2018, and by end-2020, had 2.5 million users (Open Banking, 2021). Sharing account data has enabled many new fintech services beyond simply price comparison and switching. For example, account aggregator services let consumers gain a more holistic view of their finances by viewing multiple accounts through a single dashboard; budgeting apps can analyse spending patterns from the account data and provide information and behavioural nudges to help people manage their money more effectively; account information can be fed directly to debt advisers and wealth managers to streamline the advice process; and overdrafts can be replaced by cheaper borrowing from fintech firms that automatically transfer loans to a person's account when the balance approaches zero.

Although many of these fintech services had started to develop before open banking, they relied on less-secure and less-stable technology. Open banking can be thought of as creating a secure pipeline directly between a person's bank account and any third-party services they want to use. While the third-party services have to be registered with, and are regulated by, the UK's Financial Conduct Authority (FCA), there are still concerns, for example, about protecting consumer data where is the data are shared beyond the immediate third-party firms involved or intercepted by fraudsters (Reynolds and Chidley, 2018).

potentially offer significant benefits to consumers, including increased competition, improved advice and improved access to a wider and more innovative range of financial products and services such as savings, investments, pensions and insurance.

(FCA, 2021)

Its consultation revealed that open finance creates additional risks concerning the use of data and emphasised the importance of appropriate regulation to manage those risks and provide consumers with the confidence to make use of the potential opportunities offered by open finance. Whilst there is general agreement on how this could be done, it will likely be implemented in a phased and proportionate manner.

3.8 Banking regulation

Banks are some of the most heavily regulated entities in the world. This is because banks play a systemically important role in the economy by providing finance to a large number of businesses and individuals, and a disruption of the banking system has real adverse economic effects such as economic recession, a decline in corporate investment, an increase in unemployment and a decline in general societal welfare (see Peek and Rosengreen, 2013; Reinhart and Rogoff, 2009). This close relationship between the health of the banking system and economic and social conditions is a main reason for the regulation and supervision of banking institutions, including deposit insurance, capital regulation, lender of last resort function and competition legislation.

Bank regulation has tended to change one crisis at a time. With every passing crisis, a new set of changes in bank regulations is often introduced. In the aftermath of the global financial crisis, a number of regulatory reforms have been put forward by the regulators. These regulations span bank capital regulation, separation of investment banking and retail banking functions, reform of competitive structures, changes in compensation of bank executives, bank conduct and consumer protection regulations (see Chapter 11 for more detail).

Some of the key regulatory changes in banking that have been implemented in recent times are discussed below.

3.8.1 Banking Act 2009

This UK legislation introduced a Special Resolution Regime (SRR) to allow UK regulators to deal with the winding up of banks in financial difficulties. The SRR gave UK regulators three stabilisation options: The Power to sell all or part of a bank's business to a private-sector buyer (either through a share or asset sale), the power to transfer all or part of a bank's business to a 'bridge bank' wholly owned by the Bank of England and the power to transfer the bank as a whole into temporary public ownership. The 2009 Act also introduced a bank insolvency procedure and a bank administration procedure. These changes were designed to give better protection to depositors as well as to safeguard the financial system from potential collapse due to the disorderly failure of banking institutions.

3.8.2 Enhanced capital standards

In Europe, the Capital Requirements Regulations (CRR) and Capital Requirements Directives (CRD IV, V), implement the Basel III international capital standards set out by the Basel Committee on Banking Supervision (BCBS). These capital standards require banks to increase the level and the quality of capital that they hold in order to cushion themselves against risks. The standards also introduce new liquidity adequacy requirements. In addition, the regulations introduce some macroprudential elements that allow regulators to protect the banking sector against the build-up of systemic risks.

3.8.3 Ring-fencing regulations

A 'ring-fencing' regime came into effect in the UK on 1 January 2019. The purpose of the regulations is to protect the provision of retail banking functions used by UK consumers by separating them from the other activities of a bank – deemed to be outside of the outside the ring fence. A key requirement of ring-fencing is that the legal entity within a banking group that provides core retail activities cannot also provide other activities such as investment and international banking. The ring-fenced bodies (RFBs) which provide such core services for customers – defined in the legislation as making and receiving payments, deposit-taking and providing overdrafts – will be subject to ring-fencing requirements which should make them less likely to fail as a result of any problems arising in the (generally riskier) investment banking business. The regime is designed to improve the financial stability of the UK banking system and to reduce the 'too-big-to-fail' problems associated with large UK banking groups, thereby reducing the impact on the tax payers and the UK financial system should large institutions fail.

Banks with more than £25 billion of core retail deposits were ring-fenced, thereby protecting around 75% of UK retail deposits held within banking groups subject to ring-fencing. About £1.2 trillion of core deposits have been placed within ring-fenced banks (Bank of England, 2021).

3.9 Conclusion

Banks play a key role in the economy. The information production and processing roles that banks play in the economy allow them to efficiently allocate resources by reducing the impact of information asymmetries in financial intermediation. Banks, as specialist institutions in the lending process, tend to focus on various segments of the lending market. This gives rise to different types of banking institutions that provide a wide variety of financial services and financial products. Their ability to specialise in market segments means that the customer is served more efficiently. Such services include the provision of savings products, payment services and lending products.

In the UK, the banking sector plays a key role in the provision of financial services. However, the top five banks dominate. In the past, this concentration of competition among a few entities, coupled with consumer unwillingness to switch between services providers, has resulted in a lack of competition and the charging of excess fees for services such as overdrafts. This has prompted the FCA to introduce changes such as open banking and open finance, which may help challenger banks to compete with traditional banks. Furthermore, advances in technology have resulted in increased pressures to change how financial services are provided. Modern developments such as digital banking and fintech are taking root and changing the way banking business is done. Moreover, these technological developments are blurring the lines between the different classifications of banks and other financial institutions.

Self-test questions

1 What is a bank?
2 Explain how different bank products help meet the needs of customers.
3 Discuss the role of banks in the economy.
4 Discuss some of the main factors that are driving change in the financial services sector.
5 Explain some of the regulatory changes that have occurred in the banking sector post the global financial crisis of 2008.

Further reading

Arnold G. (2014) *The financial times guide to banking.* 1st Edition. Pearson FT publishing, edition 1. United Kingdom.
Cassis Y., Grossman R. S. & Schenk C. R. (2016) *The Oxford handbook of banking and financial history*, Oxford University Press. United Kingdom.

Reference list

Bank of England (2021) *List of MFIs-Updated* 2 June 2021. Available at https://www.bankofengland.co.uk/statistics/data-collection/institutions-in-the-uk-banking-sector (Accessed 4 June 2021).
Bats J. V. & Houben A. C. F. J. (2020), Bank based versus market based financing: implications for systemic risk. *Journal of Banking and Finance* 114 (2020), 105776.
BIS (2020) *Enabling Open finance through API. Consultative group on innovation and the digital economy.* BIS representative office for the Americas. December 2020.
Bush O., Knott S. & Peacock C. (2014) Why is the UK banking system so big and is that a problem? *Bank of England Quarterly Bulletin 2014*, 54, 4, 385-395.

Competition and Markets Authority (2014) *Personal current account and small business banking face full competition investigation,* Press release 6 November. Available at: https://www.gov.uk/government/news/personal-current-account-and-small-business-banking-face-full-competition-investigation (Accessed 25 June 2021).

CMA (Competition & Markets Authority) (2016) Retail banking market investigation: final report, Competition and Markets Authority.

Competition and Markets Authority (2017) Retail banking market investigation. The Retail Banking Market Investigation Order 2017. Available at: https://assets.publishing.service.gov.uk/media/5893063bed915d06e1000000/retail-banking-market-investigation-order-2017.pdf (Accessed 25 June 2021).

Diamond D. W. (1984) Financial intermediation and delegated monitoring. *Review of Economic Studies* 51 (1984) L1 393–414. The Society for Economic Analysis Limited.

Ehrentraud J., Ocampo D. G. & Vega C. Q. (2020) *Regulating fintech financing: digital banks and fintech platforms, FSI insights on policy implementation No 27,* August 2020, Financial Stability Institute, Bank of International Settlements.

FCA (2018) *Strategic review of retail banking models: progress report.* June 2018. Available at: https://www.fca.org.uk/publication/multi-firm-reviews/strategic-review-retail-banking-business-models-progress-report.pdf (Accessed 4 June 2021).

FCA (2019) Call for input: Open finance. December, 2019. Available at: https://www.fca.org.uk/publication/call-for-input/call-for-input-open-finance.pdf (Accessed 26 June 2021).

FCA (2020) Sector views 2020. Available at: https://www.fca.org.uk/publication/corporate/sector-views-2020.pdf#page=10 (Accessed 4 June 2021).

FCA (2021) FCA publishes feedback to Call for Input on open finance. Available at: https://www.fca.org.uk/news/news-stories/fca-publishes-feedback-call-input-open-finance (Accessed 27 June 2021).

Gorton G. & Whinton A. (2002) *Financial intermediation, NBER working papers, Working paper 8928,* National Bureau of Economic Research. Available at: https://www.nber.org/system/files/working_papers/w8928/w8928.pdf (Accessed 4 June 2021).

Gu C, Monnet C. Nosal E. & Wright R. (2020) *On the stability of banking and other financial intermediation, BIS working paper No 862,* Bank of International Settlements, Monetary and Economic Department. Available at: https://www.bis.org/publ/work862.pdf (Accessed 4 June 2021).

Hutton G. & Shalchi A. (2021) *Financial Services contribution to the UK economy, Briefing paper Number 6193,* 1 February 2021, House of Commons Library.

James C. (1996) Bank debt restructuring and the composition of exchange offers in financial distress. *The Journal of Finance* 52 2, 711–727.

Mishkin F. S. (2019) *The economics of money, banking, and financial markets.* 12th Edition. Pearson. United Kingdom.

Norrestad F. (2021) *Banking sector total assets as percentage of GDP in the United Kingdom 2012–2019,* Statista. Available at: https://www.statista.com/statistics/810185/total-banking-assets-as-share-of-gdp-united-kingdom/ (Accessed 4 June 2021).

Open Banking (2021) *Three years since PSD2 marked the start of Open Banking, the UK has built a world-leading ecosystem,* News release, 13 January. Available at: https://www.openbanking.org.uk/about-us/latest-news/three-years-since-psd2-marked-the-start-of-open-banking-the-uk-has-built-a-world-leading-ecosystem/ (Accessed 25 June 2021).

Peek J. & Rosengren E. S. (2013) *The role of banks in the transmission of monetary policy. Discussion Papers N013–5.* Federal Reserve Bank of Boston.

Reinhart C. M & Rogoff K. S. (2009) *This time is different: eight centuries of financial folly,* Economics Books, Princeton University Press. Princeton and Oxford.

Reynolds, F. and Chidley, M. (2018) *Consumer priorities for open banking.* Available at: https://www.openbanking.org.uk/wp-content/uploads/Consumer-Priorities-for-Open-Banking-report-June-2019.pdf (Accessed 25 June 2021).

4

INSURANCE

Lien Luu

Key points

- Insurance plays two key functions – absorbing risks and stabilising a household's income over its life cycle
- Role of insurance is not well understood, resulting in under-insurance of big risks and over-insurance of smaller risks

---

Insurance plays two key functions over the life cycle of a consumer. The first important function is absorbing risks and protecting policyholders from potential losses in exchange for a premium. Non–life insurance companies offer policies (known as property and casualty in the US and Canada) that protect individuals, businesses and their physical assets from losses caused by fire, theft, weather perils, negligence and other events. Non–life insurance companies focus on motor, marine, personal liability and property coverage, but many are now competing with life insurance companies in the sale of health and medical insurance. Lloyds' of London, a renowned global insurance marketplace, also insures specialist and unique risks, such as David Beckham's legs, Daniel Craig's body, Troy Polamalu's hair, Bruce Springsteen's voice and Elizabeth Taylor's jewellery.

A second paramount role of insurance is protecting consumers from the risk of losing their income as a result of death, disability, retirement or depletion of resources. Life insurance companies offer life insurance and income protection policies to mitigate the financial impact of premature death and disability, retirement savings plans to help individuals accumulate assets and annuities to prevent running out of money in retirement.

DOI: 10.4324/9781003227663-4

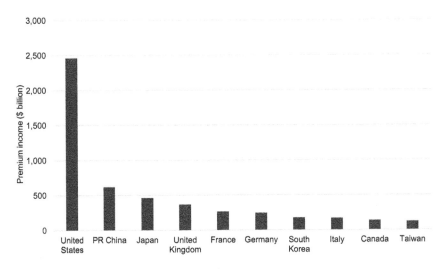

FIGURE 4.1 Largest global insurance markets.
Source: Insurance Information Institute, 2021.

These roles allow insurance companies to accumulate a vast amount of financial assets and enable them to become important institutional investors. In the UK, the insurance industry manages £1.8 trillion of investments, equivalent to around 25% of the UK's total net worth (ABI, 2021b). In 2019, insurance companies collected a total global premium of US$6.3 trillion, or 7.2% of global gross domestic product, with US$2.916 trillion (46%) from life insurance premiums and US$3.376 trillion (54%) from non-life. The largest market for insurance was the USA with more than $2.4 trillion in premiums, followed by China ($617 billion), Japan ($459 billion) and UK ($366 billion); see Figure 4.1 (Insurance Information Institute, 2021a).

There is also a difference in the amount of consumer spending on insurance in advanced and developing countries. In advanced mature economies, the premium per capita (also known as insurance density) is more than US$3,621, while the comparable expenditure per person in emerging market economies is just US$129 (Zurich, 2015). Insurance spending is positively related to income and wealth.

This chapter examines the importance of insurance to consumers in three ways: managing risks, saving for retirement and providing retirement income.

Learning outcomes

- Understand various personal risks and the role of insurance in risk mitigation.
- Examine the importance of saving for retirement, different ways to provide an income in retirement and the critical role of insurance companies.

4.1 Risk management

4.1.1 Risks

Insurance plays a critical role in helping households mitigate against a wide range of risks. According to Redhead (2008), individuals and households face six types of risks:

1 Sickness, disability and death
2 Unemployment
3 Property: Loss or damage from fire, flood earthquake
4 Consumer durable risk: Cars are vulnerable to theft or accidental damage, and accidents
5 Liability risks: Risk of a financial claim through negligence (e.g. motorists can be held legally liable for the negligent operation of their vehicles; dog owners can be held liable if their dog bites someone; property owners may be held liable if visitors to their premises get hurt; professionals such as accountants, lawyers, doctors and financial advisers can be sued by clients for negligence or malpractice)
6 Financial asset risk. The risk that the value of investments may fall, but this risk is not insurable (Redhead, 2008, pp.20–21).

4.1.2 Principles of insurance

Insurance protects individuals and businesses only from pure risks. These can be defined as risks which only have adverse (loss) or neutral outcome (no loss), but not gain. This is known as the principle of indemnity, which seeks to restore the insured back to its financial position before the loss without rewarding or penalising the insured for its loss. Examples of pure risks include accidents, damage to property from fire, flood or earthquake. However, life insurance contracts do not represent indemnity contracts because human life is not quantifiable. In addition, speculative risks are not insurable because there is a possibility of loss or gain. For example, there is a chance of making a loss or gain when investing in shares or stock, and so this is not insurable.

Insurance contracts are also based on the principle of fair presentation (changed from the utmost good faith). Due to the existence of asymmetric information, the insured is required to disclose all relevant factors when applying for insurance, otherwise non-disclosure can lead to the policy being annulled later. For example, homeowners need to disclose issues such as subsidence, flooding or burglary when applying for home insurance, while those who apply for life and health insurance have to declare factors such as smoking, hereditary diseases and dangerous sports.

A third important principle of insurance is insurable interest, where the insured needs to have some pecuniary interest in the subject matter of the insurance to reduce the risk of moral hazard. For example, the policyholder must have some vested interest in a property in order to buy property insurance, so that if the property is damaged, they will incur some financial losses. A husband and wife have an unlimited insurable interest in each other and can take out a life insurance policy on each other, but not on other people who they do not have a financial interest in.

Different risks have different impact and probability of occurrence. Some risks have a low chance of occurrence before a certain time (e.g. dying before age 65) but their impact can be devastating. Insurance companies can insure these risks, and transferring them gives consumers peace of mind. Frequent and high-impact risks may not be insurable (e.g. those who have suffered a heart attack are likely to suffer another – this risk is not insurable or is very expensive to insure) and consumers need to rely on savings or other assets to deal with these. Low-impact risks are not worth insuring, and the best solution is to use savings to compensate any financial loss.

4.1.3 What insurance and protection products do people buy in UK?

An analysis of the patterns of insurance purchase shows that consumers tend to overestimate some risks, while underestimating others. According to the FCA's Financial Lives survey (FCA, 2021a, p.60), a high proportion of households have car insurance (68%) and buildings insurance (61%). This is not surprising because these are compulsory, required by law and the lender, respectively. However, it is surprising that a high proportion of households have contents insurance (66%). This is popular because the price is relatively low in relation to the cost of replacement, the policy cover is relatively simple and policyholders receive tangible benefits and enjoyment when a claim is made (Figure 4.2).

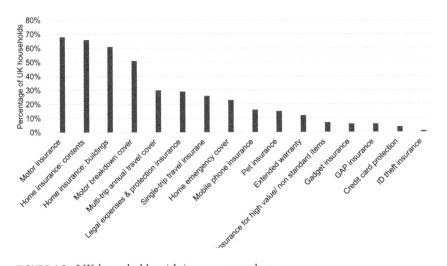

FIGURE 4.2 UK households with insurance products.
Source: FCA, 2021, p.60.

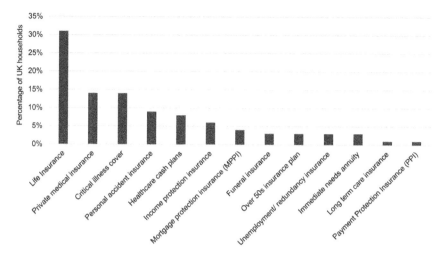

FIGURE 4.3 UK households with protection products.
Source: FCA, 2021, p.60.

Figure 4.3 shows the percentage of UK households who buy insurance to protect themselves against accident, sickness, death and unemployment. Only a third of households have life insurance, 14% private medical insurance and critical illness, 6% income protection and 3% unemployment insurance. The take-up of these policies is low, partly because they are more complex and more expensive than insurance products discussed above (Figure 4.2).

Many people opt to accept the risk rather than pay for insurance. This could be due to several factors. There is a lack of satisfaction from buying insurance which, unlike other services and products, does not provide any immediate benefits. Many people therefore may perceive buying insurance as a waste of money as they do not receive anything in return (Madura, 2014, p.312). It could also be due to ignorance or indifference, as many people do not want to think of the unpleasant aspects of life such as death and poor health. Spending money on goods and services that provide an immediate benefit brings more pleasure. The intangible nature of life insurance also makes it difficult for many people to appreciate the benefits, as these are only realised after an individual has died.

4.1.4 Reasons why protection is important

Yet, protection against premature death and disability is critical for three key reasons. First, our biggest asset is our human capital, or the present value of our future earnings, and this is determined by our skills, experience, qualifications, health, personality, social attributes, talents and ability. Our ability to earn a future income can be lost through premature death or impaired by poor health and disability (Luu, 2017, 2019 a and b).

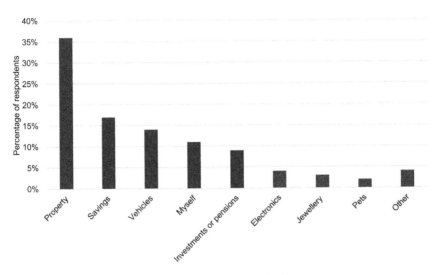

FIGURE 4.4 Perception of biggest assets in financial value.
Source: Legal and General, *Deadline to Breadline 2020*, p.26.

Many people underestimate the value of their human capital. Legal and General's Deadline to Breadline 2020 report found that 89% of people in the UK do not see themselves (their earning potential) as their largest financial asset. They see their property, savings and vehicles/cars to have a higher financial value, leading them to insure these assets, but not themselves (Figure 4.4).

In reality, human capital (earnings over your lifetime) is the biggest and the most important asset any individual can own. In the UK, the average working household's annual income is just under £35,000, and so the average worker could earn over £1.4 million in their lifetime. These figures show that individuals are worth significantly more than the average home (£232,000), the average price of a used car (£10,000) and the average savings pot (£2,700) (Legal and General, 2020, p.26). The value of human capital, therefore, has been overlooked, and this explains the existence of a massive insurance protection gap.

A second compelling reason why protection is necessary is due to the need to support dependents, such as a spouse and children. The death of a partner presents financial difficulties for many people. In the UK, a survey from Royal London found that over two-thirds of people who had lost their partner over the previous five years were practically unprepared for the monetary loss. One in five people said the impact of having a lower income was the most difficult element to deal with (Royal London, 2015). Life insurance is also necessary to ensure funds are available to repay debts. As a mortgage debt is secured on the property, lenders have a right to take back the property if mortgage repayments are not met. Research shows that surviving families with a mortgage feel insecure about their home after the premature death of the breadwinner. Some are forced to sell at low price, while others have to move in with family (Corden, Hirst and Nice, 2008).

Personal protection is also imperative because many households do not have much savings to cope with the unexpected. In 2020, 1 in 10 Brits (9%) had no savings at all, a third less than £600 in savings and 41% did not have enough savings to live for a month without an income. The average person in the UK had £2,700 saved (Legal and General, 2020), but many people feel that they need £12,200 of savings to make them feel financially secure for one year. Legal and General believe that, based on typical monthly outgoings, the amount required to give financial security for one year is much higher, at £30,000 (Legal and General, 2020, p.8).

Many households in other countries also have a low level of savings. In the US, average household savings are $16,420, but 69% of adult Americans have less than $1,000 in a savings account and 54% of those between age 45–54 have no savings. In Australia, 13.4 million people do not have emergency savings to fall back on if they were unable to earn an income for more than three months (Twiggs, 2019; Urosevic, 2021). When savings are limited, the need for insurance is even greater as households cannot rely on their own resources.

4.2 Risk of premature death

4.2.1 Causes of premature death

Every individual faces the risk of dying young (before the age of 65), also known as mortality risk or premature death. The Japanese life insurance market is the third largest in the world. Nearly 90% of Japanese households carry life insurance policies (EY, 2019, p.5). In contrast, only 54% of US households and a third of UK households have life insurance.

The probability of death before the age of 65 in the UK is low (1% or less), but some causes are unpredictable, such as road accidents. Every year, more than 150,000 people suffer from injuries on the road, with nearly 2,000 killed. Globally, approximately 1.35 million people are killed on the road every year (Center for Disease Control and Prevention, 2020; Department for Transport, 2021). More people die from preventable causes. In the UK, more than 100,000 people die prematurely every year due to an unhealthy lifestyle: smoking, drinking too much alcohol, poor diet, lack of physical activity or being overweight (Department of Health, 2014). On a global scale, these are also the major causes of premature death (Figure 4.5).

Many people are worried about premature death because it can result in serious financial problems for the survivors due to the loss of the breadwinner's future earnings (leading to a possible reduction in standard of living), the incurrence of additional expenses (e.g. funeral) and the reduced ability of the surviving spouse to work, caused by grief and increased responsibilities.

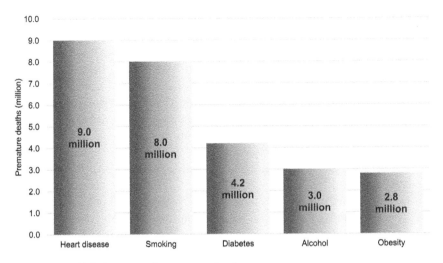

FIGURE 4.5 Global causes of premature death.
Source: World Health Organization, 2021.

4.2.2 Life insurance as hedge against financial impact of premature death

The best hedge against the financial impact of premature death or mortality risk is life insurance. The lump sum payout gives survivors the money to pay off debts or to buy an income. The financial payout allows children to continue their education and mortgage payments to be repaid even if the breadwinner dies during the early adult years. In other words, the primary function of life insurance is to provide for various household needs (e.g. funeral expenses, pay outstanding debts, buy a replacement income to maintain lifestyle, pay inheritance tax, support a business), prevent a fall in household's standard of living and stabilise the household unit (Goldsmith, 1983, p.474).

There are three main types of life insurance policy: term life insurance, endowment insurance and whole of life. Term life insurance is relatively cheap because it is pure insurance, as the sum assured will be paid only if the life assured dies within the term. If they do not, no payment is made as the policy has no surrender or cash-in value, and the policy then expires. Term assurance can be bought for a minimum of one year to a maximum of 50 years (the insured must be 90 years old or younger when the policy ends (Table 4.1).

Endowment insurance is an investment product that you buy from a life assurance company. It is set up as regular savings plan and pays out a lump sum at the end of a set period or on death during the term of the policy. It was popular in the 1980s in the UK when a million policies were sold in a single year. However, it is not very popular now due to a mis-selling scandal in the 1990s and the absence of a guaranteed lump sum. A policy might stipulate an amount that you might be paid, but this is all dependent on investment performance. A poor investment

TABLE 4.1 Different types of life insurance policies

Types of life insurance	Main features
Term life insurance	• Cover for a period of time. • Lump sum payout. • Relatively cheap. • No cash in or surrender value (e.g. no refund on premiums if there is no claim). • Different types – level, decreasing, increasing.
Decreasing term insurance	• Popular with homeowners who have a repayment mortgage, as level of life insurance coverage declines at the same rate as the mortgage balance. • Popular with families with young children who need high level of insurance in the earlier years when the children are young and less when they are older.
Family income benefit	• Type of term insurance. • Pays income for period remaining after death (e.g. term chosen may be until youngest child reaches 23). • Relatively cheap.
Endowment policy	• Mainly used for investment rather than protection. • Often regular savings plans but can also be single-premium investments. • Pay out at end of term or on death (but single premium policies can pay income). • Payout can be guaranteed (without-profits policy), but more often not guaranteed and dependent on investment performance (with-profits and unit-linked policies).
Whole of life	• Can be used for protection or investment. • Cover for the whole of life. • Usually regular premium policies when used for protection; more expensive than term insurance. • Lump sum payout may be guaranteed or dependent on investment performance. • Single-premium policies often used for investment and then have low level of life cover; may pay out a lump sum or income.

performance could drastically reduce the payout, which means that you could have a shortfall if you were using the insurance to save for a specific goal, such as paying off your mortgage. This happened in the UK, where payouts fell by 78% over 25 years, forcing mortgagees to sell their homes, dip into their pension pots or rethink their retirement plans (Green, 2020; Peachey, 2013).

Whole of life is an investment-type life insurance and is more expensive than term life insurance as there will be a guaranteed payout. This means that when a policy is cancelled, there is a surrender or cash-in value.

Some financial planners recommend consumers buy term insurance and invest the difference (difference between term and whole of life premium). Some experts recommend that individuals build their financial security over their lifetime by taking out a base amount of life insurance to pay for funeral, burial and other expenses on death, then add multiple term assurance policies when they begin to have dependants. These policies should be layered so that individual policies can be stopped as the need for life insurance declines. By the time an individual reaches retirement, all policies can be stopped, as it is assumed that an individual has built up sufficient wealth to provide for survivors' needs (Garman and Forgue, 2018, p.379).

However, whole of life policies are expensive and are generally deemed poor value. Since death is certain and funeral costs are relatively low (up to £10k), normal savings are typically a better approach.

4.3 Protection against incapacity through sickness or accident

The risk of poor health – or more formally known as morbidity risk – is a far greater risk than the risk of premature death (Luu, 2019b). In addition to the risk of injuries on the road, many people in the UK also suffer from work-related causes. The Health and Safety Executive (HES) reports that more than 1.6 million workers in the UK suffered from work-related ill-health in 2019–2020, caused by stress, depression or anxiety (51%); musculoskeletal disorders (30%); and other types of illness (19%). As a result, 32.5 million working days were lost, costing more than £16 billion annually (HES, 2020). Mental health has also become a prominent issue, and 300,000 people with a long-term mental health problem lose their jobs each year (Farmer and Stevenson, 2017).

The risk of developing a critical illness is also real. A male non-smoker aged 40, for example, is 4.1 times more likely to suffer from a critical illness than premature death before reaching the age of 65. In the UK, there are 7.4 million people living with heart and circulatory diseases and 2.5 million with cancer, the latter estimated to increase to 4 million by 2030 (Smith, 2020).

Critical illness causes financial strains on individuals, as they may not be able to work full-time, if at all, while their expenses rise. They might have to spend more money on healthcare costs, buy new clothes due to weight loss/gain and pay more for heating (Smith, 2020). Indeed, Royal London reported in 2017 that 3.5 million people who were diagnosed with a critical illness between 2012 and 2017 were not able to cope financially (Royal London, 2017). Having a critical illness policy can help alleviate financial stress in times of need.

4.3.1 Income protection as hedge against the financial impact of disability

There are two types of policies to protect individuals against disability: income protection and critical illness.

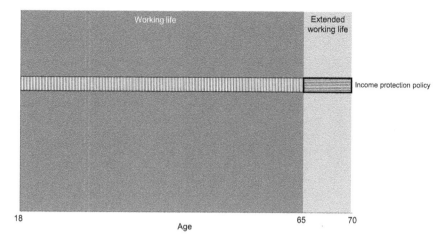

FIGURE 4.6 Role of income protection as replacement income.
Source: author's own diagram.

Income protection is designed to provide a replacement income during the whole of an individual's working life or a set period of years. If someone starts an income protection policy at the age 18 to the age 65, they could have protection for 47 years provided they continue the premiums, as can be seen in Figure 4.6. However, as many people are now working beyond 65, insurers offer cover to the age of 70, giving policyholders 52 years of protection. Income protection insurance is costly, and so insurance companies now offer 'budget' policies as a cheaper alternative, which pay out for a shorter period (five years, or until retirement if sooner).

There are two ways to calculate the level of income cover needed.

1   The salary approach: Using this approach, an individual can apply for maximum cover allowed by an insurer, usually 50–70% of gross salary. This is designed so that you do not profit from being unable to work.
2   The expenditure approach: If your income is much higher than your expenditure, you could make the premium more affordable by buying cover based on your annual expenses (rather than salary). For example, you earn £100,000 a year but your annual expenditure is £35,000. If you buy cover based on this lower amount, the premium is more affordable and sustainable.

Income protection premiums are determined by a wide range of factors, such as state of health, type of occupation and the level of income needed. In addition, premiums are also affected by the factors set out in Table 4.2.

A major drawback of an income protection policy is that the amount of cover you can buy is linked to your salary. If you have no earnings, the amount of cover

TABLE 4.2 Factors affecting income protection premiums

Factors affecting income protection premiums	Description
Deferral period	Waiting time before pay-out from insurance company – 4, 8, 13, 26 or 52 weeks. The longer the deferred period, the lower the premium. Deferred period is often chosen to coincide with the end of sick pay from work.
Term of policy	The number of years of cover also determines premium. The older we get, the higher the risk of illness. Policy that ends at age 70 is more expensive than 60 or 65.
Many people have a bias towards minimising small, initial losses. For example, they prefer to have a shorter waiting period. However, it is recommended that it is better to have a longer term so that there is cover when the risk rises as we get older.
Waiver of premium	A waiver of premium rider is an insurance policy clause that waives premium payments if the policyholder becomes critically ill, seriously injured or disabled (in other words, they do not need to pay the premium). The inclusion of this increases the cost.
Definition of incapacity	**Own occupation**: when an individual is unable to continue one's own occupation. This is the best definition but the most expensive.
Suited occupation: unable to follow any occupation to which one is suited in accordance with one's education, training or experience.
Any occupation: totally unable to follow any occupation.
Inflation protection	Premiums are higher if the level of cover increases every year in line with inflation.

you can buy will be restricted. A critical illness policy, therefore, may be more suitable for some individuals because it is not linked to earnings.

4.3.2 Critical illness as hedge against financial impact of disability

An income protection policy pays a monthly income to enable you to meet expenses. However, you might also need a lump sum to pay off debts or pay for treatments or adjustments to the home (e.g. wheelchair access). A critical illness policy is designed to give you a one-off lump sum on a diagnosis of a range of critical conditions (up to 40 or more conditions and some insurers cover over 100), such as stroke, cancer and heart attack. In 2019, cancer was the biggest single reason for an individual critical illness claim (ABI, 2020). According to the FCA, 14% of individuals in the UK have a critical illness policy, in comparison to 16% who have phone insurance (FCA, 2020, p.60).

A critical illness policy often requires a 14–30 day survival period – that is, an individual must survive this period for the insurance company to pay out. If they do not survive the minimum period, there is no pay out. For this reason, a critical illness policy is often combined with life insurance, so that payment will be made on the diagnosis of a critical condition or death.

If financial resources were not an issue, it would be advisable to take out both a critical illness policy and an income protection policy. However, the ideal amount of cover might not be affordable. For individuals with a good level of income, income protection might be suitable as it provides a replacement income for an extensive period of time and covers a wider range of conditions (e.g. stress, back pain). However, for others with little or no income, a critical illness policy may be more suitable, as the amount of cover is not determined by salary.

In summary, insurance gives us a financial tool to hedge against two of the greatest risks in life: mortality (death) and morbidity (ill-health). Premature death and prolonged illness can cause severe financial havoc, such as a loss of family home, a decline in living standard and a descent into poverty. Without any protection plan in place, individuals may live a life filled with financial anguish and fears, worrying how their family might cope should these risks materialise. Insurance therefore has a valuable role to play, because it offers not only tangible benefits in the form of a potential financial pay-out but also intangible benefits such as peace of mind and financial security.

4.4 Saving for retirement

As life expectancy increases and people spend a longer period of time in retirement, saving for retirement has become increasingly more important. According to the ONS, men reaching age 65 between 2017 and 2019 could expect to live another 18.8 years and women another 21.1 years (ONS, 2020b).

In 2020, people in the UK became entitled to a state pension from the age of 66, but on average this only provides around 29% of their pre-retirement income, in comparison to 36.8% for Japan, 50% for the USA and Canada and 92% for Italy, as can be seen in Figure 4.7 (OECD, 2019). To ensure a comfortable living standard and avoid poverty, most individuals in the UK therefore need to save to make up for the shortfall in income.

4.4.1 How much income do individuals need in retirement?

The consumer magazine, *Which*, has commissioned research into the cost of retirement lifestyles and how much saving is needed to fund these. It finds that a single person requires £13,000 per year to cover basic expenses, £19,000 for a comfortable lifestyle and £31,000 for a luxury one, on top of a full state pension. A two-person household requires slightly more income, between £5,000 and £10,000, than a single household. The costs of different lifestyles in retirement are summarised in Table 4.3.

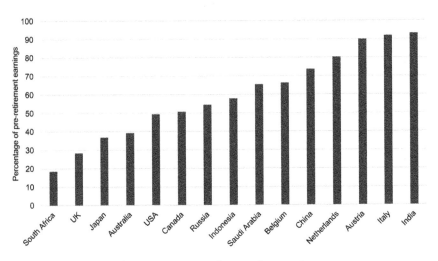

FIGURE 4.7 State pension as percentage of pre-retirement income.
Source: OECD, 2019.

People in the UK, however, are not saving enough for retirement. A report by Deloitte (2020, p.6) shows that a single person needs to have pension savings in excess of £150,000 (assuming full state pension entitlement) if they want an income of £18,500 per year to live a comfortable life in retirement. *Which* believes that individuals need to save a bigger fund – £169,175 for a comfortable lifestyle and £456,500 for a luxurious lifestyle. However, around 70% of consumers currently aged between 50 and State Pension age have DC (defined contribution) savings below £24,400 and DB (defined benefit) entitlement of less than £7,000 per year. Therefore, many consumers have an income shortfall in retirement.

The level of monthly saving is determined by the age when saving begins. The earlier you start to save, the less you need to save per month. If you wish to accumulate a fund £169,175, a sum deemed necessary to supplement state pension to provide a comfortable lifestyle, you need to save £213 per month if you start at age 20, compared to £647 if saving begins at age 50. Likewise, if you wish to accumulate a sum of £456,500, this requires a monthly saving of £570 at the

TABLE 4.3 Costs of different lifestyles in retirement

Lifestyle	Singles	Two-person household
Essentials: covers basic expenditure	£13,000	£18,000
Comfortable: covers basic expenditure and some luxuries, such as European holidays, hobbies and eating out	£19,000	£26,000
Luxurious: enough to pay for basic expenditure, plus long-haul trips and a new car every five years	£31,000	£41,000

Source: Davies, 2021.

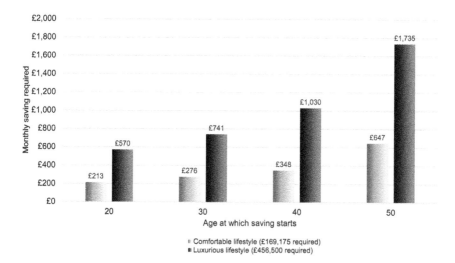

FIGURE 4.8 Monthly savings required at different ages.
Source: author's diagram using calculations from *Which*, 2021.

age of 20, in comparison to £1,735 at age 50 (see Figure 4.8). This is due to the power of compound interest.

4.4.2 Global retirement savings

The value of global retirement savings was estimated at US$50 trillion at the end of 2019, with the largest market to be found in the US, followed by the UK and Canada (Table 4.4).

There are two key ways for individuals to save for retirement in the UK: contribute to a pension scheme set up by their employer or open a private pension plan. Employers offer two types of pensions: defined benefit (DB) and defined

TABLE 4.4 Value of retirement savings

Country	Value of retirement savings (in trillions)	% of OECD
Worldwide	$50.00	98.4%
US	$32.2	65.0%
UK	$3.6	7.3%
Canada	$2.8	5.6%
Australia	$1.9	3.8%
Netherlands	$1.8	3.6%
Japan	$1.5	2.9%
Switzerland	$1.1	2.3%
Other 30 OECD countries		9.0%

Source: OECD, 2020, pp.9–12.

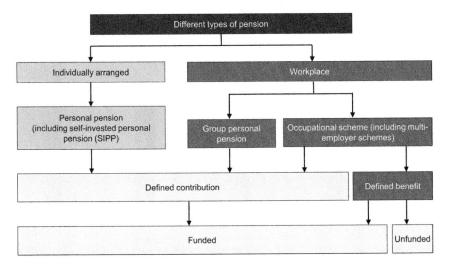

FIGURE 4.9 Different types of pension schemes.
Source: Adapted from ONS 2020c UK Pension Surveys.

contribution (DC). DB pension scheme (also known as salary-related) is often perceived as the best type of pension because employers bear the main risks and offer employees a promised income based on a fraction of their salary for each year they work for a company (the accrual rate). There are two types of DB schemes: funded schemes where the pension funds accumulate financial assets to pay retirement benefits, and unfunded schemes or pay-as-you-go scheme where they use contributions from current employees to pay benefits to retired members (Figure 4.9).

DB pension schemes were the norm after the Second World War, but by 2018 many private schemes had been closed for existing and new members (Stittle, 2018). Many employers now offer defined contribution pensions (also known as money purchase), where income in retirement is determined by the level of contributions, investment returns and charges. By moving to defined contribution pension schemes, employers are shifting the responsibility for retirement provision to employees who now bear all the risks (investment, annuity and longevity).

DC employers may offer a group personal pension, where the responsibility of running an occupational-defined contribution scheme is outsourced to an insurer. In this type of pension scheme, the contract is between the employee and the insurer, even though the employer has facilitated the arrangement.

If an individual has no access to a workplace pension, they can set up a personal pension plan with an insurer. This plan gives individuals more control over their retirement savings and an earlier access (they can take money out earlier than occupational schemes). However, the disadvantage is that they do not receive employer contributions.

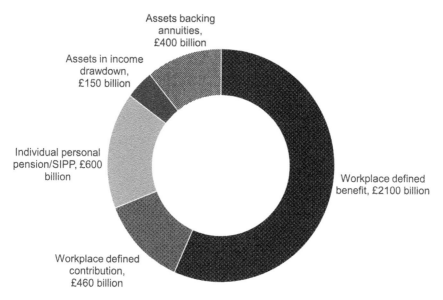

Assets backing
annuities,
£400 billion

Assets in income
drawdown,
£150 billion

Individual personal
pension/SIPP, £600
billion

Workplace defined
benefit, £2100 billion

Workplace defined
contribution,
£460 billion

FIGURE 4.10 Overview of UK's pension system.
Source: The Investment Association, 2020, p.56.

According to the Investment Association's estimate, the UK pension market was
worth approximately £3.8 trillion at the end of December 2019 (see Figure 4.10).
The total includes all assets in DB and DC, and personal pensions. Occupational
pension schemes manage £2.56 trillions of assets, but the value of DB pensions is
nearly five times bigger than DC. Insurance companies control £1.15 trillions of
retirement savings in the UK. This includes savings of retirees (£550 billion) and
non-retirees (£600 billion) (The Investment Association, 2020, p.56).

The FCA's Financial Lives Survey shows that the percentage of UK adults saving
for retirement has increased from 51% in 2017 and to 58% (equivalent to 30.2 million
adults) in 2020. However, the survey shows that there was still a significant number
of adults (9.6 million or 24%) with no membership of a pension scheme. Demographic groups with the lowest pension ownership included 18–21-year-olds (only
16% have a pension plan), the unemployed (28% compared with 80% of all adults in
work) and the self-employed (55% compared with 85% of employees) (Table 4.5).

In addition to the concern about the number of people not part of a pension
scheme, there are also worries that even when they are members of a pension
scheme many people are not saving enough for a comfortable retirement. The
Pensions and Lifetime Savings Association (PLSA) found that 18 million UK
adults do not know if they are saving enough into their pensions. The World
Economic Forum has warned that retired people in the UK will, on average,
outlive their savings by more than ten years (Riley, 2020). Indeed, the average
pension pot in the UK (approximately £50,000) is only enough to cover two
years of income for an average earner (PWC, 2018, p.9).

TABLE 4.5 Membership in different pension schemes

Type of pension	Number	Percentage
DC	20.8 million	40%
DB	11.4 million	22%
DB and DC	1.9 million	4%
No pension	9.6 million	24%
Do not know		7%

Source: FCA, 2021, p.55.

4.4.3 Retirement savings gap

Inadequate income in retirement is a real global concern. Many people face the prospect of poverty in retirement because they are not saving enough. There is a gap between what people save and what they need for an adequate standard of living in retirement, known as the 'savings gap'. In eight countries with some of the largest pension markets or populations, including the UK, Australia, Canada, China, India, Japan, Netherlands and the USA, the retirement savings gap is projected to balloon from $70 trillion in 2015 to $400 trillion by 2050 (World Economic Forum, 2019, p.7) (Table 4.6).

In the UK, there are various estimates of the savings gap. In 2015, Deloitte forecast that the savings gap would reach £350 billion by 2050 and recommended UK savers to put away an additional £10,000 per year (Deloitte, 2015). In 2018, PWC estimated that the gap in 2015 in fact was £6 trillion, and that it would quadruple to £25 trillion by 2050. However, PWC argued that the UK's population has limited capacity, or propensity, to save long term for two reasons: real earnings have been flat over the past decade, and household indebtedness has increased (PWC, 2018, p.9). By 2019, the World Economic Forum estimated the savings gap in the UK at $8 trillion in 2015, and expected it to quadruple to $33 trillion by 2050 (World Economic Forum, 2019, p.9).

TABLE 4.6 Retirement savings gap around the world

Country	Savings gap 2015 – US$ trillion	Savings gap 2050 – US$ trillion
US	$28	$137
China	$11	$119
India	$3	$85
UK	$8	$33
Japan	$11	$26
Canada	$3	$13
Australia	$1	$9
Netherlands	$2	$6
Total	$70	$400

Source: World Economic Forum, 2019, p.7.

A number of causes of the savings gap have been identified, including longer life expectancy; closure of defined benefit schemes; rising healthcare and long-term care costs; low savings as a result of a preference to spend today rather than save for tomorrow (myopic financial behaviour); and a lack of knowledge of how much has been saved (or needs to be saved) (Actuarial Post, 2021). At an individual level, it is difficult to estimate how much saving is necessary because the date of death is uncertain, and so cannot be mathematically calculated. However, it can be precisely modelled for *groups* of individuals, which is why annuities work (see discussion below on annuities). Efforts to promote more saving for retirement also need to focus on financial literacy, which is linked to higher household wealth and a higher propensity to save (National Bureau of Economic Research, 2008).

4.5 Annuities market

Insufficient savings and increasing life expectancy mean that individuals face the risk of running out of money in retirement. Insurance companies therefore offer annuities to mitigate against longevity risk. An annuity is a type of retirement income that you can buy with part of your pension pot, and so you exchange a lump sum for a guaranteed income, either for life or for a set period. Economic models suggest that risk-averse individuals would prefer to buy an annuity to prevent outliving their savings. However, few households purchase an annuity. Lockwood (2012) reports that less than 5% of a sample of single retirees in the US own an annuity; while Inkmann et al. (2011) show that only 6% of older households in the UK voluntarily purchase an annuity. This conundrum has been dubbed the annuity puzzle (O'Dea and Sturrock, 2020, p.1).

Prior to 2014, individuals reaching retirement in the UK had to buy an annuity with their pension fund. However, the introduction of Pension Freedoms in April 2015 removed the requirement to buy an annuity altogether, and gave those above the age of 55 (the earliest age when individuals could take money from their personal pensions) the option to draw down any amount from their DC pension pot and pay only their marginal income tax rate. This led to a dramatic fall in the sale of annuities, as can be seen in Figure 4.11. In 2009, 466,000 annuities were sold in the UK, but the number fell dramatically to 82,000 in 2015. By 2019, only 65,000 annuities were sold (FCA, 2020; PPI, 2020, p.24).

Research by the government shows that not everyone sees an annuity as a good deal (Department of Work and Pensions, 2020). Some do not like the fact that they are based on calculations of life expectancy, as expected longer life expectancies mean poorer annuity rates and therefore lower annuity income. They feel that an annuity provides a relatively low annual income.

Indeed, consumers see annuities as investments rather than as insurance. This means that low annuity rates make annuities unattractive and expensive versus other options (income drawdown). Table 4.7 compares the lump sum required to provide the same level of income for annuity and income drawdown. If we

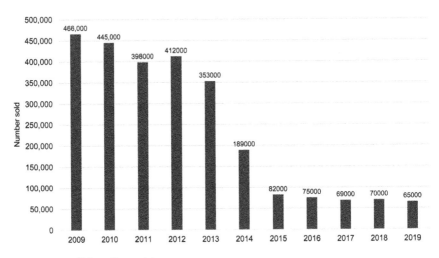

FIGURE 4.11 Sales of annuities.
Source: PPI, 2020.

TABLE 4.7 Annuity and income drawdown compared

Level of income	Amounts required to buy annuity	Amounts required for income drawdown
£25,000	£262,500	£169,175
£40,000	£718,300	£456,500

Source: Davies, 2021.

see annuities as an investment, they are expensive, costing 55–57% more than income drawdown.

However, if we see annuities as insurance, they are a better value, offering a guaranteed income until death without the fear of running out of money.

Brown (2007) has offered several behavioural explanations as to why annuities are not popular, even though they may be the best method in providing a secure retirement income. Brown believes consumer aversion is driven primarily by complexity of the annuity product market, confusion and various psychological biases. For example, loss aversion makes consumers see annuities as a risky gamble, believing that they might not live long enough to get back the initial investment. The fear of regret might lead an individual to exaggerate the probability of dying young after buying an annuity and prevent them from making a rational decision. The fear of loss of control of one's assets means consumers prefer to hold wealth rather than receive an income (Brown, 2007, pp.22–26; Lowe, 2014, p.7).

These psychological biases mean that income drawdown contracts have become more popular. This is a method of taking retirement income where individuals take some money from their pension funds (known as tax-free cash) and invest the remaining funds. This involves taking an investment risk, with well-performing investments leading to a higher level of retirement income and falling investments a lower income, but investors retain control over their pension funds.

Between 2010 and 2014, around 20,000 new contracts were sold each year. By 2014, when the Pension Freedoms were introduced, the number of sales doubled to almost 40,000 new contracts. Since then, sales of income drawdown contracts have increased by nearly 300%, as 116,000 new contracts were taken out in 2019 with a total value of £9.3 billion (Pension Policy Institute, 2020, p.32). The fall in popularity of annuities and the rise of income drawdowns mean that individuals have to manage their own investment and longevity risk.

In the five years between 2015 and 2020, it is reported that more than £40 billion has been withdrawn from pension savings (Copper-Ind, 2021). Research shows that those who took money out from their pension used it in four ways: top up their employment income to pay bills or clear debts, support adult children, invest in other vehicles to improve their financial security in retirement (e.g. buy property) and fund their semi-retirement or retirement (Department of Work and Pensions, 2020).

The Pension Freedoms have also encouraged individuals with defined benefit pensions to consider transferring their pension benefits to a defined contribution arrangement, where they could take advantage of the Pension Freedoms. According to the FCA, financial services firms advised on a total value of £30.3 billion of benefits between October 2018 and March 2020. This was made up of £20.1 billion in recommendations 'to transfer' and £10.2 billion in recommendations 'not to transfer'. There is a big disparity between the average fund size of those advised to transfer out of their DB scheme (£405,178) versus the average fund of those advised not to transfer (£267,814) (FCA, 2021b).

4.6 Individual Savings Accounts (ISAs)

Besides pension plans, another popular method for retirement saving is an Individual Savings Account (ISAs) and Lifetime Individual Savings Account (LISA). Unlike pension plans where the policyholders can only withdraw the funds at retirement date (earliest is 55), ISAs are flexible and can be accessed any time. Although there is no tax relief on contributions, there is no tax to pay when withdrawing funds. For these reasons, pension plans and ISAs are often seen as two sides of the same coin. The differences are summarised in Table 4.8.

Evidence shows that risk-taking and long-term investing are necessary ingredients for wealth accumulation, and a small proportion of ISA investors in the UK have become ISA millionaires. The three biggest investment platforms in the UK have 1,365 ISA millionaire clients between them: Interactive Investor 731, Hargreaves Lansdown 579 and AJ Bell 55. Their average age is 71 on both Hargreaves and Interactive, and 69 on AJ Bell, underlining the fact that their secret of success lies in decades of investing in stocks and shares. With their ISA millionaire status, these investors could feasibly take out a £40,000 income each

TABLE 4.8 ISAs and pensions compared

Features	ISA	LISA	Pension plans
Contribution limits	£20,000 per annum	£4,000 per annum (counts towards the normal £20,000 ISA limit)	£40,000 per annum
Tax relief on contributions	None	None	Yes – 20%, 40%, 45%
Bonus	None	25% bonus	Yes (tax relief)
Age eligible	Cash ISA from age 16 Stocks and shares ISA 18 No upper age limit	18–39 (can pay until age 50)	Birth to 75 years
Contribution levels	Flat rate for all. Not related to salary or income	Flat rate for all. Not related to salary or income	No income – max gross contribution £3,600 (or £2,880 net per year) Or 100% of salary (dividends and rental income are not considered pensionable income) Or max £40,000 (or £4K in MPAA)
Age of access	No restrictions	Can only use to pay for house deposit or from age 60. You can take out earlier but subject to a penalty.	Earliest is currently at age 55
Tax on withdrawals	None	None	25% of the fund is tax-free, and the remaining amount is taxed at marginal rates
Types	Cash ISA, stocks and shares ISA		Personal pension plan (PPP), self-invested personal pension (SIPP), group personal pension (GPP), DB and DC.
Limits on fund	No upper limit		Subjected to lifetime allowance

year tax-free, without touching their capital, assuming a 4% yield on their pot (Cook, 2020; Phillipps, 2021).

With an annual allowance of £20,000 each year, investors could become an ISA millionaire in 22.5 years, assuming 7% investment growth and that the allowance doesn't change. This means the ISA millionaires of the future will be younger than before.

4.7 Equity release

Insurance companies also offer equity release products to help consumers supplement their income needs in retirement. Some people may not have saved much in their pension fund, but they may have substantial equity in their home. As property prices rise and their wealth increases, more people are taking out some of their property wealth to supplement their needs in retirement.

Equity release customers have three types of needs:

1 *Refinancing*: They may want to refinance to pay off existing mortgages or unsecured debt.
2 *Future planning*: They may want to give an inheritance early as part of estate planning. For example, they might want to give their children or grandchildren money now to pay for a house deposit rather than wait until they die.
3 *Aspirational*: They may want to raise money to enable them to supplement their finances with their housing wealth so that they can enjoy their life more (Jackson-Obot, 2020).

Equity release providers are all insurance companies, but equity release products are not insurance. There are two ways to release wealth from a property – take out a loan against part of the equity with a lifetime mortgage or sell part of it with a home reversion plan.

A lifetime mortgage is a loan that is repaid when the borrower dies or enters long-term care. At that point, the property is sold and the lender receives their proceeds from the sale of the property. This is a more popular way to release equity because the borrower still owns the property and might benefit from any increase in its value. In practice, interest usually 'rolls up' – that is, it is added to the loan. This means the amount owed grows at a compound rate. It makes sense to opt for a plan with a no-negative-equity guarantee so that the amount owed cannot exceed the total value of the home. Nevertheless, someone who survives for a significant time after taking out a lifetime mortgage will not necessarily have any equity left.

With a home reversion plan, an individual sells a portion of their home but retains the right to live there rent-free, and thus loses ownership and any future increase in value. When they die or enter long-term care, their house will be sold and the home reversion provider will get their share of the proceeds.

Cash can be drawn down when required or lent as one lump sum at the start of the contract. In 2020, 43% of the 40,337 new equity release plans were lump sum lifetime mortgages.

The amount a consumer is able to take out from their property is determined by age. The maximum loan to value (LTV) is low for younger borrowers but rises as they get older. The maximum loan to value for those aged 55 has been calculated at 18.5%, increasing to 29.6% for a 65-year old customer, 31.5% for those over 70 and 47.1% for those over 90 (Equity Release Council 2019; Sharma French and McKillop, 2020).

Equity release enabled homeowners to raise £3.94 billion in 2018, but the amount has been decreasing, totalling £3.92 billion in 2019 and £3.89 billion in 2020. However, the average lump sum lifetime mortgage agreed has increased from £101,000 in 2019 to £104,500 in 2020 (Equity Release Council, 2021).

Equity release is concentrated in areas where property values are high, such as London, South East and South West, which made up 59% of lending compared to 14% in the North (Sharma, French and McKillop, 2020).

Research into the equity release markets in 11 countries in Europe, as well as the US and Australia, shows that over $15 billion of equity is released per year for homeowners, but by 2031, the global equity release market is expected to increase by more than threefold, to more than $50 billion in annual releases (National Reverse Mortgage Lenders Association, 2021). In other words, consumers are increasingly tapping into their property wealth as a way to deal with the retirement savings gap.

4.8 Conclusion

Insurance plays a powerful role in protecting individuals over their life cycle from risks and disruptions to income caused by premature death, disability, unemployment, retirement and inadequate income. However, consumers underrate some risks (e.g. human capital) while overestimating others (e.g. contents), resulting in under- and overinsurance. A greater understanding of insurance, its role, features and products will enable consumers to make a more effective use of this tool in stabilising their income over their lifetime.

Questions

1   What are the key risks individuals face? What are the strategies to deal with these?
2   How important is human capital for an individual?
3   What are the key types of life and health insurance policies to mitigate against the financial impact of premature death and disability?
4   Why is saving for retirement important?

5   Compare and contrast the pros and cons of defined benefit, defined contribution, personal pension plans and ISAs.

6   Why are annuities a good hedge against longevity risk? How do psychological biases affect the decision to buy an annuity?

Further readings

Annuities

Brown, J.R., 2007, 'Rational and behavioural perspectives on the role of annuities in retirement planning'. Available at https://www.nber.org/system/files/working_papers/w13537/w13537.pdf.

Glasgow, F., 2021, 'Should you buy an annuity at retirement', Morningstar. Available at https://www.morningstar.co.uk/uk/news/209179/should-you-buy-an-annuity-at-retirement.aspx. [Accessed 30 May 2021].

Lowe, J., 2014, 'Whither UK annuities: why lifetime annuities should still be part of good financial advice in the post-pension-liberalisation world'. Available at https://ilcuk.org.uk/wp-content/uploads/2018/10/ILC-Whither-annuities-2.pdf.

Protection

Goldsmith, A., 1983, 'Household life cycle protection: human capital versus life insurance', *Journal of Risk and Insurance*, 50, pp.473–486.

Legal and General, 2020, *Deadline to Breadline 2020: Myths and misconceptions*. Available at https://prod-epi.legalandgeneral.com/landg-assets/adviser/files/protection/sales-aid/deadline-to-breadline-report-2020.pdf. [Accessed 30 May 2021].

Luu, L., 2017, 'Insuring risks', in L. Luu, J. Lowe, J. Butler and T. Byrne, *Essential Personal Finance: A Practical Guide for Students* (Routledge, London), Chapter 6, pp.120–144.

Luu, L., 2019a, 'Protecting against dying too young', in J. Lowe, J. Butler and L. Luu, *Essential Personal Finance: A Practical Guide for Employees* (Routledge, London), Chapter 4, pp.83–109.

Luu, L., 2019b, 'Protecting your income', in J. Lowe, J. Butler and L. Luu, *Essential Personal Finance: A Practical Guide for Employees* (Routledge, London), Chapter 5, pp.110–135.

Pensions

The Investment Association, 2020, Investment Management in the UK 2019–20: *The Investment Association Annual Survey*. Available at https://www.theia.org/sites/default/files/2020-09/20200924-imsfullreport.pdf. [Accessed 30 May 2021].

Pensions Policy Institute, 2020, *The DC Future Book*. Available at https://www.pensionspolicyinstitute.org.uk/media/3615/20200923-the-dc-future-book-in-association-with-cti-2020-edition.pdf.

Insurance

House of Commons Committee on Exiting European Union, 2017, 'Insurance and pensions sector report'. Available at https://www.parliament.uk/globalassets/documents/commons-committees/Exiting-the-European-Union/17-19/Sectoral-Analyses/20.Insurance-and-Pensions-Report.pdf. [Accessed 30 May 2021].

References

ABI, 2020, 'Record 98.3% of protection claims paid out in 2019'. Available at https://www.abi.org.uk/news/news-articles/2020/05/record-98.3-of-protection-claims-paid-out-in-2019/. [Accessed 30 May 2021].

ABI, 2021a, *UK Insurance: Long-term Savings Keyfacts: February 2021*. Available at https://www.abi.org.uk/globalassets/files/publications/public/key-facts/abi_key_facts_2021.pdf. [Accessed 30 May 2021].

ABI, 2021b, 'Insurers as investors' [online]. Available at https://www.abi.org.uk/data-and-resources/tools-and-resources/regulation/insurers-as-investors/. [Accessed 30 May 2021].

Actuarial Post, 2021, 'UK savings gap to reach £350 billion by 2050'. Available at https://www.actuarialpost.co.uk/article/uk-savings-gap-to-reach-%C2%A3350-billion-by-2050-8489.htm. [Accessed 30 May 2021].

Brown, J.R., 2007, 'Rational and behavioural perspectives on the role of annuities in retirement planning'. Available at https://www.nber.org/system/files/working_papers/w13537/w13537.pdf. [Accessed 30 May 2021].

Center for Disease Control and Prevention, 2020, 'Road traffic injuries and deaths—A global problem'. Available at https://www.cdc.gov/injury/features/global-road-safety/index.html. [Accessed 30 June 2021].

Cook, L., 2020, 'Using ISAs to fund your retirement'. Available at https://www.ft.com/content/7ea0369f-27d8-4de1-b292-cfb64c7ada8c. [Accessed 30 May 2021].

Copper-Ind, C., 2021, '£9.4bn withdrawn from UK pensions during 2020', *International Investment*. Available at https://www.internationalinvestment.net/news/4026471/gbp-4bn-withdrawn-uk-pensions-2020. [Accessed 30 May 2021].

Corden, A., Hirst, M. and Nice, K., 2008, *Financial Implications of Death of a Partner*, Working Paper No. ESRC 2288 12.08. Available at www. york.ac.uk/inst/spru/research/pdf/Bereavement.pdf, p. 107. [Accessed 30 May 2021].

Davies, P., 2021, 'How much will you need to retire?' *Which*. Available at https://www.which.co.uk/money/pensions-and-retirement/starting-to-plan-your-retirement/how-much-will-you-need-to-retire-atu0z9k0lw3p. [Accessed 30 May 2021].

Deloitte, 2015, 'UK savings gap to reach £350 billion by 2050 Annual savings gap per person, on average, to increase between 2015 and 2050 from £8,000 to £10,000'. Available at https://www2.deloitte.com/uk/en/pages/press-releases/articles/uk-savings-gap-to-reach-350b-by-2050.html. [Accessed 30 May 2021].

Deloitte, 2020, 'The future of retirement: opportunities for product innovation in the retirement income market'. Available at https://www2.deloitte.com/content/dam/Deloitte/uk/Documents/financial-services/deloitte-uk-retirement-innovation.pdf. [Accessed 30 May 2021].

Department of Health, 2014, *Living Well for Longer: National Support for Local Action to reduce Premature Avoidable Mortality*. Available at https://assets.publishing.service.gov.uk/government/uploads/system/uploads/attachment_data/file/307703/LW4L.pdf. [Accessed 30 May 2021].

Department for Transport, 2021, 'Reported road casualties in Great Britain: provisional estimates year ending June 2020'. Available at https://assets.publishing.service.gov.uk/government/uploads/system/uploads/attachment_data/file/956524/road-casualties-year-ending-june-2020.pdf. [Accessed 30 June 2021].

Department of Work and Pensions, 2020, Pension freedoms: a qualitative research study of individuals' decumulation journeys. Available at https://www.gov.uk/government/publications/pension-freedoms-a-qualitative-research-study-of-individuals-decumulation-journeys/pension-freedoms-a-qualitative-research-study-of-individuals-decumula-tion-journeys. [Accessed 30 May 2021].

Equity Release Council, 2019, *Equity Release Market Report 2019*. Available at https://www.equityreleasecouncil.com/news/equity-release-council-publishes-spring-2019-equi-ty-release/. [Accessed 30 May 2021].

Equity Release Council, 2021, *Q4 and FY 2020 Equity Release Market Statistic*. Available at https://www.equityreleasecouncil.com/news/q4-and-fy-2020-equity-release-mar-ket-statistic/#:~:text=Across%202020%20as%20a%20whole, %C2%A33.94bn%20 in%202018. [Accessed 30 May 2021].

EY, 2019, *2020 Japan Insurance Outlook Trends and Imperatives Shaping the Life and Non-life Markets*. Available at https://assets.ey.com/content/dam/ey-sites/ey-com/en_gl/top-ics/insurance/insurance-outlook-pdfs/ey-global-insurance-outlook-japan.pdf. [Ac-cessed 30 May 2021].

Farmer, P. and Stevenson, D., 2017, *Thriving at Work: The Stevenson / Farmer Review of Mental Health and Employers* [online]. Available at https:// assets.publishing.service. gov.uk/government/uploads/system/uploads/ attachment_data/file/658145. [Ac-cessed 30 May 2021].

FCA, 2020, *Retirement Income Market data 2019–20*. Available at https://www.fca.org.uk/ data/retirement-income-market-data. [Accessed 30 May 2021].

FCA, 2021a, *Financial Lives 2020 Survey: The Impact of Coronavirus*. Available at https:// www.fca.org.uk/publication/research/financial-lives-survey-2020.pdf. [Accessed 30 May 2021].

FCA, 2021b, *Defined Benefit Pension Transfers Market Data October 2018-March 2020*. Avail-able at https://www.fca.org.uk/data/defined-benefit-pension-transfers-market-data-october-2018-march-2020. [Accessed 30 May 2021].

Garman, E.T. and Forgue, R.E., 2018, *Personal Finance* (Cengage Learning, UK and USA).

Goldsmith, A., 1983, 'Household life cycle protection: human capital versus life insur-ance', *Journal of Risk and Insurance*, 50, pp.473–486.

Green, N., 2020, 'What is an Endowment policy and should I get one?'. Available at https://www.unbiased.co.uk/life/pensions-retirement/what-is-an-endowment-poli-cy-and-should-i-get-one. [Accessed 30 May 2021].

Health and Safety Executive (HES), 2020, *Health and Safety at Work: Summary Statistics for Great Britain 2020* [online]. Available at https://www.hse. gov.uk/statistics/overall/ hssh1920.pdf [Accessed 30 May 2021].

Inkmann, J., Lopes, P., and Michaelides, A., 2011, 'How deep is the annuity market par-ticipation puzzle?', *The Review of Financial Services*, 24(1), pp.279–319.

Insurance Information Institute, 2021a, 'World insurance marketplace'. Available at https://www.iii.org/publications/insurance-handbook/economic-and-financial-data/world-insurance-marketplace. [Accessed 30 May 2021].

Insurance Information Institute, 2021b, 'Facts and statistics: life insurance'. Available at https://www.iii.org/fact-statistic/facts-statistics-life-insurance#:~:text=DOWN-LOAD%20TO%20PDF-, Life%20insurance%20ownership, LIMRA's%202020%20 Insurance%20Barometer%20Study. [Accessed 30 May 2021].

Jackson-Obot, I., 2020, 'What has changed in the equity release market,' *FT Adviser*. Available at https://www.ftadviser.com/mortgages/2020/09/01/what-has-changed-in-the-equity-release-market/?page=2. [Accessed 30 May 2021].

Legal and General, 2020, *Deadline to Breadline 2020: Myths and Misconceptions*. Available at https://prod-epi.legalandgeneral.com/landg-assets/adviser/files/protection/sales-aid/deadline-to-breadline-report-2020.pdf. [Accessed 30 May 2021].

Lockwood, L.M., 2012, 'Bequest motives and the annuity puzzle', *Review of Economic Dynamics*, 15, pp.226–243

Lowe, J., 2014, 'Whither UK annuities: why lifetime annuities should still be part of good financial advice in the post-pension-liberalisation world'. Available at https://ilcuk.org.uk/wp-content/uploads/2018/10/ILC-Whither-annuities-2.pdf. [Accessed 30 May 2021].

Luu, L., 2017, 'Insuring risks', in L. Luu, J. Lowe, J. Butler and T. Byrne, *Essential Personal Finance: A Practical Guide for Students* (Routledge, London), Chapter 6, pp.120–144.

Luu, L., 2019a, 'Protecting against dying too young', in J. Lowe, J. Butler and L. Luu, *Essential Personal Finance: A Practical Guide for Employees* (Routledge, London), Chapter 4, pp.83–109.

Luu, L., 2019b, 'Protecting your income', in J. Lowe, J. Butler and L. Luu, *Essential Personal Finance: A Practical Guide for Employees* (Routledge, London), Chapter 5, pp.110–135.

Madura, J., 2014, *Personal Finance* (Pearson, London & New York).

National Bureau of Economic Research, 2008, 'Financial literacy, planning, and retirement saving'. Available at https://www.nber.org/bah/2008no2/financial-literacy-planning-and-retirement-saving#:~:text=They%20find%20that%20those%20who, for%20retirement%20many%20years%20later.&text=Most%20of%20the%20evidence%20suggests, in%20employer%2Dprovided%20pension%20plans. [Accessed 30 May 2021].

National Reverse Mortgage Lenders Association, 2021, 'Global equity release market forecast to more than treble by 2031'. Available at https://www.prnewswire.com/news-releases/global-equity-release-market-forecast-to-more-than-treble-by-2031-301217526.html. [Accessed 30 May 2021].

O'Dea, C. and Sturrock, D., 2020, *Survival Pessimism and the Demand for Annuities*, Institute for Fiscal Studies. Available at https://ifs.org.uk/uploads/WP201902-Survival-pessimism-and-the-demand-for-annuities.pdf. [Accessed 30 May 2021].

OECD, 2019, *Net Pension Replacement Rates*. Available at https://data.oecd.org/pension/net-pension-replacement-rates.htm. [Accessed 30 May 2021].

OECD, 2020, 'Pension markets in focus 2020'. Available at www.oecd.org/finance/pensionmarketsinfocus.htm. [Accessed 30 May 2021].

Office of National Statistics, 2020a, *Individual Savings Account (ISA) Statistics*. Available at https://assets.publishing.service.gov.uk/government/uploads/system/uploads/attachment_data/file/894771/ISA_Statistics_Release_June_2020.pdf. [Accessed 30 May 2021].

Office of National Statistics, 2020b, *National Life Tables – Life Expectancy in the UK: 2017 to 2019*. Available at https://www.ons.gov.uk/peoplepopulationandcommunity/birthsdeathsandmarriages/lifeexpectancies/bulletins/nationallifetablesunitedkingdom/2017to2019#:~:text=Life%20expectancy%20at%20age%2065%20years%20was%2018.8%20years%20for, comparison%20with%202016%20to%202018. [Accessed 30 May 2021].

Office of National Statistics, 2020c, *UK Pension Surveys: Redevelopment and 2019 Result*. Available at https://www.ons.gov.uk/economy/investmentspensionsandtrusts/articles/ukpensionsurveys/redevelopmentand2019results. [Accessed 30 May 2021].

Peachey, K., 2013, 'Endowment mortgages: legacy of a scandal'. Available at https://www.bbc.co.uk/news/business-20858236#:~:text=The%20rise%20and%20fall%20of, getting%20on%20the%20property%20ladder. [Accessed 30 May 2021].

Pensions Policy Institute, 2020, *The DC Future Book*. Available at https://www.pension-spolicyinstitute.org.uk/media/3615/20200923-the-dc-future-book-in-association-with-cti-2020-edition.pdf.[Accessed 30 May 2021].

Phillipps, J., 2021, 'The secrets of the ISA millionaires'. Available at https://citywire.co.uk/funds-insider/news/the-secrets-of-the-isa-millionaires/a1470332. [Accessed 30 May 2021].

PWC, 2018, 'UK life & pensions: a roadmap to succeed in a fast-changing sector: navigating the future'. Available at https://www.pwc.co.uk/insurance/documents/life-insurance.pdf. [Accessed 30 May 2021].

Redhead, K., 2008, *Personal Finance and Investments: A Behavioural Finance Perspective* (Routledge, London & New York).

Riley, A., 2020, 'How to address the global retirement savings gap'. Available at https://reba.global/content/how-to-address-the-global-retirement-savings-gap. [Accessed 30 May 2021].

Royal London, 2015, *Losing a Partner: The Financial and Practical Consequences*. Available at https://www.royallondon.com/siteassets/site-docs/media-centre/press/losing-a-partner-report-part-2.pdf. [Accessed 30 May 2021].

Royal London, 2017, *Reality Bites: The Cost of Critical Illness* [online]. Available at https://adviser.royallondon.com/globalassets/docs/protection/ brp8pd0004-critical-illness-report.pdf [Accessed 30 May 2021].

Sharma, T., French, D. and McKillop, D., 2020, 'Risk and equity release mortgages in the UK' in *The Journal of Real Estate Finance Economics*. Available at https://doi.org/10.1007/s11146-020-09793-2. [Accessed 30 May 2021].

Smith, J., 2020, *Critical Illness Cover* (Royal London) [online]. Available at https://studio.royallondon.com/docs/reportcic-example.pdf [Accessed 30 May 2021].

Stittle, P., 2018, 'Britain's great pension robbery: how defined benefits schemes became a thing of the past'. Available at https://www.independent.co.uk/news/business/analysis-and-features/pension-retirement-defined-benefit-contribution-funds-risky-a8479426.html. [Accessed 30 May 2021].

The Investment Association, 2020, Investment Management in the UK 2019–20: *The Investment Association Annual Survey*. Available at https://www.theia.org/sites/default/files/2020-09/20200924-imsfullreport.pdf. [Accessed 30 May 2021].

Twiggs, H., 2019, 'Over 13 million Aussies without a financial backup plan or emergency savings'. Available at https://www.comparethemarket.com.au/news/over-13-million-aussies-without-a-financial-backup-plan-or-emergency-savings/. [Accessed 30 May 2021].

Urosevic, M., 2021, '21+ American savings Statistic to Know in 2021'. Available at https://spendmenot.com/blog/american-savings-statistics/. [Accessed 30 May 2021].

World Economic Forum, 2019, 'Investing in (and or) our future'. Available at http://www3.weforum.org/docs/WEF_Investing_in_our_Future_report_2019.pdf. [Accessed 30 May 2021].

World Health Organization, 2021, 'Factsheets'. Available at https://www.who.int/newsroom/fact-sheets. [Accessed 30 May 2021].

Zurich, 2015, 'Insurance – a global view: markets, participants and Challenges'. Available at https://www.zurich.com/new-joiner/-/media/969FAE61E59D415CBBE39799C9459F65.ashx. [Accessed 30 May 2021].

5

INVESTMENTS

Jordan Wong

Key points summary

- Building an investment strategy starts with identifying an individual's goals.
- The building blocks of an investment strategy are asset classes which are characterised by different risk and return features.
- Assets may be combined in a portfolio to target the desired combination of risk and return; economic theory underpins the type of portfolio investors might choose.
- The overall return that investors may get depends also on the charges they pay, tax treatment and potentially the impact of financial advice.

Around the world, people invest to help themselves and their families achieve goals, such as access to healthcare, education for their children and security in old age. Investing can take many forms – for example, in parts of Asia, gold jewellery has been a traditional store of value for centuries (The Economist, 2010). In higher-income countries, investing typically means holding the types of securities introduced in Chapter 2, such as bonds and equities, though property is also a significant store of wealth. Globally, household wealth (net of debts) stood at $418.3 trillion at the end of 2020, equivalent to $79,952 per person (of which around $50,000 was in financial assets). However, the distribution of wealth is heavily skewed, with 55% of the world's population having less than $10,000 (Credit Suisse, 2021).

Personal investing has become more important than ever in some countries due to changes in pension provision. These are the countries, like the US, the

DOI: 10.4324/9781003227663-5

UK, Israel and Italy (OECD, 2020), which had a history of **salary-related pen-sion schemes**, where employers promised their workers a specified income in retirement. Many private sector employers have stopped offering these and moved to **money purchase schemes**, where employees instead build up a per-sonal pot of savings. In other words, employers have shifted the responsibility for investment decisions and investment risks to their employees.

Investing for retirement is an important aim, but individuals also invest to grow their wealth, fulfil specific financial goals or obtain sources of **passive income**, and so achieve financial independence. Retail investors typically do this not by investing directly in the securities you looked at in Chapter 2 but by placing their money in the hands of professional fund managers (see Box 5.1). Globally, for retail and institutional investors combined, total assets under man-agement were worth an estimated $110 trillion in 2020 (PwC, 2020).

In everyday language 'investing' is a term used to mean: 'putting money into financial schemes, shares, property, or a commercial venture with the expec-tation of achieving a profit' (Oxford Dictionaries, 2021). While the goal for many investors is to make a profit, there is no magic formula to achieve this.

BOX 5.1 ASSETS UNDER MANAGEMENT

There is a wide range of ways in which investors can buy into profession-ally managed portfolios of investments. Firstly, most pension schemes are 'funded', which means that the promised income is backed by a fund of in-vestments or that the pension pot you are building up is housed in investment funds (that you may have chosen for yourself). For non-retirement savings, you might choose to invest through some type of **collective investment scheme**, for example:

- **Mutual fund, unit trust or open-ended investment company (OEIC)**: You invest through the organisation managing the fund. The price of sales and purchases closely reflects the value of the assets in the fund.
- **Exchange traded fund (ETF)**: You invest by buying and selling shares in the ETF through a stock exchange. The price of the shares closely re-flects the value of the assets in the fund.
- **Investment trust**: You invest by buying and selling shares in the trust through a stock exchange. The price of the shares is affected by the de-mand for them relative to the number of sellers, and they may trade at a premium or a discount to the value of the assets in the fund.

These and similar schemes are referred to in this chapter under the collective term 'investment funds'.

Risk is an inherent part of investing and is synonymous with the chance of loss as well as gain. For example, in 2020, investment in an equity fund of Neil Woodford, once a star fund manager, left investors with a 40% loss, instead of the 31% profit that was potentially achievable had they invested in a similar fund elsewhere (Collinson, 2020) – you can read more about the Woodford debacle in Chapter 10. Thus, investing is a broad, vast and complex topic. The aim of this chapter is twofold: to develop your understanding of the nature of, and theory behind, some common investment strategies; and to provide you with some practical investment principles to help with your own investing.

Learning outcomes

The learning outcomes for this chapter are to:

- Understand how securities and other assets, particularly when combined in a diversified portfolio, can help individuals achieve a variety of life goals.
- Be aware of the main economic theories that underpin different investment strategies.
- Be able to describe the key factors that can influence the return investors may get from investments, including risk, charges, tax and financial advice.

5.1 Investment goals

As an investor, before you begin your journey to invest, the first step is to identify your goals. This is important because it affects your choice of investments, how long you can invest for and how much risk you can take. There are many reasons why people wish to save and invest. A famous UK economist, John Maynard Keynes (1936), identified eight motives which can be broadly translated today as:

1 Uncertainty: Money to deal with the unexpected (e.g. car repairs, job loss, poor health).
2 Retirement: To save for retirement.
3 Interest and appreciation: To receive a return because higher consumption later on is preferred to more consumption today.
4 Big expenditure: To pay for a major expense such as house deposit, home improvements, wedding or major purchases (car or electrical goods).
5 Independence: Money for financial independence.
6 Business ventures: To fund speculative or business ventures.
7 Inheritance: To have money to give away as inheritance.
8 Frugality: Some people prefer to live a frugal life and so accumulate surplus income.

These goals can be classified into three categories as illustrated in Figure 5.1. The time horizon of your goals is one of the key factors determining whether

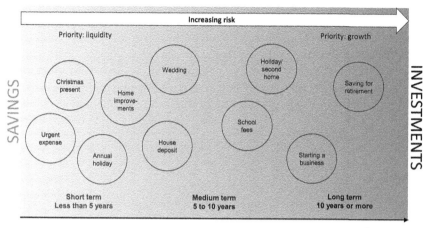

FIGURE 5.1 Goals and their relationship to investing.
Source: author's diagram.

you should consider putting money into savings (cash products) where liquidity is likely to be your priority, or into investments where you can prioritise getting higher returns. Investing is different from saving because the former typically involves a longer timescale and a higher amount of risk.

5.1.1 Investment behaviour in the UK

In the UK, the amount of money saved for retirement is much greater than saving for other purposes. According to the FCA (2020), 35 million consumers have pension savings valued at £2.8 trillion in total. Pension savings benefit from tax advantages (see Section 5.5.2) and, in most cases, contributions from employers, so in general they are the most efficient way to save for retirement.

The other main tax-incentivised saving scheme in the UK is the Individual Savings Account (ISA), which can hold either cash or investments. Saving through ISAs is likely mainly to be for purposes other than retirement and the totals saved are lower than for pensions. For example, there were 22 million adult ISA holders with holdings worth £584 billion in 2017–2018, but of these 70% subscribed only to cash ISAs; cash ISAs were worth 46% of the total ISA market value and stocks and shares ISAs 54% (HMRC, 2020, Tables 9.6 and 9.7). Data from the FCA (2021a) suggested that the number of people with an ISA account had increased to more than 28.4 million by 2020 and that there was a fundamental difference in investment behaviour among the different income groups, with higher-income groups showing a stronger preference for stocks and shares ISAs, while lower-income groups were biased towards cash ISAs. This difference is significant because it affects future returns and tends to perpetuate differences in the level of wealth of different income groups.

5.2 Asset classes and risk

The initial thought when someone mentions the word 'investment' tends to be the sort of securities, like stocks and shares, considered in Chapter 2 of this book. However, for investment planning and management, securities and other assets are divided into a spectrum of different asset classes that typically offer investors different combinations of risk and expected reward. The main asset classes in broadly ascending order of capital risk are cash, fixed income/credit, property, equities and alternative assets.

5.2.1 Cash

Cash can include a variety of different products ranging from cash and savings account available through financial institutions such as banks through to money market funds (discussed in Chapter 2, Section 2.5.1).

Cash is an integral part of building an investment portfolio for a number of reasons. Firstly, it does not pose any capital risk, that is (in most cases) there is no loss of the original amount invested, meaning that cash has a stable value in nominal terms, although in the long-term, its real value may be eroded by inflation. Cash is also easily accessible (liquid), and, in a long-term investment portfolio, this can add additional diversification by providing a ready pool of resources for taking advantage of any market opportunities that arise. It can also be used to pay out income or to cover potential ongoing fees without the need to realise any other investments during poor market conditions.

Cash can also have a societal role by providing a pool of money for specific communities, for example where **credit unions** make it feasible to offer affordable lending to low-income households (Initiative for Responsible Investment at Harvard University, 2011).

5.2.2 Fixed income/credit

This asset class traditionally comprises the fixed-income securities (mainly government and corporate bonds) discussed in Section 2.2 of Chapter 2. In recent years, 'credit' has emerged as a wider asset class that, in addition to fixed-income securities, includes, for example, asset-backed securities, property-finance lending and even **peer-to-peer lending** (which you will look at in detail in Chapter 7). These sorts of investments still involve an investor acting as a lender (in other words, a creditor) to the firm or institution that wants to raise money. These investments can be accessed either through investment funds or in some cases directly.

Investments within the credit asset class can come with varying degrees of risk. Typically, government bonds are considered to be low risk as a government is unlikely to default in developed economies with a well-developed financial system. However, investing in government bonds in countries with a poor credit rating or a weak financial system can lead to loss if they default on their sovereign debts. Greece, for example, partially defaulted on its payments in 2012, and other countries, such as Sudan and Argentina, have also defaulted in recent times, leading to economic turmoil in those countries (Schwalbach, 2018). Investors usually demand a higher interest rate where they perceive the risk of default to be high.

As you saw in Chapter 2, the other key risk associated with fixed interest securities, particularly government and corporate bonds, is interest rate risk. Bonds typically have a fixed interest rate until redemption. If competing interest rates were to increase during the period before redemption, the bond price would fall because bonds would be deemed less valuable since an investor would be able to purchase other assets offering a higher return. However, the opposite could also occur in that the bond may become more valuable if general interest rates decrease.

The risk/return characteristics of this asset class means that it is unlikely to outperform equities in the long term but is lower risk than equity investments and is therefore an important part of an overall investment portfolio strategy, particularly as there is typically a negative relationship between the return from fixed interest and other asset classes such as equities. During times when equities may be falling, fixed interest may experience stronger returns acting as a good counterbalance.

Many investors invest a proportion of their wealth in fixed-income securities as it gives them the peace of mind that comes from stability and capital preservation. It is possible to generate a steady, known income stream to potentially provide them with some form of financial security.

5.2.3 Property

There are many different sectors within the property asset class that investors can invest in. Residential property which private investors tend to invest in directly in the form of buy-to-let properties is a highly popular investment, especially within the UK. The fact that investors are able to own a physical asset over which they have some control is attractive. In England alone, around 4.6 million homes were rented from private landlords between 2016 and 2018, representing 20% of total households in England, with a further 3.95 million renting social housing (GOV.UK, 2021a, 2021b).

However, when referring to property as a long-term investment, it typically means commercial property such as high-street retail properties, office buildings and warehouses. Again, investors can invest directly into commercial property, but this may prove difficult unless significant capital is available to purchase the building. Therefore, investment in this asset class is typically through buying the shares of listed property companies or through investment funds. The latter also enable access to other areas of the property sector such as student property, social housing, ground rent funds and care homes, providing opportunities for more niche investment into this asset class.

Investing in the property asset class can provide investors with stability and good yields over the long term as most properties are held with long leasehold terms. Commercial property investments, however, are exposed to economic and market risks as seen during the global pandemic that started in 2020, whereby many commercial properties had to be closed as part of lockdown restrictions. This, along with new-found ways of working from home and a shift in work patterns, means that commercial property might not be as much in demand as it once was, which could undermine some commercial property returns. However, social housing and care homes are not exposed to market conditions in the same way and may be considered less risky than other types of commercial property.

Liquidity can be a risk to all property investments, with potentially long timescales for sales. This is one reason why many investors opt to hold property through investment funds. Shares in investment trusts, for example, can be sold on the stock exchange; however, investors may have to accept a low price for unpopular shares. In theory, property unit trusts and OEICs also provide easy access to cashing in an investment since they aim to provide daily dealing. However, there have been times when property funds have been suspended by fund managers due to the volume of investors wanting their money back exceeding the fund's ability to liquidate its property holdings. In situations like these, fund managers are allowed to suspend trading in order to manage cashflows and allow time for an orderly sell-off of property if required.

On the investment risk spectrum, the property asset class is lower than equities but higher than fixed income.

5.2.4 Equities

As you saw in Chapter 2, investors who purchase equities (also called shares) become shareholders, effectively part-owners of the company they invest in. As shareholders, investors hope to see the share price rise to reflect the growth of the company and potentially to receive dividend payments as a result of the company generating and distributing profits each year.

An investor can invest in the shares of a company directly or through an investment fund that holds a basket of different companies' shares. There are several advantages to choosing the investment fund route. Firstly, as noted in Chapter 2, risk can be reduced and managed by holding the shares of many rather than one company. However, for a small investor, splitting their capital across many different shares would mean dealing in relatively small amounts, which could be costly. Investment funds provide a lower cost way to hold a portfolio of many shares. Also, the administration involved in buying shares in overseas companies is burdensome and avoided by using an investment fund. Furthermore, not many small investors have the time, skills or inclination to research and/or select from the universe of equities on offer, a task that is delegated in a fund to the fund manager.

Equities are an important aspect of an investment portfolio and are the driver to producing long-term returns, beating inflation and other key asset classes. For example, over any ten-year period, UK equities outperform cash 91% of the time and outperform bonds 77% of the time (Barclays Research, 2019). However, compared to other asset classes, equities tend to be higher risk. These risks can be specific to the company that issued the shares and the sector within which it operates, and also wider economic risks that affect the market as a whole. Typically, large companies tend to be less risky than smaller companies, as the former are well-developed, long-standing companies, whilst the latter are often start-up companies with very little liquidity and short trading records and hence more likely to fail. However, smaller companies can offer great potential for growth and therefore can produce higher returns than large companies.

5.2.5 Alternatives

The alternatives asset class includes investments that do not fall under any of the previous asset classes discussed above. These can typically include commodities such as gold, copper, nickel, the renewable energy sector, infrastructure investments and derivatives. Therefore, the risks involved within these sectors could potentially be greater or less than those asset classes above.

Alternative investments can be used in a portfolio to offset risks present in other asset classes. For example, commodities such as gold are deemed to be higher risk than equities. However, gold's inclusion within an investment portfolio can balance the risk as its price tends to move in a way unrelated to equity prices. Investing in alternative investments can also expose an investor to different sectors which may not be easily accessible in other asset classes.

5.2.6 Investors and risk

The risk of an asset class (or particular investments within it) can be measured statistically by looking at how widely the price of the assets concerned has fluctuated in the past. However, there is no direct way of matching these quite mechanical statistical measures to the way that investors perceive risk which is personal and subjective.

Moreover, statistical measures focus on capital risk and, while that is often how investors think about risk too – in other words, the risk that they might lose some or all the money they invested or returns they had already accrued – in fact, there are other and often greater risks than losses due to falling prices. These include inflation risk, when their money loses its purchasing power because of rising prices; shortfall risk, when investors are unable to achieve their goal because the return they can get is too low; and longevity risk, when their savings run out before the end of their life. Many people erroneously believe that cash is safe, not realising that, for long-term goals, it is often the riskiest asset class, as it cannot achieve enough return for most investors to beat inflation and meet their goals. So, perversely, a cautious investment strategy could in fact be the riskiest.

Against this need to embrace risk in order to stand a good chance of achieving their goals, investors (and their advisers) need to consider two aspects of risk from the individual's perspective:

- **Attitude towards risk (ATR)**: This refers to how comfortable or fearful an individual feels taking on risk. Before investing, an investor should always find out their attitude to risk. Psychometric risk-profiling assessments are a useful tool to gauge a person's behavioural or attitudinal traits. Attitude to investment risk is measured by soliciting an individual's attitude or behavioural response towards specified investment scenarios, usually through a questionnaire. These questionnaires will often produce a result in the form of an outcome or a score to determine the level of risk that an individual is willing to take. FinaMetrica questionnaire, for example, has 25 questions. The higher the score, the more risk the investor is likely to be comfortable with and so the more of their money might be invested in higher-risk assets, such as equities.
- **Capacity for loss**: This measures an individual's ability to absorb falls in the value of their investments (or the income from them). In other words, it assesses how much an individual can afford to lose before their standard of living is impacted. Capacity for loss is more objective than attitude to risk as it can be quantified, and it can be higher or lower than attitude to risk.

No one investment or asset class is likely to exactly match an individual's goals, circumstances, ATR and capacity for loss. Therefore, in most cases, devising a suitable investment strategy involves combining assets in a portfolio that targets the required balance of risk and return. Economic theory provides some pointers on how to do this.

5.3 Building a portfolio

The goal of investing for many investors is to make a profit. This involves targeting a reasonable return while at the same time controlling the risk of losses to an acceptable level. You can manage risk and return more effectively if you build a portfolio that combines multiple investments from within or across the different asset classes. There are three influential investment theories from the world of financial economics that shed light on creating an effective portfolio.

5.3.1 The theory behind diversification

Modern portfolio theory (MPT) was initially developed by Nobel Prize-winning US economist, Harry Markowitz (1952). It starts from the relationship between risk and expected return: a desire for a higher return means the investor has to take more risk, while a low-risk investor can expect only a low return. Markowitz worked out the way to construct the most efficient portfolios, where efficiency means gaining the highest possible return given a particular level of risk or being exposed to the lowest possible level of risk given a particular level of expected return.

If every possible portfolio were plotted on a chart that related risk to expected return, they would all lie within a bullet-shaped curve, like the one in Figure 5.2, and the most efficient portfolios would lie on the top part of that curve, which is called the efficient frontier.

For portfolios on the efficient frontier, the assets combine in such a way that there is a more than proportional increase in return for taking on risk. The key is the extent to which the returns on the assets tend to move in sync, which can be measured by a statistical metric called the 'correlation coefficient'. It takes a value from −1 to +1, where −1 means the returns move in exactly equal and opposite directions and +1 means the returns move exactly in line with each other. The best results are when the correlation between assets is negative (the returns from the assets tend to move in opposite directions), but good results can still be achieved where there is no correlation (value 0); and, even if the returns move in the same direction (positive correlation), provided they are not perfectly in step with each other, there will still be some more-than-proportionate improvement in return for taking on extra risk. For example, Guggenheim (2021) estimates that the historical correlation between international equities and cash is −0.15, bonds slightly negative at −0.02 and commodities +0.60. This suggests that any combination of these assets would produce some efficiencies (since they all have correlation coefficients of less than +1), but the most efficient portfolio could be constructed by combining equities and cash (since −0.15 is the closest to −1). The level of risk and return in the portfolio also varies with the proportion (called the

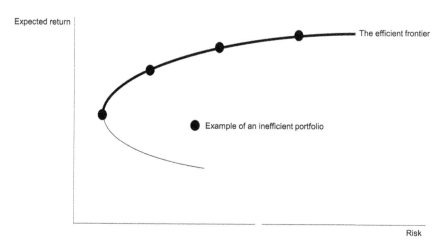

FIGURE 5.2   The set of efficient portfolios.
Source: author's diagram.

weighting) of the different assets. For example, a portfolio investing 80% in equities and 20% in bonds has a higher risk – and so the potential to deliver a higher return – than a portfolio with only 60% in equities and 40% in bonds.

To summarise, Markowitz theory suggests that, having chosen the desired level of risk (from the horizontal scale in Figure 5.2), the investor should identify the portfolio located on the efficient frontier that corresponds to that level of risk. An investor who is comfortable with a different level of risk will select a different portfolio but again from the set that lies on the efficient frontier.

There are limitations to the efficient frontier in that it assumes the investor is purely interested in risk as measured by average variations in past returns and does not incorporate other factors which may affect risk (such as whether risks are frequent but small or infrequent but large). Moreover, being based on historical data, it is not necessarily an indication of future outcomes. Finally, the model does not include transaction costs or tax which will affect the overall return (see Sections 5.5.1 and 5.5.2).

5.3.2 A theory of equity valuation and returns

William Sharpe (1970), another Nobel Prize-winning financial economist, took MPT a step further, establishing the capital asset pricing model (CAPM). He theorised that risk has two elements:

- **Systematic risk**: This is also called market risk. It is the risk of losses that affect all the assets in a market, for example, because of macroeconomic factors like interest rate changes, inflation and recession.
- **Specific risk**: The risk of losses arising because of factors related to a particular investment, such as the type of products a firm produces and how it finances its activities.

Sharpe argued that diversification cannot reduce systematic risk, but rational investors can easily diversify specific risk by holding a number of different securities in a portfolio. Therefore, investors cannot expect to be rewarded for specific risk, only the security's market risk. Sharpe developed a formula to calculate the return that an investor is expected to receive by taking on the market risk as follows:

$$ER = Rf + \beta(Rm - Rf)$$

Where:

ER = Expected return on investment
Rf = Risk-free return
β = The beta of the security (i.e. the market/systematic risk)
Rm = Expected return from the market
$(Rm - Rf)$ = Market risk premium

The return on the risk-free asset is the reward for having to wait to get the invested sum back (called 'pure time preference'). It is typically assumed to be the return from very short-term government money market securities: these offer a fixed return, so there is no capital risk; being very short-term, there is no inflation risk; and, with the government as issuer, credit risk is deemed to be nil. The market risk premium is thus the reward for taking on the additional risks associated with investing in the market or asset class concerned.

By definition, the market has a beta of 1. But market risk is, broadly speaking, the average of the risk of all the securities that make up the market, so some securities will have above average risk, while others will have below average risk. The beta (β) of an investment reflects the extent to which the investment's return moves up and down with the market. Based on the CAPM theory:

- An investment with a beta of 1 will move up and down exactly in line with the market.
- An investment with a beta greater than 1 will move in the same direction as the market but will be more exaggerated. If the market falls, the investment's fall will be greater; if the market goes up, the investment will go up by more than the market. The investment could be deemed as a more aggressive investment.
- An investment with a beta value of less than 1 will move up and down in line with the market, but by a lesser amount. The investment could be deemed as a more defensive investment.

The expected return calculation above is widely used by investment professionals, and the answer it provides can be used as the discount rate in the discounted cash flow calculations that you looked at in Section 2.3.3 of Chapter 2.

5.3.3 A theory of passive investing

Sharpe (1970) also used CAPM to show how it was possible to construct portfolios that produce returns superior even to those on the efficient frontier by borrowing and investing at the risk-free rate.

In Figure 5.3, the line labelled 'capital market line' describes all the portfolios that can be constructed by combining one of the portfolios on the efficient frontier with the risk-free asset (which, for convenience, let's call cash). For example, the investor could put all their money in cash and they would get the risk-free return indicated where the capital market line meets the vertical axis. Alternatively, they could put all their money into the portfolio on the efficient frontier (the market portfolio), in which case they would expect to get return ER_1 and take on risk R_1. A further option would be to borrow at the risk-free rate so that the borrowed money could also be invested in the market portfolio to create a portfolio with, say, expected return ER_2 and risk R_2.

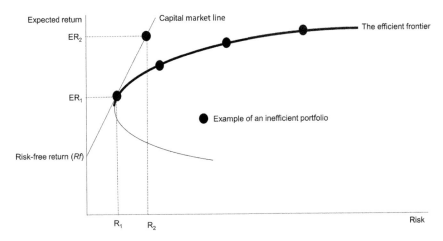

FIGURE 5.3 Superior portfolios possible under CAPM.
Source: author's diagram.

The important point to note in Figure 5.3 is that all the portfolios on the capital market line, except for the market portfolio itself, offer superior combinations of risk and return to the portfolios on the efficient frontier. Therefore, rather than tailoring risk and return by looking for differently diversified portfolios, why not simply hold the market portfolio combined with saving or borrowing cash? That, in essence, is the justification for the strategy of **passive management**, where fund managers simply aim to track a stock market index, explored in Section 5.4.2.

5.3.4 Are markets efficient?

Although MPT and CAPM are theoretical models, they are broadly accepted as providing a good basis for understanding how effective portfolio strategies can work. However, they have been criticised for being based on a number of assumptions that do not necessarily hold in the real world, in particular:

- Information is free and available to all investors.
- There are no transaction costs or taxes.
- In the case of CAPM, that all investors can save and borrow at a risk-free rate.
- Investors are rational and risk-averse.

In other words, the theories rely on markets working efficiently, but is that the case? Eugene Fama, another US economist and Nobel laureate, in a theory dubbed the Efficient Markets Hypothesis (EMH; Fama, 1970), proposed that securities markets adapt rapidly to new developments, so that prices at any point in time already reflect all known information, making it impossible to predict future price movements. He described three possible forms of the EMH:

- **Weak form**: Today's stock prices reflect all the data of past prices. This means there is no way to predict future price movements based on the past.
- **Semi-strong form**: Today's prices reflect all publicly known information, and so it is not possible to predict prices based on analysis and forecasts.
- **Strong form**: Today's prices reflect all information, including that which is not publicly available, so that it is not even possible to profit from having insider information.

Fama's empirical work suggested that the semi-strong form of EMH is widely applicable. EMH is powerful because it influences investment strategies and the question of whether returns can be enhanced through active stock picking or tracking the market.

MPT, CAPM and EMH also rely on the assumption that investors interpret information and act on it rationally. However, behavioural finance shows that investors do not make optimal decisions due to psychological biases. The most relevant types of bias to investment markets are:

- **Loss aversion**: Investors weigh losses twice as heavily as potential gains and therefore may tend to be overweight in investments with low risk.
- **Herding**: Investors tend to follow the crowd rather than to carry out independent research or seek out professional advice. An example is the surge in popularity of bitcoin in 2021, when people invested in the cryptocurrency as a result of social media hype without fully carrying out research on the asset.
- **Hot-hand fallacy**: This is an assumption that the winners of the past will carry on being winners in the future. This explains why investors favour star fund managers, believing that they will carry on making good returns indefinitely.

BOX 5.2 STOCK PICKING TO PRODUCE ALPHA

Alpha (α) is defined as the difference (positive or negative) between the return expected from a security, given its beta, and the return it actually produces. In other words, it is any additional return that cannot be attributed to movements in the overall market. In CAPM and EMH, there is no reward for alpha because rational investors would instantly buy overperforming stocks, thus eroding the advantage as their price rose (or sell off underperforming stocks whose price would fall), so alpha is eliminated.

Alpha, as a measure of the under- or outperformance of an investment compared to a market benchmark, has been adopted as a measure of an investment manager's stock-picking ability. It quantifies the value that may have been added by an investment manager through the **active management** of a particular investment fund.

Behavioural biases can also affect whole markets, potentially making these markets less efficient and stable, especially during times of crisis.

5.4 Investment strategies

The theories in Section 5.3 and other considerations underpin a number of practical investment strategies.

5.4.1 Asset allocation

Producing an optimal mix of assets, known as asset allocation, is believed to be responsible for 90% of differences in the return from investment portfolios (Brinson et al., 1995).

There are two aspects to asset allocation: strategic asset allocation or tactical asset allocation with market timing. Strategic asset allocation involves an allocation within the portfolio into the major asset classes in accordance with the investor's long-term objectives. The purpose of this procedure is not to beat the market, but to create an asset mix that creates an optimal balance between expected return and investor's risk tolerance over the long-term horizon.

Tactical asset allocation attempts to add value to strategic asset allocation through looking for short-term opportunities to generate an extra return from financial markets. The process is based on overweighting those asset classes that are undervalued and underweighting the ones which are overvalued. While the decision-making process for a strategic asset allocation is based on long-term expectations of asset class returns, tactical asset allocation is influenced by business cycles and market sentiment (Dziwok, 2014). However, tactical asset allocation is only used in active management.

5.4.2 Active versus passive investing

The topic of active versus passive investing has been highly debated for a long time, and it still continues. Each side has very good arguments for and against its uses (see, for example, Rathbones, 2017). There are those who believe that returns greater than the market can be achieved through market timing, and effective stock-picking through active management. However, other investors believe that the outperformance by active managers occurred by luck rather than skill and believe that they are not able to pick enough winners consistently to justify their higher management fees. These investors believe that passive investing is a more effective strategy.

Passive investing involves choosing investments where the investment manager will buy and hold stocks in a particular market (or use derivatives to the same effect) wholly to track the performance of a particular market or sector, called an index. Investment funds that follow this principle are typically known as index funds or tracker funds. Because the purpose of passive investing involves buying and holding investments for a long period rather than frequent dealing, passive investments tend to be lower in cost than actively managed funds. Since passive investors believe that it is impossible to outperform the market consistently, passive investing is expected to outperform active investing because of the cost savings, and there is some evidence that this may be true. However, some active fund managers do seem to outperform the markets consistently, albeit at a higher cost to the investor. Therefore, some suggest that a blend of active and passive investments could be used to maximise investment returns.

5.4.3 Timing or time in the markets?

Attempting to buy into market trough and to sell on the peaks to make extra gains sounds attractive as an idea, and many people spend disproportionate amounts of time engaged in it. The problem is that markets never behave in the way you want them to, and successfully identifying the highest and lowest points – known as 'timing the market' – is fraught with difficulty and, if the EMH holds, impossible.

The Covid-19 pandemic of 2020 provides an example. Many UK investors panicked and blindly sold their investments as the virus dragged equity prices down to low levels. Instead, if investors had held their nerves and remained in the market, they would have given their investments time to recover and by 2021 regained a large part of their losses, as demonstrated in Figure 5.4.

When analysing long-term trends in market data, investment markets do recover from major distresses and downturns. Although it is easier said than done, a widely quoted adage from investment professionals is that investors should look

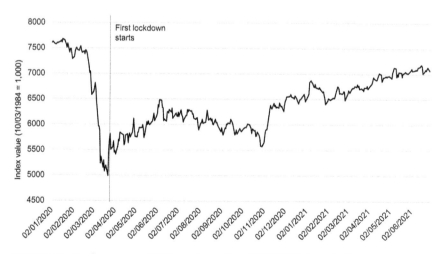

FIGURE 5.4 Performance of UK stock market (FT-SE100 index) during pandemic, 2020–2021.

Source: author's chart based on data from Yahoo Finance (2021).

BOX 5.3 POUND COST AVERAGING AND RAVAGING

If it is impossible to predict the best time to invest a lump sum in the markets, many experts recommend instead investing smaller sums on a regular basis. This in effect diversifies your investing over time, reducing the risk of getting the timing badly wrong (or spectacularly right). A statistical property of this strategy is that, when prices are low, a regular fixed sum buys more shares than when prices are high. This means that the average price of the shares in your portfolio (weighted by the amounts you have bought) is lower than the straight arithmetical average market price of the shares. This statistical property is referred to as 'pound cost averaging'.

While investors grasp the advantages of regular investing, they often overlook that the reverse may hold true when cashing in investments. This is a particular problem for investors drawing income from a pot of savings such as a pension fund. If investors stick to drawing a fixed regular sum when share prices are low, a larger number of shares will need to be sold than when prices are high. Moreover, once cashed in, there is no way for the portfolio to recover those losses when the market bounces back. This can have a devastating impact on the long-term value of the portfolio called 'pound cost ravaging'. Experts recommend instead reducing or suspending withdrawals when market prices are low. They have also recommended to use an income reserve, whereby an amount of cash equivalent to a set period of regular withdrawals, for example 12, 24 or 36 months, is held within the portfolio so that during market downturns, shares are not required to be sold in order to fund the withdrawals. When markets are doing well, profits should be taken to top up the income reserve, and when markets are low, the income reserve is used and not topped back until markets have recovered.

---

at 'time in the markets' rather than 'timing the market'. In other words, long-term investing generally provides better outcomes for investors than trying to time the market at different stages to try and gain better returns.

5.4.4 Review and rebalance

When investing in a portfolio of investments containing different asset classes, the asset allocation of that portfolio will deviate over time as investment values fluctuate. At any given time, the portfolio could become more or less risky than the initial asset allocation, and it is therefore important to rebalance the portfolio back to its initial asset allocation so that the risk associated with the portfolio is in line with the individual's attitude to risk and goals.

Reverting back to the initial asset allocation involves selling assets that have performed well over the period and buying assets that have performed not as well, which reinforces the principle of buying low and selling high Ie. By following this principle, there is a greater probability of achieving higher risk-adjusted returns.

How often a portfolio should be rebalanced is also crucial given that there are costs involved in buying and selling investments. There should also be some time to allow investments to settle within the portfolio rather than 'churning' the investments. Research suggests that the optimum rebalancing period is annually (Tokat and Wicas, 2007).

5.5 Other factors influencing returns

We have discussed several key considerations that have an effect on the level of returns that could be achieved and ways that returns can be maximised through the use of diversification, asset allocation and time in the market, taking account of different theories of portfolio construction and the behaviour of investors. However, there are additional factors that either inhibit or can improve the overall investment return, such as charges, tax and advice.

5.5.1 Charges

There are many different layers of charges involved in investing from and can be in the form of an initial or ongoing charges. The main types of charges are as follows:

- **Investment management charges**: Investing in funds will typically involve fund managers which manage the investments, and they will typically charge a percentage per annum on the amount invested with that specific fund manager. Fund management fees can range between 0% and 2% per annum. Some funds, particularly those aiming to offer higher returns through the use of derivatives, charge a performance fee, say 25% of the return. There are also other costs that are borne direct by the investment fund (but nevertheless feed through into lower returns for investors), such as dealing charges and custodian fees.
- **Platform provider charges**: Modern-day technology has allowed investments to be held much more efficiently through online platforms. These platforms allow ease of dealing and administration of investments, and there is typically an ongoing annual charge for this service or a fixed annual fee. These fees can typically range between 0.01% and 1% a year or, in some cases, a flat fee of say £10 a month. Some platforms levy an exit charge if the user wants to switch their holdings to another platform provider.

- **Adviser charges**: If an adviser is appointed to actively manage the portfolio on behalf of an individual, there is usually an ongoing charge. The service that an adviser can provide alongside investment management can vary and the level of fees can be vastly different between different firms.

Fees need to be considered as part of an efficient investment portfolio strategy as these can significantly reduce the net investment return particularly over the long term.

5.5.2 Tax considerations

Investment returns can typically be achieved in two forms: income and growth. Investments may pay income in the form of interest, dividends or a mixture of both. Some investments will pay this to investors in the form of cash, while others will automatically reinvest income back into the investment. Nevertheless, in the latter case, the investor is deemed to have received an income payment. There may be tax to pay on income. In addition, gains from an investment increasing in value may also be taxable.

In the UK, an investor has certain allowances in which they can accrue some income and capital gains without paying any tax. If the income or a gain exceeds these allowances in a given year, a tax liability may be due which will affect the overall net return achieved on the investments. However, the UK system also has a variety of 'tax wrappers', meaning arrangements that alter the tax treatment of investments, usually giving partial or complete exemption from tax. The most widely used tax wrappers are pension schemes, ISAs and insurance-based investment bonds. These tax wrappers shelter investments from tax in different ways, depending on which tax wrapper is used. Investors should consider using these wrappers so that their investments are sheltered from immediate tax and potential future tax due to legislative changes and to ensure that sums invested can be accessed in the most efficient way when needed.

BOX 5.4 TAX WRAPPERS

Consider a box of chocolates with different types of chocolate, each individually wrapped. The wrapper shelters the chocolate from any unwanted materials contaminating the chocolate and ensures that it will taste good. This analogy works in the same way when considering sheltering investments by use of tax wrappers. The chocolates in this case are the investments and the wrapper is a tax wrapper shielding the investments from tax. By doing so, you can maximise returns to avoid incurring a tax liability which is an expense that will impact the overall investment return.

5.5.3 The value of a financial adviser

Investors have two choices when they want to invest: they can invest for themselves or seek the help of a financial adviser. Although investment platforms make dealing and information readily accessible to do-it-yourself investors, individuals do not necessarily have the time and skills to carry out thorough analysis or to make fully informed choices, leading potentially to poor decisions. Getting advice from an adviser who has knowledge and experience within the industry may provide better outcomes in several ways:

- **Asset allocation**: Advisers can help to build an effective investment portfolio through the strategic and tactical asset allocation for a client, and this is fundamental to investment success. It takes time and significant research to do this, which a typical investor cannot easily do.
- **Rebalancing**: As investment values fluctuate, the asset allocation of the portfolio can deviate from the initial asset allocation set out. Assets may have risen or fallen in value, and regular rebalancing of the portfolio can help to ensure that the portfolio remains aligned with the client's risk profile to help achieve their goals.
- **An impartial outlook**: As discussed above, there are a number of different behaviours that investors possess which can cause a bias to their decision-making. Seeking a professional, who is not emotionally invested in those assets and can look at the bigger picture for the client, can often lead to a critical piece of advice and help clients avoid making detrimental decisions.
- **Tax-efficient planning**: Many advisers will couple investment management with tax planning. An adviser will look at ways to hold investments in the most tax-efficient way, and, by saving tax, this ultimately leads to a higher overall return on a client's investment.
- **Implementing withdrawal strategies**: Clients may look to draw on their investment portfolio to fund their goals. Advisers can add value by analysing and recommending how best to take the required withdrawal to save unnecessary costs and tax.

Advice comes at a cost, which generally varies depending on complexity as well as amounts invested. However, research by fund manager, Vanguard, suggests that a typical adviser, applying the methods above, could add approximately 3% a year in net returns for a client, handsomely outweighing the costs in the long term (Kinniry et al., 2019).

5.6 Investment and the rise of ESG

Global ESG assets are on track to exceed $53 trillion by 2025, representing more than a third of the $140.5 trillion in projected total assets under management.

(Bloomberg Intelligence, 2021)

In recent times, there has been an increasing demand from investors to own portfolios that align with their values. This has brought the concept ESG (environmental, social and governance) investment to the fore – underpinned at a global level by initiatives such as the UN Principles for Responsible Investment (PRI, 2021) and the Financial Stability Board's Task Force on Climate-related Financial Disclosures (TCFD, 2021). In the UK, the Financial Conduct Authority has begun to undertake various initiatives concerning climate change and sustainable finance, including risk reporting requirements for asset and wealth managers (FCA, 2021b).

The social impact of a business can create or damage reputational value (contrast publicity about 'fair wages' as opposed to 'child labour'); governance scandals can wipe out the value of organisations, as in the case of Wirecard (Better Finance, 2020); and it can be argued that a planet ravaged by climate change is unlikely to be able to provide any investment returns at all. While there may be debate about the relationship between ESG characteristics and investment performance (Armstrong, 2020; Giese et al., 2019), it is nevertheless the case that ESG investing appears to be here to stay. In 2021, PwC announced an increase in global headcount of 100,000 people over five years as part of a $12 bn investment aimed to capturing a thriving market for ESG advice (Edgecliffe-Johnson and O'Dwyer, 2021). There are also a range of organisations that have sprung up around the promotion and measurement of ESG standards and engagement (Murray, 2021).

Importantly, it is not just the risk–return characteristics of ESG portfolios that are driving these developments. Investors are also motivated simply by values – seeking to align their portfolio with their norms and beliefs, or by impact investing – wanting their investments to bring about social or environmental change. The experience of the pandemic and the focus of many governments on pursuing a 'green' economic recovery is only likely to increase the significance of these developments for the financial services sector.

5.7 Conclusion

Investments are diverse and useful for achieving a multiplicity of goals. Unsurprisingly, then, this is a wide and sometimes complex topic, with different and at times competing views on how investors can maximise their returns. There are different factors to consider when looking at investments and there is not a right or wrong way to strategise investing, since, ultimately, the investors' aims, preferences and risk tolerance are individual and subjective. However, following certain key principles and understanding the different aspects of investments and the underlying theories associated can increase the probability of maximising returns and avoiding unnecessary risks. Potentially, the chances may be even greater if professional advice is obtained, and that is the topic to which the next chapter turns.

Further reading

For an entertaining and classic read about the efficiency of markets:
Malkiel, B.J. (2019) *A random walk down Wall Street. The time-tested strategy for successful investing*, New York: W.W. Norton & Company.
For an introduction to the UK taxation of investment income and gains and ISAs:
Low Income Tax Reform Group (LITRG) (2021) Savings and tax Available at: https://www.litrg.org.uk/tax-guides/savers-property-owners-and-other-tax-issues/savings-and-tax

References

Armstrong, R. (2020) *The fallacy of ESG investing.* Financial Times. 2rd October 2020. Available at: https://www.ft.com/content/9e3e1d8b-bf9f-4d8c-baee-0b25c3113319 (Accessed 1st July 2021).

Barclays Research (2019) *Barclays equity gilts study 2019*, 64th edition, London: Barclays Research.

Better Finance (2020) *Wirecard AG: an outrageous case of corporate governance, external auditing and supervisory failures, once again at the expense of investors and pension savers.* Press Release, 1st July 2020. Available at: https://betterfinance.eu/wp-content/uploads/PR-Wirecard-An-outrageous-case-of-accumulated-failures-01072020.pdf (Accessed 1st July 2021).

Bloomberg Intelligence (2021) *ESG assets may hit $53 trillion by 2025, a third of global AUM.* 23rd February 2021. Available at: https://www.bloomberg.com/professional/blog/esg-assets-may-hit-53-trillion-by-2025-a-third-of-global-aum/ (Accessed 1st July 2021).

Brinson, G.P., Hood, L.R. and Beebower, G.L. (1995) 'Determinants of portfolio performance' in *Financial Analysts Journal*, Vol 51, Issue 1, pp.133–138.

Collinson, P. (2020) 'Neil Woodford investors take hefty loss as payouts begin' in *The Guardian.* Available at: https://www.theguardian.com/business/2020/jan/28/neil-woodford-investors-loss-payouts (Accessed 28th June 2021).

Credit Suisse (2021) *Global wealth report 2021.* Available at: https://www.credit-suisse.com/about-us/en/reports-research/global-wealth-report.html (Accessed 28th June 2021).

Dziwok, E. (2014) 'Asset allocation strategy in investment portfolio construction – a comparative analysis' in *Journal of Economics & Management*, Vol 18. Available at: https://www.researchgate.net/publication/321770525_Asset_Allocation_Strategy_in_Investment_Portfolio_Construction_-_A_Comparative_Analysis (Accessed 29th June 2021).

The Economist (2010) *Gold. Store of value.* Available at: https://www.economist.com/briefing/2010/07/08/store-of-value (Accessed 28th June 2021).

Edgecliffe-Johnson, A. and O'Dwyer, M. (2021) *PwC to boost headcount by 100,000 over five years.* Financial Tines. 15th June 2021. Available at: https://www.ft.com/content/b79e4cd4-e288-4083-a976-47f3e89a0209 (Accessed 1st July 2021).

Fama, E. (1970) 'Efficient capital markets: a review of theory and empirical works' in *Journal of Finance*, Vol 25, May 1970, pp.383–417.

Financial Conduct Authority (FCA) (2020) *Sector views.* Available at: https://www.fca.org.uk/publication/corporate/sector-views-2020.pdf (Accessed 28th June 2021).

Financial Conduct Authority (FCA) (2021a) *Financial Lives 2020 survey: the impact of coronavirus.* Available at: https://www.fca.org.uk/publication/research/financial-lives-survey-2020.pdf (Accessed 28th June 2021).

FCA (2021b) Climate change and sustainable finance. Financial Conduct Authority. Available at: https://www.fca.org.uk/firms/climate-change-sustainable-finance (Accessed 1st July 2021).

Giese, G., Lee, L., Melas, D., Nagy, Z. and Nishikawa, L. (2019) 'Foundations of ESG investing: How ESG affects equity valuation, risk, and performance' in *The Journal of Portfolio Management*, July 2019, Vol 45, Issue 5, pp.69–83; https://doi.org/10.3905/jpm.2019.45.5.069.

GOV.UK (2021a) *Renting from a private landlord.* Available at: https://www.ethnicity-facts-figures.service.gov.uk/housing/owning-and-renting/renting-from-a-private-landlord/latest (Accessed 28th May 2021).

GOV.UK (2021b) *Renting social housing.* Available at: https://www.ethnicity-facts-figures.service.gov.uk/housing/social-housing/renting-from-a-local-authority-or-housing-association-social-housing/latest (Accessed 28th May 2021).

Guggenheim (2021) *Asset class correlation map.* Available at: https://www.guggenheiminvestments.com/mutual-funds/resources/interactive-tools/asset-class-correlation-map (Accessed 28th June 2021).

HM Revenue & Customs (HMRC) (2020) *Individual Savings Account (ISA) statistics.* Available at: https://assets.publishing.service.gov.uk/government/uploads/system/uploads/attachment_data/file/894771/ISA_Statistics_Release_June_2020.pdf (Accessed 28th June 2021).

Initiative for Responsible Investment at Harvard University (2011) *Understanding cash as an asset class within a theory of responsible investment.* Available at: https://iri.hks.harvard.edu/files/iri/files/march_2011_cash_as_an_asset_class.pdf (Accessed 28th June 2021).

Keynes, J. M. (1936) *The general theory of employment, interest and money.* London: MacMillan. Available at: http://innovbfa.viabloga.com/files/JM_Keynes___Livre___The_general_theory_of_employment_interest_and_money___1936.pdf (Accessed 15 April 2021).

Kinniry, F.M., Jaconetti, C.M., DiJoseph, M.A., Zilbering, Y. and Bennyhof, D.G. (2019) *Putting a value on your value: quantifying Vanguard Advisor's Alpha ®.* Available at: https://advisors.vanguard.com/iwe/pdf/ISGQVAA.pdf (Accessed 29th June 2021).

Markowitz, H. (1952) 'Portfolio Selection' in *Journal of Finance*, Vol 7, Issue 1 (March 1952), pp.77–91.

Murray, S (2021) *ESG stays on trend despite data minefield.* Financial Times 25th June, 2021. Available at: https://www.ft.com/content/f74c2ea5-eaff-4d59-bb51-aafe09f15a75 (Accessed 1st July 2021).

Organisation for Economic Cooperation and Development (OECD) (2020) '9. Structure of funded and private pension schemes' in *Pensions at a glance, 2019. OECD and G20 indicators*, p.216. Available at: https://www.oecd-ilibrary.org/docserver/b6d3dcfc-en.pdf?expires=1624871844&id=id&accname=guest&checksum=F1F492C0278EB-DE97F377418474CBEB3 (Accessed 28th June 2021).

Oxford Dictionaries (2021) 'Invest' in *ENG (UK)*. Available at: https://premium.oxforddictionaries.com/definition/english/invest?q=investing (Accessed 28th June 2021).

PRI (2021) *About the PRI.* Principles for Responsible Investment. Available at: https://www.unpri.org/pri/about-the-pri (Accessed 1st July 2021).

PwC (2020) *Asset and wealth management revolution: the power to shape the future.* Available at: https://www.pwc.com/gx/en/industries/financial-services/assets/wealth-management-2-0-data-tool/pwc_awm_revolution_2020.pdf (Accessed 28th June 2021).

Rathbones (2017) *Active vs passive investing – the great investment debate*. Available at: https://www.rathbones.com/sites/default/files/literature/pdfs/rathbones_active_vs_passive_investing_james_pettit_investment_report_full_website.pdf (Accessed 29th June 2021).

Schwalbach, L. (2018) 'Déjà vu? Argentina is on track to default…again' in *Minnesota Journal of International Law*. Available at: https://minnjil.org/2018/11/13/deja-vu-argentina-is-on-track-to-default-again/ (Accessed 28th May 2021).

Sharpe, W.F. (1970) *Portfolio theory and capital markets*. New York: McGraw-Hill.

TCFD (2021) *Our goal*. Task Force On Climate-related Financial Disclosures. Available at: https://www.fsb-tcfd.org/about/#our-goal (Accessed 1st July 2021).

Tokat, Y. and Wicas, N.W. (2007) 'Portfolio rebalancing in theory and practice' in *The Journal of Investing*, Summer 2007, Vol 16, Issue 2, pp.52–59. https://doi.org/10.3905/joi.2007.686411

Yahoo Finance (2021) *FTSE 100*. Available at: https://finance.yahoo.com/quote/%5EFTSE%3FP%3DFTSE/history?period1=1577836800&period2=1624924800&interval=1d&filter=history&frequency=1d&includeAdjustedClose=true (Accessed 29th June 2021).

6

FINANCIAL ADVICE

Lien Luu

Key points

- Personal financial advisory sector includes guidance, advice, planning and wealth management.
- Financial advisory brings financial and emotional benefits, but there are barriers to advice due to a lack of understanding of the different services, perceived high costs, lack of trust and a shortage of advisers.
- Financial advisory services tend to serve those with a high level of wealth and income, education and risk tolerance.

6.1 Introduction

The financial advisory sector is one of the most important areas in financial services, which helps consumers make informed investment decisions, manage their wealth, insure against risks and plan for the future. On a global level, wealth managers/ financial advisers manage around US$55 trillion of investments in 2019, accounting for 14–15% of the US$399 trillion in global wealth (include properties) (Lee, 2019, Credit Suisse, 2020). In the UK, financial advisers and wealth managers manage approximately £272 billion and £942 billion of assets, respectively, a total of £1.2 trillion of assets or 12% of the £10 trillion national wealth in the UK (PIMFA, 2021).

Good financial advice confers both financial and emotional benefits. Research by Royal London shows that using a financial adviser improves the wealth of a

DOI: 10.4324/9781003227663-6

consumer on average by £47,000 after ten years. Engagement with a financial adviser also makes consumers feel more in control of their money, confident about the future and better prepared to deal with shocks in life (Royal London, 2021). In other words, financial advice can bring a greater level of personal happiness as a result of financial benefits, increased peace of mind and feeling of financial security. Yet, many people do not have access to financial advice: 73% of Australians, 85% of Americans and around 90% of British do not receive financial advice (Mckenna, 2020; FCA, 2018).

This chapter aims to provide an overview of financial advisory sector by examining the different types of advisory service, benefits of financial advice, reasons for an increased need for financial advice and barriers to access.

Learning outcomes

1   Understand different types of service in financial advisory sector.
2   Analyse the benefits of, and barriers to, advice.
3   Distinguish between financial advice and financial planning.
4   Explore the reasons why consumers need financial planning and factors affecting its use.
5   Examine the number of advisers worldwide.

6.2 What is financial advice?

The financial advisory sector consists of three key components: guidance, advice and planning, as shown below (Figure 6.1).

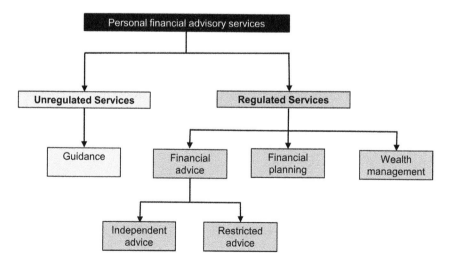

FIGURE 6.1   Spectrum of personal financial advisory services.

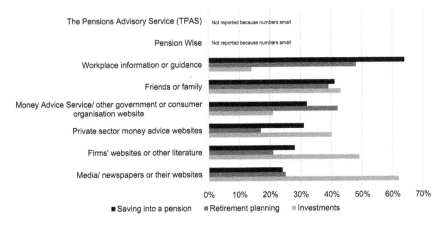

FIGURE 6.2 Sources of information and guidance.

Source: FCA, 2018, p.82 (multiple answers are allowed; ★ data not available).

6.2.1 Guidance

At one end of the scale is guidance. This is a free service, designed to empower consumers who have limited assets (the Financial Conduct Authority (FCA) defines limited assets as less than £10,000 available to invest) or simple needs (e.g. an appropriate product for 'rainy day' savings) by providing them with sufficient information so that they can make their own choices. This is not regulated and is offered by government-sponsored bodies (e.g. MoneyHelper), independent organisations (Citizens Advice Bureau) as well as banks and building societies.

Consumers need guidance on a wide range of financial issues. Research by the FCA shows that they seek information and guidance on investments from non-government sources (such as provider websites, media/ newspapers or private sector money advice websites and even families and friends) but look to their workplace and governmental bodies for information about retirement planning (e.g. Money and Pensions Service, Citizens Advice and GOV.UK). Nevertheless, nearly half take no action directly as a result of the information or guidance they receive, perhaps because they are at an early stage in the decision-making process and are simply seeking to educate themselves and understand their options (FCA, 2018, p.82) (Figure 6.2).

6.2.2 Advice

Financial advice refers to a professional service where consumers receive advice about what financial products to buy after an adviser analyses their circumstances and financial goals. It is personal, tailored to the needs of a client, and there is a fee involved. In the UK, financial advice is regulated by the FCA, an independent financial regulatory body, whose objectives are consumer protection, enhancement of integrity of the UK financial system and promotion of effective competition in the interests of consumers.

The FCA's research shows that people need advice relating to pensions (67%), such as changing where their pension(s) is invested (23%), transferring their pension(s) (17%) and setting up a new pension(s) (14%). Consumers also want investment advice (44%), such as non-pension investments for retirement (25%) and switching funds/ assets in existing investments(s) (20%) (FCA, 2018, p.30).

The overwhelming majority of the UK population does not have access to financial advice. In 2018, for example, only 4.5 million UK adults or around 9% received advice (an increase of 1.3 million from 2017) and 46.5 million did not (91%). Of these 46.5 million, 18.2 million (36% of the UK population) people having more than £10,000 of investable assets, according to the FCA's criteria, might need financial advice (FCA, 2018, p.9; Fantato, 2018; Jones, 2018) (Figure 6.3).

In 2021, it appears that a higher proportion of the UK population now receives financial advice, due to increasing demand as a result of increasing complexities of pensions, volatile equity markets and the desire to pass wealth to the next generation, and efforts by insurance companies to boost, encourage and educate the number of financial advisers. The insurance company, Royal London, reports that in 2021, 26% (13.7 million) of the UK population received financial advice and 74% (39 million) did not. In other words, the percentage of people getting financial access may have increased by 17% between 2018 and 2021 (Royal London, 2021).

However, there is an advice gap, defined as those who are open to advice but not receiving it. Royal London believes that 3.9 million people, or 10% of the

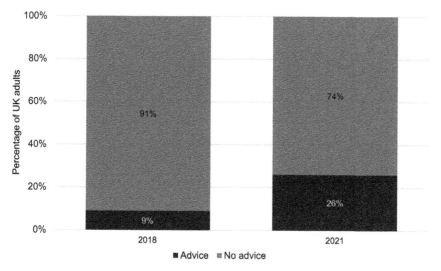

FIGURE 6.3 Percentage of UK adults who receive advice.
Source: FCA, 2018; Royal London, 2021.

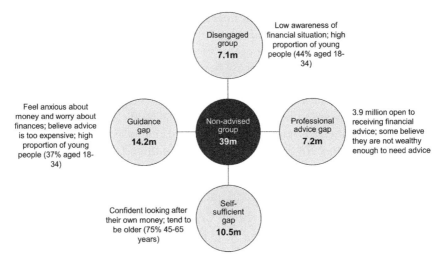

FIGURE 6.4 Different groups of non-advised consumers.
Source: Royal London, 2021.

non-advised population, are open to advice and have sufficient assets to qualify for it (Figure 6.4).

There are several barriers to advice. Findings from research by the FCA and Royal London both indicate that many people do not use a financial adviser because they believe they can look after their own money and do not need to use one. According to Royal London, a significant percentage do not use a financial adviser due to high cost and a lack of trust, factors which the FCA did not find as such significant barriers (Figure 6.5).

Vanguard, the world's second largest asset manager, believes that the cost of advice is a barrier, as the total fund management and advice costs more than 2% per year of assets under management (Walne, 2021). However, the required wealth threshold poses as an even greater barrier than fee. Although the FCA sees £10,000 of investable assets as the threshold for financial advice, financial advisory firms feel that consumers need to have £50,000 of investable assets or more before they would consider taking them on. Indeed, 20% of firms surveyed by Royal London in 2021 said that they would not take on clients with less than £100,000. Increasing regulation and the cost of professional indemnity insurance are believed to push up the cost of financial advice (Royal London, 2021).

A lack of access to financial advice has many implications. Moss, for example, argues that this results in consumers paying more than necessary for particular products, not saving enough towards future expenditure, particularly in retirement, and may be unnecessarily exposing them to the financial implications of mortality and morbidity risks such as long-term illness or premature death. This will have an impact on the 'welfare bill' and perhaps more importantly the lives of those who suffer these events (Moss, 2013, p.247).

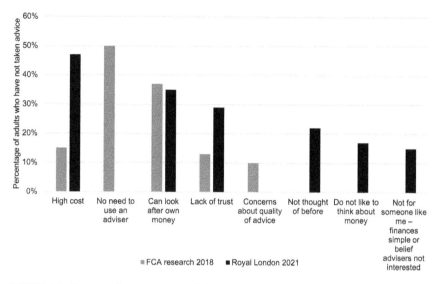

FIGURE 6.5 Reasons for not taking advice.
Sources: Royal London, 2021, p.8; FCA, 2018, p.42.

6.2.3 *Planning*

Financial planning involves helping consumers develop a bespoke financial roadmap to achieve their goals and objectives with the available resources using six steps, as recommended by the Financial Planning Standards Board (FPSB):

1   Establishing relationship and defining scope of engagement
2   Identifying client goals
3   Assessing client's financial situation
4   Preparing a financial plan
5   Implementing the recommendations based on the financial plan
6   Reviewing and revising the plan at regular intervals

It is more holistic and often incorporates financial advice, as a client may need their planner to recommend suitable financial products to help them achieve their broader goals. As a result, the terms 'financial planning' and 'financial advice' are often used interchangeably.

However, financial planning and financial advice are different in their focus. The aim of financial planning is to help clients plan their future and organise financial affairs to achieve financial and lifestyle objectives, while the goal of financial advice is to find suitable financial products to help clients achieve these goals. In other words, financial planning is about discovering where a client wants to get to, and financial products are instruments that help the client to get there. Financial planning may not need financial advice, but financial advice without financial planning may not produce the best outcome. The differences are discussed more fully below.

Wealth management is designed for clients who are wealthy and have complex needs. It includes financial planning, financial advice, as well as estate, trust, and tax planning, philanthropy and family legacy. Wealth management becomes regulated if financial advice is provided. The discussion in this chapter focuses on financial advice and planning.

6.3 Differences between financial advice and financial planning

The distinction between financial advice and financial planning is important because this affects the nature of interaction with a client; the focus of client meetings; the outcomes; and the scope, length and nature of engagement. The differences between a financial advisor and financial planner can be summarised as follows (Figure 6.6).

The benefits derived from financial planning and financial advice are also different. Financial planning confers intangible benefits such as psychological well-being, enhanced life satisfaction and greater financial resilience through the use of problem-focused financial coping strategy, while financial advice focuses mostly on tangible benefits, such as more saving, higher risk investing (which might result in higher retirement income) and choosing the most appropriate retirement income product.

6.4 Different types of planning – life planning, value-based and lifestyle planning

There is a growing desire to help clients merge money with non-financial aspects of their life and financial planning has now evolved to embrace life, values-based and lifestyle planning. In his book *Financial Planning 3.0,* Richard Wagner believes that: 'So much of the financial planner's work takes place in conversations about feelings,

	Financial planning	Financial Advice
Focus	What do you want to achieve in life? Identify life/goals and long term needs	How and where to invest? Focus on short term needs
Outcome	A financial plan/ roadmap to achieve goals	Acquisition of financial products
Benefits	Psychological well-being & enhanced life satisfaction due to greater sense of control Financial satisfaction as a result of getting financial house in order & tracking progress towards goals	Achieve financial goals by saving more and taking more risks with investments One off advice and therefore no ongoing relationship or fees.

FIGURE 6.6 Differences between financial planning and financial advice.

dreams, meaning and purpose' (quoted in Thompson, 2017). In other words, financial planning is about helping clients achieve their dreams and find meaning and purpose in life, rather than advising solely about money, investing and financial products.

6.4.1 Kinder life planning

Life planning, founded by George Kinder, for example, is based on the premise that clients seek to live a life of meaning and purpose. A fundamental task of a life planner is to help a client discover their aspirations. Life planning therefore focuses on helping clients first identify their desires, dreams, goals, values and passions, before moving on to examine how their resources can be employed to achieve these.

To help a client discover their dreams, goals, values and passions, a life planner trained by Kinder presents a client with three scenarios:

1   *Imagine you are financially secure, that you have enough money to take care of your needs, now and in the future. How would you live your life? Would you change anything?* This question is powerful because many individuals place unnecessary constraints on their ability to achieve their goals and doubt if they have enough money to attain what they want to do. This question therefore encourages individuals to focus on their aspirations, desires, values and dreams by removing money from the equation.
2   *Imagine that you visit your doctor, who tells you that you have only 5–10 years to live. You won't ever feel sick, but you will have no notice of the moment of your death. What will you do in the time you have remaining? Will you change your life and how will you do it?* This near-death experience is designed to encourage people to evaluate what is important to them. As many people lead a busy life, they may forget what is really important to them and may keep procrastinating to do the things they really want to do in life, such as travelling, spending more time with their families or pursuing meaningful careers.
3   *Imagine that your doctor shocks you with the news that you only have 24 hours to live. Ask yourself: What did you miss? Who did you not get to be? What did you not get to do?* This third question is the most emotionally charged and prompts individuals to take actions to address any unfulfilled dreams (Armson, 2016) (Kinder, 2014).

6.4.2 Values-based financial planning

Like George Kinder, Bill Bachrach sees money as a means to an end and seeks to help individuals discover what is important to them by asking the following question: *What is important about money to you?* Using a Financial Roadmap in client meetings, a financial planner establishes a hierarchy of values (e.g. family, independence, financial security, financial freedom) and identifies the available resources to help clients achieve their financial goals, which, in turn, will allow individuals to experience their values around money. This is known as a values-based approach to financial planning (Bachrach, 2000).

6.4.3 Lifestyle financial planning

In addition to life planning, some planners in the UK embrace Lifestyle Financial Planning, originally found by Arun Abey of iPac in 1983. In the UK, this approach is championed by Paul Armson, who set up *Inspiring Advisers* to train advisers to become lifestyle financial planners, with the aim of helping clients achieve and maintain their desired lifestyle at the earliest opportunity.

Lifestyle financial planning first seeks to identify a client's bucket list (i.e. things you want to do in life) and then look at financial assets available to help clients achieve their goals in life and to make sure that there will always be enough money to maintain their lifestyle, however long they live.

Lifestyle financial planning uses lifetime financial forecasting software to help clients answer questions such as:

- How much money do I need to achieve my goals?
- When can I afford to stop working?
- How much can I give away to my children and still maintain my lifestyle?
- How much investment risk should I take to achieve my goals?
- How much do I need to sell my business to achieve my goals?

Some financial planners may not feel comfortable dealing with emotional aspects and following a prescriptive approach to client meetings. They prefer to ask more generic questions such as:

- What brings you here today?
- If you could create a perfect world, what would it look like?
- How do you visualise your life in your 50s, 60s, 70s, 80s and later?

These are powerful questions that don't appear to be asking emotional questions but usually illicit life-focused or emotional answers while putting the planner and client more at ease.

In summary, there are three main types of services available to consumers: free guidance for those with limited assets, financial advice for those who require help with financial products and financial planning for those who want help in planning their future. Many people would benefit from financial planning, but a lack of awareness of this service presents a significant barrier to access.

6.5 Why do consumers need financial planning?

6.5.1 Achievement of goals

Professor Thomas Warschauer (2002, p.205) argues that financial planning is a middle-class need because middle-class families and individuals cannot achieve their goals without proper planning. Wealthy individuals, on the other hand, have sufficient wealth to meet all their financial goals, and may be more interested in sustaining wealth from one generation to another, rather than chasing risky returns. Low-income individuals tend to have financial problems that require advice in cash/debt management and are less likely to have sufficient resources to achieve financial goals such as investing. In addition, most financial advisers/planners are not interested in low-income clients because they are not a good business prospect. However, some planners and advisers offer pro bono work. In the UK, the annual financial planning week gives consumers an opportunity to get free guidance from financial planners and advisers, while government initiatives like Help-to-Save try to encourage goals even if income is low.

An important task of a financial planner is to help clients set goals. Goal setting is a central part of financial planning, and its key purpose is to identify a client's future orientation and life purpose. In doing so, goal setting provides clients with a structure and focus and motivates them to take action.

Goals can be broken down into non-financial and financial goals (Figure 6.7). Non-financial goals include personal, moral, family, social, religious and political aspirations, while financial goals involve the pursuit of financial independence and the consumption of goods and services.

There is a close relationship between these goals. Non-financial aspirations influence the kinds of financial goals individuals seek to achieve, while the ability to attain financial goals affects the amount of time and resources available to pursue non-financial goals. For example, a lack of money might engender financial stress in a family, which, in turn, might lead to divorce, affecting happiness and well-being of the family members. While having money does not guarantee

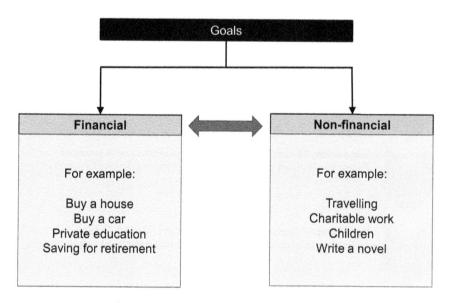

FIGURE 6.7 Types of goals.

a happy life, it can ease financial stress and remove a primary source of non-financial problems.

There are many financial goals, but the common ones include paying off debt, saving for retirement, building an emergency fund, buying a home, saving for a vacation, starting a business and achieving financial security.

Different age groups have different types of goals, as shown in Figure 6.8. Young and single people between 20 and 30 years old, for example, need to pay off debt, save money for an emergency fund and protect their human capital. The financial planning priorities for individuals with children between 30 and 45 years are more comprehensive, requiring them to take actions to protect themselves and their dependants. They therefore need to protect their human capital and save for the unexpected as well as plan for retirement and catastrophic events such as premature death. As the children leave home, the financial planning priorities focus on supporting them and saving for retirement. Once they retire, individuals need to ensure that they have sufficient income to live on, and that they can pass on their wealth efficiently if they have surplus (Figure 6.8).

For many people, the most important financial goal is financial independence: that is, having enough income and resources to be self-reliant. This goal is too broad and unhelpful in the task of planning. However, financial independence can be seen as being made up of two concrete goals: a consumption goal (current and future) and a savings goal. A consumption goal is about having enough money to pay for goods and services now and in the future. A savings goal, on the other hand, is about putting a portion of income away and saving for the

20–30 years
- **Life events**: start working, buy first car, buy first home
- **Financial planning priorities**: manage debt, emergency fund, income protection

30–45 years
- **Life events**: Marriage, children, earnings potential increases
- **Financial planning priorities**: emergency fund, life insurance, income protection, saving for retirement

45–60 years
- **Life events**: Children leaving home, career change, early retirement
- **Financial planning priorities**: retirement planning, financial support for children

60 years +
- **Life events**: Retirement, travels, new hobbies, grandchildren
- **Financial planning priorities**: estate planning, retirement income planning

FIGURE 6.8 Financial planning priorities for different age groups.

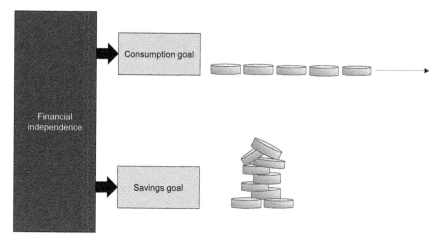

FIGURE 6.9 Financial independence and related goals.

future. People save for many reasons, including meeting consumption needs in retirement, leaving a legacy or investing to increase the value of assets (Frasca, 2009, pp.4–5). A client can be said to be financially independent if they achieve these two goals (Figure 6.9).

After identifying goals, the next task is prioritisation. As financial resources are not infinite, a client can only achieve their goals if these are prioritised and achieved in stages. Goals are commonly classified into three categories:

1 *Short-term goals*: These include saving for a holiday, paying off debts and money for Christmas. Some regard short-term as the timescale within a year, while others see it as between 0 and 3 years.
2 *Intermediate goals*: These include savings for a wedding, a house deposit, holiday home or school fees. Some see the medium term as timeframe between 3 and 7 years, while others are between 3 and 5 years.
3 *Long-term goals*: These include saving for retirement, buying a second home, setting up a business or taking early retirement. Some see long term as something that is five, seven or ten years away, while others see long term as something 15–20 years away.

As short, medium or long term can be interpreted in different ways, it is important to state clearly the timeframe these terms referred to.

Besides setting the timeframe, the attainment of goals also requires that these are:

-   *Specific*: the nature of the goals is clear
-   *Measurable*: goals are quantified and a specific amount is attached
-   *Action-oriented*: the financial actions involved are clear

- *Realistic*: involving goals based on income and life situation
- *Time-related*: timeframe to achieve the goal

In other words, goals must be SMART.

6.5.2 Key benefits of financial planning

Financial planning services offer clients many valuable financial benefits, by first helping them to identify their goals and objectives and then putting in place a strategic plan to achieve this. The financial plan includes several key elements: an emergency fund to deal with life's unexpected, debt management to reduce the psychological burden and financial worries, risk reduction to ensure assets are protected, diversified investments to minimise financial risks and tax planning to maximise the retention of income and capital by an individual. By implementing these steps, the financial planner helps a client achieve peace of mind, financial security, control and satisfaction (Figure 6.10).

Financial planners also offer a range of other valuable services, such as helping individuals smooth their income, insure against risks and broaden investment opportunities (Claessens, 2006).

FIGURE 6.10 Benefits of financial planning.
Source: Warschauer, Sciglimpaglia, 2012, 195–208.

6.5.3 Smooth consumption

For many consumers in developed countries, an important function of financial planning is to help them smooth consumption over their lifetime. In other words, individuals need help to save money when they are working, for the period in retirement when they do not have a salary. According to the life cycle theory, originally developed by Franco Modigliani in 1954, an individual typically goes through three phases (Figure 6.11):

1   **Borrowing phase**: In the early years an individual will typically borrow or rely on inheritance to fund consumption,
2   **Saving phase**: In the main working years, an individual will spend less than he earns and therefore saves. He invests these savings in assets and accumulates wealth to be used in future years.
3   **Dis-saving phase**: After retirement, an individual will consume more than he earns and therefore will rely on his savings to fund consumption. He may also wish to leave an inheritance.

Financial planning is essential because the income earned in the saving phase needs to meet both present and future needs. Individuals need to use their income to pay for current living costs and expenses, and save to accumulate a sizeable fund to pay for an extensive period in retirement. Medical advances have enabled us to live longer than people living in the past, and the average life expectancy in the UK in 2021 is 81.52 years, although many people are expected to live beyond this age.

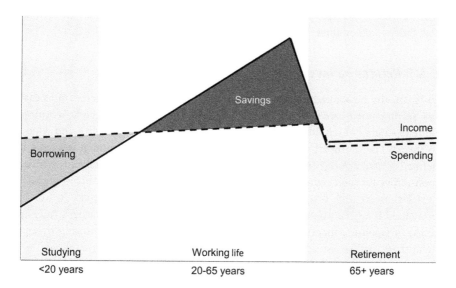

FIGURE 6.11   Spending and saving over the life cycle.

Retirement planning is becoming more important for three reasons. First, the age when people receive their state pension in the UK rose to 66 in 2020, and this is expected to increase even further to 68. Not many people would want to work until this age, and so private savings are essential to provide a replacement income until they can collect a state pension. Second, state pension in the UK only provides around 29% of pre-retirement earnings, and so this is inadequate to provide a comfortable retirement (OECD, 2019). Third, given the life expectancy and state pension age, many people in the UK will spend 15 years or more in retirement, and so need a sizeable fund to meet their needs.

Rising longevity is unprecedented because people are living longer than they ever have before. Planning for the distant, long-term future is a recent phenomenon as it was not necessary in the past. As people live longer, they now need to make plans with a longer future in mind. However, individuals have a myopic bias and tend to focus on short-term needs. Financial planners therefore help individuals save for retirement, by making them think about the future and showing them how much they need to save to achieve their goal.

6.5.4 Healthcare funding

With rising life expectancy, there is a greater risk of poor health in old age, and the fear of unexpected healthcare costs is one of the biggest drivers for financial planning in Asia. Most Chinese, Singaporean and Taiwanese investors surveyed by Legg Mason (69%, 64% and 63%, respectively) see their biggest obstacle to living a desired lifestyle in retirement is a catastrophic event that will lead them to use up their retirement funds. Many therefore seek to use a financial adviser to help them manage their resources. In 2014, Legg Mason's global investment survey showed that some 87% of respondents in China who did not have a financial adviser said that they would be interested in working with one in the future (Ho, 2014).

6.5.5 Returns on investments

In Japan, the prolonged period of low economic growth and interest rates that has accompanied rapid population ageing over the past two decades requires more Japanese households to decide more carefully how much to save and where to invest. For example, many Japanese corporations have begun to implement defined contribution corporate pension plans, forcing workers to take greater responsibility for their own saving. However, many Japanese do not invest enough in riskier assets, such as stocks or investment trusts – they represent just 16% of all household financial assets as of December 2018. The Financial Services Agency (FSA) of Japan is concerned about this and has been actively promoting investment trusts (riskier assets). However, the uptake will depend on households' access to financial knowledge and advice. To improve financial knowledge quickly, it is common for many households in developed countries to turn to financial advisers for help and guidance (Fujiki, 2019).

6.6 Factors affecting the use of financial planners and financial advisers

Zeka et al. (2015) argue that four factors influence the use of financial planners. First, there must be an awareness of a product or service before an individual adopts or makes use of a service. Improved awareness of financial planning can influence the intention to use one. Second, the perceived image of the profession also affects the use of services. Poor image leads to a low uptake of a service, and financial planning and advice suffer from it. One stereotype is that financial planners do not act in the interest of their clients, but instead recommend products and services which promote their own interests. In addition, financial planners are still associated with salespeople who manipulate individuals into investing in poor and unsuitable financial products. This poor image results in a low level of trust.

Research by PWC in 2014 showed that there was a low level of trust in financial services. While 79% trusted nurses and 76% general practitioners, only 32% trusted retail banks, 28% financial advisers, 27% insurance providers, 12% fund managers and 15% trusted investment banks. However, it is believed that greater transparency, honesty, changes to remuneration and improved internal governance can help promote a higher level of trust (PWC, 2014).

Lastly, the rewards that individuals expect to receive from financial planners can influence their intentions to use these services. The benefits of engaging a financial planner include receiving education about financial issues and financial information to make informed financial decisions, having a roadmap to achieve goals, accessing financial advice (on retirement funding, investments and tax planning) and getting help to deal with difficult financial-economic situations. However, a greater awareness of these benefits will encourage more individuals to use the service (Figure 6.12).

The use of financial planning and advice is also affected by the complexity of the financial situation, income and wealth, education, risk tolerance and government policy.

Complexity of financial situation: Hanna (2011, pp.40–41) argues that the need for financial planning services is likely to be determined by the ability of a household to do its own planning, which is related to the complexity of its financial situation as well as its knowledge and cognitive ability. Simpler types of households (e.g. a single, young person with no savings) may have less need for financial planning services, while more complex households might have a greater need (e.g. an older household with higher income and assets).

Age: Complexity of financial situation is likely to increase with age, and so there is a positive relationship between age and demand for advice (Robb et al., 2012, p.302). This means that young people under the age of 30 are unlikely to use a financial planner, partly due to the perception of a lack of financial resources to merit it. Yet, as discussed in Chapter 4 on insurance, they have substantial wealth in human capital, and financial planning can help them protect

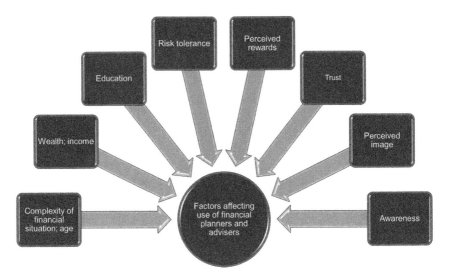

FIGURE 6.12 Factors affecting the use of financial planners and advisers.
Sources: Zeka et al., 2016, pp.76–92; Robb et al., 2012; Hanna, 2011, pp.36–62.

this intangible asset. In fact, as Hanna (2011, p.59) has pointed out, it is reasonable to expect a decrease in the use of financial planners by elderly households because future benefits are declining due to more limited remaining life expectancies. However, they are more attractive to financial planners due to their greater level of financial resources.

Wealth and financial assets: Wealthier households with a high level of net worth and level of financial assets, especially liquid assets, are more likely to use a financial planner because they have resources to pay for professional advice and receive more benefits from that advice due to their greater level of financial assets. In addition, the opportunity costs are higher for wealthy households. Financial decisions require households to consider trade-offs between individual decision-making (time-intensive) and professional advice (resource-intensive). As choices become more complicated and options more numerous, individuals need more time and knowledge to make an informed decision, thereby raising costs. Wealthier households therefore prefer to opt for professional advice.

Income: High-income households also have a higher likelihood of using a financial planner, again partly due to the complexity of household needs, higher opportunity costs and the ability to pay fees.

Education: Research shows that there is a positive relationship between education and the probability of seeking financial advice. This is a paradox because educated individuals may possess the knowledge and confidence to manage their own financial affairs. Yet they are more likely to use a financial planner, perhaps because they are more likely to recognise the need and the benefits of using a financial planner. In addition, it is possible that educated individuals may place a high value on future benefits of financial planning due to their greater future orientation and want to avoid the costs associated with poor financial decisions (Robb et al., 2012, pp.302–303; Hanna, 2011, pp.41, 49, 60). This means that less-educated affluent households might be underserved by financial planners, and yet they might find it more challenging to manage their financial affairs than more educated households.

Risk tolerance: There is a relationship between risk tolerance and the likelihood of using a financial planner. Hanna (2011, pp.40, 53) found that individuals with an extreme risk tolerance (substantial risk tolerance or no risk tolerance) are unlikely to use a financial planner. Those who are likely to use a financial planner are those willing to take average or above average risk. Yet, households with low-risk tolerance should have a higher demand for financial planning services than those with high-risk tolerance because a financial planner can help them mitigate against the risks of inflation and inability of achieving their goals by not taking enough risk.

Research by the FCA (2018) confirms that the provision of financial planning and advice in the UK is biased in several ways:

- *Gender bias*: More men receive advice than women
- *Age bias*: The propensity to advice increases markedly with age
- *Retirement bias*: Retirees are more likely to receive advice than those who are still working
- *Education bias*: Adults with higher education attainment are more likely to have advice
- *Wealth bias*: The propensity to seek advice increases significantly with wealth (FCA, 2018, p.26)

In summary, there is a bias in the financial advisory sector towards older, wealthier and more educated individuals, and younger and less-educated individuals are underserved by financial planners. This bias is compounded by the shortage of advisers and planners.

6.7 Size of financial advisory sector

There are not enough financial planners and advisers to serve consumers around the world. In the US, Egan et al. (2016) reported that there were 650,000 financial advisers in 2015, while Blanchett (2019) states that there were 1 million advisers. However, Cerulli Associates estimates there are only about 300,000 financial advisers in the US. With an average of 57 clients per advisor, only 17 million out of 125 million US households or 15% have access to financial advice. Of these advisers, only about one-fourth (or 82,000) are financial planners with a Certified Financial Planner (CFP) certification, serving about 5 million households or the top 4% of US households (Kitces, 2018).

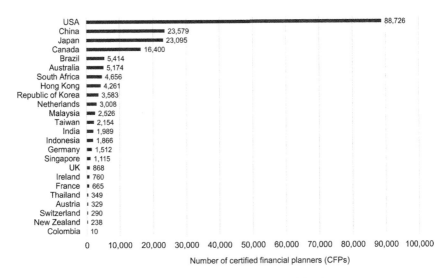

FIGURE 6.13 Number of certified financial planners worldwide in 2020.
Sources: FPSB, 2020b.

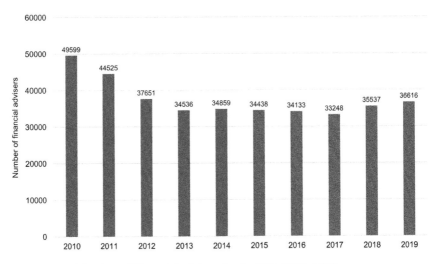

FIGURE 6.14 Number of financial advisers in the UK, 2010–2019.
Source: Angeloni, 2020.

The Financial Planning Standards Board (FPSB), a global organisation responsible for setting standards and promoting financial planning, estimates that there were 192,762 certified financial planners (CFP) in 2020, unlikely to be adequate to serve a world population of 7.8 billion. The biggest regions for certified financial planners are North America (the USA and Canada) accounting for 55%, followed by Asia with 36%, Europe 4%, Africa 2% and the Middle East 1% (Figure 6.13).

In some countries, the number of CFPs has increased between 2019 and 2020: Taiwan (17.3%), Brazil and Malaysia (15.8%), Thailand (8.4%), Singapore (7.9%), Ireland (7%), China (6.9%), Japan (3.8%) and the US (2.7%). In other countries, the number of CFPs is declining: France (51%), the Republic of Korea (7.4%), Australia (6.3%) and the UK (3.2%).

The figures above show that financial planning is not as strong as financial advice in some countries, such as the UK. In 2019, for example, there were only 897 certified financial planners (CFP) in the UK, falling to 868 in 2020, but the number of financial advisers was approximately 36,000.

The number of advisers in the UK has seen significant changes. As Figure 6.14 shows, the number fell by a third between 2010 and 2013, as a result of the introduction of the Retail Distribution Review, which banned commissions and established a minimum qualification level (Level 4 qualification – diploma in financial planning). The number of financial advisers appears to be increasing again since 2018. However, growth is likely to be slow due to the imminent retirement of many advisers. In the US, only 25% of advisers are under 44, suggesting that 75% are over this age. The average age of a financial adviser is 52 and 37% are looking to retire in the next ten years (Sergeant, 2019).

In the UK, there is a recruitment crisis in the financial advice profession. The average age of advisors is 55 years, and almost a third of UK advisers say they expect to retire in the next five years, and six-in-ten in the next ten years. This is equivalent to more than 15,000 advisers leaving the profession in this timeframe (Purkess, 2019). It is estimated that only 18,000 advisers will be working in ten years. This is a worrying trend, as this will limit the number of consumers who can access financial advice. Unless there is a replenishment, it is believed that only 1 million consumers in the UK will be able to access financial advice in ten years (Mortimer, 2019).

6.8 Who is qualified to give advice?

Financial planners and advisers play a key role in managing clients' savings and assets. However, there is a long history of abuse. As a result, financial advice is now a heavily regulated profession. A wide range of regulatory strategies is used to provide consumers with protection when they rely on financial advisers to make financial decisions, as can be seen in Figure 6.15.

On the one end of the scale are information strategies, such as disclosure and consumer education, aimed at empowering consumers. At the other end are entry regulations, which restrict who can offer advice (qualification requirements) and the terms on which it may be offered (product regulation). In between these two measures lie conduct and prudential regulation (Armour et al., 2016; see also Chapter 11) (Figure 6.15).

Entry regulation: This strategy requires regulators to set minimum standards criteria and screen entry into the industry. Entry regulations are 'good' in a

FIGURE 6.15 Framework of regulation of advisers.
Source: author's own diagram.

sense because they can raise standards, but can be bad because they are a barrier to entry that restricts competition; see Chapter 11 for more detail.

In the past, financial advisers/ planners were not expected to have a degree and professional certifications. Now, a degree is a standard requirement along with a professional qualification, required in countries such as the US and Australia. In the UK, financial advisers are only expected to have a Level 4 qualification (equivalent to the first year of a degree), but it is expected that a Level 6 qualification (equivalent to a degree) will soon be the standard requirement. Advisers in the UK are required to engage in continuous professional development (35 hours a year) and their licences and details are registered on the regulator's website, while in Australia 40 hours are needed.

Prudential regulation: The provision of financial advice, by itself, does not give rise to concerns about systemic risks. However, where advice is combined with custody of client assets, firms are subjected to certain rules, such as capital adequacy requirements (see Chapter 11) and the requirement to ensure the segregation and safe custody of investors' funds, so that client's assets are not mingled with the adviser's assets.

Governance: Financial services firms are required to have in place sound administrative and accounting procedures; internal control mechanisms; effective procedures for risk assessment; and effective arrangements for information processing, record-keeping and the safeguarding of client assets.

Disclosure: Information asymmetry distorts the relationship between an adviser and a client, and so regulators seek to rectify the balance by subjecting advisers to disclosure rules. This is designed to empower investors to make better decisions for themselves. However, it is doubtful that disclosure can prevent investors from falling prey to opportunistic advisers and recommendation of inappropriate products.

Conduct: Disclosure has been combined with other regulatory tools that regulate the relationship between the adviser and the investor. These rules aim to regulate how a firm carries out its role, including regulation of the quality of the services being provided. They impose standards of good behaviour (conduct rules) on advisers. These include suitability rules, best execution rules and rules designed to manage the conflicts of interest that arise in the adviser–investor relationship.

Nearly all financial planners and advisers in the UK are regulated by the FCA. The FCA regulations provide the main framework within which the financial planning process operates. The FCA Handbook contains detailed rules on principles for business, senior management arrangements, code of practice for those approved to work as advisers by the regulator, and training and competency.

Professional bodies also seek to promote good conduct of advisers by putting in place a Code of Conduct. The Chartered Institute of Securities and Investment's (CISI) Code of Conduct, for example, lays down several principles:

- *Personal Accountability*: planners are expected to uphold the highest levels of personal and professional standards at all times, acting with integrity, honesty, due skill, care and diligence to avoid causing damage to the reputation to the firm, professional body and the financial services profession
- *Client focus*: put the interests of clients and customers first by treating them fairly, never seeking personal advantage from confidential information
- *Conflict of interest*: manage conflicts of interest
- *Professional development*: strive for professional excellence
- *Aware of capabilities*: decline to act on any matter which an adviser is not competent or qualified
- *Respect others and the environment*: treat everyone fairly and with respect, embracing diversity and inclusion and consider the environmental impact of one's work (CISI, 2021).

Compensation: Measures are put in place to compensate investors who suffer loss at the hands of investment firms. In the UK, the Financial Services Compensation Scheme was set up in 2001, to pay compensation to consumers if an authorised firm is unable to pay claims against it.

6.9 Conclusion

Access to financial advice and financial planning can bring financial and emotional benefits. While financial advice helps consumers save more and take more risks with their investments, financial planning enhances psychological well-being, financial and life satisfaction, and happiness. Yet, the financial advisory sector is still biased towards advice and there is a lack of public awareness of financial planning services. The lack of access to financial advice and financial planning is a key concern, as this increases the gap in wealth and well-being between those with and without the privilege.

Self-test questions

1   What are the financial and emotional benefits of financial advice?
2   Discuss the range of services available to consumers, and which one do you think is the most valuable? Discuss the differences between financial advice and financial planning.
3   Why do people need financial planning?

4   What factors determine the demand for financial planning?
5   What factors contribute to the advice gap? How can this be addressed?
6   How do you increase the number of advisers?

Further readings

Armson, P.D., 2016, *Enough: How Much Money Do You Need for the Rest of Your Life?* (Envision Your Money Limited, Great Britain).

Bachrach, B., 2000, *Values-Based Financial Planning: The Art of Creating and Inspiring Financial Strategy*, (Aim High, San Diego).

Claessens, S., 2006, 'Access to financial services: A review of the issues and public policy objectives', *The World Bank Research Observer*, Vol. 21, Issue 2 (Fall 2006), pp.207–240.

Hanna, S., 2011, 'The demand for financial planning services', *Journal of Personal Finance*, Vol. 10, Issue 1, pp.36–62.

Kinder, G., 2014, *Life Planning for You: How to Design & Deliver the Life of Your Dreams*, (Serenity Point Press, USA).

Robb, C., Babiarz, P., Woodyard, A., 2012, 'The demand for financial professionals' advice: The role of financial knowledge, satisfaction, and confidence', *Financial Services Review*, Vol. 21, pp.291–305.

Royal London, 2021, *Exploring the Advice Gap: The Opportunities, the Challenges and the Need to Work Together.* Available at https://adviser.royallondon.com/globalassets/docs/adviser/misc/br4pd0007-exploring-the-advice-gap-research-report.pdf.

Warschauer, T., 2002, 'The role of universities in the development of the personal financial planning profession', *Financial Services* Review, Vol. 11, Issue 3, pp.201–216.

Warschauer, T., Sciglimpaglia, D., 2012, 'The economic benefits of personal financial planning: An empirical analysis', *Financial Services Review*, Vol. 21, pp.195–208.

Zeka, B., Goliath, J., Antoni, X., Lillah, R., 2016, 'The factors influencing the use of financial planners', *Journal of Economic and Financial Services*, Vol. 9, Issue 1 (April 2016), pp.76–92.

References

Angeloni, C., 2020, 'Fewer IFAs in the UK for first time', *International Adviser.* Available at https://international-adviser.com/fewer-ifas-in-the-uk-for-first-time/. [Accessed 3 June 2021].

Armour, J., Awrey, D., Davies, P., Enriques, L., Gordon, J.N., Mayer, C., Payne, J., 2016, *Principles of Financial Regulation* (Oxford University Press, Oxford).

Armson, P.D., 2016, *Enough: How Much Money Do You Need for the Rest of Your Life?* (Envision Your Money Limited, Great Britain).

Bachrach, B., 2000, *Values-Based Financial Planning: The Art of Creating and Inspiring Financial Strategy*, (Aim High, San Diego).

Blanchett, D., 2019, 'Financially sound households use financial planners, not transactional advisers', *Journal of Financial Planning*, Vol. 32, Issue 4, pp.30–40.

CISI, 2021, 'Code of Conduct'. Available at https://www.cisi.org/cisiweb2/cisi-website/integrity-ethics/code-of-conduct. [Accessed 3 June 2021].

Claessens, S., 2006, 'Access to financial services: A review of the issues and public policy objectives', *The World Bank Research Observer*, Vol. 21, Issue 2 (Fall 2006), pp.207–240. Available at https://openknowledge.worldbank.org/bitstream/handle/10986/16428/767600JRN0WBRO00Box374387B00PUBLIC0.pdf?sequence=1&isAllowed=y. [Accessed 2 June 2021].

Credit Suisse, 2020, *The Global wealth report 2020*. Available at https://www.credit-suisse. com/about-us/en/reports-research/global-wealth-report.html. [Accessed 2 June 2021].

Egan, M., Matvos, G., Seru, A., 2016, 'The market for financial adviser misconduct', NBER Working Paper Series, 22050. Available at https://www.nber.org/system/ files/working_papers/w22050/w22050.pdf. [Accessed 6 July 2021].

Fantato, D., 2018, 'FCA finds third of adults need advice but don't access it', *Financial Times*. Available at https://www.ftadviser.com/your-industry/2018/09/25/fca-finds-third-of-adults-need-advice-but-don-t-access-it/. [Accessed 2 June 2021].

FCA, 2018, *The Changing Shape of the Consumer Market for Advice: Interim Consumer Research to Inform the Financial Advice Market Review (FAMR)*. Available at https://www. fca.org.uk/publication/research/famr-interim-consumer-research-report-2018.pdf. [Accessed 2 June 2021].

Financial Planning Standards Board, 2020a, 'Number of certified financial planner professionals worldwide tops 192,000'. Available at https://www.fpsb.org/news/num-ber-of-certified-financial-planner-professionals-worldwide-tops-192000/. [Accessed 2 June 2021].

Financial Planning Standards Board, 2020b, 'Growth of certified financial planner professionals 2020'. Available at https://www.fpsb.org/wp-content/uploads/2021/03/ FPSB-Growth-of-CFP-Professionals-in-20201024_1-1-486x1024.jpg. [Accessed 2 June 2021].

Frasca, R., 2009, *Personal Finance: An Integrated Planning Approach*. (Pearson, London, 8th Edition).

Fujiki, H., 2019, 'Who needs Guidance from a Financial Adviser? Evidence from Japan'. Available at https://www.researchgate.net/publication/335825561_Who_Needs_Guidance_ from_a_Financial_Adviser_Evidence_from_Japan. [Accessed 2 June 2021].

Hanna, S., 2011, 'The demand for financial planning services', *Journal of Personal Finance*, Vol. 10, Issue 1, pp.36–62.

Ho, M., 2014, 'Chinese demand growing for financial advice', *Asian Investor*. Available at https://www.asianinvestor.net/article/chinese-demand-growing-for-financial-ad-vice/383714. [Accessed 2 June 2021].

Jones, R., 2018, '1.3 m more people taking financial advice in 2018: FCA', *Financial Reporter*. Available at https://www.financialreporter.co.uk/finance-news/13m-more-people-taking-financial-advice-in-2018-fca.html. [Accessed 2 June 2021].

Kinder, G., 2014, *Life Planning for You: How to Design & Deliver the Life of Your Dreams*, (Serenity Point Press, USA).

Kitces, M., 2018, 'How "Robo" technology tools are causing fee deflation but not fee compression'. Available at https://www.kitces.com/blog/fee-compression-fee-defla-tion-robo-advisor-cost-savings-productivity-efficiency/. [Accessed 2 June 2021].

Lee, M., 2019, 'How the Global wealth management industry is evolving', *EY*. Available at https://www.ey.com/en_gl/wealth-asset-management/how-the-global-wealth-management-industry-is-evolving. [Accessed 2 June 2021].

Mckenna, S., 2020, 'Three factors driving the global advice gap'. Available at https:// www.ssctech.com/blog/three-factors-driving-the-global-advice-gap-1. [Accessed 2 June 2021].

Mortimer, R., 2019, 'One in five advisers to exit industry in next five years', *FTAdviser*. Available at https://www.ftadviser.com/your-industry/2019/01/15/one-in-five-ad-visers-to-exit-industry-in-next-five-years/. [Accessed 3 June 2021].

Moss, J.G.R., 2013, *Personal Financial Planning Advice: Barriers to Access*, PhD thesis Birmingham University. Available at https://www.birmingham.ac.uk/Documents/ college-social-sciences/social-policy/CHASM/briefing-papers/2014/personal-fi-nancial-planning-advice-barriers-to-access.pdf. [Accessed 2 June 2021].

OECD, 2019, 'Net pension replacement rates'. Available at https://data.oecd.org/pension/net-pension-replacement-rates.htm. [Accessed 2 June 2021].

Personal Investment Management & Financial Advice (PIMFA), 2021, 'Industry statistics'. Available at https://www.pimfa.co.uk/about-us/industry-statistics/. [Accessed 2 June 2021].

Purkess, L., 2019, 'Advice gap on verge of crisis as 15,000 advisers to retire', *Citywire*. Available at https://citywire.co.uk/new-model-adviser/news/advice-gap-on-verge-of-crisis-as-15000-advisers-to-retire/a1257097. [Accessed 3 June 2021].

PWC, 2014, 'Stand out for the right reasons how financial services lost its mojo – And how it can get it back'. Available at https://www.pwc.co.uk/assets/pdf/fsrr-consumer-survey-final.pdf. [Accessed 2 June 2021].

Robb, C., Babiarz, P., Woodyard, A., 2012, 'The demand for financial professionals' advice: The role of financial knowledge, satisfaction, and confidence', *Financial Services Review*, Vol. 21, pp.291–305.

Royal London, 2021, *Exploring the Advice Gap: The Opportunities, the Challenges and the Need to Work Together*. Available at https://adviser.royallondon.com/globalassets/docs/adviser/misc/br4pd0007-exploring-the-advice-gap-research-report.pdf. [Accessed 2 June 2021].

Sergeant, J., 2019, '37% of financial advisors expected to retire over next decade', *Financial Advisor*. Available at https://www.fa-mag.com/news/the-financial-advisory-space-stands-to-lose-one-third-of-advisors-to-retirement-in-the-next-decade-52579.html?section=3. [Accessed 3 June 2021].

Thompson, B., 2017, '10 questions your financial advisor should ask you', *Forbes*. Available at https://www.forbes.com/sites/brianthompson1/2017/10/08/10-questions-your-financial-advisor-should-ask-you/?sh=6f4d457c159d. [Accessed 28 June 2021].

Walne, T., 2021, 'US investment giant Vanguard lays down gauntlet to savings world by slashing the price of financial advice', *This Is Money*. Available at https://www.thisismoney.co.uk/money/investing/article-9482093/Vanguard-slashes-price-financial-advice.html. [Accessed 2 June 2021].

Warschauer, T., 2002, 'The role of universities in the development of the personal financial planning profession', *Financial Services* Review, Vol. 11, Issue 3, pp.201–216.

Warschauer, T., Sciglimpaglia, D., 2012, 'The economic benefits of personal financial planning: An empirical analysis', *Financial Services Review*, Vol. 21, pp.195–208.

Zeka, B., Goliath, J., Antoni, X., Lillah, R., 2016, 'The factors influencing the use of financial planners', *Journal of Economic and Financial Services*, Vol. 9, Issue 1 (April 2016), pp.76–92.

7

FINANCIAL TECHNOLOGY (FINTECH)

Lien Luu, Pythagoras N. Petratos, Thang Nguyen and Viet Le

Key points summary

- Financial technology has been used in finance for a long time, but the current fintech (3.0) is distinguished by its reliance on artificial intelligence, machine learning, blockchain and mobile technologies.
- Changing consumer preferences, greater access to information technology, wider use of mobile technology and the global financial crisis have contributed to the rapid growth of fintech 3.0.
- Technologies transforming consumers' interaction with financial services are those relating to payments, alternative finance, insurance (InsurTech), wealth management (WealthTech) and, indirectly, regulatory compliance (RegTech).
- While conferring benefits such as faster decisions, better customer experience and financial inclusion, fintech increases risks, particularly cybersecurity threats.

Developments in financial technology (fintech) have transformed financial services in the last decade and revolutionised the way consumers interact with the sector. Fintech has improved consumer experience by providing faster payments, more secure transactions, user-friendly interfaces and personalised products and services, and by lowering costs. However, fintech increases cybersecurity risk and sub-optimal financial decision-making process. This chapter looks at the origins of fintech, its growth and its advantages and disadvantages, before moving on to examine technological innovations in payments, alternative finance, insurance, wealth management and compliance.

DOI: 10.4324/9781003227663-7

Learning outcomes

- Understand the definition, nature, growth and types of fintech and the reasons for its emergence.
- Understand key areas of fintech – alternative finance, payments, Wealth-Tech, InsurTech, RegTech.
- Analyse the impact of these changes on consumers.

7.1 The emergence of fintech

At its simplest level, fintech can be defined as the use of technology to enhance or automate financial services. However, the rise of fintech is seen to be closely linked with the 2008 global financial crisis. This leads Cortina and Schmukler (2018) to define fintech as a new industry that relies on innovative technologies and business models to deliver financial services outside the traditional financial sector. The authors trace the emergence of fintech to 2008 when tighter regulation of the traditional banking system, combined with greater access to information technology and wider use of mobile services, spurred its growth. However, fintech has a deeper history.

Arner et al. (2016) argue that, although fintech received widespread interest after 2014, the interconnection between finance and technology can be traced back to the nineteenth century. Fintech has evolved over three distinct phases: fintech 1.0 (1866–1967) with the emergence of the first age of financial globalisation; fintech 2.0 (1967–2008), the development of traditional digital financial services; fintech 3.0, the supremacy of the mobile phone and blockchain technology; and fintech 3.5, the spread to emerging/ developing countries. In other words, technological changes have been evolutionary, rather than revolutionary (Figure 7.1).

An analysis of the fintech development highlights three pertinent points. Fintech is a Western development, pioneered by developed countries, predominantly the US and the UK. In 2020, for example, the US received by far the largest investment, $79.25 billion, equivalent to 75% of the total global fintech investment, while London, the second world leader in fintech, $3.8 billion or 3.6% of the total global fintech investment (KPMG, 2021, p.32; England, 2021). This is not surprising because research shows that fintech start-ups require a well-developed economy, availability of venture capital, a suitable infrastructure (e.g. secure internet servers and mobile telephone services for fintech 3.0) and a pool of skilled labour force (Haddad & Hornuf, 2019). However, in recent years, fintech has spread to Asian countries, particularly China and India. In 2020, India received $2.7 billion (2.6%) of global fintech investment, and China $1.6 billion (1.5%) (KPMG, 2021, 63–64).

The role of traditional financial services firms in the fintech development should not be underrated. Indeed, they are an integral part, with Barclays Bank responsible for the introduction of ATM in 1967 and Nottingham Building

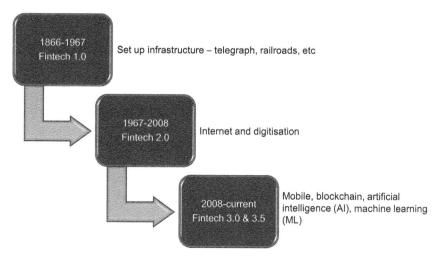

FIGURE 7.1 Evolution of fintech.
Source: Arner et al. (2016).

Society for online banking in 1983 (Arneris, Buckley, pp.9–10). Moreover, traditional banks increasingly see fintech start-ups as partners and enablers rather than disruptors and competitors. They realise the need to utilise technology to grow their business, retain their existing customers and attract new ones. Fintech companies also see the importance of partnerships, as incumbent firms can provide access to a client base, client trust, brand recognition, capital, licenses and a global infrastructure (Cortina & Schmukler, 2018, p.4). These mutual benefits have led to the acquisition of fintech firms by traditional financial services players. In November 2019, the UK Lloyds Banking Group announced a strategic partnership with Thought Machine, an innovative fintech company, to accelerate the digital transformation of its business. In 2020, American Express bought Kabbage, US fintech lender, and Mastercard agreed to buy Finicity, a provider of real-time access to financial insights. Traditional players also acquire fintech firms to expand their business globally. In June 2021, JP Morgan, America's biggest bank, bought Nutmeg, the British digital wealth manager, for £700 million to kickstart its consumer business in the UK.

The 2008 global financial crisis has accelerated the development of fintech (3.0). The global financial crisis created widespread distrust of banks because they were blamed for the subprime mortgage crisis due to their 'predatory' lending practices. It also resulted in the unemployment of many financial professionals, thus producing an underutilised, financially educated workforce, which provided a ready pool of talent for fintech firms. The financial crisis stifled employment opportunities for fresh educated graduates, pushing them to look for opportunities elsewhere. In short, Arner et al. (2016) see the emergence of fintech 3.0 as a reaction to the financial crisis in the West.

7.1.1 Fintech technologies

Although the use of technology in financial services is not novel, what is distinctive about fintech 3.0 is the exploitation of four powerful technologies (Figure 7.2).

Artificial intelligence (AI) is widely used to verify customers' identities quickly, automatically and securely, using facial recognition. Users can confirm their identity online by taking a selfie and uploading a photo of their ID document. The AI technology Optical Character Recognition (OCR) then scans the photos to see whether they match. OCR tech can also read contracts and other documents, in a greater quantity and faster speed than a human.

Perhaps the most useful aspect of AI for a consumer is its role as a virtual financial adviser. Many financial apps analyse users' finances and compare their personal expenditure with their income, savings goals and monthly bills; however, Cleo, the fastest growing fintech app, takes this further. It acts as a digital financial adviser by giving users financial insights via chat, like the way we talk to a friend on WhatsApp and Facebook Messenger. Using NLP technology, a chatbot can communicate with users in a friendly, relatable way about their personal finances (Smartosc Global, 2021).

Financial institutions (peer-to-peer lenders and traditional banks) utilise machine learning (ML) to develop a better method of credit scoring so that they can help increase lending without additional risks. ML provides a more accurate way to predict a borrower's ability to pay because it uses a wider range of data and relies on more complex calculations than conventional models. Rather than

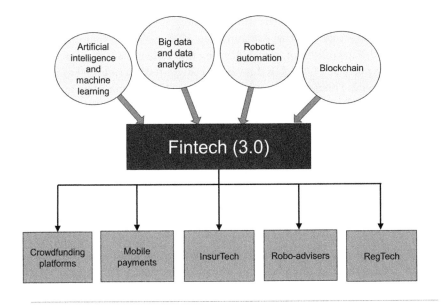

FIGURE 7.2 Technologies behind fintech 3.0 and fintech applications.
Source: adapted from CFI, 2021.

relying on financial history, a credit scoring system based on ML algorithms uses thousands of factors, such as data from social profiles, telecommunications companies, utilities, rent payments and even health checkup records. It then compares aggregated data points with those of other customers to generate an accurate risk score. If a risk score is under the threshold set by the lender, a loan will be approved automatically. The use of ML reduces risks for lenders, as well as increasing access to credit for borrowers previously overlooked.

ML is also being used to prevent fraud, as it can evaluate enormous data sets of simultaneous transactions in real time. By running ML algorithms, the system can detect unusual activity, for example, in an online transaction. This reduces fraud and cybercrime and increases consumer confidence.

The chatbot is an excellent example of a ML application. As chatbots learn from each interaction, the conversations they hold become more helpful and personalised (Oleksyuk, 2019). Intelligent, human-like, client-oriented and available 24/7, the use of chatbot enhances customer service.

Big data refers to large, diverse and complex data sets, and can be used to understand consumer preferences, spending habits and investment behaviour, as well as predict future trends. Big data has several applications in financial services:

- **Car insurance in combination with the internet of things** (black-box in car): The use of big data to enhance consumer protection (e.g. car recovery in case of theft) and allow individual pricing (based on driving style).
- **Personalised Wealth Management Advice**: The use of big data to identify customer goals, family situation, risk attitude, financial situation and financial goals and propose automatically investment advice, tax advice and financial planning based on these insights.
- **Personal Financial Management**: The use of big data to automatically classify financial transactions in categories, propose budget plans in line with customer's goals and compare budget plans and actual spending with people of similar profile.
- **Algorithmic trading**: Analyse massive amounts of market data in fractions of a second to identify investment opportunities. (Lochy, 2019).

Robotic process automation (RPA), software tools that partially or fully automate human activities that are manual, rule-based and repetitive, is another powerful technology in fintech. It is used to perform tasks such as data entry, process standard transactions or respond to simple customer service queries like 'where is X on the website?' and 'how do I reset my password?'. Another important application of RPA is robo-adviser, a popular fintech application that automates financial advice and investment management (Telus International, 2019). This makes investing more accessible and cheaper.

The adoption of blockchain technology is also transforming consumers' use of financial services. Blockchain is a database technology that works on a network such as the internet, and it is secure because it cannot be forged or tampered with.

Any data that are recorded on a blockchain can be tracked in real time, leaving a very detailed audit trail (Haller Grønbæk, 2016). For consumers, blockchain means enhanced security and transparent financial records. It also enables swift transfers of funds, as transactions can be done in minutes or seconds instead of a week or longer. It reduces costs, as intermediaries (e.g. custodian banks which transfer money between banks) are removed and peer-to-peer transactions become possible. It brings great convenience, as smart contracts powered by blockchain automatically execute insurance claims once certain pre-set conditions have been met.

However, blockchain has drawbacks. Mining (a process of adding transactions to the large distributed public ledger of existing transactions) uses as much computing power as a small country so it is environmentally unsustainable; while the anonymity of blockchain-currency transactions attracts organised crime, triggering increasing calls for digital currencies to be regulated (e.g. China has recently banned the involvement of many firms in this sector).

7.1.2 Applications of fintech

Harnessing the power of these technologies, Fintech 3.0 focuses on five key areas:

1 *Finance and investment*: Technological innovations in this area focus on alternative financing methods, particularly crowdfunding and P2P lending. Fintech is also increasingly involved in areas such as robo-advisory services.
2 *Financial operations and risk management*: Technologies such as *RegTech* focus on the automation of compliance processes and offer a fast and cost-effective management of large amounts of data, such as transaction records and compliance documents.
3 *Payments and infrastructure*: Digital and mobile payments have become increasingly important to support a wide range of needs, such as trading, cross-border transfers and commerce, especially e-commerce.
4 *Data security and monetisation*: The digitised nature of the financial industry means it is vulnerable to cybercrime. Many fintech solutions focus on developing automated tools to manage an array of financial crime threats, such as preventing fraud, hacking, money laundering and terrorism financing.
5 *Consumer interface*: Technologies in this area help firms engage with customers, with a digital front-end considered to be the key. For example, a banking app helps a customer manage bank accounts and savings, pay bills, apply for a loan, transfer money – all available at their fingertips with a single login using a PIN or facial ID (Finextra, 2016).

In short, fintech not only augments, streamlines and digitises processes, products and services, but it also improves the user experience by providing faster speed, greater convenience and a single platform to access financial services products and services.

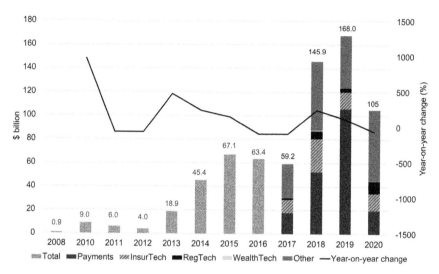

FIGURE 7.3   Investments in fintech 2008–2020.

Source: authors' table based on data from Gelis and Woods (2014), Statista (2021a) and KPMG (2021).

7.1.3 Investments in fintech

Fintech has experienced remarkable growth since the global financial crisis, as a result of disruptions to the traditional financial sector. In 2008, global investment in fintech was $928 million, growing to a peak of $168 billion in 2019, more than an 18,000% increase in ten years. The periods of greatest growth were 2008–2010 with a 969% increase, 2012–2015 with 286% and 2017–2018 with 246%. In other periods, investments in fintech declined – 2011–2012 and 2016–2017. Fintech, thus, grows in a zig-zag, nonlinear pattern. In total, fintech has received approximately $684 billion of global investment (Figure 7.3).

The distribution of global investments among different segments of fintech is not even. Payments and insurance technologies have received the highest amount of investment, approximately $196 billion and $68.2 billion, respectively, over four years, while RegTech and WealthTech smaller amounts – $22.1 and $1.6 billion, respectively. This reflects the varying global usage of fintech services, with payments and transfers most widely used (50%), followed by insurance (24%), savings and investments (20%) and financial planning (10%) (Center Forward, 2016).

7.1.4 The benefits and risks of fintech

Fintech has been growing rapidly, thanks to its recognised benefits. One key advantage of fintech is its rapid speed, with processes that used to take days, weeks or even months now being done in minutes. Whether it is a bank loan or an overseas money transfer, consumers can apply online anytime, anywhere, and get decisions in minutes. The faster speed is made possible by the use of powerful technologies, as well as the decentralised nature of fintech, which works as a peer-to-peer ecosystem without a central authority and financial intermediation. Peer-to-peer lending, for example, brings savers/lenders in direct contact with borrowers and removes the bureaucratic procedures involved in using intermediaries (e.g. banks and financial institutions – see Chapter 3). Savers can make decisions about who they want to lend to and what projects they want to fund. Fintech thus empowers consumers.

Fintech also promotes financial inclusion (see Chapter 8), reaching out to consumers unserved by traditional institutions – for example, robo-advisers allow consumers with as little as a pound to invest in the stock market. Mobile money platforms allow unbanked consumers to make and receive payments much faster and cheaper than in the past. Blockchain technology also enhances financial inclusion because it has the potential to improve property ownership through blockchain registries, which generate proof of collateral and thus improves access to credit (Walden, 2020; Cortina & Schmukler, 2018, p.3).

However, the use of fintech raises concerns about increased risks such as cybersecurity, which, in turn, may impact systemic risk and financial stability. The financial sector is highly exposed to cyber risk because financial institutions are dependent on interconnected networks and critical infrastructures (payment and settlement systems, trading platforms). Furthermore, many financial institutions have legacy systems that make them vulnerable to cyberattacks, and this is enhanced by the increasing sophistication of cybercriminals (Bouveret, 2018).

Emerging technologies such as fintech are particularly vulnerable to cyberattacks due to their greater reliance on technology and weaker risk management processes. Greater use of technology enhances vulnerability because it increases the range and entry points into the financial system for hackers to target. Between 2013 and 2018, cyberattacks on fintech firms (mainly online exchanges allowing trading of bitcoins and providing wallet services) have resulted in US$1.45 billion in losses due to fraud (Bouveret, 2018). Cybercrimes undermine consumers' confidence and trust in financial services. In response, investment in cybersecurity has increased 20 times between 2012 and 2020, from $0.1 billion in 2012 to $2 billion in 2020 (KPMG, 2021, p.24). Chapter 10 discusses a range of measures that consumers can use to protect themselves against financial crimes.

Reliance on technology also produces other undesirable outcomes. The use of complex AI/ML algorithms may result in firms having less control over business decisions, as they do not understand how decisions are made (Jagtiani & John, 2018). For consumers, the reliance on AI/ML also rules out discretion in the decision-making process, and this may disadvantage some consumers. For example, a mortgage applicant who does not fit the standard profile may receive a more sympathetic outcome from an underwriter considering their circumstances on a discretionary basis rather than from an automated system.

In addition, the ability of individuals to make near-instantaneous financial decisions, based on immediate availability of information and recommendations, may not produce optimal outcomes. Financial decisions are complex and consumers need time for research, reflection, guidance or advice. This is essential because, as Chapter 4 has made clear, our behavioural biases cloud our judgement. The most common pitfalls include mental accounting errors, overconfidence, anchoring, herd behaviour, loss aversion and framing. Instantaneity in financial decisions, while satisfying our desire for immediate gratification, may not produce the best results.

This chapter now explores these key areas of fintech in more detail: payments, alternative finance, InsurTech, WealthTech and RegTech.

7.2 Fintech and payments

The payments sector is one of the most important areas of the global economy, as business and commerce can be severely delayed if the payment system is not efficiently deployed. However, the traditional payments system is built on several intermediaries such as Automated Clearing Houses and intermediary banks, and the process is costly and slow.

However, faster, easier and cheaper transactions are required to support the exponential growth in e-commerce. Between 2014 and 2021, e-commerce rose by 366%, from $1.336 trillion in 2014 to $4.891 trillion in 2021. It is expected to grow further to $5.424 trillion in 2022, $5.9 trillion in 2023 and $6.388 trillion in 2024 (Statista, 2020a). Consumers also need a faster and cheaper method of sending money abroad. The UN estimates that more than 258 million people are living outside their country of birth in 2017, and the annual global remittance flow is worth $540 billion. In addition, more and more people are travelling overseas, and they want easier, more convenient and cheaper ways to spend money on their travels. In 1950, there were 25 million tourist arrivals, and by 2019 this has risen to more than 1.46 billion, a 58-fold increase, spending $2.37 trillion on their overseas trips (World Bank, 2021; Statista, 2021b; Roser, 2017; INED, 2018).

There are several significant innovations in payments and transfers. In payments, innovations use the existing payment infrastructure and focus on improving the user experience by leveraging mobile devices and connectivity. However, the area of transfers has seen greater innovations, with the emergence of innovative mobile money solutions such as M-Pesa (discussed in more detail in Chapter 8), allowing peer-to-peer transactions to take place via mobile devices without a need for a bank account. This is likely to promote financial inclusion, by permitting consumers without a bank account to participate in the financial system. New business models such as Azimo and Transferwise have also revolutionised cross-border transfers. By matching transactions with the other users sending money in the opposite direction, high fees typically associated with international transfers have fallen.

The most striking innovation in payments and transfers is the application of the powerful blockchain technology, a decentralised payment system which does not require a third party to validate transactions. Instead, the transactions are validated and logged by a network of computers. The application of blockchain technology in payments brings several benefits, including faster speed, greater efficiency and enhanced security (due to creation of a log of transactions) (Cortina & Schmukler, 2018, p.2).

The global payments revenue nearly doubled between 2010 and 2019, from US$1.1 trillion to US$2.0 trillion by 2019. However, in 2020, the revenue fell to an estimated US$1.9 trillion, as a result of reduced spending caused by the global pandemic. The greatest growth in payments occurred in Asia-Pacific, where revenue trebled between 2010 and 2019 (Figure 7.4).

Methods of payment have changed drastically over the last century. Traditionally, cash, coin or bartered goods were the main currencies, and the transfer of value was direct, passed between hands that were known to each other and trusted. This all changed with the introduction of non-physical money transfers: telegraph transfers, then credit cards, Automated Clearing Houses and, most recently, the introduction of online banking, mobile wallets and contactless payments (Cahill, 2021). Indeed, the digital revolution has resulted in the rise of mobile payments as the most important payment method in the modern digital economy, where payments and transactions are rapidly transmitted from fixed locations to anytime and anywhere (Antovski & Gusev, 2003), and this is discussed in more depth in Chapter 8.

The global pandemic has accelerated the shift away from cash, as its use was discouraged due to the fear of contracting Covid-19. The use of cash declined

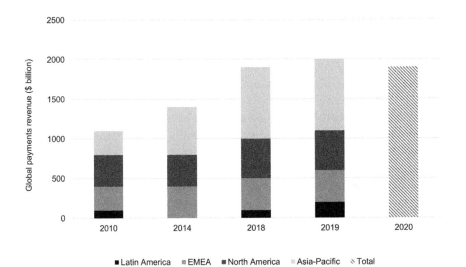

FIGURE 7.4   Global payments revenue, 2010 and 2019.
Source: McKinsey and Company, 2020, pp.4–5.

drastically in China, and by 2020 cash was only used in 41% transactions, down from 99% in 2010. This trend can also be seen in Sweden, where the use of cash fell from 56% in 2010 to 9% in 2020; in the Netherlands from 52% to 14%; and in the US from 51% to 28% (McKinsey & Company, 2020, p.6, France-Presse, 2020)). Thus, the pandemic helped spur the growth of contactless payments. According to UK Finance, cash now makes up just 23% of transactions in the UK, after debit cards and credit cards, while cards and contactless payments now account for more than half of all transactions conducted in the UK (Nixon, 2020). The global contactless payment market size is expected to nearly double in five years, increasing from $10.3 billion in 2020 to $18 billion by 2025, or at a compound annual growth rate (CAGR) of 11.7% (Lulic, 2020).

The emergence of open banking has also revolutionised payments. Payment service providers can now take payments direct from a bank account without the need to register or use any plastic card. Account information service providers can also use data from bank accounts to provide value-added services such as account aggregation. While providing convenience, open banking increases the risk of consumers losing control of their financial data.

The decline of cash has accelerated the growth of electronic money (e-money) as a digital alternative to cash. It allows users to make cashless payments with money stored on a card or a phone, or over the internet. E-money is experiencing tremendous growth, to the point that it is expected to take over from cash and bank deposits in the coming years, led by e-money providers like Alipay and Paypal. E-money is expected to be better integrated into our digital lives especially as cross-border transfers of e-money would become cheaper and faster than the transfers of cash and bank deposits. While e-money can reduce crime rates (as there is no tangible money to steal) and money laundering (because there is always a digital trail), and it is easier to spend globally, its use makes us completely reliant on technology and the internet, disadvantages the older generations who may prefer using cash and increases the risk of cyberattacks and overspending (Keeton, 2019).

One type of e-money is a digital wallet, an electronic device or an online service, that enables individuals or businesses to make transactions electronically. It stores the payment information of users for different payment modes on various websites, along with other items such as gift coupons and driver's licences. A digital wallet is also known as an e-wallet. A surge of growth in adoption of digital wallets means that e-wallets are expected to be the leading e-commerce payment method globally over the next five years. The ecosystem is constantly expanding, with Apple Pay, Google Pay and Samsung Pay continuing to grow in popularity (LS Retail, 2020)

The second type of e-money is mobile payments. Traditional cross-border payment costs are high and can become considerably more expensive because the current international payment setup consists of a number of financial intermediaries, and a large proportion of transactions still require human input. Most international transfers are done via SWIFT (Society for Worldwide Interbank

Financial Telecommunication). The whole process for a cross-border payment is expensive and time-consuming. As a result, a new market entrant, M-Pesa (a mobile money service owned by Vodafone), was first introduced in 2007. M-Pesa offers a safe, fast and low-cost way to pay, receive, transfer and store money overseas. It is now present in ten countries. Mobile money service companies recently established include Revolut, Transferwise and Stripe.

A new generation of supermarkets is offering consumers ultimate convenience and completely automated payment options, such as Amazon Go. In the Amazon Go stores, shoppers simply pick up the products they want and leave without having to check out. Unlike most shops, there are no registers or cashier; Amazon uses a combination of artificial intelligence, computer vision and data pulled from multiple sensors to ensure customers are only charged for goods they pick up. Cameras are used to track items as they are taken from the shelves. The purchase price is automatically withdrawn from the customer's bank account after ten minutes of inactivity.

Cryptocurrencies, such as Bitcoin, Ethereum and Ripple, are being adopted as a payment method. Many companies accept these as a valid payment method through Bitrefill. Founded in 2014, the company wants to help people pay with their cryptocurrencies. Consumers can buy vouchers, gift-cards and credits and then spend them in 3,000 retailers and providers, including well-known names such as John Lewis, M&S, Sainsburys, B&Q, Currys PC World, Uber Eats and Deliveroo (Tayeb, 2021; Bitrefill, 2021). Tesla originally also accepted Bitcoin as a payment method for its cars, before a change of heart due to environmental concerns.

Central banks around the world are also considering adopting digital currencies. In 2020, the People's Bank of China began a real-world trial of the central bank digital currency – the digital renminbi – in one district of Shenzhen. In the West, a group of central banks, including the Federal Reserve, European Central Bank and Bank of England, set out a framework and requirements for offering central bank digital currencies (KPMG, 2021, p.6; Keswani, 2020).

In summary, methods of payments have changed in response to technological innovations, the growth of e-commerce, the effects of the global pandemic and the growing desire for a faster and more efficient means of paying for goods and services. As a result, they have become more diverse, digital and invisible.

7.3 Alternative finance and crowdfunding

Another important area in fintech is alternative finance, emerging to fill the gap left by falling bank lending after the global financial crisis. Alternative finance refers to fundraising and investment activities that have emerged outside of the incumbent banking systems and traditional capital markets, though banks themselves are now among the P2P lenders (Cambridge Centre for Alternative Finance, 2020). There are two types of alternative finance: BigTech and fintech, worth US$572 billion and US$223 billion, respectively, in 2019 (Cornelli et al., 2021, p.31) (Figure 7.5).

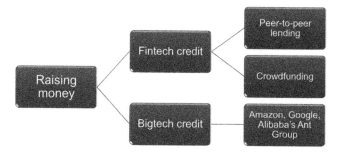

FIGURE 7.5   Fintech and BigTech credit.
Source: author's own diagram.

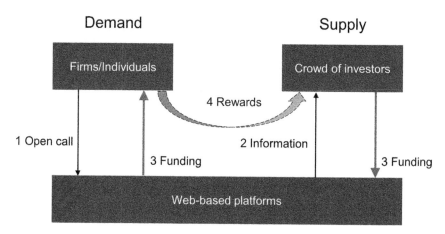

FIGURE 7.6   Conceptual framework of crowdfunding.
Source: author's own diagram.

Fintech credit refers to credit activity facilitated by electronic (online) platforms that are not operated by commercial banks. It includes peer-to-peer lending and crowdfunding. BigTech credit, on the other hand, refers to credit facilities offered by BigTech companies whose primary activity is digital services, rather than financial services, and who have established networks from non-financial business lines (e.g. e-commerce). In recent years, many BigTech firms have begun to offer credit to their users, either directly or in partnership with traditional financial institutions. The largest markets for BigTech credit in absolute terms are China, Japan, Korea and the US (Cornelli et al., 2021, pp.30–31). The remaining discussion focuses on Fintech credit.

The use of technology has made it possible to raise money through crowdfunding, defined by Mollick (2014) as the 'efforts by entrepreneurial individuals and groups to fund their ventures by drawing on relatively small contributions from a relatively large number of individuals using the internet, without the standard financial intermediaries' (Figure 7.6).

Typically, within this new capital raising system, fundraisers collect funding from the 'crowd' of investors via an online marketplace called a platform. The so-called crowdfunding, which began as a means of raising funds for artistic and creative projects, now encompasses a much broader range of activities from small charitable projects to entrepreneurs seeking hundreds of thousands of dollars in seed capital (Mollick, 2014). There are two types of crowdfunding: debt-based and non-debt-based.

7.3.1 Debt-based crowdfunding – peer-to peer-lending

Investors lend money to other individuals (peer-to-peer or 'P2P') or businesses (peer-to-business or 'P2B'). Loans can be asset-backed, secured or unsecured and offer financial returns to investors in the form of interest, in addition to the repayment of the original capital sum. The term 'peer to peer', however, is misleading because most of the loans include funding from a wide range of investors and financial institutions.

Peer-to-peer lending differs from traditional lending because it simply offers a digital platform to connect borrowers and lenders and does not bear the risk of default. These lending platforms have no physical branches and provide faster loan applications, though their loans are smaller and shorter term. They also do not rely on traditional credit scoring systems, but instead use ML and algorithms to assess credit risk, accelerate processes and lower costs (Cortina & Schmukler, 2018, p.2).

7.3.2 Other types of crowdfunding

Rather than lending money, crowdfunding offers other ways to raise capital, and there are three types: reward-based, equity-based and donation-based.

Reward-based or reward crowdfunding is used by diverse range of organisations, from non-profit art and humanitarian activities to entrepreneurs seeking start-up funds and seed capital for their businesses (Agrawal et al., 2013). Founders may therefore be individuals, start-ups or small businesses. Specialist reward-based platforms include Kickstarter and Indiegogo, which are among the two most prominent and well-known crowdfunding platforms globally. Funders of reward-based campaigns receive material rewards (non-financial such as early access to products) of increasing value if their contribution exceeds certain tiered monetary thresholds. With average amounts raised ranging from around $5,000 to $10,000 (Cox & Nguyen, 2018), reward-based crowdfunding is expected to fill the gap in the very early stage of firm development when entrepreneurs have already exhausted their personal funds and capital from FFFs (acronym for family, friends and fools).

Equity crowdfunding is the most recent development in crowdfunding and has perhaps the greatest potential for entrepreneurs and small firms. Indeed, founders of equity crowdfunding projects are typically established smaller businesses that are already engaged in activities and want to raise money from the crowd to extend and develop their company. The funding targets and actual amounts raised in equity crowdfunding are larger than those in reward-based crowdfunding and may serve to fill the gap before firms can gain access to funding from venture capitalists. There are a number of significant issues and complexities relating to equity crowdfunding that pose challenges for small firms, including the level of legal complexity and information asymmetry between project founders and funders (Vismara, 2018) and the generally illiquid nature of assets (Ahlers et al., 2015). Funders in equity crowdfunding are similar to other investors who receive an equity stake or similar consideration such as a portion of future profits, royalties and shares of profit from any IPO (Hornuf & Neuenkirch, 2017). Equity crowdfunding may, therefore, be a means by which start-ups and small businesses can begin the process of book building.

Donation-based crowdfunding is perhaps the simplest form of crowdfunding, where projects are mostly community, humanitarian or non-profit. Founders of the projects are mostly charitable organisations or individuals in need, although they also include social entrepreneurs. Contributors to donation-based projects act as donors and do not receive any direct material return in exchange for their contribution. One combination of donation and lending crowdfunding is a variant known as pro-social lending, in which funders receive back their capital but with very little or no interest. Contributors towards this type of crowdfunding have more in common with donors than investors, given that they do not receive any financial or material benefits for their participation and bear the risk of losing their principal sum if the borrower is unable to make repayments. Examples of pro-social lending platforms include *Kiva* and *Lendwithcare*.

7.3.3 Developments in crowdfunding

There are two new developments in crowdfunding. The first is the initial coin offerings (ICO) in which a blockchain-based issuer sells cryptographically secured digital assets (called tokens) to investors (Howell et al., 2020). The underlying concept of ICO is very similar to crowdfunding except that investors pay for their investment using digital currency (rather than fiat money) and will be rewarded with cryptographical token. The digital token rewarded provides investors consumptive rights to access a product and services (Howell et al., 2020). The ICO market grew explosively in 2017 and 2018 and has been seen as a quick and easy way to raise funding outside the scope of traditional regulatory frameworks (Scaglioni, 2020). This advantage, nevertheless, does not come without cost as the (ICO) market has been notorious with scams and frauds and gradually losing its appeal.

The second is the securities token offerings (STOs), which are seen as a market response to the fraudulent issues of ICOs. STOs involve the issuance of tokens which represent a conventional security. More specifically, the equity tokens may entitle investors to voting and/or dividend rights, while debt tokens may grant rights to interest and principal payment (Scaglioni, 2020). Altogether, as a new development of the crowdfunding market, it is still too early to say whether the STOs will continue to thrive as a separate type of crowdfunding or combine with the 'traditional' types to become a totally new crowdfunding category.

In summary, the credit markets have been transformed by alternative ways to raise finance: BigTech credit and Fintech credit. This includes peer-to-peer lending, crowdfunding and initial and securities coin offerings.

7.4 WealthTech

WealthTech is generally seen as a subsection of fintech, devoted to enhancing wealth management and the retail investment process. Although robo advisers are the most visible and prominent part of WealthTech, the term also includes technology derived from wealth management firms, research tools that generate investment solutions and platforms to support financial advisers (Vieira, 2017). While robo-advisers grew after 2010, their origin can be dated to 1996, when William F. Sharpe, the winner of the 1990 Nobel Prize in economics, co-founded the first robo-adviser called Financial Engines, which was sold in 2018 for $3 billion (Pender, 2018). However, the technology used may have been different from that used currently, which relies on artificial intelligence, ML, social networks and cloud computing.

Several factors contribute to the increasing demand for WealthTech. The financial crisis of 2008 shows that traditional financial institutions cannot be trusted. In the old days, consumers trusted banks and felt their money was safe and secure. However, this had evaporated with the financial crisis, which produced repossessions, loss of savings and a run on the banks. This, along with openness to technology, swayed consumers, especially millennials, to turn to tech companies to manage their money (Rooney, 2018).

There has also been a massive shift from active to passive investing, as investors move away from costly, actively managed funds, facilitating the rise of WealthTech as passive funds are more suitable for automation. In March 2020, passive funds accounted for 41% of combined US mutual funds and ETF assets under management (AUM), in comparison to 3% in 1995 and 14% in 2005 (Parsons, 2020, Anadu et al., 2020, p.4).

Some millennials turn to WealthTech because they like the convenience of modern technology (e.g. apps). Younger generations find it more useful to use online apps than to give their advisors a call or make an appointment. They also want greater accessibility to their financial information and like the convenience of accessing information anytime, anywhere, via their smartphones. They also prefer to use a variety of communication tools, such as Skype or Facetime, rather than having face-to-face meetings (The Wealth Mosaic, 2019, p.9; Drake Star, 2020, p.3).

The desire for personalised and customised advice also enhances the appeal of WealthTech. The algorithms behind personalisation draw on several sources, including information provided by a client online, the data from their transactions and their online behaviour over a period of time. The insights from this information enable digital platforms to establish an investor's needs and recommend investment strategies or model portfolios with little or no human intervention (The Wealth Mosaic, 2019, p.9). This reduces costs and makes investing affordable.

Indeed, unlike traditional financial advice, investing with a robo-adviser is very accessible. Research shows that an investor needs to have around £50,000 to invest to make it economical for a financial adviser to take them on as a client. In contrast, investors can invest spare change or as little as £1 with a robo adviser (such as Moneybox). The result is that robo advisers democratise financial advice and promote financial inclusion by serving previously underserved segments of the market by automating savings and advice (The Wealth Mosaic, 2019, p.27).

The most important aspect of WealthTech is robo advisers, which are automated digital platforms using machine-learning algorithms to determine the ideal investment portfolios for customers, based on their risk preferences and individual profile. They are popular because they are personalised, cheaper, faster and less susceptible to human biases than traditional services (Brown & Frost, 2021, Lewis, 2021). In addition to investment strategy recommendations, robo advisers can also offer portfolio monitoring, rebalancing, diversification and retirement planning.

In 2019, Forbes reported that robo advisers were expected to manage around $1 trillion by 2020, increasing to $4.6 trillion by 2022 in the US alone. However, this forecast may have been overestimated, as assets under management reached just $1.4 trillion in 2021 (Statista, 2020b; Cheng, 2019).

The biggest market for robo -advisers is the US, with 75% of the global market share or $1.05 trillion in assets under management in 2020. It is estimated that there are 200 robo-advisers in the US, in comparison to 20 in the UK and 20 in China. Industry leaders include Betterment, Wealthfront, Personal Capital, Nutmeg, FutureAdvisor and the Vanguard Group.

China is the second largest robo-advisory market with an estimated $312 billion in assets under management, followed by the UK with $24.4 billion, Germany with $14 billion and Canada with $8.2 billion (Payments Next, 2021). In the last few years, the number of investors using robo-adviser financial planning services all around the world grew by almost 5.5 times, reaching 70.5 million in 2020. This is expected to reach 147 million by 2023 (Wealth Adviser, 2020).

The use of robo-advisers promotes financial inclusion because it allows consumers with little money to invest in the stock market, known as micro-investing. Money Box, for instance, is an example of so-called 'round-up' app, allowing users to invest their spare change.

In recent years, financial planning apps have been launched to help consumers plan their future. *Personal ProjeXion*, for example, seeks to help clients establish answers to three important questions:

- Will I have enough money?
- Can I have my desired lifestyle?
- Can I retire early?

Source: PersonalProjeXion (2020)

In summary, technological innovations in wealth management relate largely to investing. Although the rise of rob-advisers has made investing easier and more accessible, consumers first need help with financial planning, so that they can establish their goals and objectives. However, technological developments in financial planning are falling behind those in the sphere of investing.

7.5 InsurTech

The rise of fintech has spurred similar developments in insurance, known as InsurTech. InsurTech emerged around 2010 and seeks to harness the power of technology to drive efficiency and make savings in insurance. The level of global interest and investment in InsurTech h has grown immensely between 2012 and 2020, increasing from $348 million in 2012 to $7,108 million in 2020, more than 2,000% in nine years. The period of greatest growth in investment is 2013–2014, when it jumped from $276 million to $2,721 million, that is, 986% increase (Figure 7.7).

Burgeoning interest in InsurTech reflects customer dissatisfaction with the traditional insurance model. One source of frustration concerns the slow and prolonged process, requiring multiple visits to an insurance broker's office, long turnaround times and long application forms before a policy can be set up. This made it difficult to take out insurance at short notice.

The digital solutions offered by InsurTech, on the other hand, are convenient and save time and costs. A digital service (e.g. Insurify) can assist customers with finding the best or cheapest deal available, while a digital insurance company can

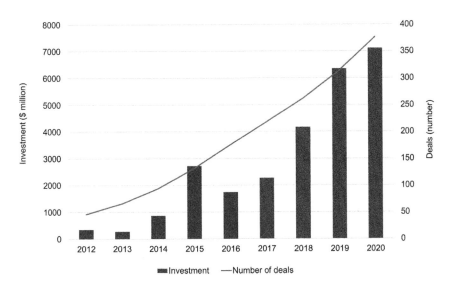

FIGURE 7.7 Investment in InsurTech, 2012 and 2020.
Source: Willis Towers Watson, (2021).

provide cheaper prices due to the elimination of the middle-man and the associated commissions paid to the brokers.

The traditional principle of pooling of risks, where a large number of customers buy cover against a certain risk (e.g. disability) by paying a premium, may result in unfair pricing. The price is determined at the point when they take out a policy, and if later they become sick, they will be subsidised by those who stay healthy and who continue to pay premiums (Marquie & Buntin, 2006). By pooling of risks, insurers can thus provide coverage for a range of customers, who may be exposed to different levels of risk, and thus low-risk customers may subsidise high-risk ones.

Using artificial intelligence innovations and algorithms, InsurTech is able to offer individualised risk pricing (based on individual risks) and dynamic pricing (no single price for a product but varies with demand in real time). It also offers value for money. Friendsurance, for example, introduces peer-to-peer finances to the insurance sector. It allows small groups of people to anonymously combine their premiums, and, if no claims are made, up to 40% of premiums will be returned.

Traditional insurance tends to offer off-the-shelf policies, which lack flexibility and are often incapable of meeting individual needs. Insurtech, on the other hand, offers bespoke products, tailored to the needs of individuals, such as usage-based insurance products or insurance on demand which provides coverage only when it is needed (e.g. car insurance premium based on actual mileage used). Customers now can buy insurance for shorter periods – a day, a month rather than a year. This creates a more flexible product, making insurance more affordable and bespoke to the needs of the individual customer (Deloitte, 2018, p.4)

InsurTech also enhances customer experience by making the claims process easier and automatic. One example is flight delay insurance products which are embedded with smart contracts, allowing automated payout when it is triggered by information extracted from the internet regarding flight delays. Automatic payout makes the claims process smooth, faster and more convenient, as well as reducing the costs associated with filing insurance claims This improved experience can enhance confidence and trust in insurers and may result in more people buying insurance (Lin & Chen, 2019, pp.9–11).

The power of InsurTech goes beyond reducing costs and improving experience. It can provide consumers with a holistic analysis of their insurance needs and shortfalls. For example, Knip, a digital insurance manager, provides users with an overview and analysis of their existing insurance policies. This is designed to automatically detect insurance gaps and recommend essential insurance.

Although InsurTech provides benefits, there are also concerns. The ability to use greater sources of information (e.g. personal data from social media or social networks) to establish a customer's risk profile raises the question of fairness and creates discrimination. While InsurTech may lead to lower insurance premiums for low-risk customers, it might result in increased costs for high-risk customers who may not be able to buy protection due to high risk or high premiums (Lin & Chen, 2019, pp.14–15).

7.6 Regulatory technology (RegTech)

The rise of RegTech has also transformed consumer experience of financial services. RegTech is believed to have emerged in 2015 when it was used in government and academic circles in the UK. From the beginning, RegTech was closely associated with fintech, because the UK regulator, in its call for input on the topic in 2016, defined it as 'a sub-set of fintech that focuses on technologies that may facilitate the delivery of regulatory requirements more efficiently and effectively than existing capabilities' (FCA, 2016, p.3). The use of technology in managing compliance is not new, but dates back at least two decades. However, what is different about RegTech is its reliance on emerging technologies such as cloud computing, application programming interfaces (APIs) and artificial intelligence (City of London & RegTech Associates, 2021, p.11).

A study by the City of London Corporation and RegTech Associates (2021) defines RegTech as the use of technology to help regulated firms meet their regulatory obligations. It argues that, because fintech is a disruptive technology while RegTech an enabler, the conflation of the two terms is problematic. In addition, RegTech is used not only by financial services but also by other highly regulated industries such as the legal sector, government, gambling, gaming, healthcare and energy. Some academics also argue that considering RegTech as part of fintech underestimates the potential of the industry, and its inherent differences in terms of origins and objectives (City of London and RegTech Associates, 2021, p.11).

Interest in the RegTech industry is growing, as can be seen in the significant global level of funding and revenue generated by the sector. It is estimated that globally the industry has attracted between $11 billion to $18.7 billion of funding between 2017 and June 2020, with UK RegTech firms receiving approximately $3 billion (City of London and RegTech Associates, 2021, pp.18, 26). In terms of revenue, one estimate put the global RegTech market revenue at $2.3 billion in 2018 and $7.2 billion by 2023, at a compounded annual growth rate of 25.4% from 2018 to 2023 (Frieder, 2019). This may be a low estimate, as revenue may already have reached $4.9 billion in 2018, and so revenue in 2023 is likely to be much higher than $7.2 billion (Cambridge Centre for Alternative Finance, 2019, p.7).

According to the Cambridge study, there were 824 RegTech firms in the UK employing 44,000 people in 2018 (Cambridge Centre for Alternative Finance, 2019, p.49). However, the City of London report shows that the number of RegTech firms in 2021 is lower, a total of 560 firms with 230 RegTech companies headquartered in the UK and 330 overseas RegTech firms either with an office in the UK or who are operating globally. However, the number of people they employ appears to have increased to approximately 68,000 people, or 2.3% of all the jobs in the UK's technology sector (City of London & RegTech Associates, 2021, pp.7, 18).

Users of RegTech are predominantly financial services firms, and this means that RegTech firms tend to locate in financial centres, with over-concentration in Europe due to the volume of EU regulations between 2014 and 2018. The top 10 markets for RegTech include the UK (63%), the US (46%), Luxembourg (12%), Switzerland (18%), Ireland (11%), Australia (23%), Singapore (23%), Japan (9%), Germany (16%) and France (17%). The United Arab Emirates is the centre of activity in the Middle East, but there is no African or South Asian country in the group of top jurisdictions (Cambridge Centre for Alternative Finance, 2019, pp.8, 25).

Several factors stimulate the growth of RegTech. Regulatory changes increased after the 2008 global financial crisis, and the accompanying volumes of regulations have rendered compliance a logistical nightmare. Thomson Reuters, for example, recorded 56,300 regulatory updates globally in 2017 (154 daily), in comparison to 17,800 in 2012 (48 daily) and 8,700 (23 daily) in 2008 (Cambridge Centre for Alternative Finance, 2019, p.20). The US Dodd Frank Act generated over 22,000 pages of regulations, while the Markets in Financial Instruments Directive (MiFID) II takes 30,000 pages and 1.5 million paragraphs to describe the rules, costing firms some €2.5 bn to interpret and rewrite the rules into business texts and computer code (Butler et al., 2018, pp.5–6). Firms also need to navigate multiple and divergent regulatory regimes simultaneously, and this increases the cost. It is believed that the cost of regulatory fragmentation and divergence to international financial firms is around 5–10% of revenues (Cambridge Centre for Alternative Finance, 2019, p.20).

Due to a high volume of regulations, compliance has become a major cost to financial services firms. Oliver Wyman estimates that 10–15% of financial services employees work on compliance and risk management, with much of the time spent on going through regulation-related paperwork. The banking industry is reported to spend $780 billion on compliance costs globally (Roy et al., 2018, p.3). Financial services firms are believed to spend 4% of their revenue on compliance, with the cost spent mainly on consultants, professional services and project cost, including technology changes (Butler et al., 2018, pp.5–6). The total direct and indirect costs of compliance have been put at 10% of GDP for the UK and 12% for the US (Cambridge Centre for Alternative Finance, 2019, p.19).

Compliance failures have also become expensive, with the sector paying £321 billion in fines and penalties in the last ten years, in addition to reputational damage and the loss of confidence by shareholders (Roy et al., 2018, p.3). Therefore, it is important to take steps to ensure compliance with the ever-changing regulation.

Interest in RegTech also comes from the need to improve existing strategies to combat financial crimes (Refinitiv, 2019). The FinCen files scandal, for example, demonstrates that many global banks have been ineffective in tackling money laundering or the movement of dirty money, and have allowed criminals to

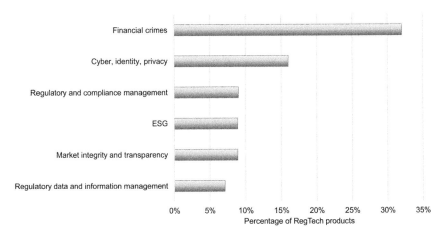

FIGURE 7.8   Main uses of RegTech.
Source: author's own diagram using data from City of London and RegTech Associates, 2021, p.14.

move vast sums of money through their banks for years (Dzhanova & Jankowicz, 2020). The global pandemic has also sped up the pace of change, as compliance teams work remotely and the fear of COVID-19 virus surviving on paper for up to 28 days renders manual and paper-based compliance ineffective (Christensen, 2020).

The main clients of RegTech are predominantly banks, followed by insurers and fintech start-ups. Research by RegTech Associates shows that the top five major uses of RegTech are: financial crimes; cyber, identity and privacy; regulatory and compliance management; ESG and market integrity and compliance management (Figure 7.8).

RegTech brings several benefits to consumers. It allows a faster onboarding process. Traditionally, to open a bank account, a customer, needs to make an appointment and bring their ID to be verified manually to ensure compliance with know-your-customer (KYC), and with anti-money laundering (AML) regulations. It is reported that it takes 24 days on average for a financial institution to complete the onboarding process, with some customer having to wait up to three months and longer (Planet Compliance, 2021). Now, identity verification can be done remotely in minutes using a mobile phone. This process involves a customer taking a photo of an ID document and a selfie for facial comparison with the photo on the ID document. A liveness detection then takes place by analysing eye blinking and lip movement (e.g. a smile) to verify the customer. Using biometrics, this method also enhances security when onboarding customers remotely, because fraudsters would find it difficult to impersonate the individual on the photo ID (Planet Compliance, 2021).

Technology also allows consumers to save a lot of time when using financial services. It is reported that new clients are contacted, on average, ten times during the onboarding process to submit anything between 5 and 100 documents. RegTech solves this problem by providing a centralised client and counterparty data platform so that up to 80% of client data and documentation can be reused across various business lines and jurisdictions (Fenergo, 2017). Thus, RegTech reduces hassles for a customer by removing the need to complete endless application forms.

RegTech also tackles financial crimes and allows consumers to use financial services with greater confidence. Feedzai, a platform to manage financial crime, for example, monitors all transactions in real time and claims that it can prevent complex fraud occurrences with accuracy. By utilising powerful ML technology, Feedzai can detect complex money laundering typologies and identify hidden relationships among transactions.

In short, RegTech brings benefits to both businesses and consumers (Barclaycard, 2021). For businesses, it means lower compliance costs, higher business effectiveness resulting in quicker and more reliable decisions and lessened risk of costly compliance failures. For consumers, RegTech means faster onboarding, greater convenience, less paperwork and fewer hassles.

7.7 Conclusion

Technology-driven financial solutions have undergone an evolution over the past 130 years, starting with technologies such as the telegraph, railroads and steamships in the late nineteenth century, followed by digitisation in the late 1960s, and the use of Big data, ML, blockchain and artificial intelligence (AI) after 2008.

The next step in the financial evolution is the application of augmented reality (AR) and virtual reality (VR). AR is the technology that blends the virtual with reality (e.g. Change My Face, for example, allows a user to upload their photo and then see how they age over time), while VR is a pure virtual world with users interacting through a VR headset (e.g. virtual bank). These technologies are used to provide a personalised, face-to-face virtual service. For example, Fidelity Investments developed a VR agent named 'Cora' to interact with users and recommend stocks based on Big Data and the individual's portfolio. Users can also interact with Cora by asking questions in a VR chat room (Cizmeci, 2021). As Chapter 6 has shown, the traditional financial services marginalise the young and less affluent, but these new technological changes may lead to the rise of the younger, technologically savvy generation of consumers as important users of financial services.

Self-test questions

1   What factors contributed to the emergence of fintech?
2   What role did the 2008 global financial crisis play in the rise of fintech?

3   Analyse the advantages and disadvantages of fintech.
4   Critically discuss the key features, pros and cons of technological innovations in payments, alternative finance, InsurTech, WealthTech and RegTech.
5   Critically discuss how fintech contributes to financial inclusion.
6   What other areas of finance need technological innovations?

Further readings

Fintech

Antovski, L., and Gusev, M. (2003). 'M-payments'. Proceedings of the 25th International Conference on Information Technology Interfaces, ITI 2003, 2003, 95–100, doi: 10.1109/ITI.2003.1225328.

Arner, D., Barberis, J., and Buckley, R., (2016), 'The Evolution of Fintech: A New Post-Crisis Paradigm?', *University of New South Wales Law Research Series.* Available at https://www.researchgate.net/publication/313365410_The_Evolution_of_Fintech_A_New_Post-Crisis_Paradigm.

Cortina, J.J., and Schmukler, S.L., (2018), 'The Fintech Revolution: A Threat to Global Banking?', *World Bank,* Research and Policy Briefs, No. 14, April 2018. Available at https://documents1.worldbank.org/curated/en/516561523035869085/pdf/125038-REVISED-A-Threat-to-Global-Banking-6-April-2018.pdf.

KPMG, (2021), *The Pulse of Fintech H2'20.* Available at https://assets.kpmg/content/dam/kpmg/xx/pdf/2021/02/pulse-of-fintech-h2-2020.pdf.

Insurtech

Lin, L., and Chen, C., (2019), 'The Promise and Perils of Insurtech', *NUS Law Working Paper 2019/021.* Available at https://papers.ssrn.com/sol3/papers.cfm?abstract_id=3463533.

Regtech

City of London & Regtech Associates, (2021), 2021: A Critical Year for RegTech. Available at https://www.theglobalcity.uk/PositiveWebsite/media/Research-reports/2021-A-Critical-Year-for-RegTech-final.pdf.

Wealthtech

Drake Star, (2020), 'Sector Report: The Rise of Wealthtech'. Available at https://s3-eu-west-1.amazonaws.com/drake-blog-content/wp-content/uploads/2016/09/02184614/20200702_WealthTech-Report_vF-1.pdf. [Accessed 18 June 2021].

The Wealth Mosaic, (2019), *UK Wealth Technology Landscape Report.* Available at https://www.thewealthmosaic.com/vendors/twm/insights/the-uk-wealth-technology-landscape-report/. [Accessed 18 June 2021].

References

Agrawal, A.K., Catalini, C., and Goldfarb, A. (2013). *Some Simple Economics of Crowdfunding.* NBER Working Paper 19133. Available at https://www.nber.org/system/files/working_papers/w19133/w19133.pdf. [Accessed 30 May 2021]

Ahlers, G.K., Cumming, D., Günther, C., and Schweizer, D. (2015). 'Signalling in Equity Crowdfunding', *Entrepreneurship Theory and Practice,* 39(4), 955–980.

Anadu, K., Kruttli, M., McCabe, P., and Osambela, E., (2020). 'The Shift from Active to Passive Investing: Potential Risks to Financial Stability?,' *Finance and Economics Discussion Series 2018–060r1*. Washington: Board of Governors of the Federal Reserve System, https://doi.org/10.17016/FEDS.2018.060r1. [Accessed 18 June 2021]

Antovski, L., and Gusev, M. (2003). M-payments. Proceedings of the 25th International Conference on Information Technology Interfaces, ITI 2003, 2003, 95–100, doi: 10.1109/ITI.2003.1225328.

Arner, D., Barberis, J., and Buckley, R., (2016), 'The Evolution of Fintech: A New Post-Crisis Paradigm?', *University of New South Wales Law Research Series*. Available at https://www.researchgate.net/publication/313365410_The_Evolution_of_Fintech_A_New_Post-Crisis_Paradigm. [Accessed 15 June 2021]

Barclaycard, (2021), 'How Regtech Can Boost Customer Experience'. Available at https://www.barclaycard.co.uk/business/accepting-payments/corporate-payment-solutions/news/regtech-customer-experience. [Accessed 16 June 2021]

Bitrefill, (2021), Available at https://www.bitrefill.com/buy/. [Accessed 9 June 2021]

Bouveret, A., (2018), *Cyber Risk for the Financial Sector: A Framework for Quantitative Assessment*, IMF Working Paper, WP/18/143. Available at https://www.imf.org/en/Publications/WP/Issues/2018/06/22/Cyber-Risk-for-the-Financial-Sector-A-Framework-for-Quantitative-Assessment-45924. [Accessed 27 June 2021]

Brown, J., and Frost, G., (2021), 'What Is a Robo-adviser?', *The Times* 19 May 2021. Available at https://www.thetimes.co.uk/money-mentor/article/robo-adviser/. [Accessed 16 June 2021]

Butler, T., North, P., and Palmer, J., (2018), *A New Paradigm for Regulatory Change and Compliance A Whitepaper by the RegTech Council*. Available at https://www.bnymellon.com/content/dam/bnymellon/documents/pdf/emea/regtech-council-weighs-in.pdf.coredownload.pdf. [Accessed 16 June 2021]

Cahill, D., (2021), 'The Unique Opportunity for Fintech in the Payments Space', *Information Age*. Available at https://www.information-age.com/the-unique-opportunity-for-fintech-in-the-payments-space-123494432/. [Accessed 16 June 2021]

Cambridge Centre for Alternative Finance, (2019) *The Global RegTech Industry Benchmark Report*. Available at https://www.jbs.cam.ac.uk/wp-content/uploads/2020/08/2019-12-ccaf-global-regtech-benchmarking-report.pdf. [Accessed 16 June 2021]

Center Forward, (2016), 'FinTech and Its Role in the Future of Financial Services'. Available at https://center-forward.org/basics/fintech-future-financial-services/. [Accessed 15 June 2021]

Cheng, M., (2019), 'The Future of Wealthtech,' *Forbes* 19 February 2019. Available at https://www.forbes.com/sites/margueritacheng/2019/02/19/the-future-of-wealthtech/?sh=2dcffc2d35e6. [Accessed 16 June 2021]

City of London & Regtech Associates, (2021), *2021: A Critical Year for RegTech*. Available at https://www.theglobalcity.uk/PositiveWebsite/media/Research-reports/2021-A-Critical-Year-for-RegTech-final.pdf. [Accessed 16 June 2021]

Cizmeci, D., (2021), 'The Next Stage in the Financial Revolution: AR and VR Solutions', *Alley Watch*. Available at https://www.alleywatch.com/2020/11/the-next-stage-in-the-financial-revolution-ar-and-vr-solutions/. [Accessed 27 June 2021]

Cornelli, G., Frost, J., Gambacorta, L., Rau, R., Wardrop, R., and Ziegler, T. (2021), 'Fintech and Big Tech Credit: What Explains the Rise of Digital Lending?' CESifo Forum 2 / 2021 March Volume 22. Available at https://www.econstor.eu/bitstream/10419/232393/1/CESifo-Forum-2021-02-p30-34.pdf. [Accessed 16 June 2021]

Corporate Finance Institute (CFI), (2021), Fintech (Financial Technology). Available at https://corporatefinanceinstitute.com/resources/knowledge/finance/fintech-financial-technology. [Accessed 22 June 2021]

Cortina, J.J., and Schmukler, S.L., (2018), 'The Fintech Revolution: A Threat to Global Banking?', *World Bank*, Research and Policy Briefs, No. 14, April 2018. Available at https://documents1.worldbank.org/curated/en/516561523035869085/pdf/125038-REVISED-A-Threat-to-Global-Banking-6-April-2018.pdf. [Accessed 15 June 2021]

Cox, J., and Nguyen, T. (2018). 'Does the Crowd Mean Business? An Analysis of Reward-based Crowdfunding and Support for Start-ups'. *Journal of Small Business and Enterprise Development*, 25(1), 147–162.

Deloitte, (2018), 'Fintech Revolution in Insurance.' Available at https://www2.deloitte.com/us/en/pages/financial-services/articles/fintech-revolution-in-insurance.html. [Accessed 18 June 2021]

Drake Star, (2020), 'Sector Report: The Rise of Wealthtech'. Available at https://s3-eu-west-1.amazonaws.com/drake-blog-content/wp-content/uploads/2016/09/02184614/20200702_WealthTech-Report_vF-1.pdf. [Accessed 18 June 2021]

Dzhanova, Y., and Jankowicz, M., (2020), 'The 11 Most Important Things in the Leaked FinCEN Files, Which Exposed $2 Trillion in Suspicious Transactions and Are Roiling the World of Finance,' *Business Insider*. Available at https://www.businessinsider.com/biggest-revelations-that-came-out-of-the-leaked-fincen-reports-2020-9?r=US&IR=T. [Accessed 16 June 2021]

England, J., (2021), 'UK Ranked Second to US for Fintech Capital Funding in 2020', *Fintech Magazine*, 21 January 2021. Available https://fintechmagazine.com/financial-services-finserv/uk-ranked-second-us-fintech-capital-funding-2020. [Accessed 15 June 2021]

FCA, (2016), *Call for Input on Supporting the Development and Adopters of RegTech*, FS16/4. Available at https://www.fca.org.uk/publication/feedback/fs-16-04.pdf. [Accessed 18 June 2021]

Fenergo, (2017), The Path to Client Lifecycle Transformation Is Paved with RegTech. Available at https://www.fenergo.com/blog/the-path-to-client-lifecycle-transformation-is-paved-with-regtech/. [Accessed 27 June 2021]

Finextra, (2016), 'The Digital Interface Is the Future of Banking'. Available at https://www.finextra.com/newsarticle/28771/the-digital-interface-is-the-future-of-banking. [Accessed 15 June 2021]

France-Presse, A., (2020), 'Chinese Banks Disinfect Banknotes to Stop Spread of Coronavirus', *Guardian*. Available at https://www.theguardian.com/world/2020/feb/15/chinese-banks-disinfect-banknotes-to-stop-spread-of-coronavirus. [Accessed 8 June 2021]

Frieder, J., (2019), 'RegTech Likely to Gain New Importance in 2019', *Accenture*. Available at https://financialservicesblog.accenture.com/regtech-likely-to-gain-new-importance-in-2019. [Accessed 18 June 2021]

Gelis, P., and Woods, T., (2014), 'The Rise of Fintech in Finance: How Fintech Is Reshaping the Finance Sector and How You Handle Your Money', *Kantox*. Available at https://docplayer.net/23789528-The-rise-of-fintech-in-finance.html. [Accessed 15 June 2021]

Haddad, C., and Hornuf, L., (2019), 'The Emergence of the Global Fintech Market: Economic and Technological Determinants', *Small Business Economics* (2019), 53. 81–105. Available at https://link.springer.com/content/pdf/10.1007/s11187-018-9991-x.pdf. [Accessed 15 June 2021]

Haller Grønbæk, M. von, (2016), 'Blockchain 2.0, Smart Contracts and Challenges,' Bird & Bird. Available at https://www.twobirds.com/~/media/pdfs/in-focus/fintech/blockchain2_0_martinvonhallergroenbaek_08_06_16.pdf. [Accessed 22 June 2021]

Hornuf, L., and Neuenkirch, M. (2017). 'Pricing Shares in Equity Crowdfunding'. *Small Business Economics*, 48, 795–811.

Howell, S.T., Niessner, M., and Yermark, D. (2020). 'Initial Coin Offerings: Financing Growth with Cryptocurrency Token Sale.' *Review of Financial Studies*, 33, 3925–3974.

INED, (2018), 'Migration Worldwide'. Available at https://www.ined.fr/en/everything_about_population/demographic-facts-sheets/focus-on/migration-worldwide/. [Accessed 16 June 2021]

Jagtiani, J., and John, K., (2018), 'Fintech: The Impact on Consumers and Regulatory Responses', *Journal of Economics and Business*, 100, 1–6. Available at https://www.researchgate.net/publication/329408296_Fintech_The_Impact_on_Consumers_and_Regulatory_Responses. [Accessed 16 June 2021]

Keeton, G., (2019), 'Exploring the Pros and Cons of a Cashless Society', *Revolut*. Available at https://blog.revolut.com/pros-cons-cashless-society/. [Accessed 27 June 2021]

Keswani, D., (2020), 'Blockchain Central Bank Digital Currency (CBDC) in Asia: Where We're Headed,' *OMG* Network. Available at https://omg.network/blockchain-cbdc-in-asia-2020/. [Accessed 20 June 2021]

KPMG, (2021), *The Pulse of Fintech H2'20*. Available at https://assets.kpmg/content/dam/kpmg/xx/pdf/2021/02/pulse-of-fintech-h2-2020.pdf. [Accessed 15 June 2021]

Lewis, R., (2021), '5 Common Behavioral Biases and How They Lead Investors to Make Bad Decisions', *Businessinsider*. Available at https://www.businessinsider.com/behavioral-biases?r=US&IR=T. [Accessed 16 June 2021]

Lin, L., and Chen, C., (2019), 'The Promise and Perils of Insurtech', *NUS Law Working Paper 2019/021*. Available at https://papers.ssrn.com/sol3/papers.cfm?abstract_id=3463533. [Accessed 16 June 2021]

Lochy, J., (2019), 'Big Data in the Financial Services Industry – From Data to Insights,' Finextra. Available at https://www.finextra.com/blogposting/17847/big-data-in-the-financial-services-industry---from-data-to-insights. [Accessed 22 June 2021]

LS Retail, (2020). 'The Future of Payments'. Available at https://www.lsretail.com/future-of-payments-ebook

Lulic, M., (2020), 'The Future of Contactless Payments: Three Predictions for the Next Five Years,' *Forbes*. Available at https://www.forbes.com/sites/forbestechcouncil/2020/08/28/the-future-of-contactless-payments-three-predictions-for-the-next-five-years/?sh=15dd8c4c316f. [Accessed 22 June 2021]

Marquie, M.S., and Buntin, M.B., (2006), 'How Much Risk Pooling Is There in the Individual Insurance Market?' *Health Services Research*, 2006 Oct, 41(5), 1782–1800. Available at https://www.ncbi.nlm.nih.gov/pmc/articles/PMC1955300/pdf/hesr0041-1782.pdf. [Accessed 18 June 2021]

McKinsey & Company, (2020), 'The 2020 McKinsey Global Payments Report'. Available at https://www.mckinsey.com/~/media/mckinsey/industries/financial%20services/our%20insights/accelerating%20winds%20of%20change%20in%20global%20payments/2020-mckinsey-global-payments-report-vf.pdf. [Accessed 16 June 2021]

Mollick, E., (2014), 'The Dynamics of Crowdfunding: An Exploratory Study', *Journal of Business Venturing*, 29(1), 1–16.

Nixon, G., (2020), 'Britain Was Going Cashless Before Coronavirus Hit, Banking Data Shows: More Than Half of Payments Last Year Were Made by Card for the First Time', *Thisismoney*. Available at https://www.thisismoney.co.uk/money/saving/article-8383733/Cash-just-23-transactions-2019-contactless-boomed.html. [Accessed 9 June 2021]

Oleksyuk, A., (2019), '5 Uses of Machine Learning in Finance and FinTech'. Available at https://medium.com/@annoleksyuk/5-uses-of-machine-learning-in-finance-and-fintech-9cf4a7530695. [Accessed 22 June 2021]

Parsons, J., (2020), 'Passive Strategies Continue to Overwhelm Asset Managers as Market Hits $11 Trillion,' *The Trade News*. Available at https://www.thetradenews.com/passive-strategies-continue-overwhelm-asset-managers-market-hits-11-trillion/. [Accessed 18 June 2021]

Payments Next, (2021), 'Robo Advisors Will Reach $2.5 Trillion in Assets Managed in 2023.' Available at https://paymentsnext.com/robo-advisors-will-reach-2-5-trillion-in-assets-managed-in-2023/. [Accessed 18 June 2021]

Pender, K., (2018), 'Financial Engines, Robo-advice Pioneer, to be Sold for $3 billion', *San Francisco Chronicle 30 April 2018*. Available at https://www.sfchronicle.com/business/networth/article/Financial-Engines-robo-advice-pioneer-sold-for-12875847.php. [Accessed 16 June 2021]

PersonalProjeXion, (2020), *The Financial Planning App for Everyone*. Available at https://www.personalprojexion.co.uk/. [Accessed 18 June 2021]

Planet Compliance, (2021), Frictionless Client Onboarding or a Case Study in Creating Business Opportunities with RegTech. Available at https://www.planetcompliance.com/frictionless-client-onboarding-or-a-case-study-in-creating-business-opportunities-with-regtech/. [Accessed 27 June 2021]

Refinitiv, (2019), 'Revealing the True Cost of Financial Crime What's Hiding in the Shadows? 2018 SURVEY REPORT'. Available at https://www.refinitiv.com/content/dam/marketing/en_us/documents/reports/true-cost-of-financial-crime-global-focus.pdf. [Accessed 16 June 2021]

Rooney, K., (2018), 'After the Crisis, a New Generation Puts Its Trust in Tech Over Traditional Banks,' *CNBC 14 September 2018*. Available at https://www.cnbc.com/2018/09/14/a-new-generation-puts-its-trust-in-tech-over-traditional-banks.html. [Accessed 18 June 2021]

Roser, M., (2017), 'Tourism'. Available at https://ourworldindata.org/tourism. [Accessed 16 June 2021]

Roy, S., Heaney, M., and Seibert, H., (2018), *RegTech on the Rise: Transforming Compliance into Competitive Advantage*, Oliver Wyman. Available at https://www.oliverwyman.com/content/dam/oliver-wyman/v2/publications/2018/may/RegTech-on-the-Rise.pdf. [Accessed 16 June 2021]

Scaglioni, L., (2020). 'Security Token Offerings – A European Perspective on Regulation', *Clifford Chance*. Available at https://www.cliffordchance.com/briefings/2020/10/security-token-offerings---a-european-perspective-on-regulation.html. [Accessed 1 July 2021]

Smartosc Global, (2021), 'Fintech & AI: 7 Ways Artificial Intelligence Is Used in Finance'. Available at https://www.smartosc.com/insights/7-ways-ai-is-used-in-fintech. [Accessed 22 June 2021]

Statista, (2020a), 'Retail E-commerce Sales Worldwide from 2014 to 2024'. Available at https://www.statista.com/statistics/379046/worldwide-retail-e-commerce-sales/. [Accessed 16 June 2021]

Statista, (2020b), 'Robo Advisors Worldwide'. Available at https://www.statista.com/outlook/dmo/fintech/personal-finance/robo-advisors/worldwide#key-market-indicators. [Accessed 18 June 2021]

Statista, (2021a), 'Total Value of Investments into Fintech Companies Worldwide from 2010 to 2020 *(in billion U.S. dollars)*'. Available at https://www.statista.com/statistics/719385/investments-into-fintech-companies-globally/. [Accessed 15 June 2021]

Statista, (2021b), 'Global Tourism Industry: Statistics and Facts.' Available at https://www.statista.com/topics/962/global-tourism/. [Accessed 16 June 2021]

Tayeb, Z., (2021), 'More Companies, Including PayPal and Xbox, Are Accepting Bitcoin and Other Cryptocurrencies as Payment. Others Are Weighing Up Their Options', *Business Insider*. Available at https://www.businessinsider.com/more-companies-accepting-bitcoin-cryptocurrency-paypal-starbucks-2021-4?r=US&IR=T. [Accessed 9 June 2021]

Telus International, (2019), 'How RPA Can Benefit Financial Services Firms'. Available at https://www.telusinternational.com/articles/rpa-benefit-financial-services. [Accessed 22 June 2021]

The Wealth Mosaic, (2019), *UK Wealth Technology Landscape Report*. Available at https://www.thewealthmosaic.com/vendors/twm/insights/the-uk-wealth-technology-landscape-report/. [Accessed 18 June 2021]

Vieira, H., (2017), 'WealthTech': The Challenges Facing the Wealth Management Industry'. Available at https://blogs.lse.ac.uk/businessreview/2017/06/16/wealthtech-the-challenges-facing-the-wealth-management-industry/. [Accessed 16 June 2021]

Vismara, S., (2018), 'Information Cascades Among Investors in Equity Crowdfunding'. *Entrepreneurship Theory and Practice*, 42(3), 467–497.

Walden, S., (2020), 'What Is Fintech and How Does It Affect How I Bank?', *Forbes Advisor*. Available at https://www.forbes.com/advisor/banking/what-is-fintech/. [Accessed 15 June 2021]

Wealth Adviser, (2020), 'US Robo-advisory Industry to Hit USD1tn Value This Year.' Available at https://www.wealthadviser.co/2020/05/18/285696/us-robo-advisory-industry-hit-usd1tn-value-year. [Accessed 18 June 2021]

Willis Towers Watson, (2021), 'Quarterly InsurTech Briefing Q4 2020: 2020 — The Most Important Year for InsurTech to Date.' Available at https://www.willistowerswatson.com/en-GB/Insights/2021/01/quarterly-insurtech-briefing-q4-2020. [Accessed 18 June 2021]

World Bank, (2021), 'Defying Predictions, Remittance Flows Remain Strong during COVID-19 Crisis'. Available at https://www.worldbank.org/en/news/press-release/2021/05/12/defying-predictions-remittance-flows-remain-strong-during-covid-19-crisis. [Accessed 16 June 2021]

8

FINANCIAL INCLUSION

Nikhil Sapre

Key points summary

- Financial exclusion is a global issue but differs across different countries: in low-income countries, the key focus is lack of access to basic banking and payment services; in higher-income countries, the focus is more on access to credit, savings, insurance and financial advice.
- Financial inclusion is a multidimensional concept that embraces access to and usage of financial products and services, and also the efficacy of the financial system.
- Major causes of financial exclusion include a lack of willingness of firms to serve less profitable, poorer and more remote communities; poor financial literacy; and demographic factors many of which intersect and are often related to low income.
- Important ways to increase financial inclusion are government policies (either direct intervention or creating the environment for financial services to develop) and the opportunities afforded by technological innovation. Particularly in higher-income countries, consumers have some – albeit limited – ways to influence their own financial inclusion.

Before the late 1990s, the term **financial inclusion** was nowhere near as topical as it is today. The attention financial inclusion has received from academics, policymakers, international development organisations and the private sector has increased considerably in the past few years. This reflects both the importance of financial services to global and national economic policies (as discussed in Chapter 1) and, from a social policy perspective, the fact that it is increasingly difficult to function as a consumer without engaging with financial services in some shape or form.

DOI: 10.4324/9781003227663-8

As a minimum, people need a payment system in order to sell their labour and buy the things they need. Beyond that, as you have seen in earlier chapters, there is a need to borrow for personal spending or to finance a business, to save as a cushion against emergencies and for life beyond work and to insure things of value such as homes, crops or human capital. Without access to these financial services, individual well-being is impaired and even the growth of whole countries may be held back.

This chapter explores the scale of financial exclusion across the globe, the impact it can have on individual well-being, the factors behind financial exclusion and how technology in particular may help to increase inclusion.

Learning outcomes

The learning outcomes for this chapter are to:

- Understand why financial inclusion is important for individual financial well-being.
- Appreciate that the terms 'financial inclusion' and 'financial exclusion' can mean different things depending on different contexts, particularly differences between lower-income and higher-income countries.
- Be able to explain some of the reasons why financial exclusion exists and some ways in which inclusion may be increased.
- Understand that financial inclusion, as well as being a driver of well-being at the individual level, can also contribute to economic growth at the macroeconomic level.

8.1 Nature and scale of financial exclusion

The banking and financial services sector is an important part of our lives. Many day-to-day activities such as paying utility bills, buying groceries or hiring a taxi are transactions that involve money and are facilitated through debit or credit cards, bank transfers or mobile payment applications. Convenient and sufficient access to financial services can enhance the ability to borrow for education or business expansion, to save for contingencies, to purchase insurance against unforeseen economic shocks or to invest for post-retirement income. Unsurprisingly then, **financial exclusion** - the inability of economic agents, such as individuals, households and firms, to access and use the financial services they need - can present difficulties for those agents' day-to-day functioning (Marshall, 2004).

8.1.1 Financial exclusion: a global issue

Across the globe, lack of access to financial services has a strong association with poverty, especially in lower-income countries. Amartya Sen, the Nobel Prize-winning economist, posits that poverty is not merely insufficient income, rather the absence of a wide range of capabilities, including security and the ability to participate in economic and political systems (Sen, 2000). Therefore, enhancing overall participation in the formal financial system is an increasingly important **development policy** objective.

In 2015, the **United Nations (UN)** member states unanimously adopted a set of 17 Sustainable Development Goals (SDGs) as a global commitment to end poverty and promote economic growth while at the same time tackling inequality and climate change (UN, no date). Financial inclusion has been identified as an enabler for seven out of the 17 goals:

- SDG 1, on eradicating poverty.
- SDG 2 on ending hunger, achieving food security and promoting sustainable agriculture.
- SDG 3 on profiting health and well-being.
- SDG 5 on achieving gender equality and economic empowerment of women.
- SDG 8 on promoting economic growth and jobs.
- SDG 9 on supporting industry, innovation and infrastructure.
- SDG 10 on reducing inequality.

Financial inclusion, potentially a direct or indirect solution to critical socio-economic issues as identified in the SDGs, continues to be in focus in the twenty-first century.

8.1.2 Who are the financially excluded?

The term 'financial inclusion' is often used to refer to ensuring the participation of the unbanked and the underbanked population in the formal financial system. 'Unbanked' refers to those who lack complete access to any kind of financial services, including a payment account at a financial institution or mobile money service. 'Underbanked' refers to those who have access to these basic financial services but may not be using them or may lack access to other mainstream facilities such as credit.

Although down from 2.5 billion in 2011 and 2 billion in 2014, World Bank data show that 1.7 billion adults remain unbanked globally as of 2017 (Demirguc-Kunt et al., 2018). As seen in Figure 8.1, financial exclusion is considerably higher in the relatively less-developed **Global South**: the larger the size of the circle, the higher the number of financially excluded in the population, with China and India having the highest figures at 224 million and 191 million, respectively. There is a significant gap between richer and poorer countries, with 94% of adults having an account in high-income developed economies, but only 63% in low-income and lower middle-income developing economies. However, both traditional and mobile accounts have been growing from 62% of adults in 2014 to 69% by 2017. In 2018, the mobile money industry saw a 20% year-on-year growth as the total number of accounts reached 866 million, adding another 143 million registered customers globally (GSMA, 2019).

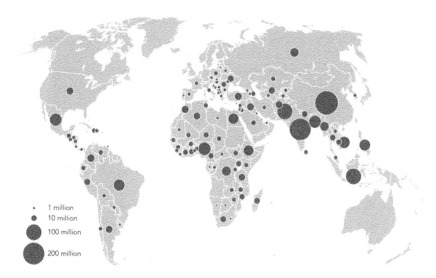

FIGURE 8.1   Adults aged 15 and more without a payment account★ (2017).
Source: Demirguc-Kunt et al. (2018), p.35.
★Bank account or mobile payment account.

The data in Figure 8.1 are part of a wider World Bank database on how adults make payments, save, borrow and manage risk, which has been published every three years since 2011. It supports the work of the Global Partnership for Financial Inclusion (GPFI), an inclusive platform for all G20 countries to carry forward work on financial inclusion, including implementation of the G20 Financial Inclusion Action Plan (FIAP), which was established in 2010. Over 50 developing countries have developed and implemented national strategies and laws to enhance financial inclusion (World Bank, 2019).

In the UK, the Financial Conduct Authority, one of the UK's financial regulators, conducts regular surveys of the financial attitudes and experiences of consumers. It estimates (FCA, 2021) that in early 2020, prior to the coronavirus pandemic, 2.3% of UK adults (1.2 million) were unbanked, of which one in ten had tried unsuccessfully to open an account in the past. Approximately 3.1 million (6%) had been refused a financial product in the last two years, most commonly credit cards, personal loans or overdrafts – this proportion rose to 10% in the eight months following the onset of the pandemic. Around one person in 11 was affected by **digital exclusion** (and so unable to access online or mobile banking) and one in ten said they would not cope in a cashless society.

8.2 The multidimensionality of financial inclusion

Among the earliest researchers to explore the concept of financial exclusion were British geographers Leyshon and Thrift (1995). They highlighted the profit-seeking, risk-averse policies that the financial services industry would deploy when faced with financial crises. These involve withdrawing services and infrastructure (such as bank branches) from lower-income countries or poorer segments of higher-income countries. The result is that even in developed countries, such as the US, Japan and some European economies, the inability to access financial products such as bank accounts and credit manifests as a geographical divide associated with income, wealth and class. This approach firmly locates financial exclusion as a **supply-side** problem, which is reinforced by an early UK regulatory view that financial exclusion is mainly due to:

> **condition exclusion**, when the conditions attached to products are unsuitable or unacceptable to consumers; **price exclusion**, where the price of products is unaffordable; **marketing exclusion**, where certain consumers are unaware of products due to marketing strategies that target others.
>
> *(Kempson et al., 2000)*

A more nuanced definition of financial exclusion recognises that **demand-side** factors are important too, as it is not only those who are unable to access financial services but also those who choose to self-exclude because the available services do not serve their purpose (Kempson and Whyley, 1999). Financial exclusion can also result from people's negative experiences or perceptions (Sinclair, 2001).

At a more systemic level, quality or effectiveness and appropriate regulation and supervision have been identified as important characteristics of an inclusive financial system (Roa, 2015). While the UK's Financial Inclusion Centre (no date) advocates the significance of a stable, competitive market environment, the United Nations underscore the need for sound and sustainable institutions that can enhance economic growth, create jobs and lead to overall development including higher financial inclusion (UNSGSA, 2009–2021).

While these disparate factors suggest that one common and universally accepted definition of financial inclusion does not exist, three major dimensions emerge (as emphasised in Figure 8.2):

- **Access**: This refers to the supply of basic financial services such as deposits, savings, credit and insurance through physical (e.g. bank branches, ATMs, building societies, credit unions, post offices) and remote access (e.g. mobile money applications, internet banking, online payment services).
- **Usage**: This refers to the demand for financial products and services by consumers (who may be individuals and firms) who have access to or wish to access but may or may not engage with the formal financial system. The level of usage can be determined by involuntary barriers (e.g. low and/or irregular income, low **financial literacy** and limited or no **Know Your Customer (KYC)** documentation) or voluntary ones (e.g. lack of trust in financial institutions, cultural and/or religious beliefs). However, low, irregular or no usage can also be a supply-side issue due to involuntary barriers related to financial institutions (for example, pricing, application procedures and collateral requirements) (Demirguc-Kunt et al., 2015).

FIGURE 8.2   Three dimensions of financial inclusion.
Source: author's diagram.

- **Efficacy**: This refers to the quality of financial products and services. It can also include inefficiencies in financial institutions' implementation of regulations, for instance narrow interpretation of the documents acceptable as proof of identity and address to satisfy KYC rules. Here, quality denotes an efficient, well-regulated market environment, comprising government and regulatory bodies as well as financial firms. In such a conducive environment, individuals and firms are able to readily identify, evaluate, access and use the financial services that suitably satisfy their needs.

Based on the three dimensions above, financial inclusion can be defined as beneficial usage of and smooth access to the formal financial system for all households and firms in an efficient market environment.

8.3 Causes and consequences of financial exclusion

Most of the early research into financial inclusion was conducted using developed countries' data and highlighted poor access, higher price and inadequate services as prominent reasons for financial exclusion. However, the issue is far more severe in the developing world, where achieving financial inclusion of the under-banked and the unbanked population is the immediate priority. For instance, 5% of adults in the US in 2014 but over 20% in Kenya did not use their accounts. In the same year, 6% of Indian adults had borrowed from a formal financial institution in the past 12 months compared to over 20% in the US and the UK (Demirguc-Kunt et al., 2015). In recent years, academic studies, using cross-country, single-country or regional data of both developing and developed countries, have identified a variety of factors that can impact financial inclusion, which are summarised in Table 8.1. These factors are briefly discussed in the sections below.

8.3.1 Geographical location

Those living in remote locations can face the barrier of distance from financial institutions. This results in limited access to banking services, which can be more acute for low-income households and small businesses in relatively underdeveloped countries as illustrated by the examples in Box 8.1.

TABLE 8.1 Factors affecting financial exclusion

Determinant	Dimension	Supply/demand
Geographical location (country/rural vs. urban)	Access	Supply-side
Bank branch outreach	Access	Supply-side
Financial literacy	Usage	Demand-side
Socio-economic and demographic factors		
Education	Usage	Demand-side
Income	Usage	Demand-side
Gender	Access and usage	Supply-side and demand-side
Age	Access and usage	Supply-side and demand-side
Race, ethnicity and nationality	Access, usage and efficacy	Supply-side and demand-side

Source: author's table.

Across both developed and less-developed countries, urban areas with better infrastructure and connectivity have few people that are financially excluded compared to rural areas (Sarma and Pais, 2011). Financial exclusion can be particularly high in rural areas due to lack of formal salaried employment opportunities, exacerbated where products and services focus on adults with a regular salary (Makesh and Kuzhuvelil, 2014).

Banks refrain from expanding in non-urban areas because the cost of servicing rural branches may not be commensurate with the financial returns they generate. Where rural dwellers have bank accounts, usage may be low because branches are inaccessible. Thus, there exists an urban–rural divide with respect to ownership and usage of bank accounts in developing countries and, albeit to a lesser extent, in developed countries too. As seen in Figure 8.3, the proportion of the rural population is considerably higher in the less-developed South Asian

BOX 8.1 FINANCIAL EXCLUSION IN BHUTAN AND NEPAL

Bhutan and Nepal are two land-locked, small, lower-middle income Asian countries situated in the remote and mountainous Himalayan region. A World Bank study (Niang et al., 2013) conducted in Bhutan showed that the formal financial system is weakly integrated into the daily life of people, hence incapable of providing services tailored to their needs. The lack of adequate financial infrastructure had reduced Bhutan to a cash-based economy. In Nepal, only 26% of households had a bank account, 38% had outstanding loans from unregulated money lenders and 69% of foreign inward remittances came through informal channels (Ferrari et al., 2007).

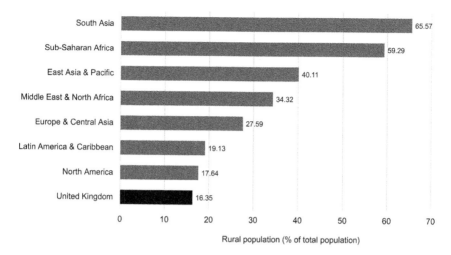

FIGURE 8.3 Rural population percentage by regions (2019).
Source: author's chart using data from World Bank (2021).

and sub-Saharan African countries, than the developed regions of Europe and North America. In contrast, in the UK, only around 10% of its rural population live ten miles or more from their nearest bank branch in 2017 (Bennett, 2020).

8.3.2 Bank-branch outreach

As you read in Chapter 1, financial deregulation removed restrictions on financial markets in many developed countries, unleashing the forces of competition. In the past, this has tended to help increase financial inclusion by expanding access to branch banking. For example, the loosening of restrictions and the deregulation of the banking sector led to an increase in the number of bank branches in the US from 13,291 in 1963 to 60,320 in 1997. However, the focus of competition has shifted in recent years with the number of bank branches per 100,000 adults remaining static in low- and middle-income countries over the period 2013 to 2019, reflecting the growing importance of mobile money (see Section 8.4.2), although over the same period the number of ATMs has grown (IMF, 2020). Meanwhile, in higher-income countries and some of the middle-income economies, the density of both bank branches and ATMs has fallen. The IMF (2020) suggests that this reflects cost-cutting measures on the part of banks and the growing popularity among customers of digital banking. In the US and UK, branch closures are reported to have focused disproportionately on those located in lower-income areas (see, for example, Davis, 2019; FCA, 2019), reducing access for communities that already tend to have higher levels of financial exclusion (see Section 8.3.4). However, it should be borne in mind that, even after closures, bank branch density is over six times higher in richer countries than in poorer ones, as shown in Figure 8.4.

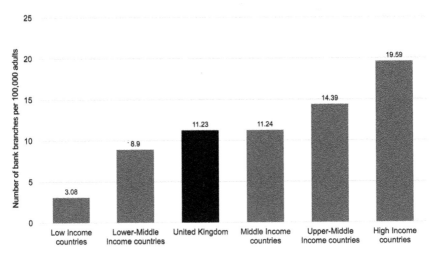

FIGURE 8.4 Density of bank branches by income groups (2019).
Source: author's chart based on data from IMF (2020).

BOX 8.2 BANK BRANCH CLOSURES IN THE UK

As Figure 8.4 shows, access to bank branches is considerably lower in the UK, compared to rest of the developed, high-income countries. The number of branches in the UK has been reduced by over 50% in the past four decades. Investing in remote banking services is more profitable with significant cost savings for banks (Collard et al., 2016; Bennett, 2020). Moreover, consumers are increasingly moving to mobile and internet banking, a trend that accelerated during the coronavirus pandemic (FCA, 2021). However, some sections of the society, such as the older population and small businesses, face barriers in adapting to the new financial technology, which can cause their financial exclusion. For instance, in the UK, roughly 20% of businesses with a turnover below £2 million use branches as their primary means of banking (FCA, 2019).

8.3.3 Financial literacy

Financial literacy is broadly defined as an understanding of basic financial concepts (such as inflation), numerical ability (e.g. calculating compound interest), attitude towards money (including spending habits, budgeting), ability to mitigate risks and knowledge of financial assets (such as bonds and stocks). Lack of financial literacy has been recognised as a key factor contributing to financial exclusion. Financial literacy can improve financial choice behaviour and increase the likelihood of investing in financial markets (Christiansen et al., 2008). Moreover, lack of basic financial education can increase vulnerability to macroeconomic shocks and lead to insolvencies (Jappelli and Padula, 2013). Little or no financial awareness often triggers greater reliance of the financially excluded population on the informal sector, for instance, pawn shops and unregulated **pay-day lenders** (Cole et al., 2013). One of the ways to ensure inclusion of such vulnerable and under-served consumers in the formal financial system is through achieving higher financial literacy. This is particularly evident from the policy initiatives of governments and regulators of both developed and emerging economies. Among 142 economies, 88% have clear mandates to improve financial inclusion, out of which 58% have specifically included achieving better financial literacy or education (Atkinson and Messy, 2013).

8.3.4 Socio-economic and demographic factors

Financially excluded individuals are less likely to have any formal educational qualification, with financial inclusion predominantly being a function of low income (Kempson et al., 2000). In all, 50% of adults in developing economies have a primary education or less, but 62% of the unbanked globally. Worldwide, only 38% of the unbanked have completed high school or post-secondary education (Demirguc-Kunt et al., 2018). Financial inclusion shares an inverse causal relationship with unemployment, with employed individuals more likely to frequently use banking services. In the UK, lower education and lower income have a negative impact on the level of financial inclusion (Devlin, 2005). Globally, 27% of the adults without an account in a financial institution lie in the poorest fifth of households, whereas 13% belong to the richest 20% of households (Demirguc-Kunt et al., 2018).

There exists a significant gender gap worldwide: compared to men, women are less likely to use basic banking services (Allen et al., 2016). In the UK, female borrowers can be more susceptible to obtaining credit from illegal and/ or informal lenders (HM Treasury, 2007c). About 980 million (56%) of all unbanked adults globally are women (Demirguc-Kunt et al., 2018). Single-parent households tend to have relatively lower usage of current accounts and insurance, which can be because lone parents (most often women) usually work fewer hours and consequently have lower incomes (Barnes et al., 2005).

Ethnic minorities and immigrants are more likely to be financially excluded due to their social identity (Kempson and Whyley 1999; Barr, 2007). Regardless of income or education, race, ethnicity and nationality have been identified as major factors determining the rate of financial exclusion in the US (Karp and Nash-Stacey, 2015).

Socio-economic and demographic factors tend to be heavily interconnected. For example, a study in Ireland showed that almost 20% of the adult population did not have a bank account and these were mostly those who were older, unemployed, disabled, single parents, had low-income and/or were poorly educated. It highlighted a strong relationship between poverty and financial exclusion (Russell et al., 2011).

8.3.5 The impact of financial exclusion in the UK

As the sections above have shown, there are many factors influencing someone's chances of financial exclusion and the factors overlap. A key intersection in the UK is low income (House of Lords Select Committee on Financial Exclusion, 2017). Research has found that low-income households pay a 'poverty premium' – in other words, incur extra costs – of almost £500 a year (Davies et al., 2016). A substantial part of this premium is related to financial or digital exclusion:

- **Paying to access money (£9 a year)**: For example, because local ATMs charge a fee, paying to use a cheque-cashing shop due to lack of access to a bank or using a fee-charging pre-paid card due to being ineligible for a debit or credit card.
- **Not paying by the cheapest billing method (£33)**: For example, because the annual premium for insurance is too high to pay in one go but paying monthly is treated as a loan and incurs interest charges.
- **Using high-cost credit (£55)**: Because a poor or non-existent **credit record** means that mainstream lenders will not serve these customers.
- **Insurance premiums related to where people live (£84)**: Because the person lives in a low-income neighbourhood often associated with higher crime levels.
- **Not switched to the best fuel tariff (£233) and paying to receive paper bills (£12)**: In some cases, because the customer is not connected to the internet or lacks digital confidence or skills, so cannot easily shop around for the best deals or operate an online account.

A survey (Lin et al., 2017) conducted in the low-income neighbourhoods of London found that 75% of those who borrowed using informal means pay a poverty premium, and 58% of those paying a premium reported going without food, gas and electricity in order to pay off their debts. Individuals with better money management skills were less likely to miss debt repayments.

Major areas of concern around financial exclusion in the UK are also lack of access to financial advice (see Chapter 6) and lack of savings. The Money and Pensions Service (2020) estimates that 11.1 million working-age people do not save regularly, of which 14% have no savings at all and 31% less than £500.

8.4 Increasing financial inclusion

This section considers three major ways of improving financial inclusion and the agents of that change: government, firms and consumers themselves. To a large extent, widening financial inclusion lies in the hands of governments either through direct intervention or by creating the environment that fosters the development and evolution of the financial system and economic growth. In both developing and developed countries, a major force for change from within the financial services sector and beyond has been technological innovation, particularly the emergence of branchless banking. This section concludes by considering what, if anything, consumers can do for themselves to improve their financial inclusion.

8.4.1 Economic policy, governance and regulation

The development of a country's financial system, financial inclusion and eco-nomic growth are closely associated, though theorists argue about the direc-tion of causality: some claim that economic growth creates demand for financial services, consequently driving financial sector development; others suggest that financial deepening mobilises savings and channels them into more productive investments causing economic growth. What is less contentious is that, for a fi-nancial system to operate effectively, it needs at least some degree of transparency and trustworthiness, and, for financial inclusion, the system needs to be acces-sible to all, not just a power elite (see Chapter 1). Therefore, political, legal and governance factors are important for financial development and participation in the formal financial system. Evidence from the developed European countries shows that a stable political system and responsive policy-making are key con-tributors to financial inclusion (Carbo et al., 2010).

Responsive policies include those that focus on industrial reforms and sec-tor-specific schemes to aid the growth of firms and employment generation, including **microfinance** initiatives. This helps to improve income levels and at the same time generates demand for financial services (Kumar, 2013).

Governments, especially in low-income countries, may also have an incentive to foster trust in the financial system where remittances (discussed in Chapter 1) make a substantial contribution to the economy, with citizens receiving the re-mittances more likely to own a savings account (Anzoategui et al., 2014). In higher-income countries, trust in financial institutions is important if govern-ments want to promote financial inclusion in the form of savings and private insurance to improve individual independence in retirement and resilience to financial shocks, reducing the likelihood of citizens falling back on state **means-tested** support.

A key question is whether governments should directly mandate financial inclusion – for example, by requiring universal access to **basic bank accounts** as is the case in Europe and the UK – or merely create the environment in which financial institutions can flourish. The former approach may be more suitable in richer countries with developed financial systems. However, some form of government intervention may be necessary, as the onus of improving inclusion cannot solely be on financial institutions, particularly in poorer countries with relatively underdeveloped financial systems. For instance, some regulators typi-cally require banks to open a certain percentage of branches in unbanked rural areas or sparsely populated smaller towns and/or prioritise lending to micro and small businesses in under-banked sectors such as agriculture.

Some question the whole idea of encouraging the underprivileged sections to make use of banking services (not only credit), especially given that policy-makers and governments have time-bound mandates to improve financial inclusion. They argue that setting targets for financial institutions can lead to flawed marketing practices, through which consumers' choice and decision-making may be adversely influenced. In a knowledge exchange research programme, which discussed aspects of financial inclusion in developed European countries and the UK, prominent financial advisory professionals were hesitant about promoting financial services to the poor, because people may end up with products they do not need or are unable to service responsibly (Sinclair, 2013). For instance, a savings product with a long-term fixed commitment may not be suitable for households that barely manage to meet their day-to-day expenses due to low or irregular incomes. Therefore, it is necessary to ascertain which services are truly necessary and suitable. To implement a blanket government policy applicable to one and all may not be the appropriate method to achieve better financial inclusion.

8.4.2 Branchless banking

Banking has steadily evolved from across-the-counter cashiers to ATMs, from cheques to telephone banking and, more recently, internet and mobile banking. Therefore, it is important to understand the association between the banking in-dustry, communication technology and financial inclusion. The banking sector is increasingly adopting cellular and digital technology, even in the developing countries, as these modes of delivery provide improved accessibility to financial services; equally, the **Information and Communication Technology (ICT)** sector has developed payment systems to rival the banks.

The ability to make financial transactions remotely has not only been ac-cepted by people globally, but internet banking is one of the most profitable e-commerce applications. There is a strong positive relationship of the increase in demand for deposits and loans with higher mobile and internet usage (Abubakar, 2014). However, the adoption of internet banking is vastly varied. While 96% of South Koreans have access to internet banking, it is used by only 18% of Indians (Barquin and Hv, 2015).

Meanwhile, mobile payment applications, which allow financial transactions without sophisticated smartphones or the internet, have bypassed traditional banking through brick-and-mortar branches or internet/mobile platforms, par-ticularly in developing countries. Therefore, it is important to understand the significant differences in financial services available through mobile phones. A mobile *banking* account is an extension of traditional banking, wherein commer-cial banks have mobile banking applications which can be used to check the ac-count balance, request money transfers, make utility bill payments and so on. By contrast, mobile money accounts allow users to store and exchange money dig-itally without directly involving a regular bank account and can be used purely over mobile networks and without access to the internet. Mobile money accounts can be broadly divided into mobile wallets and mobile payments. While mobile wallets (e.g. eWallet or Stocard) can simply store money on a mobile device and do not allow transactions, mobile payment applications (e.g. Apple Pay or PayPal) typically allow both storing and transacting through mobile cellular devices.

Digital payments whether through internet banking or mobile money are a fast growing area: between 2014 and 2017, the share of adults across the globe making digital payments increased from 41% to 52% (Demirguc-Kunt et al., 2018). However, take-up within populations varies. For example, Figure 8.5 highlights a strong correlation between age and the usage of internet banking in Great Britain, as older populations have been slower to switch to new technology-driven financial services.

As noted earlier in the chapter, the growth of branchless banking has not simply been due to cost-cutting exercises by the banks. Consumers have actively adopted online and mobile banking, attracted by 24–7 accessibility, better service quality, lower price and superior product features such as paper-free transactions and money management.

Branchless banking can also help to overcome the urban–rural divide discussed in Section 8.3.1 as demonstrated by the examples of mobile money adoption in Box 8.3. As well as convenient payment services, branchless banking can provide liquidity to poorer, rural populations who may have savings in illiquid assets such as gold. Conversion of illiquid assets to cash or directly using them to make purchases in times of crisis may be difficult or may cause loss of value. Products like mobile wallets (e.g. Rush) can help deal with such issues by enabling gold deposits to be partially cashed and converted to currency at the

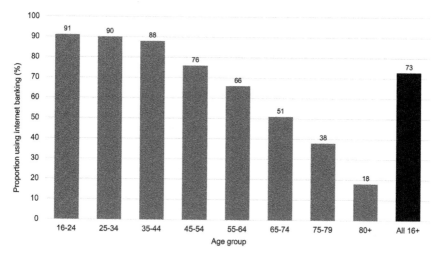

FIGURE 8.5 Internet banking usage by age group in Great Britain (2019).
Source: author's chart based on data from ONS (2019).

BOX 8.3 INNOVATIVE ADOPTION OF BRANCHLESS BANKING

M-Pesa: Evident from the success of M-Pesa in Kenya, a mobile money platform, cellular technology has contributed more to increasing the access of financial services in remote locations than traditional branch banking. Since its launch in 2007, the research found that more than 70% of the adult population in Kenya regularly use mobile banking services and more than 75% of households have at least one regular user (Jack and Suri, 2014). The research also showed that because M-Pesa enables the swift transfer of remittances between family members, when households are faced with an unexpected shock to income, their consumption barely changes compared with a 10% fall for non-M-Pesa users. The success of M-Pesa inspired entrepreneurs in Asia, Latin America and other parts of Africa to develop similar mobile platforms that facilitate payments and remittances (for instance, Paytm and PhonePe in India and Alipay and Tenpay in China).

Banking correspondent model: Banks appoint individuals, non-government organisations (NGOs), microfinance institutions (MFIs) and private firms as non-bank agents to act as their intermediaries to the unbanked rural population. The main aim of this model is the provision of branchless banking with literally doorstep delivery of financial products and services. These services range from filling of forms and advice to the collection of loan repayments and making small-value payments and deposits on customers' behalf. Brazil's correspondent banking model has provided point-of-sale devices to over 95,000 shops for faster and cheaper transactions. India had a total of 337,678 banking correspondents in 2014, with roughly one correspondent for two villages. Particularly striking about these statistics is that a large proportion of its users have moved from the pure cash economy to using any form of formal financial product for the first time.

---

point of purchase. ICT-based payment services can also provide privacy and self-sufficiency, especially for women (Morawczynski, 2009).

Internet and mobile banking do also have some drawbacks. First-time users may lack faith in electronic transactions where tangible money is not seen and exchanged. This is often rooted in the fear of funds being stolen or lost partially or entirely. Misuse of confidential personal information is another reason inhibiting users from accepting technology-based financial services. However, this risk can be both perceived and real in nature, with respect to both internet banking and mobile banking (Roy et al., 2017; Hua and Huang, 2020). Moreover, these issues may arise from the possible overarching reasons for self-exclusion and demand-side barriers to usage of financial services discussed earlier, such as lack of trust in the financial system, preconceived notions, cultural beliefs and lower financial literacy.

8.4.3 What consumers can do to tackle financial exclusion

Section 8.2 identified three dimensions of financial exclusion: access, usage and efficacy. Collard et al. (2016) noted that consumers often feel powerless in the face of access issues. However, there are some limited ways in which they may improve their chances of financial inclusion, for example:

- **Basic bank accounts**. In the European Union and the UK, consumers have the right to ask for a basic transactions account even if they are turned down for a full current account. Banks often do not advertise or promote the availability of basic bank accounts, so consumers need to know they exist and be prepared to ask for them.
- **Building a credit score**. A lack of credit in the past means that mainstream lenders have insufficient information to gauge a person's creditworthiness. A way to overcome this problem is to take out a 'credit-builder' credit card. These have a relatively high interest rate, but by borrowing and repaying in full on a regular basis, the cardholder can keep down the cost while building up a credit record that may open the door to lower-cost mainstream credit in the future.
- **Using fintech products**. Fintech is coming up with many new solutions to consumer problems. You have seen in Section 8.4.2 that it is a major way to reach the unbanked and underbanked. In higher-income countries, fintech is driving alternative ways to assess creditworthiness based on records of, for example, managing rental payments or other non-standard financial commitments.

Consumers potentially have greater control over the usage dimension of financial inclusion, and again fintech is offering ways to work with the grain of behavioural traits that may stand in the way of self-inclusion. For example, budgeting apps allow consumers to monitor, analyse and control spending, and 'round-up' apps enable everyday payments to be rounded up to the nearest pound or dollar with the excess being paid automatically into a savings account.

Considering efficacy, consumers collectively have the power to influence the quality and pricing of products and services by engaging actively in markets, shopping around, switching and using their right of exit when products are found wanting.

8.5 Conclusion

The main motivation for promoting financial inclusion as a development policy objective is the inability of the unbanked and the underbanked to derive benefits from the formal financial system that the rest of the world population takes for granted. In developed countries, the focus of financial inclusion is more on access to affordable credit, savings products and insurance to improve financial resilience and also to financial advice. However, access to a bank account remains key because in addition to providing payment mechanisms, it frequently unlocks access to other financial services such as saving, borrowing and insurance.

Financial inclusion is a multidimensional concept that may be defined as having three aspects: access, usage and efficacy. The factors influencing financial exclusion are numerous and inter-related, with low income in particular intersecting with other factors such as the unwillingness of traditional branch-banking to serve sparse rural communities.

For governments in developing countries, financial inclusion is part of the nexus between the financial system and economic growth, including, for example, access to finance for entrepreneurs and services to facilitate remittances. In higher-income countries, financial inclusion is often part of social policies aimed at maintaining and increasing individual financial well-being and reducing reliance on the state. Governments may take a direct role in promoting financial inclusion or concentrate more on creating the conditions for the financial services sector to develop and evolve. Although digital exclusion is a related issue, in general the development of digital payment services and other technology-related financial services has a positive effect on financial inclusion. Individual consumers also have some limited ways in which they may influence their own financial inclusion.

Self-test questions

1   What are the three dimensions of financial inclusion?
2   Describe the main differences between the concept of financial inclusion applied to lower-income countries and to higher-income countries.
3   Discuss one advantage and one disadvantage of branchless banking from the consumer perspective.

Further reading

For global perspectives of financial inclusion, publications from the World Bank and International Monetary Fund, including:

Barajas, A., Beck, T., Belhaj, M., Naceur, S. B., Cerra, V., and Qureshi, M. S. (2020). *Financial inclusion: what have we learned so far? What do we have to learn?* Available at: https://www.elibrary.imf.org/view/journals/001/2020/157/article-A001-en.xml (Accessed: 16 June 2021).

Demirguc-Kunt, A., Klapper, L., and Singer, D. (2017). *Financial inclusion and inclusive growth: A review of recent empirical evidence,* World Bank Policy Research. Available at: https://elibrary.worldbank.org/doi/abs/10.1596/1813-9450-8040 (Accessed: 16 June 2021).

Sahay, M. R., von Allmen, M. U. E., Lahreche, M. A., Khera, P., Ogawa, M. S., Bazarbash, M., and Beaton, M. K. (2020). *The promise of fintech: Financial inclusion in the post COVID-19 era.* Available at: https://www.imf.org/en/Publications/Departmental-Papers-Policy-Papers/Issues/2020/06/29/The-Promise-of-Fintech-Financial-Inclusion-in-the-Post-COVID-19-Era-48623 (Accessed: 16 June 2021).

For more about financial inclusion in the UK:

HM Treasury and Department for Work and Pensions (2020) *Financial inclusion report 2019–20.* Available at: https://www.gov.uk/government/publications/financial-inclusion-report-2019-2020 (Accessed: 16 June 2021).

References

Abubakar, A. (2014) 'The effects of electronic banking on growth of deposit money banks' in *Nigeria. European Journal of Business and Management*, Vol 33 No 6, pp.79–89. Available at: https://citeseerx.ist.psu.edu/viewdoc/download?doi=10.1.1.685.5947&rep=rep1&type=pdf (Accessed: 17 June 2021).

Allen, F., Demirguc-Kunt, A., Klapper, L., and Peria, M. S. M. (2016) 'The foundations of financial inclusion: Understanding ownership and use of formal accounts' in *Journal of Financial Intermediation*, Vol 27 No 7, pp.1–30. Available at: https://doi.org/10.1016/j.jfi.2015.12.003.

Anzoategui, D., Demirguç-Kunt, A., and Peria, M. S. (2014) 'Remittances and financial inclusion: Evidence from El Salvador' in *World Development*, Vol 54. Available at: https://doi.org/10.1016/j.worlddev.2013.10.006.

Atkinson, A., and Messy, F. A. (2013) *Promoting financial inclusion through financial education: OECD/INFE evidence, policies and practice.* Available at: https://www.oecd-ilibrary.org/content/paper/5k3xz6m88smp-en?crawler=true (Accessed: 17 June 2021).

Barnes, M., Lyon, N., Morris, S., Robinson, V., and Yau, Y. (2005) *Family life in Britain: findings from the 2003 Families and Children Study (FACS)*, Department for Work and Pensions Research Report No 250. Available at: http://praha.vupsv.cz/fulltext/ul_577.pdf (Accessed: 17 June 2021).

Barquin, S., and Hv, V. (2015). *Digital banking in Asia: What do consumers really want?* Available at: https://www.mckinsey.com/featured-insights/asia-pacific/digital-banking-in-asia-what-do-consumers-really-want# (Accessed: 17 June 2021).

Barr, M. S. (2007) 'Banking the poor: Overcoming the financial services mismatch' in Crain, M., Edwards, J., and Kalleberg, A. L.(eds) (2007) *Ending poverty in America: How to restore the American dream*, New York: New Press, pp.144–150.

Bennett, O. (2020) *Bank branches: why are they closing and what is the impact?* Available at: https://commonslibrary.parliament.uk/research-briefings/cbp-8740/ (Accessed: 17 June 2021).

Carbo, S., Gardener, E. P., and Molyneux, P. (2010) 'Financial exclusion in Europe' in *Public Money & Management*, Vol 27 No 1, pp.21–27. Available at: https://www.tandfonline.com/doi/abs/10.1111/j.1467-9302.2007.00551.x.

Christiansen, C., Joensen, J. S., and Rangvid, J. (2008) 'Are economists more likely to hold stocks?' in *Review of Finance*, Vol 12 No 3, pp.465–496. Available at: https://doi.org/10.1093/rof/rfm026.

Cole, S., Sampson, T., and Zia, B. (2013) 'Valuing financial literacy' in Cull, R., Demirguc-Kunt, A., and Morduch J. (eds) (2013) *Banking the world: Empirical foundations of financial inclusion*, Massachusetts: MIT Press, pp.415–428.

Collard, S., Coppack, M., Lowe, J., and Sarkar, S. (2016) *Access to financial services in the UK*, FCA Occasional Paper 17. Available at: https://www.fca.org.uk/publication/occasional-papers/occasional-paper-17.pdf (Accessed: 15 June 2021).

Davies, S., Finney, A., and Hartfree, Y. (2016) *Paying to be poor: Uncovering the scale and nature of the poverty premium*. Available at: https://www.bristol.ac.uk/media-library/sites/geography/pfrc/pfrc1615-poverty-premium-report.pdf (Accessed 15 June 2021).

Davis, M. F. (2019) *JP Morgan leads banks' flight from poor neighbourhoods*. Available at: https://www.bloomberg.com/news/articles/2019-03-06/as-u-s-banks-shut-branches-jpmorgan-leads-shift-toward-wealthy (Accessed: 15 June 2021).

Demirguc-Kunt, A., Klapper, L., Singer, D., Ansar, S., and Hess, J. (2018) *The global findex database 2017: Measuring financial inclusion and the fintech revolution*. Washington, DC: World Bank. doi:10.1596/978-1-4648-1259-0. License: Creative Commons Attribution CC BY 3.0 IGO. Also available at: https://globalfindex.worldbank.org/ (Accessed: 14 June 2021).

Demirguc-Kunt, A., Klapper, L., Singer, D., and Van Oudheusden, P. (2015) *The global findex database 2014: Measuring financial inclusion around the world*. Available at: https://documents.worldbank.org/en/publication/documents-reports/documentdetail/187761468179367706/the-global-findex-database-2014-measuring-financial-inclusion-around-the-world (Accessed: 12 June 2021).

Devlin, J. F. (2005) 'A detailed study of financial exclusion in the UK' in *Journal of Consumer Policy*, Vol 28 No 1, pp.75–108. Available at: https://doi.org/10.1007/s10603-004-7313-y.

Ferrari, A., Shrestha, S. R., and Jaffrin, G. (2007). *Access to financial services in Nepal*. Available at: https://doi.org/10.1596/978-0-8213-6989-0 (Accessed: 17 June 2021).

Financial Conduct Authority (FCA) (2019) *When bank closures bite: The picture across the UK*. Available at: https://www.fca.org.uk/insight/when-bank-closures-bite (Accessed: 17 June 2021).

Financial Conduct Authority (FCA) (2021) *Financial lives 2020 survey: The impact of coronavirus. Key findings from the FCA's Financial Lives 2020 survey and October 2020 Covid-19 panel survey*. Available at: https://www.fca.org.uk/publication/research/financial-lives-survey-2020.pdf#page=29 (Accessed: 14 June 2021).

GSMA. (2019) *State of the industry report on mobile money*. Available at: https://www.gsma.com/mobilefordevelopment/wp-content/uploads/2019/02/2018-State-of-the-Industry-Report-on-Mobile-Money.pdf (Accessed: 17 June 2021).

HM Treasury (2007c) *Financial Inclusion: An Action Plan for 2008–11*. London: HM Treasury.

House of Lords Select Committee on Financial Exclusion (2017) *Tackling financial exclusion: A country that works for everyone?* Available at: https://publications.parliament.uk/pa/ld201617/ldselect/ldfinexcl/132/13202.htm (Accessed: 15 June 2021).

Hua, X., and Huang, Y. (2020) 'Understanding China's fintech sector: Development, impacts and risks' in *The European Journal of Finance*, 1–13. Available at: https://doi.org/10.1080/0965254X.2016.1148771.

International Monetary Fund (IMF) (2020) *Financial access survey 2020. Trends and developments*. Available at: https://data.imf.org/?sk=E5DCAB7E-A5CA-4892-A6EA-598B5463A34C (Accessed: 15 June 2021).

Jack, W., and Suri, T. (2014) 'Risk sharing and transaction costs: Evidence from Kenya's mobile money revolution' in *The American Economic Review*, January, Vol104 No 1, pp.183–223. Available at: https://www.jstor.org/stable/42920692.

Jappelli, T., and Padula, M. (2013) 'Investment in financial literacy and saving decisions' in *Journal of Banking & Finance*, Vol 37 No 8, pp.2779–2792. Available at: https://doi.org/10.1016/j.jbankfin.2013.03.019.

Karp, N., and Nash-Stacey, B. (2015) *Technology, opportunity & access: Understanding financial inclusion in the US*, BBVA Research paper 15/25. Available at: https://www.bbva.com/wp-content/uploads/en/2016/06/WP15-25_FinancialInclusion_MSA.pdf (Accessed: 17 June 2021).

Kempson, E., and Whyley, C. (1999). *Kept out or opted out: Understanding and combating financial exclusion*. Bristol: The Policy Press. Available at: https://www.bristol.ac.uk/media-library/sites/geography/migrated/documents/pfrc9902.pdf (Accessed: 17 June 2021).

Kempson, H. E., Whyley, C. M., Caskey, J., and Collard, S. B. (2000) *In or out? Financial exclusion: A literature and research review*, Financial Services Authority Consumer Research 3. Available at: http://www.bristol.ac.uk/media-library/sites/geography/migrated/documents/pfrc0002.pdf (Accessed: 17 June 2021).

Kumar, N. (2013) 'Financial inclusion and its determinants: Evidence from India' in *Journal of Financial Economic Policy*, Vol 5 No 1, pp.4–19.

Leyshon, L., and Thrift, N. (1995) 'Geographies of financial exclusion: Financial abandonment in Britain and the United States' in *Transactions of the Institute of British Geographers*, Vol 20, No 3 (1995), pp.312–341. Available at: https://www.jstor.org/stable/622654.

Lin, X., Bennett, H., Santos, U., Sapre, N., Randall, S., and Brown, C. (2017) *An extra 7 years before I'm debt free: The effect of the poverty premium on debt advice service users*, Toynbee Hall research report. Available at: https://financialhealthexchange.org.uk/wp-content/uploads/2017/01/Poverty-Premium-Research-Report.pdf (Accessed: 17 Jun 2021).

Makesh, K. G., and Kuzhuvelil, M. K. (2014) 'Financial inclusion: A literature on its causes and effects' in *International Journal of Applied Financial Management Perspectives*, Vol 3 No 1, pp.745–750.

Marshall, J. N. (2004) 'Financial institutions in disadvantaged areas: A comparative analysis of policies encouraging financial inclusion in Britain and the United States' in *Environment and Planning A: Economy and Space*, Vol 36 No 2, pp.241–261. Available at: https://doi.org/10.1068/a3664.

Money and Pensions Service (2020) *The UK strategy for financial wellbeing*. Available at: https://moneyandpensionsservice.org.uk/wp-content/uploads/2020/01/UK-Strategy-for-Financial-Wellbeing-2020-2030-Money-and-Pensions-Service.pdf (Accessed: 15 June 2021).

Morawczynski, O. (2009) 'Exploring the usage and impact of "transformational" mobile financial services: The case of M-PESA in Kenya' in *Journal of Eastern African Studies*, Vol 3 No 3, pp.509–525.

Niang, C. T., Andrianaivo, M., Diaz, K. S., and Zekri, S. (2013) *Financial literacy, financial inclusion, and consumer protection*. Available at: https://elibrary.worldbank.org/doi/abs/10.1596/9780821398340_CH03 (Accessed: 17 June 2021).

Office for National Statistics (ONS) (2019) *Internet banking, by age group, Great Britain, 2019*. Available at: https://www.ons.gov.uk/peoplepopulationandcommunity/householdcharacteristics/homeinternetandsocialmediausage/adhocs/10822internetbankingbyagegroupgreatbritain2019 (Accessed: 15 June 2021).

Roa, M. J. (2015) *Financial inclusion in Latin America and the Caribbean: Access, usage and quality*, Centre for Latin American Monetary Studies (CEMLA) Research Papers 19. Available at: https://www.responsiblefinanceforum.org/wp-content/uploads/inv-2015-04-19.pdf (Accessed: 17 June 2021).

Roy, S. K., Balaji, M. S., Kesharwani, A., and Sekhon, H. (2017) 'Predicting Internet banking adoption in India: A perceived risk perspective' in *Journal of Strategic Marketing*, Vol 25 No 5, pp.418–438. Available at: https://doi.org/10.1080/09652 54X.2016.1148771.

Russell, H., Maître, B., and Donnelly, N. (2011) *Financial exclusion and over-indebtedness in Irish households*. Social Inclusion Research Report No 1. Available at: https://www. esri.ie/publications/financial-exclusion-and-over-indebtedness-in-irish-households (Accessed: 17 June 2021).

Sarma, M., and Pais, J. (2011). 'Financial inclusion and development' in *Journal of International Development*, Vol 23, pp.613–628. doi: 10.1002/jid.1698.

Sen, A. (2000) *Development as freedom*. New York: Anchor Books.

Sinclair, S. (2013) 'Financial inclusion and social financialisation: Britain in a European context' in *International Journal of Sociology and Social Policy*, Vol 33 No 11, pp.658–676.

Sinclair, S. P. (2001) *Financial exclusion: An introductory survey*. Available at: https://www. academia.edu/7086629/Financial_Exclusion_An_Introductory_Survey (Accessed: 17 June 2021).

United Nations (UN) (no date) 'The 17 Goals' in *Sustainable development*. Available at: https://sdgs.un.org/goals (Accessed: 14 June 2021).

World Bank (2019) *National financial inclusion strategies resource center*. Available at: https:// www.worldbank.org/en/topic/financialinclusion/brief/financial-inclusion-strategies-resource-center (Accessed: 17 June 2021).

World Bank (2021) 'World development indicators' in *DataBank*. Available at: https://databank.worldbank.org/source/world-development-indicators (Accessed: 15 June 2021).

9

FINANCIAL SERVICES AND THE ROLE OF GOVERNMENT

Jonquil Lowe

Key points summary

- The role of government is important for personal financial planning in three ways: fostering trust in the financial system, through its social policies and its management of the economy.
- The actions of government in these three areas influence individual and household confidence in the financial system, the nature and amount of financial products and services they need privately to arrange and the cost and outcome of financial decisions.

Whichever financial services you use – insurance, credit, a mortgage, savings, investments, retirement planning, advice, and so on – you are affected in multiple ways by the policies and actions of governments. Governments may be involved in some or all of the following areas:

- Setting a framework of legislation to enable trust in the financial system.
- Deciding on the provision of public goods and services and social welfare policies. This will influence the nature and amount of financial products and services that you need to arrange for yourself, and your ability to access them.
- Setting the economic context including key factors such as interest rates and inflation that impact all aspects of your finances.
- Issuing government securities that you might decide to include in your portfolio either directly or through investment funds and pension schemes.

DOI: 10.4324/9781003227663-9

TABLE 9.1 Direct effects of government on personal financial decisions

Personal financial decision areas	Role of government				
	Trust in the financial system	Public goods and services	Social welfare policies	Economic context	Government securities
Income			√	√	
Insurance	√	√	√		
Credit	√		√	√	
Mortgages	√		√	√	
Savings	√		√	√	
Investments	√	√	√	√	√
Retirement planning	√		√	√	
Financial advice	√		√		

Table 9.1 summarises the direct interaction of these various roles with the types of personal financial decisions that you make. However, it is important to be aware that *indirectly* the economic context trumps all, comprehensively affecting businesses as well as consumers, and so influencing the nature, cost and availability of the financial services and products on offer.

This chapter examines the roles of government set out in Table 9.1 both in general terms, drawing on examples from around the world, and with a more detailed look at how the role of the UK government may affect your financial opportunities and outcomes.

Learning outcomes

The learning outcomes for this chapter are to:

- Recognise the importance of legislation and government policies in shaping financial opportunities for individuals and households.
- Understand the implications of social policies and state provision of goods and services, such as health services, education and welfare, for individual and household personal financial decision-making.
- Develop an awareness of how differing economic contexts affect the well-being of, and opportunities for, individuals and households.

9.1 Trust in the financial system

The precise roles of governments and the extent to which they impact on your life are largely a matter of political ideology. Those on the political right tend to favour a small state with a minimum of government interference; those on the political left see a larger role for government, addressing, for example, the social issues you will examine in Section 9.2. Yet even the advocates of a small state rely on the government to make and enforce laws that underpin the working of the system. The most fundamental of these concerns is the ownership of property and the functioning of markets which are discussed in the sections below.

Governments may also delegate powers to regulators whose remit typically includes fostering trust in the financial system. This and other roles of regulation are discussed in Chapter 11.

9.1.1 Ownership of property

In most countries, governments enshrine in law recognition of the ownership of private property, together with the rights and obligations of owners. However, ownership is a complex concept. British legal theorist Anthony Honoré (1921–2019) identified 11 characteristics that together constitute full ownership (Honoré, 1961):

- **Right to possess**. This means the right to exclusive control over the asset (or thing) in question.
- **Right to use**. This means your personal use of the asset.
- **Right to security**. In the sense that your entitlement is indefinite.
- **Right to manage**. While the first three rights above focus on your own use of the asset, you are not limited to that. You also have the right to decide how and by whom the property may be used, for example, leasing or lending the things you own, often with restrictions attached. When firms do this, the terms and conditions are typically set out in a contract. For example, when you take out a mortgage, the lender typically owns the majority share of the property but grants you the right to live in it provided you make the mortgage payments and keep the home insured.
- **Residuary character**. This refers to the asset reverting back to the ultimate owner if, for example, the term of a lease expires or the conditions of a loan are not met.
- **Right to income**. This is closely related to your right to use an asset – in fact, being able to, say, live in (use) a home that you own is sometimes treated as **imputed income**, meaning the rent you would otherwise have had to pay. If you let someone else use your asset or money, then the interest, dividends or rents you receive can be thought of as reward for giving up your personal use. This aspect of ownership is an essential basis of saving with a bank, or investing in bonds, shares and buy-to-let property.
- **Right to capital**. This refers to your right to use up or dispose of the asset as you choose.
- **Transmissibility**. This means that the asset is passed on to your heirs, which underpins inheritance planning.
- **Absence of term**. The idea that the asset can carry on being passed on to subsequent heirs without any time limit.

- **Prohibition of harmful use**. Owners don't just have rights but also obligations, including not causing harm with their assets. Recognising that this may nevertheless sometimes happen by accident, owners may be obliged or wise to have **third-party insurance**, for example, when driving or to cover visitors to their home.
- **Liability to execution**. In some circumstances, your assets can be seized, for example, if you default on your debts. Without this, it is unlikely that there would be any credit products.

As you can see, many of these characteristics are necessary for financial products and services (and most other industry and trade) to function. So, the existence and enforcement of laws that recognise and protect ownership and contracts governing how assets are managed, used and transferred are important prerequisites for fostering trust in the system.

9.1.2 Free markets

Advocates of a small state believe that freely operating private markets are the best way to allocate a society's resources efficiently. This ideology emerged during the first industrial revolution in eighteenth-century Britain and is associated particularly with the Scottish philosopher and economist Adam Smith (1723–1790). He famously asserted that the actions of the butcher, brewer and baker in pursuing their own commercial interests would simultaneously also best serve the common good (Smith, 1776). Moreover, Smith saw interference by government in this process as likely to be harmful, holding back growth and prosperity; in his view, it is better, then, to adopt a liberal approach of leaving the economy to the markets (sometimes called **laissez faire**).

In Western economies, particularly the US and the UK, this liberal approach was adopted until the 1930s when the Great Depression, characterised by failing businesses and mass unemployment, called into question the ability of markets to generate acceptable, let alone best, social outcomes in all situations. It triggered a paradigm shift in the way governments approach economic management (see Section 9.3). However, since the mid-1980s, market-based ideology has again become dominant in what is often called a **neoliberal** approach to economic organisation. The free-market model is not confined to the industrialised countries of the West, but has also been adopted by many emerging economies, often through the influence of the international organisations established by the West during the 1940s, such as the International Monetary Fund (IMF) and the World Bank.

Even countries, such as China, that culturally and historically have a communist tradition - with a heavy emphasis on central planning of the economy at a regional level (Chenggang, 2021) - have adopted market-oriented systems in recent times, albeit with substantial state ownership of business which is much less common in the West. Although China is in the process of privatising some of its state-owned enterprises (SOEs), they were still estimated to account for around a quarter of China's GDP in 2017 (Zhang, 2019).

Free-market ideology rests on the idea that the price established by the interaction of buyers and sellers correctly signals the value that society places on the goods and services being traded. However, this happy coincidence of private wants and the social good requires some strong conditions, for example:

- There is free entry to the market, so, if high levels of profit are being made, new entrants swell production and price falls back until all suppliers make just enough profit (which economists call 'normal profit') to stay in business.
- All suppliers are price-takers, meaning that none has sufficient market power to charge more.
- All buyers and sellers have the same perfect information about the goods and services they are trading, so they can accurately judge their value.

Markets that operate in this way are said to be in **perfect competition**. But even a cursory glance at the real world suggests that most markets are imperfect. As such, even regimes that believe in small government intervene, for example, to prevent or break up giant firms that gain control of a market (as in the headlines in Figure 9.1) and to improve the flow of information.

A particular concern in the markets for financial securities and financial products and services is **asymmetric information** – in other words, one party to a transaction having information that is not available to others. Typically, the issuer of a security or the provider of a service will have much better information about their business and products than you will as an investor or customer. On the other hand, if you want to borrow or take out insurance, you may have better information about the chance of your defaulting on a loan or making an insurance claim than the prospective lender or insurer. Governments can tackle

CMA Back Open Banking in Attempt to Boost Competition
MoneyExpert 10 August 2016 (Lord, 2016)

China slaps Alibaba with $2.8 billion fine in anti-monopoly probe
CNBC 9 April 2021 (Wang, 2021)

A US antitrust suit might break up Google. Good – it's the Standard Oil of our day
Guardian 21 October 2020 (Miller, 2020)

FIGURE 9.1 Governments may intervene to bring markets closer to the competitive ideal.

BOX 9.1 THE PROBLEM OF ADVERSE SELECTION

In the extreme, asymmetric information can prevent markets from thriving at all if it results in **adverse selection**, a situation where only the worst products or most risky buyers are left in the market.

The US economist George Akerlof analysed adverse selection in his seminal paper *The market for lemons* (Akerlof, 1970), taking the example of second-hand cars. Lacking sufficient information on which to judge quality, buyers will assume products are average and pitch the price they are willing to pay accordingly. Sellers of high-quality products will then shun the market because they cannot get more than the average price. Therefore, the overall quality of what is on offer will decline and so buyers will revise downwards the price they will pay, deterring yet more of the better sellers, and so the vicious cycle continues. One way out of the problem is for buyers to rely on intermediaries whose role is to research the quality of what is on offer to determine a fair price – a rationale, for example, for investors using fund managers.

You have already met the problem of adverse selection where it is buyers who have the better information in the context of insurance in Chapter 3. Insurers try to tackle this by requiring applicants to disclose information relevant to the risk they pose and then setting different premiums for different customers according to their individual risk. Governments can also intervene by making cover a legal requirement, thus preventing anyone, including those who perceive themselves as 'good risks', from opting out. This is common, for example, with motor insurance.

---

asymmetric information in a variety of ways, for example by directly or indirectly (say, through a statutory regulator) making and enforcing rules about the publication and use of information in financial markets. Commonly, these include making **insider dealing** a criminal offence (see Chapter 10 for more on this) and requiring firms to comply with international accounting standards and to provide consumers with details about risks and charges before they sign up.

9.2 Public goods and social policies

A market-based system expresses the wishes of all the buyers and sellers who are willing and able to participate. Like taking part in an election, you are casting a vote for how society uses its resources each time you buy something. However, financial markets do not represent those who are:

- unable to take part, for example, because their income is too low (or due to the other causes of financial exclusion that you considered in Chapter 8), or

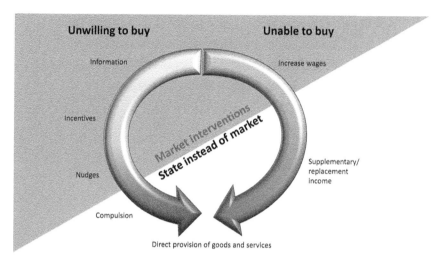

FIGURE 9.2 Social policy approaches and options.
Source: author's diagram.

- unwilling to take part even though:
  - they may personally regret it later. For example, behavioural traits such as **present bias** and **inertia** can cause individuals to save too little and too late for retirement; or
  - society as a whole would benefit if they did (as with **merit goods**). For example, left to their own devices, individuals might choose to spend less on education than required for an advanced high-skills economy.

Governments wishing to address these issues have essentially two approaches: intervene in the relevant markets or supplement/replace the market. The particular policy options they use will depend on whether the focus is ability or willingness to take part. This is summarised in Figure 9.2, working from lighter-touch interventions at the top to the more extreme at the bottom. The options are discussed in the sections which follow.

9.2.1 Policies to tackle low income (inability to buy)

Most people of working age rely on employment for the bulk of their income and so earnings are the essential foundation of financial well-being.

Unlike financial services markets where you are a buyer, in the labour market you are the seller and the wage rate is the price of your labour. In a free market, there is no guarantee that the wage you can get will be enough to live on, let alone fulfil your less immediate financial plans. One policy option governments can adopt is to ensure that employers pay their employees at least a minimum rate. Most countries around the world have a statutory national minimum wage

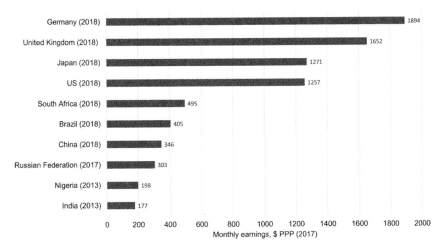

FIGURE 9.3 Statutory minimum wage for selected countries, latest year available.
ILO note: In cases where a national minimum wage is not mandated, the minimum wage in place in the capital or major city is used. In some cases, an average of multiple regional minimum wages is used.
Source: authors' chart using data from ILO (2021).

or, as in India, a more complex system of statutory regional minima (Dezan Shira & Associates, 2020). However, notable exceptions in 2014 were Singapore, Ethiopia and the United Arab Emirates (ILO, 2016). A further exception is Sweden, a high-income economy with a strong tradition of workers' unions where, rather than a statutory basis, minimum wages are negotiated locally.

Figure 9.3 compares the minimum wage for selected countries. To enable a meaningful comparison, the data are shown on a US dollar **purchasing power parity** (PPP) basis. This means that, in each case, the minimum wage in local currency has been both converted to US dollars and adjusted for the relative cost of living in each country based, in this case, on price levels in 2017.

Proponents of a minimum wage claim that it not only relieves in-work poverty but also boosts the whole economy by ensuring households can spend on consumption – this will be discussed further in Section 9.3.

Critics of a minimum wage and strong workers' unions claim that setting the price of labour above what it would be in a free market must (as in any market) reduce demand, and so create unemployment. They also suggest that the policy is poorly targeted since many low earners are either young and just starting out on their careers or are secondary earners in households that are not poor. Moreover, many people on low incomes are not in work at all and so cannot benefit. The UK has also seen a rise in people working in the gig economy, who traditionally have not been covered by minimum wage legislation, although this is starting to be challenged in the courts ('Uber BV and others (appellants) vs. Aslam and others (Respondents)', 2021).

Instead of, or in addition to, a minimum wage, governments can opt to pay cash benefits to low-income households. This is the heart of what is usually referred to as a country's **welfare state**. In a seminal study, Danish sociologist, Gøsta Esping-Andersen, has classified advanced economies' welfare states into three distinct types according to the geographical regions where they are often seen (Esping-Andersen, 1990):

- **Anglo-Saxon (e.g. US)**: Benefits tend to be low and means-tested, providing a meagre safety net for those who cannot work (because of, say, unemployment, health problems or old age) or whose wages are low. There is often stigma attached to claiming benefits – sometimes actively promoted by right-of-centre political parties through phrases such as 'hard-working families' as a contrast to benefit claimants. This helps to maintain incentives to work.
- **Continental (e.g. Germany)**: Characterised by compulsory state insurance, so that entitlement to claim benefits is based on having paid contributions into the system. Since ability to pay the contributions generally requires having an income from work, this system also maintains incentives to engage with the labour market. Often, the more generous benefits depend on having certain types of work, such as public-sector jobs.
- **Scandinavian (e.g. Sweden)**: The ideal is that citizens are guaranteed sufficient levels of support when they cannot work, including being out of the labour market while caring for children, without means-testing or contribution conditions. Higher levels of general taxation are needed to fund the system.

In practice, few countries exactly match one of the three descriptions, often adopting a mix of the three approaches but leaning towards one of the categories.

Esping-Andersen's classification highlights the conflicting aims of welfare policies in relieving poverty while maintaining incentives to work and containing the cost to the state – sometimes called the 'iron triangle of welfare' (summarised in Figure 9.4).

The more generous the state welfare system, the less need you personally have to build up a savings buffer or take out in private insurances, such as redundancy cover and income protection.

To the extent that low income is caused by a lack of qualifications and skills for better-paid jobs, a further option for governments is to make at least a minimum level of education compulsory. Worldwide, the World Bank (2018) estimates that median wages increase by around 10% for each extra year of schooling. In developed countries, compulsory education typically applies to children up to at least age 16 and often 18, is free of charge and is provided in state schools. However, provision in less-developed countries is often patchy, with, for example, lower compulsory school ages, fees and the cost of books that may be unaffordable, lack of attendance and barriers to education for girls (World Bank, 2018, 2021a).

Reduce poverty
Generous benefits available
to all who need them

Contain public cost
Low means-tested and/or
contributory benefits

Maintain work incentives
Limited eligibility and/or
contributory benefits

FIGURE 9.4 The iron triangle of welfare.
Source: author's diagram.

Similarly, for social reasons, such as poverty relief and equality, but also for economic reasons, such as promoting a more productive workforce, governments may choose to provide a state-run health service.

The availability of state-provided education and health services reduces the need for individuals to invest privately to fund these or to take out private medical insurance.

9.2.2 Policies to tackle unwillingness to buy

When consumers are able to buy the financial products and services they need but are not taking them up in the numbers or scale that a government would like, it has a variety of options as shown earlier in Figure 9.2. An area where all these options can be seen at work is saving for retirement, for example:

- **Information**. Governments may establish or encourage the provision of information to individuals about their need for income in later life, their options and/or their own personal savings to date. The aim is to spur individuals to take note and take action.
- **Incentives**. Governments may encourage desirable behaviour using the tax system. For example, many countries provide tax reliefs for saving through pension schemes (see Chapter 4).
- **Nudges**. This is a more recent innovation informed by behavioural economics and made popular by US economists, Richard Thaler and Cass Sunstein (2009). It involves changing the default so that, if no action is taken, the result is the preferred option. For example, in the case of retirement planning, instead of the default being failing to save, individuals are automatically enrolled into a pension scheme but able to opt out if they take action to do so.

- **Compulsion**. This is the most paternalistic approach, with the government making decisions for individuals. For example, most countries have a mandatory state pension system that all workers are obliged to pay into and which provides at least some income once a specified age (typically mid-60s) is reached.

These government approaches are an important factor in financial planning. For example, it makes sense to take advantage of tax incentives provided they align with your financial goals, and the availability of a state pension may reduce the amount you need to save privately to reach your retirement income goal.

9.2.3 Social policies in the UK

To tackle poverty, the UK has a long-standing focus on 'making work pay', and this is supported by a mosaic of policies.

Firstly, the UK has had a statutory minimum wage since 1999, which, in 2019, equalled 55% of the **median** wage of full-time workers (OECD, 2021).

Secondly, the UK has a complex system of both in-work state benefits to top up low earnings and out-of-work benefits for those who cannot work. This includes a compulsory state pension scheme funded through National Insurance contributions paid by workers and credited to some groups who cannot work (such as carers of young children and frail adults). Most state benefits are administered by a central government department, the Department for Work and Pensions, though some operate at local council level, such as help with rents and relief from **Council Tax** for households on low income. By law, employers are required to administer and pay some in-work benefits for their employees, such as sick pay.

Free state schooling is mandatory for children until age 16. In England (but not the rest of the UK), those who do leave at 16 must continue with further education or training (e.g. as an apprentice) until age 18 (Gov.uk, 2021a). Higher education is optional but encouraged through a system of student loans (the details of which vary across the four nations of the UK). Unlike other forms of borrowing, repayment of student loans pauses if the individual's income is below a specified threshold and the remaining balance is written off completely after a specified term. For example, in England, the threshold for repayments was just over £27,000 in early 2021 and the balance was written off after 30 years (Gov. uk, 2021b).

The National Health Service (NHS) is free to all citizens at the point of use and funded largely through a **progressive** tax system (meaning that the proportion of income taken in tax increases as income increases).

Traditionally, the UK's financial services regulators focused on the provision of information to consumers. However, there has been an increasing awareness that, while necessary for informed decision-making and well-functioning free markets, this is insufficient on its own to prompt people to take the best actions for their financial well-being. In part, the government has sought to tackle this by establishing a free-to-use national guidance service (called MoneyHelper, run by the Money and Pensions Service) which has three strands: debt advice, general money guidance and approaching retirement guidance.

Saving is encouraged through two main tax-incentivised arrangements: individual savings accounts (ISAs) and pension schemes and plans (see Chapter 4). Given that the tax system is progressive, the system of reliefs is inevitably regressive, meaning that the reliefs give greatest benefit to those with higher incomes.

Following the example of the US, the UK is one of a handful of countries that have adopted the nudge principle by introducing a system of automatic enrolment into pension schemes from 2012 onwards. Employers are obliged to place most of their employees in a workplace private pension scheme and, if they opt out, to re-enrol them every three years. In addition to the tax reliefs for pension schemes, employers must contribute at least part of the amount saved, so automatic enrolment is beneficial for most employees. Automatic enrolment does not apply to self-employed workers.

9.3 Managing the economy and public debt

Before the Great Depression of the 1930s (mentioned in Section 9.1.2), governments viewed the economy simply as a network of markets. Since markets were believed to work efficiently if left alone, so too the economy as a whole was assumed to operate most efficiently with the least intervention from the government.

In response to the Great Depression, UK economist John Maynard Keynes (1883–1946) argued that, on the contrary, to get out of a depression, governments needed to spend (Keynes, 1936). Keynes' solution is not just history – it has been very evident around the globe, firstly in debates about the response to the Global Financial Crisis, and, a decade later, as a major policy response to the coronavirus pandemic that started in 2019.

However, government spending is just one policy lever available to the authorities to manage the economy in the short to medium term; another is monetary policy, operated by central banks. Moreover, governments to a greater or lesser degree may adopt policies intended to create long-term growth which has a major impact on your employment and income prospects and also the decisions you make about where to invest.

9.3.1 Governments and economic growth

Economic growth – typically defined as increases in annual GDP – is typically considered one of the hallmarks of a successful government. There are, broadly speaking, four sources of economic growth that can be illustrated with the help of Figure 9.5, which shows what economists call the 'circular flow of income'.

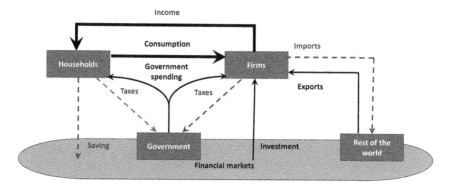

FIGURE 9.5 The circular flow of income in an economy.
Source: author's diagram.

Figure 9.5 shows how money flows between the four high-level sectors of the economy: households, firms, the government and the rest of the world. What counts as spending for one sector is received as income by another sector; broadly speaking, by totalling up either all the income or all the spending, you arrive at GDP.

The biggest flow is spending on consumption by households – accounting, for example, in the UK for some 70% of GDP (ONS, 2020). Consumption would be even higher, but for the three 'leakages' (shown by the dashed lines in Figure 9.5) from household income: money paid to the government in taxes, money that households spend on imported goods from abroad (rather than boosting national firms) and money that households decide to save for the future rather than spend now (net of amounts they borrow which increase current spending). Similarly, the leakages can occur from the firms' sector where they import products or components from abroad, decide to save and have to pay taxes to government.

However, there are also three injections into the economy that can boost national income: investment by firms to increase their output which feeds through into increases in employment, wages and spending by households; demand from abroad that similarly provides jobs and incomes for the domestic economy; and spending by government either direct to households (providing public sector jobs or welfare payments) or with firms (such as building schools, roads and hospitals).

The savings and borrowings of households, firms and governments both at home and abroad are channelled through the financial markets that we looked at in Chapter 2.

Economies tend to grow in different ways depending on their stage of development and their natural endowments. For example, eighteenth-century Britain and mid-twentieth-century China both grew by switching from largely agricultural to industrial economies. Investment in machinery and the shift of labour from rural to urban areas increased the efficiency and output of these economies (Hill, 1975; Chenggang, 2021).

China grew rapidly by exporting much of the resulting manufactured outputs to the rest of the world. By contrast, the Middle East, which has huge natural endowments of oil, grew during the last century largely by exporting this commodity to the rest of the world but has diversified the base of its growth in more recent decades, as seen, for example, in the United Arab Emirates which has developed substantial trade, financial and travel hubs (World Bank, 2021b).

Economies that industrialised early, such as the US, UK and Europe, are now highly dependent on consumption to fuel continuing growth and the same is now true of maturing economies such as China. However, expanding consumption puts pressure on the environment, causing some experts to question whether perpetual economic growth is possible (Kallis, 2018), while others believe that it is, provided the world switches to green, sustainable forms of production and consumption (World Economic Forum, 2021). You may be playing a part in this debate through the ways in which you choose to invest (see Chapter 5).

Another important consideration is who benefits from growth. In the more neoliberal regimes, such as the US, it is often assumed that economic growth, while favouring those who do well out of free markets, nevertheless benefits all as wealth 'trickles down' through the rest of the economy. However, this assumption is strongly contested by more left-leaning theorists, for example, US Nobel-Prize-winning economist Joseph Stiglitz (2013) and French economist Thomas Piketty (2014), who see free markets as the cause of increasing inequality and inevitable concentration of wealth in fewer hands.

9.3.2 Fiscal policy: the role of government spending

Fiscal policy is partly about governments managing their finances day-to-day, in other words ensuring there is enough revenue coming in (mainly from taxes) to finance government spending on all its normal functions, such as creating and enforcing the law and running its social programmes.

However, fiscal policy is also a major tool that governments can use to manage fluctuations in the economy. The great insight of Keynes back in the 1930s was that firms do not make investment decisions based just on how much they will have to pay for funds in financial markets. They also need to feel confident that their investments will be profitable. In a depression or more minor economic downturn, firms' 'animal spirits' take a dive and, however cheap it is to borrow, they may simply hold back from investing. Meanwhile, households become fearful about losing their jobs and tend to increase their **precautionary savings**. They can do this only by cutting back on current consumption. When firms see the demand for their products and services falling, they become even more reluctant to invest and may indeed start cutting jobs. Thus, the economy becomes stuck in a slump or even a worsening downward spiral.

The way out of this trap, Keynes argued, is for the government to step in and replace the spending that would have come from firms and households until their confidence in the economy resumes. Moreover, the government spending cannot be financed by raising taxes, since that would simply take back from households and firms the increased buying power that government spending is meant to be pumping into the economy. Government spending to get out of a slump needs to be financed by borrowing, with government spending exceeding the amount raised in taxes, called a **fiscal deficit**.

To some extent, the fiscal deficit increases in any case during an economic downturn because of the action of **automatic stabilisers** that are built into the tax-and-benefit system. For example, as the number of unemployed individuals rises, the amount the government pays out in unemployment benefits increases and simultaneously the amount raised in income tax falls. Where a bigger boost to the economy is needed, traditionally the government spending targets big infrastructure projects that create jobs today and new assets (like roads, dams and railways) that are expected to have lasting social benefit. However, as you have seen during the coronavirus pandemic, during economic crises, governments may even inject cash directly into households and firms to stop them from becoming insolvent.

Figure 9.6 shows the fiscal deficit (negative values) or surplus (positive values) for selected countries over the period 2001–2020. It clearly shows how their fiscal deficits expanded in response to recent crises.

Governments borrow to finance fiscal deficits by issuing the type of fixed-interest securities (often called 'government bonds') that you learned about in Chapter 2. In large, established economies government bonds are considered to be low-risk investments because, ultimately, the government can raise taxes or, if the country has its own currency, even issue new money to make the interest and redemption payments. However, not all government debt is so secure –

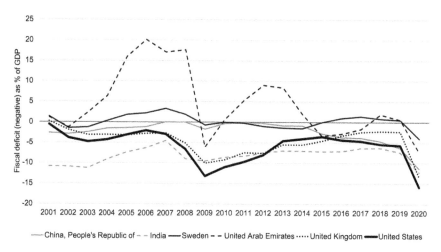

FIGURE 9.6 Government fiscal deficits for selected countries, 2001–2020.
Source: author's chart based on data from IMF (2021).

for example, there have been government defaults in Russia (1998), Argentina (2001) and Greece (2015).

Keynesian-style fiscal policy was widely used until the 1970s not just to manage crises but also to fine-tune the economy to keep it at near-full employment as it went through the swings of each **business cycle**. However, it was difficult to do this with precision: stimulate the economy too much and inflation was the result; and, once households and firms started to expect inflation, cutting back on the government stimulus put the brakes on the economy but did not dampen inflation – a situation called **stagflation**. This called for other economic tools, in particular **monetary policy**.

9.3.3 Monetary policy: managing inflation

Central banks may have a variety of functions: issuing currency, acting as banker to commercial banks, prudential regulation of the financial system and implementing the government's monetary policy.

Many central banks are independent, meaning that although the overall objectives of monetary policy may be set by the government, the central bank has freedom in how it manages the economy to meet those objectives. A common objective for central banks is to keep inflation at a low and stable rate; some examples are shown in Table 9.2. Usually, the target is symmetrical in that central banks are as keen to avoid very low or even negative inflation as they are to avoid high inflation. High inflation erodes the buying power of incomes and savings unless they are fully indexed; it can also squeeze profits if rising costs cannot be passed on, and so can depress the economy (the stagflation mentioned earlier). But **deflation** (negative inflation) can also depress economic activity if consumers decide to put off purchases because they expect future prices to be lower. Moreover, it can be much harder to cut nominal wages and other costs than

TABLE 9.2 Central bank inflation targets and inflation for selected countries

Country	Inflation target, 2021 % a year	Inflation rate, 2019 % a year
Brazil	3.75% (+ or – 1.5%)	3.73
China	Around 3%	2.90
Eurozone	Less than 2%	1.45
India	4% (+ or – 2%)	7.66
Japan	2%	0.48
Nigeria	6–9%	11.40
South Africa	3–6%	4.12
Sweden	2%	1.78
UK	2%	1.74
USA	2%	1.81

Source: author's table based on data from Central Bank News (2021) and World Bank (2021c).

merely leave them unchanged, so a little bit of inflation is generally considered good for the economy because it allows small adjustments to real values to happen easily through the action of rising prices.

A key policy lever that central banks use to influence inflation is the interest rate. In conventional monetary policy, central banks adjust the interest rate (often called **bank rate**) that they pay commercial banks who lodge money with the central bank. What the commercial banks must get then ripples through the economy influencing all other rates (and so asset prices too). A low interest rate may encourage households to borrow to spend and firms to borrow to invest, stimulating the economy. As long as there is spare capacity, the economy grows without inflation, but once everyone who wants one has a job, inflationary pressure builds up. Raising interest rates dampens the economy and brings prices back down.

Conventional monetary policy breaks down once the interest rate has been cut to zero or close to this lower bound (see Box 9.2).

Faced with low or zero rates since the Global Financial Crisis, many central banks have turned to **unconventional monetary policy**. The aim is still to push down interest rates in order to stimulate the economy. However, the mode of intervention is different. Instead of adjusting its own base rate, the central bank becomes a buyer in the market for government securities and, in some cases, corporate bonds as well. The extra demand for these fixed-interest securities pushes their price up and, as you saw in Chapter 2, must mean that their rate of return falls. The aim is to persuade private investors to switch away from these reduced returns and instead invest in equities and other higher-yielding investments that may encourage firms and hence the economy to grow. However, investors also seek higher yields elsewhere, for example the property market, and so unconventional monetary policies have been associated with speculative **asset price bubbles** (Blot et al., 2017).

BOX 9.2 NEGATIVE INTEREST RATES

Although it is possible for a central bank to set negative interest rates – and a few central banks, notably in Japan, the eurozone, Denmark and Switzerland have done this (Global Rates, 2021) – in practice, it is quite experimental. Evidence to date suggests that negative rates have not increased inflation or stimulated economic growth (see, for example, Yoshino et al., 2017).

A negative rate turns interest rates on their head, charging savers and potentially paying borrowers. Savers may decide to avoid the charges by holding physical cash instead. Moreover, banks claim that their systems need to be adapted before they can deal with negative rates (Jones and Withers, 2020).

A controversial aspect of unconventional monetary policies is that the central bank makes the asset purchases out of money that it has, in effect, newly created. Traditionally, printing money – and particularly cycling that money back to the government, for example by buying its debt – have been considered unsound ways to manage an economy and liable to lead to inflation (as more money chases the same number of goods and services). However, up to early 2021, rising inflation had not emerged.

9.4 Conclusion

This chapter has given an insight into the diverse roles of government and the many ways in which they may influence your financial well-being.

A primary task is to instil confidence in the economy and its markets, including financial markets. Laws protecting private property and making contracts enforceable are an important foundation of that trust.

Governments may also take on a social welfare function, tackling issues like poverty and inequality, either out of ideology or as a minimum to ensure the economy has a healthy, productive workforce. The degree to which governments provide public services and benefit payments determines to some extent the amount and type of private financial planning you need to undertake. Governments may also incentivize certain types of behaviour, such as saving for retirement.

Finally, governments manage the economy, typically to generate economic growth with a low and stable rate of inflation, and also take more radical steps in the event of economic crises. In this role, domestic government actions have important implications for your income and employment prospects, the cost of borrowing and the return from your savings and investments. The actions of governments in other countries may influence your choice of where to invest an internationally diversified portfolio.

Self-test questions

1 Explain one advantage and one disadvantage of a free-market system in financial services from the consumer perspective.
2 Thinking about a country you know well, can you identify any elements from the three types of welfare state that Esping-Andersen (1990) describes?
3 Thinking about the circular flow of income, what are the four key ways in which an economy might seek to grow?

Further reading

Bank of England: https://www.bankofengland.co.uk/
CoreEcon, Economics for a changing world: https://www.core-econ.org/
Institute for Fiscal Studies: https://ifs.org.uk/
Rethinking Economics: https://www.rethinkeconomics.org/

References

Akerlof, G. A. (1970) 'The Market for "Lemons": Quality Uncertainty and the Market Mechanism', *The Quarterly Journal of Economics* 84(3), pp.488–500.

Blot, C., Hubert, P. and Labondance, F. (2017) *Monetary policy and asset price bubbles*, Economic Working Papers 2018-5, University of Paris. Available at: https://ideas.repec.org/p/drm/wpaper/2018-5.html (Accessed 12 April 2021).

Central Bank News (2021) *Inflation targets*. Available at: http://www.centralbanknews.info/p/inflation-targets.html (Accessed 12 April 2021).

Chenggang, X. (2021) 'How China's economy actually works' in *New Economics Thinking (INET)*. Available at: https://www.youtube.com/watch?v=_j4Ru918V4w (Accessed 6 May 2021).

Dezan Shira & Associates (2020) 'A guide to minimum wage in India in 2021) in *India Briefing*, 23 November. Available at: https://www.india-briefing.com/news/guide-minimum-wage-india-2021-19406.html/#:~:text=How%20is%20the%20minimum%20wage, (US%2462)%20per%20month. (Accessed 10 April 2021).

Esping-Andersen, G. (1990) 'Three worlds of welfare capitalism' in Pierson, C., Castles, F.G. and Naumann, I.K. (eds) (2015) *The Welfare State Reader*, 3rd edition, pp.136–150, Cambridge: Polity Press.

Global-rates.com (2021) *Central banks – summary of current interest rates*. Available at: https://www.global-rates.com/en/interest-rates/central-banks/central-banks.aspx (Accessed 12 April 2021).

Gov.uk (2021a) *School leaving age*. Available at: https://www.gov.uk/know-when-you-can-leave-school (Accessed 12 April 2021).

Gov.uk (2021b) *Repaying your student loan*. Available at: https://www.gov.uk/repaying-your-student-loan (Accessed 12 April 2021).

Hill, C. (1975) *The Pelican economic history of Britain, Volume 2: 1530–1780 reformation to industrial revolution*, Harmondsworth: Penguin Books.

Honoré, A.M. (1961) *Ownership*. Available at: http://fs2.american.edu/dfagel/www/OwnershipSmaller.pdf (Accessed 30 March 2021).

International Labour Organisation (ILO) (2016) *Minimum Wage Policy Guide*. Available at: https://www.ilo.org/global/docs/WCMS_508566/lang--en/index.htm (Accessed 10 April 2021).

International Labour Organisation (ILO) (2021) 'Statutory nominal gross monthly minimum wage' in *Data*. Available at: https://ilostat.ilo.org/data/ (Accessed 12 April 2021).

International Monetary Fund (IMF) (2021) 'Net lending/borrowing (also referred to as overall balance)' in *IMF DataMapper*. Available at: https://www.imf.org/external/datamapper/GGXCNL_G01_GDP_PT@FM/ADVEC/FM_EMG/FM_LIDC (Accessed 12 April 2021).

Jones, H. and Withers, I. (2020) 'Move to negative rates in UK may not work, HSBC warns' in *Reuters*. Available at: https://www.reuters.com/article/uk-britain-banks-rates-idUKKBN28O2GQ (Accessed 12 April 2021).

Kallis, G. (2018) *Degrowth*, Newcastle upon Tyne: Agenda Publishing.

Keynes, J.M. (1936) *The general theory of employment, interest and money*. London: MacMillan. Also available at: http://innovbfa.viabloga.com/files/JM_Keynes___Livre___The_general_theory_of_employment_interest_and_money___1936.pdf (Accessed 15 April 2021).

Lord, D. (2016) 'CMA back open banking in attempt to boost competition' in *MoneyExpert*, 10 August. Available at: https://www.moneyexpert.com/news/cma-back-open-banking-attempt-boost-competition/ (Accessed 10 April 2021).

Miller, S. (2020) 'A US antitrust suit might break up Google. Good – it's the Standard Oil of our day' in *The Guardian*, 21 October. Available at: https://www.theguardian.com/commentisfree/2020/oct/21/google-antitrust-monopoly-power-us-politics (Accessed 10 April 2021).

Office for National Statistics (2020) *UK national accounts, the Blue Book: 2020.* Available at: https://www.ons.gov.uk/releases/uknationalaccountsthebluebook2020 (Accessed: 6 May 2021).

Organisation for Economic Cooperation and Development (OECD) (2021) 'Minimum relative to average wages of full-time workers' on *OECD.Stat*. Available at: https://stats.oecd.org/Index.aspx?DataSetCode=MIN2AVE (Accessed 12 April 2021).

Piketty, T. (2014) *Capital in the twenty-first century*, English translation by Goldhammer, A., Cambridge: The Belknap Press of Harvard University Press.

Smith, A. (1776) *An enquiry into the nature and causes of the wealth of nations.* Edited by Edwin Cannan. Facsimile of 5th edition, London: Methuen & Co, 1961, Volume 1.

Stiglitz, J. (2013) *The price of inequality*, London: Penguin.

Thaler, R. and Sunstein, C. (2009) *Nudge*, Revised British edition, London: Penguin Books.

'Uber BV and others (appellants) vs Aslam and others (Respondents)' (2021) The Supreme Court Case ID: UK SC 2019/0029 in *The Supreme Court Case details*. Available at: https://www.supremecourt.uk/cases/uksc-2019-0029.html (Accessed 12 April 2021).

Wang, C. (2021) 'China slaps Alibaba with $2.8 billion fine in anti-monopoly probe' in *CBNC*, 9 April. Available at: https://www.cnbc.com/2021/04/09/china-fines-alibaba-in-anti-monopoly-probe.html (Accessed 10 April 2021).

World Bank (2018) *Learning to realize education's promise.* Available at: https://www.worldbank.org/en/publication/wdr2018 (Accessed 11 April 2021).

World Bank (2021a) *Girls education*. Available at: https://www.worldbank.org/en/topic/girlseducation. (Accessed 11 April 2021).

World Bank (2021b) *United Arab emirates*. Available at: https://thedocs.worldbank.org/en/doc/5bae5632e2d8425830fbf0bac721cce3-0280012021/original/17-mpo-sm21-united-arab-emirates-kcm3.pdf (Accessed 6 May 2021).

World Bank (2021c) *Inflation, consumer prices (annual %)*. Available at https://data.worldbank.org/indicator/FP.CPI.TOTL.ZG (Accessed 12 April 2021).

World Economic Forum (2021) *Green new deals*. Available at: https://intelligence.weforum.org/topics/a1G680000004C93EAE?tab=publications&utm_source=sfmc&utm_medium=email&utm_campaign=2745759_Agenda_weekly-7May2021&utm_term= (Accessed 7 May 2021).

Yoshino, N., Taghizadeh-Hesary, F. and Miyamoto, H. (2017) *The effectiveness of Japan's negative interest rate policy*, Asian Development Bank Institute Working Paper No. 652, January. Available at: https://www.adb.org/sites/default/files/publication/225371/adbi-wp652.pdf (Accessed 12 April 2021).

Zhang, C. (2019) *How much do State-Owned Enterprises contribute to China's GDP and employment?*. Available at: http://documents1.worldbank.org/curated/en/449701565248091726/pdf/How-Much-Do-State-Owned-Enterprises-Contribute-to-China-s-GDP-and-Employment.pdf (Accessed 8 April 2021).

10

FINANCIAL CRIMES

Jonquil Lowe

Key points summary

- Trust between customer and provider is implicit in most financial services which contributes towards opportunities for crime.
- Financial crime lies on a spectrum of behaviours that may cause consumer detriment. Whether or not some types of behaviour amount to a crime may change over time and can differ depending on whether it is viewed from an industry or consumer perspective.
- Financial crimes can result in widespread economic damage.
- Scammers exploit innate human behavioural traits, and so one form of protection against scams involves identifying and diffusing the emotional response.

If you purchase a loaf of bread, you can judge its quality before you buy. Even if its taste subsequently disappoints, you have lost very little and can switch to another brand or baker next time. Financial services are fundamentally very different:

- Asymmetric information means you may have only a rough idea of what you are buying,
- The long-term nature of many services, or contingent nature in the case of insurance, means that you may not know whether the service is any good until years or decades after you have signed up,
- Many of these services are bought infrequently, so you have little opportunity to build knowledge and experience to help you improve your selection and
- Switching existing services may be costly and administratively onerous.

DOI: 10.4324/9781003227663-10

For all these reasons, it is essential that consumers can trust the services they are buying and the professionals through whom they buy. Financial crimes both exploit and undermine that trust, causing financial and often emotional harm to the people who are affected, and sometimes wider economic damage as well.

This chapter explores how financial crimes impact your personal finances and what you can do to guard against them.

Learning outcomes

The learning outcomes for this chapter are to:

- Appreciate that there is a spectrum of behaviour from unethical to criminal and that this may change over time.
- Understand some of the reasons why financial crime happens.
- Be aware of the main impacts of financial crime and some ways to protect against it.

10.1 The scale and nature of financial crime

Financial crime is diverse, widespread and worldwide. A survey of large global companies found that 47% had been victims of financial crimes, such as **money laundering** and fraud, in the previous 12 months (Refinitiv, 2019). In England and Wales alone, it's estimated that fraud costs individuals £4.7 billion a year, and businesses and the public sector another £5.9 billion (Gov.uk, 2019).

Such data are likely to be an underestimate since financial crimes may go unreported by victims out of a misplaced sense of shame and gullibility in the case of individuals and fear of reputational damage in the case of firms. Moreover, measuring the extent of financial crime depends on what is included in its definition.

When firms talk about financial crime, they often mean crimes against the firm itself (such as theft by employees or cyberattacks by hackers), crimes perpetrated by the employees for whom they are responsible (such as bribery and **insider dealing**) and the use of the firm by organised criminals or terrorists to launder the proceeds of other crimes (e.g. drug dealing, arms trading and human trafficking) and to finance their activities. While these crimes may seem remote from individual consumers, as you will see shortly, both the crimes and associated remedies do have implications for ordinary individuals conducting their financial affairs.

Talk to consumers about financial crime and they are more likely to think of scammers cold calling and **phishing** to steal bank account details or pension savings. These types of crime cause a more direct and obvious harm to individuals.

However, consumers may also suffer detriment in their normal dealings with legitimate financial services firms in ways that may later be outlawed by new legislation or regulations. For example, insider dealing is now outlawed in many

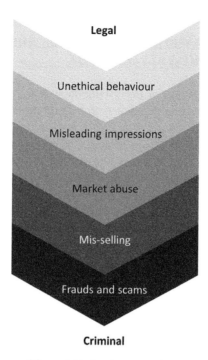

Legal

Unethical behaviour

Misleading impressions

Market abuse

Mis-selling

Frauds and scams

Criminal

FIGURE 10.1   A spectrum of financial behaviours causing consumer detriment.
Source: author's diagram.

countries but was made illegal in the UK only in 1980 (Companies Act 1980, s.68). Before that, it was widely practised and argued by some (see, for example, Manne, 2005) as an important contribution to the flow of information, which contributes to making markets more efficient (see Chapter 9). Therefore, financial crimes in their widest sense can be thought of as lying somewhere on a spectrum of adverse behaviour that ranges from legal, albeit falling short of ethical, to clearly criminal, as illustrated in Figure 10.1, with the point at which activities are deemed to be 'criminal' capable of shifting.

10.1.1 Unethical behaviour

What counts as ethical is a complex philosophical issue. In general, a society has norms of acceptable behaviour that frame the way its members conduct themselves but also adapt over time as attitudes and conduct evolve.

However, the same norms do not necessarily apply across all sectors of a society and firms may have their own distinct culture. Regulation – which you will examine in Chapter 11 – can set rules, but it is much harder to shift the culture within firms. In the UK, there is an overarching regulatory requirement for financial firms to 'treat customers fairly' (TCF) but, to some extent, what counts as fair is open to interpretation (as shown in the example in Box 10.1). There is

---

BOX 10.1 A CULTURAL DIVIDE: HOME AND MOTOR INSURANCE RENEWALS IN THE UK

What seems like unethical or unfair behaviour from a consumer perspective may simply be sound practice from a profit-maximising business perspective.

In the UK, for decades it was common for insurers to compete for new customers by offering heavily discounted premiums for home and motor policies, but then recouping this through increases to the premium each subsequent year – a practice called **price walking**. Although existing customers could shop around and switch provider at renewal, a large proportion did not do so.

From a consumer perspective, it seemed that existing customers were being penalised, contrary to their expectation that loyalty would be valued and rewarded by the firm. However, some firms took the view that:

> offering lower rates to new customers is simply a form of cross-subsidisation that is practised by firms in many sectors...there is an inherent value to customers to not having to shop around and transfer and this should be reflected in the price they pay (i.e they should pay more)...if firms were not permitted to behave in this way the result would be less innovation.
>
> (Jackie Wells & Associates, 2013, p.22)

The regulator carried out a market study, estimating that price walking contributed to consumers paying an extra £1.2 billion a year compared with premiums that accurately reflected risk, and proposed measures to restrict price walking in future (FCA, 2020).

---

pressure from the UK consumer-advocacy movement to replace TCF with a stronger statutory **duty of care** towards consumers (FCA, 2019).

10.1.2 Misleading impressions

In general, if an investor has not relied on professional advice, then they have only themselves to blame if their investment later disappoints. However, the case study in Box 10.2 illustrates some of the problems in determining if *caveat emptor* (the principle of let the buyer beware) applies, or, alternatively, if there might be others to blame and a right to redress. The crux of the case is whether investors had a fair opportunity to understand what they were buying or was the fund on offer being misrepresented as something it was not.

BOX 10.2 AN ATYPICAL INVESTMENT FUND

Neil Woodford built a reputation as a star fund manager in the UK during 26 years with the firm Invesco Perpetual. Therefore, he attracted a loyal following of retail investors when, in 2014, he left to set up his own fund management company.

Woodford Investment Management offered, among other funds, a popular LF Woodford Equity Income Fund. It was structured as an **open-ended fund** that investors could buy and sell at any time. Equity income funds usually aim to provide investors with regular income from dividends paid by the companies held by the fund (Investment Association, 2020). In the UK, they must have at least 80% of assets invested in equities, and normally pay a yield relative to a relevant market index of 90% or more on an annual basis and 100% or more on a rolling three-year basis (Investment Association, 2021).

At the start, the Woodford fund was similar to other funds in the sector, mostly holding shares in large, listed companies (Economist Intelligence Unit, 2019). However, it rapidly evolved into a less typical structure, with large dividend-paying companies accounting for only half of the fund's investments and the rest comprising riskier, small and in some cases unquoted companies that paid no dividends but were judged by Woodford to be undervalued and offering growth potential (Ferguson, 2016). Information about this unusual equity income portfolio was available to investors if they chose to check.

Following a run of poor performance, investors started to withdraw their money, requiring the fund to cash in some of the assets. Struggling to find buyers for the small company holdings, Woodford was forced to sell part of the larger company holdings. This further skewed the fund, reducing the dividend income and pushing the unquoted holdings above a 10% cap required by regulations, although Woodford did not disclose this at the time (Hill, 2019; FCA, 2021a). By mid-2019, unable to cope with the tide of withdrawals, trading in the fund was suspended.

Woodford was sacked and a decision taken to wind up the fund (Link Fund Solutions, 2019). At the time of writing in spring 2021, thousands of investors trapped in the fund stood to lose £1 billion (Walker, 2021). Investors were planning to sue both the firm, Link Fund Solutions (the **authorised corporate director**), which was meant to supervise the fund (Harcus Parker, 2021), and the investment platform, Hargreaves Lansdown, which had promoted the Woodford Fund right up to its collapse through a list of favoured funds that nevertheless fell short of giving financial advice (Clark, 2021). The regulator had not yet published any details or results of its investigation into the matter (FCA, 2021b).

10.1.3 Market abuse

Market abuse covers a range of sins. It typically includes, for example, insider dealing, where an individual uses information before it becomes publicly available to make a profit. It also includes the more invasive act of manipulating the prices in a market.

Market abuse may seem at first sight to be a victimless crime. Consider the inside dealer practice of **front running**. This occurs when, say, a broker has orders from clients to buy equities in a company that collectively are enough to move its market price, and before enacting the client orders the broker trades on their own account to profit from the subsequent price movement. If the size of the broker's trade is too small to displace other buyers or move the price, it can be argued that no one has lost: the clients still get their shares at the price they had expected to pay; the investors who sold shares to the broker similarly achieved the sale they wanted at the price they had expected. However, the sellers would no doubt have held out for the higher price if they'd had access to the same information as the broker. So, part of the justification for making insider dealing illegal is that allowing asymmetric information to flourish would undermine investors' confidence in the market since the risk of the prices available to the general public being out of step with the assets' intrinsic value would be increased. In essence, all uninformed investors become the victims of cheating by the inside dealers (Klaw and Mayer, 2021).

BOX 10.3 LIBOR-FIXING

The London Interbank Offered Rate (LIBOR) is a set of interest rates reflecting the cost of banks borrowing from their peers. There are rates for different terms and different currencies. While originally administered from London, the rates are used worldwide.

LIBOR is not based on actual loans between banks. Rather, a worldwide panel of the 15 or so biggest banks each day submits an estimate of the rates it reckons it would pay if it had to borrow. The highest and lowest submissions are ignored and the average of the remaining sets LIBOR for that day. All the submissions are published alongside the LIBOR rates.

LIBOR is important because it acts as a guide – or benchmark – for setting the price of a wide variety of other financial contracts, especially derivatives and many types of borrowing. The latter includes credit cards, mortgages and student loans because, although they are seldom linked directly to LIBOR, what banks themselves pay to borrow influences what they charge others.

In 2008, as the Global Financial Crisis (GFC) – see Box 1.1 – raged, observers noticed that LIBOR rates seemed suspiciously low and this triggered investigations by regulators in the US and elsewhere (Vaughan and Finch, 2017). Over the next few years, investigators discovered that between 2005 and 2010, contrary to a variety of regulations, several banks and **interbank brokers** had been involved in the frequent manipulation of their daily LIBOR submissions – the manipulations were routine with little effort to conceal them (Edmonds, 2014).

In the period up to 2008, the manipulations (both up and down) were typically requested by the banks' in-house derivative traders in order to increase profits. During the GFC, the submissions were massaged downwards to manage public opinion, since a high LIBOR submission would suggest that a bank was having difficulty borrowing and might be on the brink of collapse.

The banks involved – Barclays, CitiGroup, Deutsche Bank, JP Morgan, Lloyds, Rabobank, RBS, Societé Generale and UBS – and two interbank brokers – ICAP and RP Martin – were fined record amounts, totalling $9 billion, by regulators in the UK, Europe and the US (Edmonds, 2014; Browning, 2021). The previously unregulated, voluntary regime for setting LIBOR has been replaced by regulations on setting benchmarks (ESMA, no date; FCA 2020|2016). Meanwhile, LIBOR is being phased out to be replaced by new benchmark rates (mostly from 2022 onwards). In the UK, manipulating benchmark interest rates has now been made a criminal offence (Financial Services Act 2012, s.91).

Some types of market abuse are more obviously wrong, as in the example in Box 10.3, but, although the impacts ripple through the economy to consumers, tracing and measuring who has lost (or won) may still be difficult or impossible.

10.1.4 Mis-selling

Mis-selling occurs where a salesperson or adviser deliberately or negligently sells a consumer a product or service that is unsuitable for them. In developed financial systems, like the UK, mis-selling is outlawed – though not always straightforward to prove. The consequences for the individual can be devastating but, as the example in Box 10.4 shows, mis-selling can even rock the whole financial system and wider economy.

10.1.5 Frauds and scams

Fraud is deliberate deception and it comes in many guises. For example, companies may commit fraud if they falsify their accounts to create a rosier picture of their business, as happened with US telecoms giant WorldCom. Over four years, WorldCom made $9.25 billion of false accounting entries in order to inflate its stock-market results (SEC, 2003). When the fraud came to light in 2002,

BOX 10.4 MORTGAGE MIS-SELLING IN THE US

In the US (as elsewhere, including the UK), the 1980s were the start of a long-term shift towards deregulation of financial services with an emphasis on competition rather than government controls to determine the products and services on offer, to whom and at what price. The mortgage market was given a boost from the 1990s onwards with the widescale adoption of mortgage securitisation. Traditionally, a mortgage lender made money from the stream of repayments from the borrower over many years. With securitisation, the lender could immediately realise a return by selling the mortgage to firms that would package lots of different mortgages to form bond-like securities to be bought by investors. Moreover, other investors and speculators could buy derivatives whose performance was linked to these mortgage-backed securities. Thus, huge investment markets, where big banks and other professionals staked large sums, were balanced on the foundation of US homeowners.

These markets were lucrative and incentivised an aggressive push to arrange ever more mortgages. Many households, which traditionally would have been unable to afford to buy their own home, so-called 'subprime' borrowers, were inappropriately sold imaginatively devised mortgage products. These included, for example, adjustable-rate mortgages (ARMs) where the interest rate, and so repayments, started at a low level but would step up later. Borrowers were persuaded that, by the time the adjustable rate rose, the value of their home would have risen so much that they could remortgage, again at a lower rate. It seemed a self-fulfilling prophecy with the push to supply mortgages contributing to ever-rising house prices (see Figure 10.2). There is also evidence of fraud by mortgage sellers – with or without the collusion of borrowers – with household income statements being inflated to pass affordability checks (Jang et al., 2014).

Then, in early 2007, the US housing bubble burst, tipping the US economy into recession. As jobs were lost and ARM interest rate rises kicked in, homeowners began to fall behind or default on their mortgages. At its peak in 2010, as Figure 10.2 shows, over 11% of mortgagees were in arrears (FRED, 2021).

Beyond these individual tragedies, the collapse of the US housing market and the rising mortgage defaults flowed through to a collapse in the value of mortgage-backed securities and many of the derivatives based on them. This caused gaping holes in bank balance sheets and the onset of the GFC. The aftermath of the crisis – in particular the austerity measures that governments took to rein in the levels of public debt accrued as a result of bailing out the financial system – affected individuals and households in many countries, especially those on low incomes.

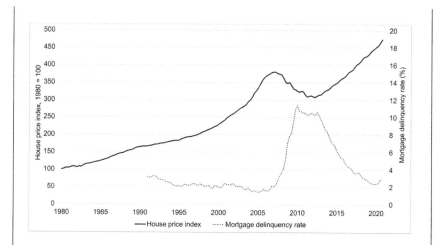

FIGURE 10.2 US house price index, 1980 to 2020.

Source: author's chart based on house price data from Federal Housing Finance Agency (2021) and mortgage delinquency (arrears) data from FRED (2021).

WorldCom filed for bankruptcy, leaving bond and share investors nursing huge losses. Subsequently, banks – accused of helping WorldCom to sell its bonds when they should have been aware of the true state of the company's finances – agreed to pay institutional and individual investors $3.6 billion compensation (*The Guardian*, 2005).

Individual employees may commit fraud against companies, sometimes with potentially devastating results for investors, as when in 1995 rogue trader Nick Leeson's unsuccessful attempts to eliminate losses on derivatives trades that had not been authorised by his employer brought down the venerable UK bank, Barings (Leeson and Whitley, 1998).

However, the frauds that often most directly affect consumers are those where they are scammed out of their money with no genuine financial product or service involved at all. Many types of scam have a long history, such as **Ponzi schemes** – of which the Madoff fraud in Box 10.5 is an example.

The online and data revolutions have opened up new ways to perpetrate scams. These are a few common examples:

- **Phishing attacks**. You receive a text or email purporting to be from a trusted source, such as your bank, a utility company, the tax authority or a postal service. It outlines a scenario that needs your urgent attention, such as a suspicious transaction on your account, a refund, court action being taken against you or a fee that must be paid before mail can be delivered. You are

BOX 10.5 BERNIE MADOFF'S PONZI SCHEME

Bernie Madoff was a well-regarded member of the US financial community, even for a time chairing the US stock exchange, NASDAQ. From 1960, he ran an eponymous firm that evolved to include wealth management.

In 1992, the US regulator, the Securities and Exchange Commission (SEC), received a complaint about the firm's claims of having made implausibly large returns risk-free for over 20 years (SEC OIG, 2009). However, SEC investigators seemed satisfied by the explanation that Madoff's returns were generated using a complex derivative-based 'split-strike conversion strategy' (Gough, 2013, p.45).

Over the years, further complaints were received, some from industry experts who pointed, among other things, to the fact that Madoff was not trading in derivatives in anything like the volume required to generate the claimed returns using the purported strategy (SEC OIG, 2009). Despite widely voiced suspicions that Madoff was operating a Ponzi scheme, the SEC failed to consider that possibility and, during several investigations, relied on evidence provided by Madoff himself, accepting vague answers such as 'some people feel the market. Some people just understand how to analyze the numbers that they're looking at' (Madoff cited in SEC OIG, 2009, p.19).

It was only 16 years later, when Madoff himself owned up, that the Ponzi scheme was formally uncovered. For decades, Madoff had simply been placing investors' money in his own business account. When an investor wanted to cash in, he would draw money from the account, which was regularly topped up as new investments flowed in. But the GFC led to a wave of withdrawals and, faced with an impossible call for $7 billion of redemptions, Madoff turned himself in (BBC, 2021a).

Investors included investment funds, banks, pension schemes and trade unions as well as individuals (Wall Street Journal, 2009). It's estimated that including the fictitious returns, the Ponzi scheme amounted to a staggering $65 billion, of which $17 billion was the amount invested, with only $14 billion subsequently recovered (BBC, 2021a). Madoff was sentenced to 150 years in jail and died there in April 2021 (BBC, 2021a).

required either to reply with requested information, typically including your banking details, or to click on a link. The link may take you to a cloned website where your information is harvested or it might download malicious software that enables fraudsters to take control of your device or capture every keystroke. Sometimes the information gathered is not enough in itself to steal your money but can be used later to give authenticity to other frauds.

- **Bank impersonation fraud**. You receive a call purportedly from your bank's fraud department. Number spoofing software may be used so that the caller ID shows a genuine bank number. Information gathered during phishing may be used to lend credibility to the call. Typically, the story is that your account has been hacked and you should log into your online account and transfer your balance to a new safe account for which the caller will give you the sort code and account number. As a result, it is you who transfers your money to the thief in an example of **authorised push payment (APP) fraud**.
- **Utility impersonation fraud**. Similarly, you may receive a call purporting to be from your broadband supplier or operating system, claiming that your router or device has been compromised. You're then led to download software to 'fix' the problem that enables the fraudster to control your device, gaining access to any online accounts.
- **Online trading platform scams**. Fraudsters pay to place ads on social media or that appear first in the list when you make a web search; they include a link to a convincing website through which you can 'invest' your money, maybe in funds or more exotic opportunities, such as cryptocurrencies (FCA, 2021c). Initially, your investments may seem to grow, a ploy to persuade you to invest more, but ultimately your money is spirited away by the fraudsters. These are online versions of conventional scams where cold callers typically phone to offer amazing investment opportunities (**boiler room scams**) or 'review' your pension savings to persuade you to hand over your cash or assets.

Phone, text and online scams are frequently operated by fraudsters based overseas, often from centres that are highly organised in much the same way as any legitimate business would be. Phishing and impersonation fraudsters do not necessarily know that you are the customer of a particular bank or other providers. They simply operate on such a large scale that some of the attacks are bound to be on target. The scams may be elaborate, with scammers willing to take time to reel in their victims. The execution of the frauds can also be agile, switching from one type of scam to another according to the circumstances the targeted individual reveals. For example, a bank impersonation fraud involved persuading the target to divulge credit card details which were then used to make a £10,000 APP fraud, possibly because the balance in the bank account itself was too low to be worth stealing (BBC, 2021b).

10.2 Why financial crime happens

For financial crimes to happen there must be perpetrators motivated and able to enact the crimes and enough targets who are susceptible to the crime to make it worthwhile. This section takes a brief look at some of theories about why financial crime happens.

10.2.1 The perpetrators of financial crime

In a seminal work, US sociologist and criminologist Donald Cressey (1919–1987) proposed what came to be known as the 'triangle of fraud' as a way of codifying three conditions required before someone, like an employee, who was in a position of trust would violate that trust: a non-sharable problem (the pressure to act), knowledge or awareness that the violation could solve the problem (opportunity) and the ability to reconcile their behaviour to themselves as compatible with their self-image (rationalisation) (Cressey, 1950).

Subsequent researchers have added further dimensions, such as capability to act (Wolfe and Hermanson, 2004) and arrogance (Marks, 2014). However, there is some overlap, depending on how each dimension is defined. In this section, I will use the model shown in Figure 10.3.

Cressey's fundamental premise was that financial crime could not be explained by any one factor; rather, a sequence of factors must apply before a trusted person tips into crime.

The first factor in the sequence, pressure, arises because of some problem that cannot be shared. Cressey (1950) talked of gambling losses or the need to display a particular position in society. Marks (2014) points to changes in corporate culture over the decades with, these days, performance-related pay and the celebration of wealth and fame as also providing pressure points – think, for example, of the pressure on fund managers, such as Woodford (see Box 10.2), to achieve and maintain 'star' status.

Many of the phishing and impersonation scams are perpetrated by individuals based in lower-income countries abroad, such as African nations and India. The pressure in those cases may stem from a lack of legal opportunities to make a

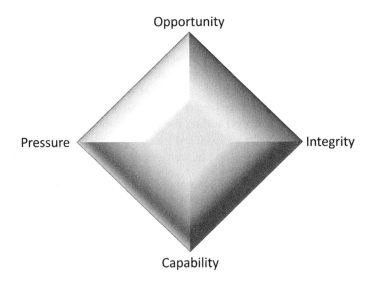

FIGURE 10.3 The fraud diamond.

Source: Author's diagram based on Wolfe and Hermanson (2004).

living, a situation exacerbated by global inequality (Ibrahim Baba Muhammed, cited in Mutua, 2020).

Opportunity and capability are closely linked. Cressey talked of the fraudster becoming aware that they could exploit the system in some way. This involves there being some flaw in the system – such as the lax oversight of the LIBOR system (see Box 10.3) – but also the individual having the position and skills to be able to exploit that flaw.

Under capability, Wolfe and Hermanson (2004) identify six traits. As well as position and being smart, fraudsters often have the following psychological traits: a strong ego and self-confidence; ability to coerce others to commit or conceal the crimes, say through bullying; ability to lie effectively and with consistency; and being able to deal well with the stress that perpetuating a fraud over long periods is likely to entail. Madoff (see Box 10.5) provides an example.

To some extent, these psychological traits overlap with the dimension of integrity, the ability to distinguish right from wrong and to adopt that as a moral compass. Cressey (1950) describes the perpetrator seeking culturally acceptable ways to describe and rationalise what they are doing, such as 'borrowing', rather than stealing. The contextualising to culture is important; in some of the examples above, such as insider dealing, price walking and LIBOR-fixing, it is easy to see that corporate culture may play a strong part in shaping what individuals within that setting see as wrong or socially unacceptable.

The model above concerns trusted people turning to untrustworthy acts. But scams in particular are often perpetrated by outsiders who may well view scamming as a rational business choice. It may just be a matter of **cost-benefit analysis**, with viability determined by a suitably weighted flow of estimated rewards versus the costs and risks

10.2.2 The targets of financial crime

Some types of financial crimes, such as market abuse and corporate fraud, are not directed at particular individuals. Financial scams are different – to work, they involve the compliance of targeted victims. Those who fall for scams often feel foolish and ashamed for being duped, but this reaction is misplaced since scammers are professionals at exploiting innate human behavioural biases.

The US psychologists, Keith Stanovich and Richard West (2000), divide thought processes into two types:

- **System 1 thinking** is fast, effortless and emotionally based, providing mental shortcuts that enable rapid decisions; and
- **System 2 thinking** is rational, slow and effortful, enabling careful analysis and more informed decisions.

Given the volume of decisions that a person must make every day, there is simply not the mental energy to engage System 2 thinking every time. The default is to rely on the System 1 shortcuts and mostly this results in satisfactory outcomes. But scammers – and also legitimate businesses, for example, through their marketing strategies – are expert at exploiting System 1 thinking for their own ends. Another US psychologist, Robert Cialdini (2007), has identified six tactics (which he calls 'weapons of influence') for doing this, which I suggest may apply to financial crimes in a variety of ways, for example:

- **Reciprocation**: We are hard-wired to feel indebted, and so repay, a gift or favour, and this also extends to concessions. For example, you might refuse an invitation from a boiler-room scam to invest a large sum, but if they drop back to suggest a smaller amount, you are more likely to agree, making your own concession in return for theirs.
- **Consistency**: Socially this is seen as a desirable trait, so we are programmed to try to ensure our actions are consistent with previously stated attitudes. To exploit this, scammers may initially engage you in seemingly innocent conversation, for example, about your desire for better returns from your savings, that make it harder to deny the sense of going along with what they subsequently offer.
- **Social proof**: We use evidence that others are doing something as reassurance that it's a good move for us too. This makes referrals from friends and endorsements, whether from celebrities or ordinary people, persuasive, and is a factor in **affinity fraud** (where scammers insinuate themselves into groups, such as religious communities, before launching a scam on their new 'friends').
- **Authority**: We tend to do without question what people or organisations in authority (or seeming to be) tell us. This tactic is clearly seen in the phishing and impersonation scams that claim to be instructions from your bank or tax authority. It can also help explain why employees may be persuaded to become complicit in, or cover up frauds, by senior colleagues.
- **Liking**: We respond positively to people we already know or warm quickly to strangers who are similar to us or compliment us. Whatever the fraud, this makes it harder to say no, and is especially useful in affinity fraud.
- **Scarcity**: The more limited the availability of opportunities is, the more highly we value them. Scammers exploit this with offers that are restricted to the select few or must be acted on today.

Your capacity to assess a scam situation rationally may be affected by both scarcity and another common tactic: posing an emergency that requires your immediate action (such as moving your bank account to safety or paying a tax penalty). Urgency prevents you from consulting others for advice or taking time to engage your System 2 thinking to unpick the scammers' claims. Moreover, research suggests that acute stress may be associated with a failure to take into account the full potential consequences of a decision (see, for example, Wemm and Wulfert, 2017).

Cialdini (2007) also notes that people's material self-interest – their desire to get a good deal – is an ever-present factor that may predispose people to be less alert to the tactics being used against them.

10.3 Protection against financial crime

In many situations, it is not possible for consumers and individual investors to access the information that could alert them to corporate fraud, market abuse and similar financial crimes, even if they had the time and capabilities to process the information (which many will not). Therefore, a great deal of the battle against financial crime relies on regulation (which you will explore in detail in Chapter 11).

Regulation can reduce opportunities for crime, promote integrity, increase the likelihood of crime being detected and, failing that, provide systems of redress for the victims of crime. On the other hand, regulations aimed at thwarting criminals can also have the unwanted side effect of making it harder for legitimate consumers to access the financial services they need – for example, where firms interpret anti-money laundering (AML) rules narrowly, requiring consumers to prove their identity and address using standard documents, such as a passport, driving licence or paper-based bills, that not everyone has (see Chapter 8).

While the online world has certainly proliferated the opportunities for scams, banks and other financial institutions use machine learning and other digital developments to track transaction patterns and detect potential frauds. But it is a battle for providers to keep ahead of the fraudsters.

Section 10.2.2 may have left you feeling that, given inbuilt behavioural biases and the expertise with which scammers play on these, there is little people can do to protect themselves. But this is not the case. Cialdini (2007) offers techniques for rebuffing scammers, mainly based on being aware of the possibility you are being played and arming yourself with rational reasons to reject your emotional response. For example, if a gift is not genuine but just a ploy, then you can reject the feeling of a duty to reciprocate; and, if your attitudes have been manipulatively gathered, you should feel under no obligation to act consistently with them. He also warns against ignoring 'red flags', those feelings of uncertainty or gut instinct that something is wrong.

In the UK, the police, regulators, financial firms and their trade bodies issue information about current scams and guidance on how to avoid them. Some of the key messages include:

- If it sounds too good to be true, then it probably is. Walk away.
- Be careful about the personal data you share, for example on social media sites. Use privacy settings to restrict access.
- Don't reply to, or click on links in, unsolicited emails.
- If you doubt the authenticity of an unsolicited phone call, hang up.

- Be suspicious of any cold call purporting to be from your bank or another authority. Check using independent contact details (not those provided by the caller) and use a different mode of contact if you can (since scammers may keep your line open, playing a recorded dial tone to fool you into thinking they have hung up).
- Be aware that genuine authorities will never ask you to disclose passwords, personal identification numbers (PINs) or one-time security codes sent to your mobile, or set up 'safe' accounts for you.
- Never allow anyone to remotely access your computer, for example to 'fix' a problem.
- Keep your software up to date.
- Don't use the same password for multiple accounts. Use strong passwords (ideally at least 16 digits with a mix of upper- and lower-case letters, numbers and punctuation characters) or a **password manager**.

If you think you have been a victim of a scam, contact the police and your bank or other relevant account providers immediately.

10.4 Conclusion

Financial crime is big business and comes in many shapes and forms. Some types appear at first sight to be victimless but nevertheless have repercussions, say, for individual investors who may be losers, although sometimes winners.

Scams are perpetrated against individuals who are always losers if the scams succeed. They involve the sophisticated exploitation of the behavioural traits that are innate to us all.

Nevertheless, there are steps that individuals can take to protect themselves against scams. However, regulation is at the forefront of preventing crime and providing routes for redress where it does occur, and it is to that topic that Chapter 11 turns.

Self-test questions

1 Outline one argument for and one argument against insider dealing being a crime.
2 What is a Ponzi scheme?
3 Search the internet for an example of a financial scam and try to analyse how it works using Cialdini's (2007) six 'weapons of persuasion'.

Further reading

Financial Conduct Authority, consultations, policies and guidance: https://www.fca.org.uk/publications

Financial Services Consumer Panel, publications: https://www.fs-cp.org.uk/fca-publications

References

BBC (2021a) *Bernie Madoff: disgraced financier dies in prison*. Available at: https://www.bbc.co.uk/news/business-56750103 (Accessed: 30 April 2021).

BBC (2021b) 'Royal Mail scam' in *You and Yours*, Radio 4, 26 April, 09:46-18:10. Available at: https://www.bbc.co.uk/programmes/m000vh53 (Accessed: 30 April 2021).

Browning, J. (2021) 'How much did Libor rigging cost? U.S. FDIC finally has an answer' in *Bloomberg*, 18 March. Available at: https://www.bloomberg.com/news/articles/2021-03-18/how-much-did-libor-rigging-cost-u-s-fdic-finally-has-an-answer (Accessed: 28 April 2021).

Cialdini, R. B. (2007) *Influence. The psychology of persuasion*.1st Collins Business Education edition. New York: Harper Collins.

Clark, J. (2021) 'Investors sue Hargreaves Lansdown over losses linked to Neil Woodford collapse' in *City AM*. Available at: https://www.cityam.com/investors-sue-hargreaves-lansdown-over-losses-linked-to-neil-woodford-collapse/ (Accessed 25 April 2021).

Companies Act 1980, ch.22. Available at: https://www.legislation.gov.uk/ukpga/1980/22/contents/enacted (Accessed 2 May 2021).

Cressey, D.R. (1950) 'The criminal violation of financial trust' in *American Sociological Review*, Vol. 15(26), December 1950, pp.738–743.

Economist Intelligence Unit (2019) 'Woodford, felled; investment management' in *The Economist*, Vol. 431(9146), p.30.

Edmonds, T. (2014) *LIBOR, public enquiries and FCA disciplinary powers*, House of Commons Briefing Paper No 06376. Available at: https://researchbriefings.files.parliament.uk/documents/SN06376/SN06376.pdf (Accessed: 27 April 2021).

European Securities and Markets Association (ESMA) (no date) *Benchmarks*. Available at: https://www.esma.europa.eu/policy-rules/benchmarks (Accessed: 28 April 2021).

Federal Housing Finance Agency (2021) 'All transactions indexes: US and Census Divisions (not seasonally adjusted)' in *House price index datasets*. Available at: https://www.fhfa.gov/DataTools/Downloads/Pages/House-Price-Index-Datasets.aspx#qat (Accessed: 30 April 2021).

Federal Reserve Economic Data (FRED) (2021) *Delinquency rate on single-family residential mortgages, booked in domestic offices, all commercial banks*, DRSFRMACBN. Available at: https://fred.stlouisfed.org/series/DRSFRMACBN (Accessed: 3 May 2021).

Ferguson, H. (2016) *Special report: CF Woodford equity income*. Available at: https://www.hl.co.uk/news/articles/archive/special-report-cf-woodford-equity-income (Accessed: 25 April 2021).

Financial Conduct Authority (2021a) 'Regulation COLL 5.2.8(4)' in *FCA Handbook*. Available at: https://www.handbook.fca.org.uk/handbook/COLL/5/2.html#D59 (Accessed: 29 April 2021).

Financial Conduct Authority (2021b) *Statement by Mark Steward, FCA Director of Enforcement and Market Oversight, on Woodford Investment Management Ltd and WCM Partners Ltd*, 17 February. Available at: https://www.fca.org.uk/news/statements/statement-mark-steward-fca-director-enforcement-market-oversight-woodford-investment-management (Accessed: 26 April 2021).

Financial Conduct Authority (2021c) *Be a ScamSmart investor*. Available at: https://www.fca.org.uk/scamsmart. (Accessed: 30 April 2021).

Financial Conduct Authority (FCA) (2020) *General insurance pricing practices. Final report*, Market study MS18/1.3. Available at: https://www.fca.org.uk/publication/market-studies/ms18-1-3.pdf (Accessed 25 April 2021).

Financial Conduct Authority (FCA) (2020|2016) UK benchmarks regulation. Available at: https://www.fca.org.uk/markets/benchmarks/regulation (Accessed: 28 April 2021).

Financial Conduct Authority (FCA) (2019) *A duty of care and potential alternative approaches: summary of responses and next steps* Feedback Statement FS19/2 Available at: https://www.fca.org.uk/publication/feedback/fs19-02.pdf (Accessed: 25 April 2021).

Financial Services Act 2012, c.21. Available at: https://www.legislation.gov.uk/ukpga/2012/21/contents/enacted (Accessed: 28 April 2021).

Gough, L. (2013) *The conmen. A history of financial fraud and the lessons you can learn*, Harlow: Pearson Education Ltd.

Gov.uk (2019) *Economic crime plan, 2019 to 2022*. Available at: https://www.gov.uk/government/publications/economic-crime-plan-2019-to-2022/economic-crime-plan-2019-to-2022-accessible-version (Accessed: 24 April 2021).

The Guardian (2005) *WorldCom investors to get $6bn and Ebbers's house*. Available at: https://www.theguardian.com/business/2005/sep/22/corporatefraud.worldcom (Accessed: 29 April 2021).

Harcus Parker (2021) *Woodford litigation*. Available at: https://woodfordclaim.com/?gclid=Cj0KCQjwppSEBhCGARIsANIs4p6022aZMTCD36nVx8wzHhhk0zzGCA25q1yY-AOqYruEvFaqvffv65kaAgbuEALw_wcB (Accessed: 25 April 2021).

Hill, C. (2019) *Woodford Equity Income – what to expect now*. Available at: https://www.hl.co.uk/news/articles/archive/woodford-equity-income-what-to-expect-now (Accessed: 25 April 2021).

Investment Association (2021) *Fund sector definitions*. Available at: https://www.theia.org/industry-data/fund-sectors/definitions (Accessed: 25 April 2021).

Investment Association (2020) *IA issues new guidance on equity income sectors in light of Covid-19*. Available at: https://www.theia.org/media/press-releases/ia-issues-new-guidance-equity-income-sectors-light-covid-19 (Accessed: 25 April 2021).

Jackie Wells & Associates (2013) *Consumer responsibility: Identifying and closing the gap*, Report prepared for the FCA Practitioner Panel. Available at: https://www.fca-pp.org.uk/sites/default/files/fca_practitioner_panel_consumer_responsibility_report_september_2013.pdf (Accessed: 25 April 2021).

Jang, W., Nelson, A.A. and Vytlacil, E. (2014) 'Liar's loan? Effects of origination channel and information falsification on mortgage delinquency' in *The Review of Economics and Statistics*, Vol. 96(1), pp.1–18.

Klaw, B.W. and Mayer, D. (2021) 'Ethics, markets, and the legalization of insider trading' in *Journal of Business Ethics*, Vol. 168(1), pp.55–70.

Leeson, N. and Whitley, E. (1998) *Rogue trader*, London: Warner Books.

Link Fund Solutions (2019) *Tuesday 15th October 2019- Investor letter regarding the winding-up of the LF Woodford Equity Income Fund*. Available at: https://equityincome.linkfundsolutions.co.uk/investor-communications/tuesday-15th-october-2019-investor-letter-regarding-the-winding-up-of-the-lf-woodford-equity-income-fund/ (Accessed: 26 April 2021).

Manne, H. G. (2005) 'Insider trading: Hayek, virtual markets and the dog that did not bark' in *Journal of Corporation Law*, Vol. 31 Fall, 2005, pp.167–185.

Marks, J.T. (2014) *Playing offense in a high-risk environment. A sophisticated approach to fighting fraud*. Available at: https://www.academia.edu/31698128/Playing_Offense_in_a_High-Risk_Environment_A_Sophisticated_Approach_to_Fighting_Fraud (Accessed 16 September 2021).

Mutua, M. (2020) *The untold stories of financial crime*. Independently published.

Refinitiv (2019) *Revealing the true cost of financial crime. 2018 survey report*. Available at: https://www.refinitiv.com/content/dam/marketing/en_us/documents/reports/true-cost-of-financial-crime-global-focus.pdf (Accessed: 24 April 2021).

Securities and Exchange Commission (2003) *Report of investigation by the Special Investigative Committee of the Board of Directors of WorldCom Inc*. Available at: https://www.sec.gov/Archives/edgar/data/723527/000093176303001862/dex991.htm#ex991902_2 (Accessed: 29 April 2021).

Securities and Exchange Commission Office of Inspector General (SEC OIG) (2009) *Report of Investigation. Case No. OIG-509. Investigation of failure of the SEC to uncover Bernard Madoff's Ponzi scheme*. Available at: https://www.sec.gov/files/oig-509-exec-summary.pdf (Accessed: 30 April 2021).

Stanovich, K.E. and West, R.F (2000) 'Individual differences in reasoning: Implications for the rationality debate' in *Behavioural and Brain Sciences* 23, pp.645–726. Available at: http://psy2.ucsd.edu/~mckenzie/StanovichBBS.pdf (Accessed: 2 May 2021).

Vaughan, L. and Finch, G. (2017) 'Libor scandal: The bankers who fixed the world's most important number' in *The Guardian*, 18 January. Available at: https://www.theguardian.com/business/2017/jan/18/libor-scandal-the-bankers-who-fixed-the-worlds-most-important-number (Accessed: 28 April 2021).

Walker (2021) 'Neil Woodford: The continuing fallout of a scandal' in *The Financial Times*, 19 March. Available online at: https://www.ft.com/content/dcc04950-f680-4210-af4e-669413501951 (Accessed: 25 April 2021).

Wall Street Journal (2009) *Madoff's victims*. Available at: https://s.wsj.net/public/resources/documents/st_madoff_victims_20081215.html (Accessed: 30 April 2021).

Wemm, S.E. and Wulfert, E. (2017) 'Effects of acute stress on decision making' in *Applied Psychophysiology and Biofeedback*, Vol. 42(1), pp.1–12.

Wolfe, D.T. and Hermanson, D.R. (2004) 'The fraud diamond: Considering the four elements of fraud' in *CPA Journal*, Vol. 74(12) (2004), pp.38–42. Also available at: https://digitalcommons.kennesaw.edu/cgi/viewcontent.cgi?referer=https://www.google.com/&httpsredir=1&article=2546&context=facpubs (Accessed: 30 April 2021).

11

REGULATION OF FINANCIAL SERVICES

Patrick John Ring

Key points summary

- There are three objectives of financial regulation: systemic stability, the soundness of individual firms and ensuring that markets work effectively (including appropriate consumer protection). The objectives and theory about how they may be achieved influence the structure of regulation.
- The main front-line tasks for regulators are to authorise appropriate firms to do business, police the perimeter between authorised and unauthorised firms and supervise and enforce compliance with specified rules.
- Consumer protection can take two forms: ex-ante protection focuses on preventing consumer detriment; ex-post protection provides routes for complaints and redress.
- Conventional regulatory measures may be supplemented with innovative approaches, such as 'nudging' consumer behaviour and trying to change the culture of firms.

It is fair to say that, in recent years, events in the financial sector have cast a strong light upon the role of national and international regulators of the financial services industry. The Global Financial Crisis (GFC) that started in 2007 – described in Box 1.1 in Chapter 1 – drew attention to the failures of financial regulation, and subsequent financial scandals in many different countries have also drawn attention both to the challenges faced by consumers in navigating their way through an increasingly complicated financial landscape, and to the behaviour of certain individuals and the culture of the firms for which they worked.

DOI: 10.4324/9781003227663-11

In this chapter, we begin by looking at the objectives of financial regulation and how that can influence the structure of national regulators. Thereafter, we focus upon the position in the UK, which itself illustrates many of the issues and dilemmas facing regulators around the world. In doing so, we concentrate on three particular issues: the regulatory concerns of front-line regulation, the role of regulators when it comes to the protection of financial services consumers and the regulation concerning the behaviour of individuals and culture of financial firms operating within the financial services sector.

Learning Outcomes

After reading this chapter you should be able to:

- Discuss the objectives of financial regulation.
- Explain the relationship between regulatory objectives and possible regulatory structures.
- Describe the main roles of front-line financial regulators.
- Critically assess the extent to which regulation can, or can be expected to, protect consumers.
- Discuss the significance of 'choice architecture' in enhancing outcomes for financial services consumers.
- Explain how regulators can attempt to influence the behaviour of financial firms and their employees, and critically assess the importance of these efforts.

11.1 Objectives and structures of regulation

The functions that banks, life insurance and investment companies, as well as many other financial services firms, perform are integral to the well-being of nations and their economies. That does not of itself provide a justification for governments introducing regulation, particularly if, as some argue, this may often make the position worse (Benston, 1998). Nevertheless, if the social costs of banks or markets failing, for example due to poor governance or lack of consumer confidence, are greater than the private costs to individual market participants themselves, there is clearly a need to consider whether regulation can serve economic and social purposes by ensuring good governance and continued confidence in markets and firms.

In general (see, for example, Goodhart et al., 1998; Georgosouli, 2007, Armour et al., 2016), debate tends to centre around the following three basic objectives: sustaining **systemic stability,** ensuring firms are financially sound and ensuring markets work effectively, including protecting consumers from avoidable harm.

11.1.1 Maintaining systemic stability

Traditionally, it was thought that the regulation safeguarding the financial position of individual institutions was sufficient to maintain the stability of the financial system – what is referred to as **microprudential regulation** (see Brunnermeier et al., 2009). The argument is that the failure of a single financial institution can lead to 'contagion' in the financial system, undermining confidence in other financial institutions, bringing about their failure and leading to a widespread crisis (a 'domino effect'). This is regarded as a particular issue for banks if they do not hold sufficient assets, or sufficiently liquid assets, to meet their liabilities. It is argued that the potential public, or social, costs of a subsequent default can be much greater than the private costs to the firm arising from the event. As public costs are not taken into account by individual firms, regulation should be used to safeguard the position. Thus, the main international standards on banking regulation, the Basel Accords (BIS, 2021), focus upon ensuring individual banks remain financially sound, to prevent the possibility of their demise creating a 'run' on other banks due to a lack of confidence in the banking system.

The GFC illustrated the limitations of this analysis (FSA, 2009). In the context of the impending collapse of a single bank, the domino effect assumes a relatively passive role for other banks. Yet it is unlikely that, in circumstances where one bank is facing financial issues in difficult market conditions, other banks would not take action themselves in relation to their own risk exposures and balance sheets; these actions could, in turn, have further negative effects on the banking system. In this way, problems can spread across the financial system affecting a wide range of institutions simultaneously (see, for example, Brunnermeier et al. (2009) pp.13–21).

As a result, it is now accepted that regulators also need to specifically address system-wide issues that have the potential to destabilise the financial system as a whole – an approach called **macroprudential regulation**. As Armour et al. (2016, p.409) neatly put it:

> The distinction between the microprudential and macroprudential approaches can be illustrated by analogy with that between medicine and public health care. Medicine is concerned with saving individual lives, public health care with protecting populations and communities as a whole.

Examples of the significance of this objective can be seen in the creation of the European Union (EU) European Systemic Risk Board and the US Financial Stability Oversight Council in the wake of the GFC.

11.1.2 Ensuring the financial soundness of individual firms

The main concern here is microprudential regulation – that is, ensuring the soundness of individual financial institutions (ECB, 2014, pp.135–140). Such regulation includes making sure institutions have enough assets or shareholder capital to absorb losses and meet their liabilities; that they have appropriate risk management systems to manage their financial risks; and that there are appropriate compensation schemes and **resolution procedures** in place to ensure that, in the event of the failure of an institution, consumers are protected and that failure does not create wider systemic problems.

The most well-known international standards relating to many of these issues are the Basel Accords for banks, set out by the Basel Committee on Banking Supervision (BIS, 2021). These are not mandatory but have been implemented by a wide range of countries (see Armour et al., 2016, Part D). In the EU, they have been implemented in member states through regulations and directives, and a similar comprehensive set of rules also governs the microprudential regulation of insurance companies under what is known as **Solvency 2** (European Commission, 2021). In the wake of the GFC, these standards incorporate additional measures designed for larger institutions that could have a significant effect on the financial system as a whole if they got into difficulties (so-called 'systemically important financial institutions'). The international standards for resolution procedures for banks and other financial institutions have been developed by the Financial Stability Board (FSB, 2014), an international standard setting board made up of the **G20** economies as well as other international institutions.

11.1.3 Protecting investors and maintaining the integrity of financial institutions and markets

Maintaining the integrity of financial institutions and markets encompasses a range of goals, most commonly maintaining competitive financial markets and preventing monopolies, securing appropriate behaviours of those working in the financial services sector and preventing financial crime such as insider dealing and money laundering (see Chapter 10). The main focus is on the business conduct of firms.

The micro- and macroprudential regulation mentioned in the previous sections also underpin these efforts. It is argued that investors, both individuals and institutional as well as other financial consumers and market participants, need to be satisfied that those markets, and the people involved in them, are dependable and are acting with integrity.

However, the concerns of this objective go beyond maintaining the dependability and integrity of markets to focus on consumer protection, and in particular retail investor protection. It is argued that financial services markets and products differ from other products and markets. While the problems that financial consumers can encounter, such as lack of comprehensible information, the possibility of being misled, lack of transparency and lack of guarantees, are attributes that could also be applied to many other kinds of goods, it is argued that 'the uniqueness of some financial products, services and contracts is that they combine all or a large number of these characteristics' (Llewellyn, 1999, p.39)

11.2 Regulatory objectives and regulatory structures

Traditionally, financial institutions have been regulated based on their legal status (institutional-based regulation), or on the kinds of activity they undertake (functional-based regulation) (see Herring and Carmassi, 2008). Typically, these approaches work best where institutions specialise in one particular function or area of business, but the late twentieth century saw the rise of financial conglomerates blurring the distinctions that have traditionally been applied across firms, products and distribution channels (see Briault, 1999).

As a result, many nations have sought to reconfigure the activities of their financial regulators around the kinds of objectives or goals discussed above. The most commonly cited example is the 'twin peaks' approach, where day-to-day regulatory functions are divided between two main regulators – one dealing with microprudential issues and the other focusing on, broadly, market conduct and consumer protection (Herring and Carmassi, 2008). The task of managing macroprudential regulation is typically seen as a separate, but coordinated, function, often under the auspices of the central bank. The logic in this approach can be seen in Figure 11.1, illustrating each of these three objectives and the regulatory functions underpinning them.

The 'twin peaks' approach was introduced in Australia as far back as 1998, although such integrating tendencies can be seen in countries as far apart as China, the UK, South Africa and the Netherlands, among others (See Schmulow, 2015;

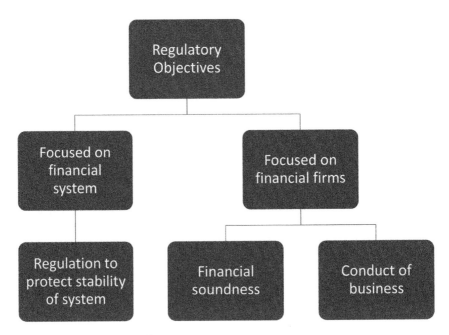

FIGURE 11.1 Regulatory objectives.
Source: author's diagram.

Godwin, 2017; Baker McKenzie, 2017; GLI, 2021). In some countries, this has led to the integration of all regulatory functions within a single regulator (for more on the structures of financial regulators see Huang and Schoenmaker, 2015).

11.3 Regulatory structure in the UK

In 2013, as a result of the Financial Services Act 2012, the UK moved from financial regulation through a single regulator to a 'twin peaks' approach. Figure 11.2 illustrates the respective roles of the Prudential Regulation Authority (PRA) and the Financial Conduct Authority (FCA) as 'front-line' regulators. The regulatory framework of statutory objectives, powers and duties for both regulators is set out in the Financial Services and Markets Act 2000 (hereinafter FSMA, 2000) as amended by subsequent legislation.

The PRA is concerned with the microprudential regulation of systemically significant financial institutions, such as banks, building societies and insurance companies, to ensure their financial soundness. The FCA is tasked with protecting consumers, ensuring orderly and transparent financial markets and promoting competition in financial services markets in the interests of consumers. The competition objective is shared with both the PRA and a government agency, the Competition and Markets Authority (CMA). The range of financial products that the FCA oversees is set out in secondary legislation and has been regularly expanded so that it now includes investments (including personal pensions and annuities), all types of insurance, mortgages, equity release, credit, payment services and even funeral plans. As the PRA is tasked only with prudential

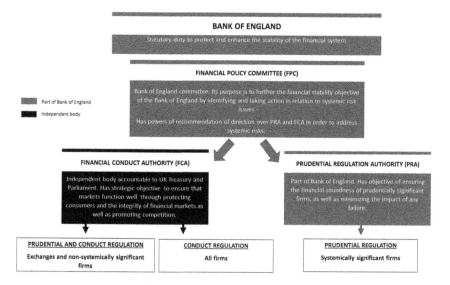

FIGURE 11.2 Structure of financial regulation under FSMA 2000.
Source: author's diagram.

regulation, it regulates systemically significant firms jointly with the FCA, which is responsible for the conduct regulation of those firms.

In an acknowledgement of the relationship between microprudential and macroprudential issues, the PRA is part of the Bank of England, which itself has a remit to promote financial stability, primarily through its Financial Policy Committee (FPC). The Bank of England Act 1998 , as amended, gives the FPC the statutory purpose of contributing to the achievement by the Bank of England of its financial stability objective, and thereby economic growth. This involves identifying, monitoring and taking action to remove or reduce **systemic risks** to protect and enhance the resilience of the UK financial system. As Figure 11.2 illustrates, as in many other countries, the UK's systemic regulatory body is at the apex of the regulatory system, and in the UK the FPC has the power to direct the PRA and FCA, as front-line regulators, to take action on a sector or system-wide basis to enhance or maintain financial stability.

11.4 Front-line financial regulation in the UK

The regulatory requirements of the PRA and the FCA are set out in the PRA Rulebook and the FCA Handbook (created and amended under powers given to them by the FSMA 2000, as amended).

Figure 11.3 sets out what may be regarded as the key functions of any front-line regulator: authorising financial firms and individuals to undertake regulated activities; preventing those who do not have authorisation from undertaking regulated activities; supervising and monitoring authorised firms and individuals; and taking enforcement action against firms and individuals who breach regulatory requirements. In the following sections, these functions are examined in relation to the UK, although the issues discussed are ones that have to be addressed by any front-line regulator.

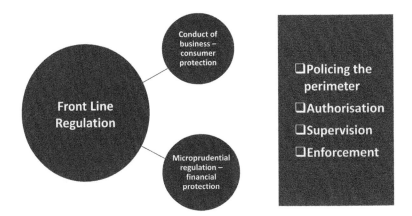

FIGURE 11.3 Front-line regulation.
Source: author's diagram.

11.4.1 Authorisation and policing the perimeter

Section 19 of the FSMA 2000 prohibits any firm from carrying on any regulated activities (defined under secondary legislation) in the UK unless it is authorised (or exempt from needing authorisation under the FSMA 2000). Individuals holding specific important functions in those firms must also be separately approved. Through authorisation/approval, regulators can ensure that firms and individuals meet minimum standards and, importantly, that they continue to meet those standards for as long as they are authorised/approved.

For a firm to obtain authorisation from the FCA, the regulator must be satisfied, both when granting authorisation and on an ongoing basis, that (FCA, 2021a):

- Its legal status and corporate structure are such that it can be regulated effectively.
- Those in control of the firm are fit and proper to undertake the activities for which authorisation is being sought.
- It has the appropriate level of resources (financial and non-financial) in order to undertake the activities for which authorisation is being sought.
- Its business model will enable business to be conducted in a way that will ensure it meets the requirements of the regulator.

Organisations falling under the remit of the PRA must apply to the PRA for authorisation, and their application will be reviewed by both the PRA (for prudential issues) and the FCA (for conduct of business issues). Where a firm does not fall within the remit of the PRA, the firm is authorised by the FCA alone, which in that case applies its own prudential requirements. This latter approach applies to the vast majority of financial firms that are not considered to be systemically significant, that is, not banks, building societies or insurance companies.

One consequence of Section 19 of the FSMA 2000 is to distinguish between regulated activity, requiring authorisation and unregulated activity that does not require authorisation (see, for example, the difference between advice and guidance discussed in Chapter 6). This distinction creates a 'perimeter' that needs to be monitored and 'policed' by the FCA under its conduct of business function. It must ensure regulated activities are undertaken only by those who are properly authorised – a key aspect of protecting consumers against unscrupulous individuals and ensuring the authorisation process is not undermined.

Drawing the general public's attention to the 'scams' of unauthorised firms (see Chapter 10) is an important element of policing the perimeter (FCA, 2018a; Steward, 2021). It is also important to ensure that consumers understand what is covered by regulatory protections and what is not, and that any new developments in the sector are adequately covered by regulation if appropriate (see, for example, FCA (2020)). A Financial Services Register is freely available, listing all authorised firms and approved individuals involved with regulated activities, and it is always advisable for consumers to check the register when deciding whether to do business with a firm.

11.4.2 Supervision and enforcement

In the face of inevitable financial constraints upon regulators, there has been an increasing emphasis to prioritise activity by assessing firms in terms of the risks they pose to regulatory objectives. This requires an understanding of the risks posed by a firm's business model and practices, as well as of the markets within which those firms operate. For microprudential regulation, it also involves a detailed understanding of the financial position of a firm, and its risk management and controls.

To achieve this, regulators must acquire sufficient information about firms and the environment in which they operate. This may be publicly available information, reports and annual returns that authorised firms are required to submit to their regulator(s), specific requests for information or investigations and on-site visits. It may also include information obtained from whistleblowers or from reports made to the regulator by consumers.

This 'risk-based' approach to regulation has several consequences. Firstly, regulators must have the necessary expertise and capacity to collect and analyse this material. Secondly, it emphasises the importance of the ex-ante activities of the regulator, that is, those activities attempting to prevent harm before it happens. Regulators must use evidence collected to make judgements about the risk posed to their objectives by firms, and challenge firms' business models and practices where necessary.

Thus, effective two-way communication with firms is important in sharing and developing good regulatory practice (PRA, 2018; FCA 2019a). Nevertheless, regulators do not have the ability to have close and continuing relationships with all firms, and the extent of contact will again be based on the potential risks posed by the size and activities of firms. As a result, regulators have increasingly developed other means to communicate wider issues or concerns to all or parts of the industry – see, for example, the PRA's and FCA's use of 'Dear CEO' letters (BDO, 2020).

As regards formal enforcement, having appropriately investigated any matter, the FCA and PRA can enforce their rules using a range of administrative, civil or criminal means. This includes restricting or withdrawing the authorisation of firms or approval of individuals, the imposition of fines and public censure through the publication of their regulatory decisions (FCA, 2019b). While breaches of the criminal law would normally be dealt with by criminal authorities, there are limited circumstances under which the regulators can bring criminal proceedings (e.g. FCA Handbook, Section ENF15).

11.5 Regulation and the protection of consumers

Under section 1C of the FSMA 2000, the FCA has a statutory objective to secure 'an appropriate degree of protection for consumers'. This is not a blanket

FIGURE 11.4 A well-functioning market for consumers.
Source: author's diagram based on FCA (2018b).

protection for consumers, and the obligation is circumscribed by the type of transaction and level of risk involved, the experience of the consumer and the 'general principle that consumers should take responsibility for their decisions' (FSMA, 2000 s.1C(d)). While in the past there has been debate about what the extent of this obligation might be (FSA, 2008), regulators have always been at pains to point out that the regulatory system is a **non-zero failure regime** (Mortimer, 2020). Notwithstanding, as of May 2021 the FCA has proposed the principle of firms having a consumer duty to all retail consumers, which will be underpinned by more detailed rules setting out its expectations (FCA, 2021b).

The FCA's general approach involves both creating a market that facilitates consumers in seeking and achieving appropriate financial outcomes (ex-ante regulation), and ensuring that there are effective mechanisms to provide redress where consumers have suffered harm as a result of the inappropriate action of others (ex-post regulation). Figure 11.4 summarises key elements of what the FCA currently envisages such a market might look like.

11.5.1 Ex-ante regulation for consumer protection

As regards ex-ante regulation, the FCA Handbook contains high-level principles for business behaviour, and Principle 6 states that 'A firm must have regard to the interests of its customers and treat them fairly'. The FCA and its predecessor, the

Summary of FCA's outcomes to ensure fair treatment of consumers

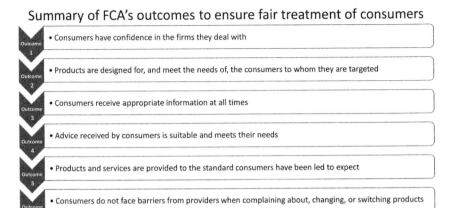

FIGURE 11.5 Fair treatment of consumers.
Source: author's diagram based on FCA (2021b).

Financial Services Authority (FSA), developed a 'Treating Customers Fairly' initiative, the aim of which was to deliver fair outcomes for retail consumers (FSA, 2004). This is now embodied in the FCA's requirement that 'All firms must be able to show consistently that fair treatment of customers is at the heart of their business model' (FCA, 2021c) and in the six consumer outcomes that it requires firms to strive to achieve (see Figure 11.5). These requirements are underpinned by detailed rules in the FCA Handbook which, among other things, address the conduct of firms and individuals, including their training and standards of behaviour; how firms develop and assess the appropriateness of their products for any market in which they intend to offer those products; and how they interact with their clients, and with consumers generally, through financial promotions, social media or otherwise.

In addition, there have also been regulatory efforts to support and empower consumers (Lowe, 2017). Originally, the FSMA 2000 gave the regulator a statutory objective to promote public understanding of the financial system. This responsibility was transferred in 2010 to the Money Advice Service (MAS) with the aim of providing a financial information and guidance service to the general public online, via telephone and through a network of advisers. Criticisms about lack of public awareness of this service, its value for money and the nature of the service provided (Rovnick and Parker, 2016) resulted in the MAS being replaced in 2019 by the Money and Pensions Service (MaPS). MaPS's core functions are pension and money guidance, debt advice, consumer protection (working with the FCA) and driving forward the UK's Strategy for Financial Wellbeing (MaPS, 2020). From June 2021, MaPS has consolidated its three former brands (Money Advice Service, The Pensions Advisory Service and PensionWise) into a single new brand called MoneyHelper.

11.5.2 Ex-post regulation for consumer protection

Where consumers encounter problems or difficulties, there is also a range of ex-post regulation designed to ensure consumers obtain appropriate redress.

11.5.2.1 Complaints

Reflecting the FCA's Outcome 6 for fair treatment of consumers (see Figure 11.5), if individual consumers have a complaint about the firm they are dealing with, the FCA Handbook requires firms to have written procedures to deal promptly and fairly with any complaint, written or oral, regardless of whether or not the complaint appears to be justified. The FCA normally expect a final response within eight weeks (FCA Handbook DISP 1.6).

If the complainant is not satisfied with the outcome, they have the right to refer the matter to the Financial Ombudsman Service (FOS) to independently review the case. The referral must be made within six months of the final response received from the financial firm complained against.

The FOS is an alternative to immediately seeking redress through the legal system, is free to complainants and is available to individual consumers and small businesses. The FOS can consider complaints about most financial products and services provided in or from the UK, including debt collection, payday loans, insurance, mortgages, financial advice and problems with claims management companies, and its rules are set out in the FCA Handbook (FCA Handbook DISP 2 and DISP 3).

The FOS can require firms to put things right in a way that may not involve paying money (e.g. correcting a credit history) as well as requiring the payment of compensation for financial loss and for the (often emotional) impact on the consumer of what went wrong. As on May 2021, the maximum financial compensation limit is £335,000. An FOS ruling is binding on the firm if the complainant accepts it, although the complainant has the option of not doing so and pursuing their case through the legal system.

There is a separate Pensions Ombudsman (PO) that deals with complaints of maladministration and disputes of fact or law concerning personal and occupational pension schemes. Any decision (a 'Determination') made by the PO is binding and enforceable in a court of law.

11.5.2.2 Compensation

The Financial Services Compensation Scheme (FSCS) is the UK's statutory fund of last resort for customers of financial services firms. This means it can pay compensation to consumers if a financial services firm has gone out of business and is unable, or likely to be unable, to pay claims against it. It thus protects individuals if a business fails and those individuals will suffer a financial loss. To qualify, the following conditions must be met:

- The firm is authorised under the FSMA 2000 and the claim relates to a regulated activity.
- The firm has a legal liability in relation to the claimant with respect to that regulated activity (this could be due to deposits held or a negligence claim).
- The claimant must have suffered actual financial loss.
- The claimant is a private individual (although some businesses and charities may be eligible, depending on the type of claim).

The FSCS includes deposit insurance. As of May 2021, if a bank, building society or credit union failed, then a depositor would be entitled to up to £85,000 (£170,000 for joint accounts) in relation to each legal entity with which money is held (the single limit applies even if that entity has several 'brands' with which money is deposited). The FSCS also protects temporary high balances of up to £1million in these accounts for six months, for example, due to a property sale or inheritance. Separate limits apply to other types of financial business and these can be found on the FSCS's website.

The FSCS provides reassurance to individuals with bank accounts, insurance products, savings and investments and pension policies, and covers a wide range of institutions, including banks, building societies, credit unions, insurance companies, mortgage providers and financial advisers. While NS&I investments are not covered by the FSCS, because NS&I is part of the government it is backed by HM Treasury, which guarantees 100% of everything invested in NS&I.

One lesson from the GFC is that to be effective in giving consumers confidence to entrust their finances with financial firms, consumers need to be aware that the FSCS exists, it has to be easy and quick to make a claim and compensation needs to be received within a reasonable time (FSCS, 2017). It is therefore no surprise that addressing these issues is a key objective of the FSCS (FSCS, 2021).

11.5.3 Beyond empowerment – choice architecture

The study of behavioural finance points to behavioural traits in individuals, such as short-termism or reactions to suffering loss, that can result in poor decisions or outcomes, no matter the information or guidance available. This has resulted in regulatory developments which could be said to alter the **choice architecture** within which retail consumers make decisions.

The term 'choice architecture' was coined by Thaler and Sunstein (2008) in their book, *Nudge*, to refer to, among other things, the deliberate structuring of a choice environment to be aligned with individuals' behavioural biases and thus to **nudge** them towards a particular (more beneficial) outcome.

An archetypical example in the UK relies on the inertia of individuals by automatically enrolling them into an employer pension scheme when they enter employment (as opposed to leaving individuals to make a voluntary decision to join). Those individuals have the option to opt out of the pension scheme, but their inertia in taking action (the same inertia which meant many did not voluntarily join a scheme) results in them remaining in the scheme and thus making private provision for their retirement (generally viewed as being in their best interests). In the UK, this has resulted in more than 10 million individuals being enrolled into a pension scheme (DWP, 2020).

The UK government has also altered the decision landscape in order to attempt to protect consumers in the face of potential harm. For example, to try and avoid individuals making poor decisions about their pension funds, in certain circumstances individuals must take advice from a qualified adviser before being allowed to make a pension transfer. The Financial Guidance and Claims Act 2018 also requires the FCA to ensure that consumers have received appropriate pension guidance or have opted out of guidance before accessing or transferring their pension savings, and the regulator will likely take similar steps in relation to the provision of financial guidance for pension investors approaching retirement (Austin, 2021).

11.6 Regulatory outcomes – the role of industry

In 2014, the FCA's Director of Supervision noted:

> …. at the firm level, particularly for the large firms that have the biggest consumer and market footprint, we are looking at how the interests of the customer and market integrity are at the heart of how their business is run – this means our focus is on the firm's business model, culture and front-line activities such as product governance and less on second-line controls. This focus on how the business is run, rather than how it is controlled, is a fundamental change and is directly linked to our outcome-focused philosophy.
>
> *(Adamson, 2014)*

As already discussed, for both the FCA and the PRA, focusing on a firm's business model is at the heart of their approach to authorisation and supervision. In turn, this requires the expertise and experience to make judgements about the implications of firms' plans and behaviours for a regulator's objectives (PRA, 2018, FCA, 2019a). The focus is on the performance of firms and the expected outcomes, and this performance-based approach has been underpinned by what is referred to as 'principle-based regulation'.

Principles have been used in UK regulation alongside detailed rules since the late 1980s. Set out in the regulatory rule books, principle-based rules are legal requirements that express fundamental regulatory standards concerning the outcomes and behaviours that regulators expect. The main set of principles that dominates the FCA Handbook is its *Principles for Business*. In the PRA Rulebook, the equivalent is its *Fundamental Rules*. Both of these are fundamental expressions of aims and intent that inform more detailed provisions in the regulators' rule books. Subject to specific rulebook requirements, the broadly framed nature of a principle-based approach allows firms to use their knowledge and expertise, in an often rapidly changing financial landscape, to decide how best to meet the outcomes that regulators expect them to achieve. This underlines the importance of a regulator's ex-ante judgements concerning the outcomes that are likely as a result of firms' business models and behaviours, a point noted in the aftermath of the GFC:

> I think there was a philosophy of regulation which emerged, not just in this country but in other countries, which was based upon too extreme a form of confidence in markets and confidence in the ideas that markets were self-correcting, which therefore believed that the fundamental role of the supervision of financial institutions, in particular banks, was to make sure that processes and procedures and systems were in place, while leaving it to the judgment of individual management to make fundamentally sensible decisions. As Alan Greenspan said, that is the intellectual framework which has received an extraordinary challenge.
>
> *Lord Turner of Ecchinswell (House of Commons*
> *Treasury Committee, 2009)*

A 'performance-based' approach therefore requires a supervisory regime capable of assessing the likelihood of firms being able to 'perform', and intervention if regulators believe (ex-ante) that firms are unlikely to meet regulators' desired outcomes. This approach also explains the prominence given by UK regulators in their supervision to the issues of firm culture and the behaviour of individuals in firms (FCA, 2018b; Suss et al., 2021).

11.6.1 Regulation and firm culture

UK regulators have for some time recognised the importance of the culture of a firm as a potential root cause of poor outcomes (Adamson, 2014). Focusing on 'culture' draws attention to how issues such as leadership, governance, purpose and values, training and rewarding staff can influence the attitudes and behaviours of staff (and vice versa) (FSA, 2007)). This, in turn, influences outcomes in the financial marketplace, and thus culture is as an indicator of the capacity, and likelihood, of firms behaving in the way expected by the regulator.

To the extent that a regulator relies on a principle-based approach, such as the 'Principles for Business' or 'Treating Customers Fairly' initiative discussed above, it is establishing the outcomes it wishes to achieve, and drawing attention to the importance of behaviours, attitudes and values in achieving those outcomes. The precise manner in which those outcomes are to be achieved; the precise nature of those attitudes, values and behaviours; and how they are embedded within a firm are to a significant degree a matter for firms themselves, but they are monitored by the regulator. In the UK, broad principles regarding behaviour are underpinned by rules and guidance within the FCA and PRA rulebooks, as well as often being further expanded upon by separate guidance or evidence of practice issued from time to time (see, for example, FSA, 2007).

This focus on culture is one way of supporting a 'performance-based' approach to regulation.

11.6.2 Regulation and individual behaviour

In the wake of problems in the UK's banking sector, in 2013 the Parliamentary Committee on Banking Standards (PCBS) recommended reinforcing the individual responsibility of the senior management of banks for the performance of their organisations (PCBS, 2013). The PCBS' recommendations resulted in the UK's Senior Managers and Certification Regime (SM&CR), which the PRA and FCA both recognise as important in supporting an appropriate culture within organisations.

11.6.2.1 SM&CR overview

The SM&CR sets out standards of conduct for all those working in financial services while making senior management in firms more responsible and accountable for their own conduct, actions and competence, and that of their staff. It places the responsibility for a firm's activities upon the most senior managers, including introducing criminal sanctions for reckless mismanagement. It has been in force for banks, building societies, credit unions and certain investment firms since March 2016 and was extended to cover all financial services firms in December 2019.

Its main provisions consist of three key pillars of obligations, and these are set out in Figure 11.6.

Senior Managers Regime

- This covers the most senior managers in a firm who have ultimate responsibility for the actions and decisions of the firm. These senior managers must be pre-approved by the regulator. Among other things, firms must produce a Statement of Responsibilities for each senior manager, clearly setting out their role and responsibilities within the firm. These statements must include specific responsibilities set out by the regulator. This enables the regulator to identify the senior manager ultimately responsible when any rule breach within the firm has happened. Senior managers may be held personally liable for any breach for which they are ultimately responsible.

Certification Regime

- This covers senior individuals who are not pre-approved by the regulator, but whose roles pose a risk of significant harm to customers, the firm or markets. These individuals must be certified as fit and proper by their firm before taking on their role, and thereafter annually or upon a significant change in their role.

Conduct Rules

- This is a set of requirements that are enforceable by the regulator and apply to all staff directly engaged in the firm's business. The standards of conduct, some of which apply to all staff and some only to senior managers, require individuals to take personal responsibility for their behaviour. There are requirements concerning reporting by firms to the regulator of breaches of the Conduct Rules.

FIGURE 11.6   The three pillars of the SM&CR regime.
Source: author's diagram.

11.7 Conclusion

The GFC drew attention not to the need for regulation, but to the effectiveness of regulation. In particular, post-GFC there has been a greater focus on the objectives of regulation, on the effectiveness of financial regulators in achieving those objectives and on the responsibilities of those working in the financial services sector to comply with both the letter and the spirit of regulatory requirements. The recognition of the need to address systemic risk post-GFC has also been reflected in the institutional practices and structures of regulation at both a national and international level, and this will likely require even greater international coordination of national regulators if such efforts are to be effective. At the same time, as discussed elsewhere in this volume, the financial services sector provides ever-increasing challenges and opportunities for consumers. As a result, the role of regulation in empowering and protecting consumers, as well as developing a market framework more likely to deliver good outcomes, is key for consumers facing those challenges and opportunities.

Of course, the implication of all of this is that, going forward, the nature of regulation and the role of regulators will also face challenges and demands. Success is likely to depend upon the skill of regulators in identifying and addressing these challenges before they become the next scandal or crisis, underscoring the importance of the issues raised in this chapter.

Self-test questions

1   Explain the importance of, and distinguish between, microprudential and macroprudential regulation.
2   What is meant by the 'regulatory perimeter'?
3   Describe the difference between ex-ante and ex-post consumer protection.

Further reading

Understanding the rationale for regulation

For an excellent analysis and critique of the economic argument for regulation, read Georgosouli, A. (2007) The debate over the economic rationale for investor protection regulation: a critical appraisal, *Journal of Financial Regulation and Compliance*, Vol. 15 No.3 pp.236–249.

Institutional structures of financial regulation

For a good analysis of the fundamental theories concerning the institutional structures of regulation, as well as discussion of the institutional structures in a range of different countries, see Huang, R.H. and Schoenmaker, D. (eds.) (2015) *Institutional Structure of Financial Regulation: Theories and international experience*. Abingdon. Routledge.

Policing the perimeter, financial scandals and regulatory supervision

For a detailed analysis of the problems that can arise due to consumer misunderstandings concerning the authorisation of firms, the suitability of their products, and the role of the regulator in policing these issues, read: Gloster, E. (2020) Report of the Independent Investigation into the Financial Conduct Authority's Regulation of London Capital & Finance plc. Available at: https://assets.publishing.service.gov.uk/government/uploads/system/uploads/attachment_data/file/945247/Gloster_Report_FINAL.pdf

The position and role of the consumer in financial services markets

For a discussion of how to deliver more effective consumer power in retail financial markets read: Lowe, J. (2017) *Consumers and competition: Delivering more effective consumer power in retail financial markets*. Financial Services Consumer Panel. London. Available at: https://www.fs-cp.org.uk/sites/default/files/fscp_consumers_and_competition_thinkpiece_finalpp_jtl_20170306.pdf

Culture in financial firms

For a series of contributions on the importance of enhancing culture in financial services firms, see: FCA (2018) Transforming Culture in Financial Services. Discussion Paper DP18/2. March 2018. London. FCA. Available at: https://www.fca.org.uk/publication/discussion/dp18-02.pdf

Useful websites

FCA Handbook: https://www.handbook.fca.org.uk/
Financial Ombudsman Service: https://www.financial-ombudsman.org.uk/
Financial Services Compensation Scheme: https://www.fscs.org.uk/
Financial Services Register: https://register.fca.org.uk/s/
Financial Stability Board: https://www.fsb.org/
Money and Pensions Service: https://www.maps.org.uk
PRA Rulebook: https://www.prarulebook.co.uk/

References

Adamson, C. (2014) *FCA one year on – effective regulation goes hand-in-hand with sustainable businesses*. Speech at the Building Societies Association, 14 May 2014. Available at: https://www.fca.org.uk/news/speeches/fca-one-year-%E2%80%93-effective-regulation-goes-hand-hand-sustainable-businesses (Accessed 8 May, 2021)

Armour, J, Awrey, D., Davies, P., Enriques, L., Gordon, J.N., Mayer, C. and Payne, J. (2016) *Principles of financial regulation*. Oxford, OUP.

Austin, A. (2021) FCA tells providers to book Pension Wise sessions for savers. *FT Adviser*, 4 May 2021. Available at: https://www.ftadviser.com/pensions/2021/05/04/fca-tells-providers-to-book-pension-wise-sessions-for-savers/ (Accessed 8 May, 2021)

Baker McKenzie (2017) *Global financial services regulatory guide*. Available at: https://globalfsrguide.bakermckenzie.com/global-financial-services-regulatory-guide (Accessed 4 May, 2021)

BDO (2020) *Number of 'Dear CEO'-style warning letters issued by the FCA and PRA hits new high.* Available at: https://www.bdo.co.uk/en-gb/news/2020/number-of-dear-ceo-style-warning-letters-issued-by-the-fca-and-pra-hits-new-high (Accessed 4 May, 2021)

Benston, G.J. (1998) *Regulating financial markets: A critique and some proposals,* Hobart Paper 135, London, The Institute of Economic Affairs.

BIS (Bank for International Settlements) (2021) *The basel committee – Overview.* Available at: https://www.bis.org/bcbs/ (Accessed 2 May, 2021)

Briault. C. (1999) *The rationale for a single financial services regulator.* London: Financial Servcies Authority

Brunnermeier, M., Crockett, A., Goodhart. C., Persaud, A. and Shin, H. (2009) *The fundamental principles of financial regulation,* Geneva Reports on the World Economy 11. Available at: https://cepr.org/sites/default/files/geneva_reports/GenevaP197.pdf (Accessed 3 May, 2021)

DWP (Department of Work and Pensions) (2020) *Automatic enrolment evaluation report 2019.* Available at: https://assets.publishing.service.gov.uk/government/uploads/system/uploads/attachment_data/file/883289/automatic-enrolment-evaluation-report-2019.pdf (Accessed 28 April, 2021)

ECB (European Central Bank) (2014) *Financial stability review May 2014.* Available at: https://www.ecb.europa.eu/pub/pdf/fsr/financialstabilityreview201405en.pdf (Accessed 3 May, 2021)

European Commission (2021) *Risk management and supervision of insurance companies (Solvency 2).* Available at: https://ec.europa.eu/info/business-economy-euro/banking-and-finance/insurance-and-pensions/risk-management-and-supervision-insurance-companies-solvency-2_en (Accessed 4 May, 2021)

FCA (Financial Conduct Authority) (2018a) *FCA mission: Approach to authorisation.* Available at: https://www.fca.org.uk/publication/corporate/our-approach-authorisation-final-report-feedback-statement.pdf (Accessed 10 May, 2021)

FCA (Financial Conduct Authority) (2018b) *FCA mission: Approach to consumers.* Available at: https://www.fca.org.uk/publication/corporate/approach-to-consumers.pdf (accessed 30 April, 2021)

FCA (Financial Conduct Authority) (2019a) *FCA mission: Approach to supervision.* Available at: https://www.fca.org.uk/publication/corporate/our-approach-supervision-final-report-feedback-statement.pdf (Accessed 1 May, 2021)

FCA (Financial Conduct Authority) (2019b) *FCA mission: Approach to enforcement.* Available at: https://www.fca.org.uk/publication/corporate/our-approach-enforcement-final-report-feedback-statement.pdf (Accessed 3 May, 2021)

FCA (Financial Conduct Authority) (2020) *Perimeter Report 2019/20.* Available at: https://www.fca.org.uk/publication/annual-reports/perimeter-report-2019-20.pdf (Accessed 28 April, 2021)

FCA (Financial Conduct Authority) (2021a) *Handbook Chapter 2: The threshold conditions.* Available at: https://www.handbook.fca.org.uk/handbook/COND/2.pdf (Accessed 8 May, 2021)

FCA (Financial Conduct Authority) (2021b) *A new consumer duty.* Consultation Paper CP21/13. May 2021. Available at: https://www.fca.org.uk/publication/consultation/cp21-13.pdf (Accessed 15 May, 2021)

FCA (Financial Conduct Authority) (2021c) *Fair treatment of customers.* Available at: https://www.fca.org.uk/firms/fair-treatment-customers (Accessed 1 May, 2021)

FSA (Financial Services Authority) (2004). *Treating customers fairly – Towards fair outcomes for consumers.* Available at: https://www.fca.org.uk/publication/archive/fsa-tcf-towards. pdf (Accessed 2, May 2021)

FSA (Financial Services Authority) (2007) *Treating customers fairly – culture.* Available at: https://www.fca.org.uk/publication/archive/fsa-tcf-culture.pdf (Accessed 24 April, 2021)

FSA (Financial Services Authority) (2009) *The turner review: A regulatory response to the global banking crisis,* March 2009, London, Financial Services Authority.

FSB (Financial Stability Board) (2014) *Key attributes of effective resolution regimes for financial institutions.* Available at: http://www.financialstabilityboard.org/2014/10/r_141015/ (Accessed 1 May, 2021)

FSCS (Financial Services Compensation Scheme) (2017) *FSCS protection has more than doubled since the financial crisis.* 14 September, 2017. Available at: https://www.fscs.org. uk/news/protection/protection-doubled-since-crash/ (Accessed 7 May, 2021)

FSCS (Financial Services Compensation Scheme) (2021) *Our mission and strategy.* Available at: https://www.fscs.org.uk/about-us/mission-and-strategy/ (Accessed 8 May, 2021)

Georgosouli, A. (2007) The debate over the economic rationale for investor protection regulation: a critical appraisal, *Journal of Financial Regulation and Compliance,* Vol. 15 No.3 pp.236–249.

GLI (2021) Banking Regulation 2021: China. Available at: https://www.globallegal-insights.com/practice-areas/banking-and-finance-laws-and-regulations/china (Accessed 1 May, 2021)

Godwin, A. (2017) Introduction to special issue – the twin peaks model of financial regulation and reform in South Africa. *Law and Financial Markets Review,* Vol. 11 No.4 pp.151–153.

Goodhart, C., Hartmann, P., Llewellyn, D., Rojas-Suarez, L. and Weisbrod, S. (1998). *Financial regulation: Why, how and where now?* London, Routledge.

Herring, R.J. and Carmassi, J. (2008) The structure of cross-sector financial supervision, *Financial Markets, Institutions and Instruments,* Vol. 17 No.1 pp.51–76.

House of Commons Treasury Committee (2009) *Banking Crisis: Volume I – Oral evidence.* London. TSO. Available at: https://publications.parliament.uk/pa/cm200809/ cmselect/cmtreasy/144/144i.pdf (Accessed 30 April, 2021) (Contains Parliamentary information licensed under the Open Parliament Licence v3.0. – see https://www. parliament.uk/site-information/copyright-parliament/open-parliament-licence/)

Huang, R.H. and Schoenmaker, D. (eds.) (2015) *Institutional Structure of Financial Regulation: Theories and international experience.* Abingdon. Routledge.

Llewellyn, D. (1999). *The economic rationale for financial regulation.* London, Financial Services Authority. Available at: https://www.fep.up.pt/disciplinas/pgaf924/PGAF/ Texto_2_David_Llewellyn.pdf (Accessed 18 May, 2021)

Lowe, J. (2017) *Consumers and competition: Delivering more effective consumer power in retail financial markets.* Financial Services Consumer Panel. London. Available at: https:// www.fs-cp.org.uk/sites/default/files/fscp_consumers_and_competition_think-piece_finalpp_jtl_20170306.pdf (Accessed 1 May, 2021)

MaPS (Money and Pensions Service) (2020) *The UK strategy for financial wellbeing: 2020–2030.* Available at: https://moneyandpensionsservice.org.uk/wp-content/ uploads/2020/01/UK-Strategy-for-Financial-Wellbeing-2020-2030-Money-and-Pensions-Service.pdf (Accessed 8 May, 2021)

Mortimer, R. (2020) FCA will not 'stop firms from failing'. *FT Adviser*, 10 November, 2020. Available at: https://www.ftadviser.com/regulation/2020/11/10/fca-will-not-stop-firms-from-failing/ (Accessed 29 March, 2021)

PCBS (2013) *Changing banking for good. Report of the Parliamentary Commission on Banking Standards. Volume I: Summary, and Conclusions and Recommendations.* Available at: https://publications.parliament.uk/pa/jt201314/jtselect/jtpcbs/27/27.pdf (Accessed 24 April, 2021)

PRA (Prudential Regulation Authority) (2018) *The prudential regulation authority's approach to banking supervision.* Available at: https://www.bankofengland.co.uk/-/media/boe/files/prudential-regulation/approach/banking-approach-2018.pdf (Accessed 1 May, 2021)

Rovnick, N. and Parker, G. (2016) 'Unfit' money advice service to be scrapped in Budget. *Financial Times.* March 16 2016. Available at: https://www.ft.com/content/604c11bc-eaef-11e5-888e-2eadd5fbc4a4 (Accessed 8 May, 2021)

Schmulow, A. (2015) *Twin peaks: A theoretical analysis.* CIFR Paper No. WP064/2015. Available at SSRN: https://ssrn.com/abstract=2625331 (Accessed 3 May, 2021)

Steward, M. (2021) *The rise in scams and the threat to a legitimate financial services industry.* Speech delivered 18th May 2021 at the City & Financial Global – FCA Investigations & Enforcement Summit. Available at: https://www.fca.org.uk/news/speeches/rise-scams-and-threat-legitimate-financial-services-industry (Accessed 22 May, 2021)

Suss, J., Bholat, D., Gillespie, A. and Reader, T. (2021) *Organisational culture and bank risk.* Bank of England Staff Working Paper No. 912. March 2021. Available at: https://www.bankofengland.co.uk/-/media/boe/files/working-paper/2021/organisational-culture-and-bank-risk.pdf?la=en&hash=81DD3E865BC0159475F-D10A78AA2293F0379FB8E (Accessed 14 May, 2021)

Thaler, R. and Sunstein, C. (2008) *Nudge: Improving decisions about health, wealth, and happiness.* New Haven: Yale University Press.

12

RISK AND FINANCIAL SERVICES

Patrick John Ring and Gbenga Adamolekun

Key points summary

- Risk is inherent in the business of financial services and creates risk management challenges for both consumers and the financial services industry.
- Lack of financial awareness or capability can leave consumers particularly vulnerable in managing their financial well-being.
- Governments, regulators and financial services firms can use the lessons of behavioural finance to mitigate the risks consumers face and produce better outcomes.
- The risk management systems and the risk culture of financial services firms and their staff are crucial in ensuring positive outcomes for those organisations, their customers and the wider economy.

12.1 Introduction

While we may not think of it in these terms, we all take risks every day – whether it be crossing the road, getting on a train or climbing a set of ladders. Research even tells us that sitting down all day (at a desk or on a couch) can have risks for our health (NHS, 2021). Yet, when it comes to our finances, we seem to be much more aware of the risks we face – whether it is losing or gaining money on an investment, becoming the victim of fraud in a financial scam, wondering whether we have enough money to cope with unforeseen events or coping with price rises in the face of changes in the economy. In managing our money, the financial services sector also has to cope with a whole range of risks, including

DOI: 10.4324/9781003227663-12

investment risks, borrowers not repaying their lending and economic turmoil. If it does not do so successfully, then this can create further problems for financial consumers.

This chapter focuses on the risks faced by retail financial services consumers, and how those consumers can, or can be helped to, manage those risks. It also looks at some of the main risks financial institutions face, and the implications if those risks are not managed properly. The discussion begins by looking at what is meant by 'risk' and why it is such a significant issue in financial services. Thereafter, some of the most common risks faced by financial services consumers are examined, as well as how such risks can be mitigated through financial capability and applying the lessons of behavioural finance. There follows a discussion of the relationship between risk and consumer trust in the financial firms they deal with, before consideration is given to how financial firms manage risks and the importance of risk management and risk culture. While the examples used to illustrate the issues discussed in this chapter relate primarily to the UK, the issues discussed in this chapter can be applied to the experience of consumers and financial services firms across the world.

Learning Outcomes

After reading this chapter you should be able to:

- Discuss the importance of risk and risk management for financial services.
- Describe and explain key risks facing financial services consumers and institutions.
- Discuss the contribution of financial capability and behavioural finance, including trust, in mitigating the risks faced by financial services consumers.
- Explain the importance of risk management systems and risk culture for financial services institutions.

12.2 Risk and its importance in the financial services sector

While there is much academic debate about what exactly is meant when we refer to the concept of 'risk', in the context of financial services it is generally understood to refer to the possibility of the outcome of an event, decision or course of action that deviates from what was expected (Lupton, 1999). For consumers, this might include the possibility of advice received not resulting in the expected tax savings, investments not securing anticipated returns or an insurance policy not providing the cover expected or desired. For a provider of financial services, it could include the risk of giving the wrong advice, suffering an IT disruption that hampers its business or employee fraud resulting in huge losses for the business. Crucially, while risks clearly exist in all areas of business and life, the very nature of financial services and their importance to our well-being means that the notion of risk plays a much more significant role in the financial services sector than in many other areas of business and consumer life.

12.2.1 Risk and the nature of financial services

It is argued that the nature of financial services products creates a unique set of risks for consumers. They are both intangible and technically sophisticated, making them complex and difficult to understand and compare, particularly when that purchase or investment is relatively infrequent, making it difficult to build up knowledge. This is compounded by the rate of change and innovation in financial markets. It also is argued that some, if not all, financial services products are 'credence' goods, meaning it is difficult to verify their quality or value at the time of purchase, and given the generally long-term nature of investments, it may be a long time before a consumer becomes aware of the real value of, or any faults or problems with, that investment. As a result, and given the complexity of financial products, consumers often rely for information on which to base their decision upon the very firms providing them with, and making profit from, those financial products. This 'asymmetric information' between the consumer and financial services firms creates the possibility for consumers to, at worst, be misled, or at least potentially make a poor decision (Lumpkin, 2010).

Of course, it may be suggested that lack of information, the possibility of being misled, infrequent purchases, lack of transparency and lack of a guarantee, all attributes linked with financial services products, are also attributes that could be applied to other goods and services. It is argued, however, that 'the uniqueness of some financial products, services and contracts is that they combine all or a large number of these characteristics' (Llewellyn, 1999:39). Additionally, in instances such as pension investments and other savings, insurance policies, mortgages and other borrowing, the decisions and investments made can have life-changing impacts on the well-being of individuals and their families. Managing these risks is therefore key for financial services consumers.

Turning to financial services firms, the essential business of banks, investment funds and insurance companies is about taking and managing risk. That is how they generate profits. For commercial banks, this may be accepting deposits or borrowing from other sources with a view to lending or investing that money to earn returns (see Chapter 3). Pension funds will be concerned with the risk of not delivering returns for investors, and in particular any guaranteed or predicted levels of return. Insurance companies underwrite the risks covered by their insurance policies in return for premiums from the insured, which are then invested as a means of generating returns in excess of payouts made in relation to the risks underwritten. For advisers and other providers of ancillary services to financial consumers, their role will be to give advice or otherwise make a judgement on how to manage financial risks in order to achieve the best outcomes for their clients or customers.

It is therefore no surprise that risk management is a fundamental part of the business of financial services firms (Hull, 2018), and this is reflected in the requirements of financial regulators (see Chapter 11). The Great Financial Crisis (GFC) of 2007–2008 illustrated the implications for the well-being of consumers, and ultimately for economies, if those risks are not managed properly.

12.3 Financial consumers and risk

There are a number of commonly identified risks that consumers face in managing their finances, and these are set out in Table 12.1.

TABLE 12.1 Common risks faced by financial services consumers

Risk faced by consumer	Explanation
Default risk	This is the risk of financial providers failing and consumers potentially losing some or all of their investment as a result.
Investment risk	Also known as 'market risk' or 'performance risk', this is the risk that investment markets will not provide the returns expected. This may arise due to a variety of market and economic conditions which are difficult to predict.
Bad faith risk	This is the risk that fraud, mis-selling or other misconduct of a financial provider or adviser will result in financial harm for consumers.
Mis-buying risk	This is the risk that consumers will make suboptimal choices as a result of the complexity of products, being poorly informed or insufficiently literate in relation to financial matters. For example, poor value for money could take the form of paying abnormally high investment management fees while receiving no better returns than average funds. This could be due to the complexity of fee structures or the problems in finding and/or comparing fee structures across different funds.

Two high-profile UK examples of default risk, that illustrate the problems that can arise for consumers where firms get into financial difficulties, are the collapse of the Equitable Life insurance company as a result of financial mismanagement (Penrose, 2004) and the failure of Northern Rock in the wake of the GFC (House of Commons Treasury Committee, 2008).

The possibility of bad faith risk arising from a combination of imbalances of information between parties, and the lack of awareness leading to consumers relying upon financial providers and advisers, has also led to some high-profile, industry-wide problems of mis-selling (see Box 12.1)

BOX 12.1 FINANCIAL PRODUCTS: MIS-SELLING AND RISK

Between 2011 and 2019 a total of £38.3 billion was paid out in compensation by financial services firms as a result of customer complaints about the way they were sold payment protection insurance (PPI) (FCA, 2021a). PPI is insurance usually sold alongside products that required repayments to be made, such as car loans or mortgages. The insurance is designed to meet the repayments in circumstances where the insured cannot, for example, in the event of redundancy, accident or illness. These policies were aggressively sold because of their profitability and were often portrayed as being 'essential' (although they were not) in relation to the loan for which they were providing cover. It transpired that the insurance policies were very expensive and often did not provide any, or adequate, cover to those to whom they were sold. Ironically, this illustrates the potential risk to consumers of a product that, in theory, should reduce their exposure to financial risks.

12.4 The vulnerability of financial services consumers

The Financial Conduct Authority's (FCA) Financial Lives Survey research (FCA, 2021b), and in particular the work it has done to understand the vulnerability of financial services consumers, underlines the potential for the risks discussed to result in harm to consumers. For example, research in 2012 found that one in seven adults has literacy skills expected of child aged 11 and that more than half of adults do not have the numeracy skills expected of an 11-year-old (Department for Business, Innovation and Skills, 2012). The FCA's research has also highlighted how old age, mental illness, long-term physical illness, caring responsibilities and disabilities can all compound the risks for consumers when managing their finances (FCA 2017). One example of this is the rise in financial

---

BOX 12.2 'PACKAGED' BANK ACCOUNTS

'Packaged' bank accounts were designed, in return for a monthly fee, to provide a package of services or features such as travel insurance, vouchers or discounts, or additional service features, alongside the bank account itself. In the UK, bank staff were often incentivised to push these accounts, whose charges could range from £5 to £25 per month, rather than normal no-fee current accounts. While these packaged accounts were suitable for many customers, by 2013 it had become apparent that, for some account holders, the insurance or other services were unsuitable, or the customer already had similar products. The regulator required providers of such products to check the suitability of these add-ons, although on reviewing these checks the regulator found that where customers complained that their account was mis-sold, the organisations complained to had only achieved a fair outcome in 44% of cases (FCA, 2016).

scams (see Chapter 10), to which the vulnerable are particularly susceptible (Holkar and Lees, 2020).

Lowe (2017) also highlights the risk of firms taking advantage of these circumstances to exert their 'market power' over consumers. One example of this is 'price obfuscation', where complex charging structures with multiple ancillary extra charges, alongside difficulty in obtaining information to make price comparisons, mean consumers may overlook or be unaware of the true cost of a product and have difficulty shopping around (see, for example, FCA, 2019). Another instance is the use of 'product bundling and add-ons', where different products or services are combined and presented as a single proposition. This can also lead to price obfuscation, concealing the true price of each element of the proposition and enabling a higher price to be charged; this has resulted in high-profile instances of consumers purchasing inappropriate products (see Box 12.2).

12.5 Consumers managing risk – capability and behaviour

The UK's 2020 strategy for financial well-being found that 22 million people say they don't know enough to plan for retirement and that 5.3 million children do not get a meaningful financial education (MaPS, 2020). The FCA's Financial Lives Survey (FCA, 2017:134) also noted that:

> One in six (17%) UK adults deem their own financial capability as particularly low. Some rate their confidence in managing money or knowledge about financial matters as 0–3 out of 10.

This is consistent with previous research (Clery et al., 2010; Macleod et al., 2012; Wicks and Horack, 2009). At the same time, research in 2018 found that over 60% of consumers thought that managing personal finances had become more difficult in the previous decade (Resolution Foundation, 2018).

As regards the young, the 2020 strategy identified the need to target parents and teachers with better resources, support and, in the case of teachers, training, and to deliver scalable solutions to enhance the awareness and capabilities of young people and create 'financial foundations' for their adult lives (MaPS, 2020:14–17).

Outside of the sphere of formal education, much of the UK government's efforts to enhance the capability of consumers to manage their finances have focused on the delivery of information and guidance through 'MoneyHelper', the brand name of the Money and Pensions Service (see Chapter 11). This is a service that is free to consumers and aims to ensure they have access to the guidance and information they need to make effective financial decisions over their lifetime.

Many consumers also use commercially available consumer comparison websites. A review of these sites in the UK (Resolution Foundation, 2018:39) concluded that their use:

> can substantially reduce the risk of people buying inappropriate, poor quality or overpriced financial products – potentially saving them a great deal

of money. More generally, using comparison sites can increase a consumer's understanding of, and confidence in, dealing with the financial services market, and therefore help increase the population's levels of financial capability.

Nevertheless, the same review also found that, generally, these sites were opaque in providing information about their commercial relationships, making it difficult to establish how some sites generated their income and how this was reflected on their sites. It also found that comparison tables needed to provide more explanation of technical terms and abbreviations and that more could be done to provide personalised information based on the circumstances of the individuals using the sites.

12.5.1 Managing risks for consumers – the contribution of behavioural finance

The discussion in the previous section assumes a position adopted in classical economics – that individuals act in a completely rational and self-interested way; so in a situation where someone does not understand a financial product or does not have relevant information, they will learn about the product or seek out that information and then make a calculated decision, taking account of all of the risks, to maximise their financial outcome. Yet research in behavioural finance has shown that this is an inaccurate portrayal of what happens, and in practice financial consumers often act in ways inconsistent with such a 'rational' approach (Dixon, 2006; Elliott et al., 2011). Based on applying psychology to the realm of economics, this perspective focuses on the mindset of individuals, looking at how they 'weigh up' alternatives, and the automatic thought processes ('rules of thumb'), habits and routines they adopt that result in what might be considered 'suboptimal' outcomes (Kahneman and Tversky, 1979). Elliott et al. (2011) identify at least 13 different ways in which these human 'biases' affect behaviour, but also discuss how these biases can be enlisted and used to help achieve better outcomes for consumers. Insights illustrating how this approach can be applied to address risks faced by consumers are set out in Table 12.2. This approach has influenced the strategy of the UK's financial regulators towards safeguarding consumer interests (FCA, 2013).

12.6 Risks to consumers and the relevance of trust

Trust is a key element for economic exchange; it is not by chance that the word "credit" comes from the Latin word 'to believe' or to 'to trust' (Sapienza et al., 2013).

Luhmann (1979) suggests that trust can be regarded as a mechanism for providing some level of certainty or security. It can provide us with confidence in relying upon others when making decisions in the present moment that will affect our (uncertain) future. Making financial plans and investment decisions

TABLE 12.2 Insights from behavioural finance

Insight	Prospect theory (also known as loss aversion)	Over-extrapolation
Basic explanation	• Evidence shows individuals value gains and losses differently, giving around twice as much weight to a potential loss compared to the same amount of a potential gain.	• Investors may make their predictions based on limited evidence or over a limited time period, taking the view that this evidence is an accurate representation of real patterns or trends.
Implications for behaviour	• Investors may be more reluctant to invest in the stock market due to the risk of loss, and thereby hold a less diversified portfolio of assets as well as lose out on the returns stocks and shares can provide.	• Investors may underestimate risk, i.e. the degree to which eventual returns may vary from their expectations, and take more risk than they can afford. • Investors may mistake initial investment gains as evidence of longer-term trends
Strategies using this insight	• Present investment options in terms of the risk of 'loss' through missing out on investment returns offered by stock market compared to other asset classes. • Place the assets of the investor in a 'default' fund managed by an experienced investment manager rather than forcing the individual investor to choose the fund or specific investments.	• Regulate the nature and timing of the information that is given to investors, e.g. in relation to past performance, and provide it in a way that is easy to understand.

draws our attention to the complex and uncertain future consequences and outcomes of our decisions in the present. As a result, one way in which financial consumers can manage these risks is to place their trust in financial product providers and advisers who they believe are better able to anticipate and manage those risks.

Trust is regarded by behavioural finance as a 'mental short cut' for making decisions (Dixon, 2006); so the question then arises about the grounds for, and therefore the appropriateness of, placing trust in a financial services provider. By placing trust in another person or institution, a consumer is relying on that other party to have their best interests at heart and deliver what they have promised. In some areas of law in the UK, such as trust law, this kind of obligation is formalised in a binding legal, or fiduciary, duty of care that trustees have in relation to the beneficiaries of a trust. In other areas of financial services there may be a regulatory duty to act in the interests of consumers, although this is not necessarily equivalent to a legal fiduciary duty (FCA, 2021c). The definition and extent of any fiduciary laws can vary from country to country (Sullivan et al., 2015).

Given the above, it is no surprise that gaining consumer trust is a key issue for financial services professionals (CII, 2018). Yet in the wake of the GFC, and other highly publicised scandals in various financial markets, trust has been a difficult issue for the financial services industry (Instinctif Partners, 2020). Research in 2021 suggests that, worldwide, trust in the sector is in decline after recovering somewhat in the wake of the GFC (Edelman, 2021), although, as Table 12.3 indicates, the position is not uniform across countries or financial sectors.

Nevertheless, if consumers are to be able to trust financial services institutions, then, among other things, this means those institutions need to be able to manage the risks that they face in delivering products and services to consumers. We now turn to examine some of the main risks they face and how they deal with them.

12.7 Financial institutions and managing risk

Financial institutions are exposed to various risks while in the business of meeting the needs of their clients. These risks can emanate from within the firm (e.g. employee fraud or IT failure) or outside of the firm (a downturn in economic conditions or a natural disaster). While internal risks can be addressed by effective risk management and governance (see Section 12.8), some external risks are unavoidable, and, at most, firms can attempt to mitigate them, for example, hold financial reserves to absorb losses (in the event of an economic downturn) or make business continuity plans to attempt to mitigate their effects (in the event of a natural disaster).

TABLE 12.3 Percentage trust in financial services sectors in 2021

Country Sector	USA	UK	Singapore	Global average
Banks	64	53	64	57
Personal Insurance	60	44	68	57
Credit Cards	59	50	60	56
Property and Casualty Insurance	54	42	58	54
Financial advisory/Asset management	52	37	57	50
Digital payments	49	39	62	58
Digital wealth management/ robo-advisory	38	24	53	42
Cryptocurrency	34	21	45	40

Source: Data taken from Edelman, 2021.

12.7.1 Operational risk

Operational risk is the risk that loss may arise as a result of the weakness of a firm's internal risk management and governance. The Basel Committee on Banking Supervision (2005) defines operational risk as the risk of loss resulting from inadequate or failed internal processes, people and systems or from external events. This may be a loss because of a firm's operating equipment, software and systems (for example where bank IT systems fail (Morrison, 2019)) or from people errors or behaviour (Jarrow, 2008). It also includes cyber risk. For an assessment of operational risk in the financial services sector, see Aldasoro et al. (2020).

Operational risks often arise due to human errors or misjudgements. This focus on people risk draws attention to the issue of conduct risk that has been at the forefront of the UK's regulatory efforts (see Chapter 11). Conduct risk was born out of the need for sound internal risk management. The consequences of operational risk can be significant, as illustrated by mis-selling scandals such as the PPI scandal discussed in Box 12.2. For a fuller discussion of the PPI case and its implications for operational risk management, see Laris (2020).

12.7.2 Market risk

Market risk refers to the probability of loss as a result of unexpected movement in prices of financial assets. This includes movement in the prices of equities, bonds, currencies, commodities, interest and exchange rates, and derivatives. As banks and other financial institutions trade in such assets and markets, they become exposed to potential losses. This may result in the institution being unable to fulfil its contractual obligations to clients, and ultimately to its demise. As a result, appropriate risk management systems are required to control the amount of risk taken, as well as to maintain sufficient capital to absorb any losses incurred. Market risk can be measured using Value at Risk (VaR), which is a statistical measure of the volatility (expected possible losses/gains) of a portfolio of assets over a given time horizon (Casu et al., 2015).

12.7.3 Credit risk

Credit risk refers to the probability of loss as a result of the failure of a borrower or other counterparty to a contract to repay the contractual debt or sum otherwise due. The most common example of credit risk is bank lending, where the bank makes profit through the repayment of the capital plus interest, but faces the risk that the borrower may be unable to repay the sum borrowed. The management of that kind of credit risk may include an assessment of the risk of each borrower, as well as placing limits on the amount of lending to individual persons, industries or countries as a means of diversifying the risk. The problems that can arise as a result of the mismanagement of credit risk were illustrated in the issues faced by HBOS bank in the UK during the GFC, where a key contributor to its failure was the mismanagement of credit risk (Bank of England, 2015).

12.7.4 Liquidity risk

Liquidity risk refers to the problems arising when an institution is unable to meet liabilities because of a mismatch between the maturity of its assets and its liabilities. This is an inherent risk for banks who take on short-term liabilities (deposits) but have assets (loans and investments) that are often much longer term. This risk is dealt with through asset and liability management (ALM), an approach designed to ensure enough liquid assets are always available to meet liabilities as they fall due. Financial difficulties can arise when firms cannot liquidate their financial assets to meet their liabilities, or have to do so at below market value, resulting in losses that can threaten the financial position of the firm (Sheng, 1999). For an example of the problems that can arise, see Upton's (2007) analysis of the collapse of Northern Rock bank.

12.8 Importance of risk management in financial institutions

Given the significance of trust for the relationship between consumers and financial services providers, it is essential that financial institutions are able to manage and mitigate the risks they take when seeking to achieve the outcomes expected by their customers. That is why the regulation of financial services places such a strong emphasis on the management of risk (BIS, 2021). The FCA's third Principle for Business states: 'A firm must take reasonable care to organise and control its affairs responsibly and effectively, with adequate risk management systems' (FCA Handbook PRIN2.1.1).

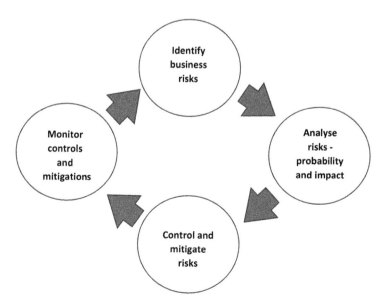

FIGURE 12.1   Risk management cycle.

Generally speaking, risk management systems will tend to follow the kind of risk management cycle set out in Figure 12.1. This requires an appropriate internal risk management framework – the processes and structures installed by an organisation to address the consequences arising from risk exposures. Such a framework provides a coherent set of guidelines to ensure appropriate action is taken to prevent or mitigate negative risk outcomes for the organisation, as well as enabling the organisation to exploit risks (i.e. opportunities) to achieve positive outcomes for itself and its customers. There is an increasing tendency for organisations to adopt an 'enterprise risk management' (ERM) approach, which not only captures all of the risks across an organisation but also seeks to understand their interdependencies and the potential effects of risk in one part of an organisation for other areas of the business, as well as the organisation as a whole (COSO, 2017). This is also likely to involve an assessment of 'risk appetite', that is, the amount of risk an organisation is willing to take and believes it can manage in pursuit of its strategic objectives (Financial Stability Board, 2013; Martens and Rittenberg, 2020).

12.8.1 Building a sound risk culture

To be effective and to ensure that it is not just a paper-based box-ticking exercise, an internal risk management structure needs to be complemented by a sound risk culture (Ring et al., 2016). Risk culture is a subcategory of an organisation's culture. The FCA (2021d) suggests that an organisational culture is represented by the 'habitual behaviours and mindsets that characterise an organisation'. Accordingly, risk culture is often regarded as being identified by how the personnel of a firm talk, act, think or approach the issue of risk in their daily business activities, and how senior management characterise an organisation's perception of, and response to, risk. Essentially, it indicates how well responsibility for an organisation's risk management policy has been integrated into its day-to-day practice. An appropriate and embedded risk culture should help ensure that the products and services offered by a business are suitable for their clients, and that it does not expose those clients, the business itself or the wider financial system to undue risk.

12.9 Future challenges

The increasingly fast-paced developments in the embedding of technology in financial services discussed in Chapter 7 affect the landscape of risks and risk management. They offer better access to financial products and can be used to enhance the risk assessment judgements of consumers and financial firms. At the same time, data privacy issues, cybercrime and the increasing challenge of managing the operational assurance of delivery systems in the face of the complexity and ubiquity of technology present risk management challenges (Carletti et al., 2020).

Perhaps the other most significant challenge for risk management in the financial services arena is 'sustainable finance', that is:

the integration of environmental, social and governance (ESG) factors in the DNA of a financial institution, from strategy to investment and credit decisions to risk management all the way to external reporting.

(PwC, 2021)

It is becoming increasingly apparent that the well-being of the world's population, including its financial well-being, is dependent on how we address global issues such as climate change and social justice. This has become apparent in the financial services sector with an increasing emphasis on sustainable finance, which requires firms to consider the impact that these global risks can have on their financial decisions, and likewise the impact that their financial decisions can have on these global risks.

12.10 Conclusion

A financial services environment in which the risks inherent in finance are managed effectively is likely to produce good outcomes for consumers, financial services providers and the economic and social health of a nation. That means the management of risk is a key issue for financial consumers, financial services firms, regulators and the government. It is clear that financial awareness and capability is key if consumers are going to be able to better manage the risks they face in seeking financial security and the well-being of themselves and their families. Evidence also indicates that an informed public is more likely to place their trust in the financial services sector (Edelman, 2021).

At the same time, the institutions that make up the financial services industry must ensure they have appropriate risk management frameworks, underpinned by suitable attitudes and behaviours, that will ensure they adequately manage risks on behalf of their customers and investors. In a global environment encompassing an array of complex social, health and climate issues, the landscape is only likely to become more challenging. Investors are increasingly demanding that their money be used for environmentally and socially purposeful activities, and environmental, social and governance (ESG) will be a source of significant continuing risk for the financial sector (Bellens and Santenac, 2021).

Self-test questions

1   Explain why consumers can be said to be vulnerable to financial risks and what those risks might be.
2   Explain the role that trust can play in helping consumers manage financial risks.
3   Distinguish between credit risk, market risk, liquidity risk and operational risk.

Further reading

Financial consumers

To gain a real insight about UK financial consumers and the potential vulnerabilities in their financial lives, read FCA (2020) Financial Lives 2020 survey: the impact of coronavirus. Available at: https://www.fca.org.uk/publications/research/financial-lives-2020-survey-impact-coronavirus

Behavioural finance

For a useful discussion of the application of behavioural finance to issues in financial services, read Chuah and Devlin (2010) Behavioural Economics and the Financial Services Consumer: A Review. Financial Services Research Forum. Nottingham University Business School. Available at: https://www.nottingham.ac.uk/business/businesscentres/gcbfi/documents/researchreports/paper69.pdf

Risk management

For an outline discussion of Enterprise Risk Management, read CIMA (2008) Enterprise Risk Management Topic Gateway Series No. 49. Available at: https://www.cimaglobal.com/Documents/ImportedDocuments/cid_tg_enterprise_risk_management_jul08.pdf.pdf
To find out more about risk culture, look at IRM (2012) Risk culture Under the Microscope: Guidance for Board. Available at: https://www.theirm.org/media/8447/risk_culture_a5_web15_oct_2012-executive-summary.pdf

References

Aldasoro, I., Gambacorta, L., Giudici, P. and Leach, T. (2020) *Operational and cyber risks in the financial sector*. BIS Working Papers No 840. Available at: https://www.bis.org/publ/work840.htm (Accessed 15th February, 2021)
Bank of England (2015) *The failure of HBOS plc (HBOS)*. A report by the Financial Conduct Authority (FCA) and the Prudential Regulation Authority (PRA). Available at: https://www.bankofengland.co.uk/-/media/boe/files/prudential-regulation/publication/hbos-complete-report (Accessed 17th June, 2021)
Basel Committee on Banking Supervision (2005) *International convergence of capital measurement and capital standards: A revised framework*. Basel, Bank for International Settlements.
Bellens, J. and Santenac, I. (2021) *How to navigate the increasingly important and complex ESG agenda,* EY. Available at: https://www.ey.com/en_gl/financial-services/how-to-navigate-the-increasingly-important-complex-esg-agenda (Accessed 19th June, 2021)
BIS (Bank for International Settlements) (2021) *Basel III: international regulatory framework for banks*. Available at: https://www.bis.org/bcbs/basel3.htm (Accessed 18th June, 2021)
Carletti, E., Claessens, S., Fatás, A. and Vives, X. (2020) *The bank business model in the post-Covid-19 world*. The Future of Banking 2. London. Centre for Economic Policy Research.
Casu, B., Girardone, C. and Molyneux, P. (2015) *Introduction to banking* (2nd Ed.) Harlow: Financial Times Prentice Hall.

CII (Chartered Insurance Institute) (2018) *Public trust in insurance: The challenge.* London. CII. Available at: https://www.cii.co.uk/media/9224356/trust-in-insurance_the-challenge_liz-barclay_final.pdf (Accessed 18th June, 2021)

Clery, E., Humphrey, A., and Bourne, T. (2010) Attitudes to pensions: The 2009 survey, Research Report No. 701, London, Department of Work and Pensions.

COSO (Committee of Sponsoring Organizations of the Treadway Commission) (2017), *Enterprise risk management: integrating with strategy and performance,* Committee of Sponsoring Organisations of the Treadway Commission, Available at https://www.coso.org/Pages/erm.aspx (Accessed 19th January, 2020).

Department for Business, Innovation and Skills (2012) *The 2011 skills for life survey: a survey of literacy, numeracy and ICT levels in England.* BIS RESEARCH PAPER NUMBER 81. December 2012

Dixon, M. (2006) *Rethinking financial capability: lessons from economic psychology and behavioural finance.* London, Institute of Public Policy.

Edelman (2021) *Edelman trust barometer 2021: Global report trust in financial services.* Available at: https://www.edelman.com/sites/g/files/aatuss191/files/2021-04/2021%20Edelman%20Trust%20Barometer%20Trust%20in%20Financial%20Services%20Global%20Report_website%20version.pdf (Accessed 19th June, 2021).

Elliott et al. (2011) *Transforming financial behaviour: developing interventions that build financial capability.* CFEB Consumer Research Report 01. July 2010. London: CFEB.

FCA (Financial Conduct Authority) (2013) *Applying behavioural economics at the Financial Conduct Authority.* Occasional Paper No. 1. April 2013. London. FCA Available at: https://www.fca.org.uk/publication/occasional-papers/occasional-paper-1.pdf (Accessed 18th June, 2021)

FCA (Financial Conduct Authority) (2016) *Packaged bank accounts.* Thematic Review TR16/8 October 2016. Available at: https://www.fca.org.uk/publication/thematic-reviews/tr16-8.pdf (Accessed 17th June, 2021)

FCA (Financial Conduct Authority) (2017) *Understanding the financial lives of UK adults: Findings from the FCA's Financial Lives Survey 2017.* London, FSA. Available at https://www.fca.org.uk/publication/research/financial-lives-survey-2017.pdf (Accessed 17th June, 2021)

FCA (2019) *Review on disclosure of costs by asset managers.* Available at: https://www.fca.org.uk/publications/multi-firm-reviews/review-disclosure-costs-asset-managers (Accessed 17th June, 2021)

FCA (Financial Conduct Authority) (2021a) *Monthly PPI refunds and compensation.* Available at: https://www.fca.org.uk/data/monthly-ppi-refunds-and-compensation (Accessed 18th June, 2021)

FCA (Financial Conduct Authority) (2021b) *Financial Lives survey.* Available at: https://www.fca.org.uk/publications/research/financial-lives (Accessed 19th June, 2021)

FCA (Financial Conduct Authority) (2021c) *A new Consumer Duty.* Consultation Paper CP21/13, May 2021. Available at: https://www.fca.org.uk/publications/consultation-papers/cp21-13-new-consumer-duty (Accessed 18th June, 2021)

Financial Conduct Authority (FCA 2021d). *Culture and governance.* Available at: https://www.fca.org.uk/firms/culture-and-governance (Accessed 18th May 2021)

Financial Stability Board (2013) *Principles for an effective risk appetite framework.* 18th November 2013. Available at: https://www.fsb.org/2013/11/r_131118/ (Accessed 18th June, 2021)

Holkar and Lees (2020) *CAUGHT IN THE WEB: Online scams and mental health.* December, 2020. London. The Money and Mental Health Policy Institute. Available at:

https://www.moneyandmentalhealth.org/wp-content/uploads/2020/12/Caught-in-the-web-full-report.pdf (Accessed 18th June, 2021)

House of Commons Treasury Committee (2008) *The run on the Rock*. Fifth Report of Session 2007–08 Volume I. London. TSO. Available at: https://publications.parliament.uk/pa/cm200708/cmselect/cmtreasy/56/56i.pdf (Accessed 18th June, 2021)

Hull, J. (2018) *Risk management and financial institutions*. 5th Ed, New Jersey, Wiley.

Instinctif Partners (2020) *Rebuilding relationships of trust in financial services*. Available at: https://instinctif.com/insights/rebuilding-relationships-trust-financial-services/0/ (Accessed 18th June, 2021)

Jarrow, R.A., 2008. Operational risk. *Journal of Banking & Finance*, 32(5), pp.870–879.

Kahneman, D. and Tversky, A. (1979). Prospect theory: An analysis of decision under risk. *Econometrica*, 47(2), pp.263–291.

Laris, G.F. (2020) Scandal or repetitive misconduct: Payment Protection Insurance (PPI) and the not so Little "Skin in Lending Games". *Seven Pillars Institute: Moral Cents*, 9(1), Winter/Spring 2020. Available at: https://sevenpillarsinstitute.org/wp-content/uploads/2020/05/PPI-Scandal-ED-2.pdf (Accessed 19th June, 2020)

Llewellyn, D. (1999). *The economic rationale for financial regulation*. London, Financial Services Authority. Available at: https://www.fep.up.pt/disciplinas/pgaf924/PGAF/Texto_2_David_Llewellyn.pdf (Accessed 18 May, 2021).

Lowe, J. (2017) *Consumers and competition: Delivering more effective consumer power in retail financial markets*. Financial Services Consumer Panel. London. Available at: https://www.fs-cp.org.uk/sites/default/files/fscp_consumers_and_competition_think-piece_finalpp_jtl_20170306.pdf (Accessed 1 May, 2021).

Luhmann, N. (1979) *Trust and power*. Chichester, John Wiley & Sons.

Lumpkin, S. (2010) Consumer protection and financial innovation: A few basic propositions. *OECD Journal: Financial Market Trends*, 2010(1), pp.117–139.

Lupton, D. (1999) *Risk*, London, Routledge.

MacLeod, P., Fitzpatrick, A., Hamlyn, B., Jones, A., Kinver, A. and Page, L. (2012) *Attitudes to pensions: The 2012 survey*. Department of Work and Pensions, Research Report No.813. London, DWP.

Martens, F. and Rittenberg, L. (2020) *Risk appetite – Critical to success*. Committee of Sponsoring Organisations of the Treadway Commission. Available at: https://www.coso.org/Documents/COSO-Guidance-Risk-Appetite-Critical-to-Success.pdf (Accessed 17th June, 2021)

MaPS (2020) *The UK Strategy for financial wellbeing: 2020–2030*. London. Money and Pensions Service. Available at: https://moneyandpensionsservice.org.uk/wp-content/uploads/2020/01/UK-Strategy-for-Financial-Wellbeing-2020-2030-Money-and-Pensions-Service.pdf (Accessed 17th June, 2021)

Morrison, C. (2019) *TSB IT meltdown cost bank £330m and 80,000 customers*. The Independent. 1st February, 2019. Available at: https://www.independent.co.uk/news/business/news/tsb-it-failure-cost-compensation-customers-switch-current-account-a8757821.html (Accessed 19th June, 2019)

NHS (2021) *Why we should sit less*. Available at https://www.nhs.uk/live-well/exercise/why-sitting-too-much-is-bad-for-us/ (Accessed 8th June 2021)

Penrose, G. (2004) *Report of the equitable life inquiry*. London. HMSO. Available at: https://assets.publishing.service.gov.uk/government/uploads/system/uploads/attachment_data/file/235298/0290.pdf (Accessed 19th June, 2021)

PwC (2021) Six key challenges for financial institutions to deal with ESG risks. Compliance and long-term value creation. Available at: https://www.pwc.nl/en/insights-and-publications/services-and-industries/financial-sector/six-key-challenges-for-financial-institutions-to-deal-with-ESG-risks.html (Accessed 26th June, 2021)

Resolution Foundation (2018) *COMPARE AND CONTRAST: How the UK comparison website market is serving financial consumers.* London, Resolution Foundation.

Ring, P.J., Bryce, C., McKinney, R. and Webb, R. (2016) Taking notice of risk culture – The regulator's approach, *Journal of Risk Research*, 19(3), pp.364–387.

Sapienza, P., Toldra-Simats, A. and Zingales, L. (2013) Understanding trust. *The Economic Journal*, 123, 1313–1332. doi:10.1111/ecoj.12036

Sheng, A., 1999, March. The framework for financial supervision: macro and micro issues. In *Strengthening the Banking System in China: Issues and Experience. A Joint BIS/PRC Conference* Held in Beijing, China, 1–2 March 1999 (No. 7, p. 154). Bank for International Settlements.

Sullivan, R., Martindale, W., Feller, E. and Bordon, A. (2015) *Fiduciary duty in the 21st Century.* Geneva, United Nations Environment Programme Finance Initiative.

Upton, M. (2007) *Northern Rock: a business model unravels.* Available at: https://www.open.edu/openlearn/money-management/money/accounting-and-finance/finance/northern-rock-business-model-unravels (Accessed 17th June, 2021)

Wicks, R. and Horack, S. (2009) *Incentives to save for retirement: understanding, perceptions and behaviour, A literature review.* Research Report No. 562, Leeds, Department for Work and Pensions.

CONCLUSION

Themes and trends in financial services

Lien Luu

Key points

- Financial services industry is rapidly changing due to technological developments, increasing customer expectations and the shocks such as the pandemic.
- Digital platforms, cryptocurrencies and decentralisation of financial systems have become conspicuous features.
- Consumers face new risks including data misuse, cybercrime and mis-selling.

As we have seen in this book, financial services form an intricate part of our lives and underpin everything we do. As Chapters 3–6 have shown, we rely on bank accounts to deposit money, receive salaries, pay our bills and manage our day-to-day finances; we use mortgages to purchase our homes; investment products to grow our assets; insurance to protect ourselves against unforeseen events; pension plans to save for our retirement; and annuities to prevent us from outliving our resources. In short, financial products are designed to serve our needs, support our aspirations and prepare us for the future.

The financial services industry is undergoing a process of radical transformation, as a result of technological innovations, changing consumer expectations and the pandemic. These changes, in turn, precipitate new risks (cybercrimes) and accentuate existing global challenges (environmental degradation, wealth inequality, low financial literacy), as outlined in Figure C.1.

This chapter examines these issues and in doing so, it builds on Chapters 7–12 by drawing attention to the future risks/challenges faced by government, regulators and consumers as they come to terms with the increasing pace of technological advances and its potential impact on financial markets in the future.

DOI: 10.4324/9781003227663-13

FIGURE C.1 Themes and trends in financial services.

Learning outcomes

- Understand key factors driving changes in financial services.
- Analyse the risks facing consumers.
- Evaluate the impact of global challenges on consumers.

C.1 Customer expectations

The financial services landscape is rapidly evolving in response to changing customer expectations, technological developments and the shock of worldwide
events like the Covid-19 pandemic. Customers' expectations towards financial
services are being driven by best practice in other sectors, such as Uber, which
has shown how a convenient, customer-focused approach can disrupt a market,
and Amazon, which seeks to meet, or even exceed, the demands of its customers
and has recently started providing deliveries as quickly as one hour after purchase
for some orders. Accustomed to these services, customers demand ease and accessibility, high-quality customer service, personalisation and near-instant gratification and resolution in financial services (Capgemini, 2020; Vishnoi, 2021).

Indeed, McKinsey believes that the 'white-glove service', traditionally offered
to wealthy customers, will be accessible to a wider market. This service is high
quality and personalised with solutions tailored to each customer's specific needs,
and is made possible by data and advanced analytics (Agarwal, Jacobson, Kline,
Obeid, 2020).

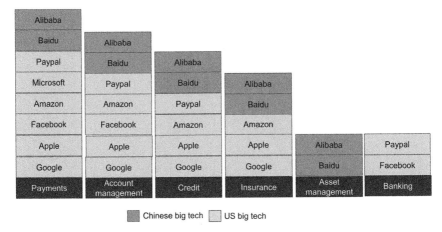

FIGURE C.2 BigTech and financial services.
Source: adapted from Wyman, 2020, p.16.

Research shows that two-thirds of millennials (67%) are open to using financial services from brands they trust, like Nike, Google and Apple (Akamai, 2021). According to Oliver Wyman (2020), many BigTech companies in the US are already offering some forms of financial services, and two even have the licence to operate as a bank. With their existing client base, they can move into other services such as mortgages, retirement and investments products. In China, BigTechs such as Baidu and Alibaba also offer asset management on top of other basic financial services products. This underlines the importance of reputation and trust to financial institutions and the work they have to do in this regard to maintain their position (see Chapter 12 Section 12.5) (Figure C.2).

C.2 Technology

As Chapter 7 on fintech has shown, technological changes are radically transforming the face of financial services, with fintech precipitating the rise of a decentralised financial system and invisible banks, as shown in Figure C.3. Blockchains and cryptocurrencies, for example, are being used to pay for financial transactions without paper money or credit cards, and some central banks (Sweden, China) are also starting to offer or are at least thinking about using national digital currencies. Robo-advisers provide portfolio management without investment managers, while mobile payments transform phones into payment cards (Akamai, 2021). Financial products and services are now available anytime, anywhere, 24/7, at the touch of button, offering convenience and satisfying desire for instant gratification (Marder, 2016; Target Group White Paper; WNS 2021).

The global pandemic has also accelerated changes in the way consumers engage with financial services. The temporary closure of banks and the scaling

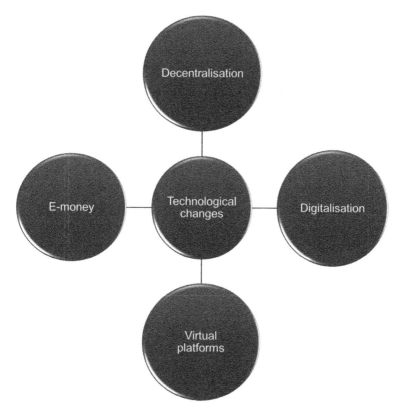

FIGURE C.3 Impact of technology.
Source: author's own diagram.

down of face-to-face operations during the lockdown forced many to turn to financial apps and digital banking. The use of financial apps rose by 72% in 2020, while 80% of consumers were reported to prefer digital banking (Target Group, White Paper, p.2).

The pandemic also accelerated the decline of cash as a method of payment, as the World Health Organization (WHO) recommended contactless payment as a way to curb the spread of the virus. Some South Koreans were reported to have taken the drastic action of burning cash to prevent the spread of the coronavirus, while Chinese banks used ultraviolet light or high temperatures to disinfect yuan bills, and then sealed and stored the cash for one to two weeks before recirculation (France-Presse, 2020). Thus, the pandemic helped spur the growth of contactless payments. According to UK Finance, cash now makes up just 23% of transactions in the UK, after debit cards and credit cards, while cards and contactless payments now account for more than half of all transactions conducted in the UK (Nixon, 2020). The global contactless payment market size is expected to nearly double in five years, increasing from $10.3 billion in 2020 to $18 billion by 2025, or at a compound annual growth rate (CAGR) of 11.7% (Forbes, 2021).

The use of contactless payments raises several concerns. First, a shift to contactless payments is reported to precipitate a rise in spending by 30%, as the non-cash method reduces the pain of paying (Cash Essentials, 2021). Second, as can be seen in Chapter 10, it also increases the risk of fraud, with criminals using a device, or a smartphone app, to read data from your contactless card, including the full 16-digit card number, the card type (Visa, MasterCard or similar), the issuing bank, the expiry date and the card owner's name, a process known as 'skimming'. With these data, criminals can commit fraud in two ways: create a cloned card with the original card details for use at older ATMs, shops or even websites with poor security checks, or sell the data. It is recommended that consumers can reduce this risk by taking the following measures: use RFID-blocking wallets, or a few sheets of thick tinfoil, to block criminals from stealing your card details using radio waves; and use systems like ApplePay and Google Wallet to give an extra level of security when paying as they do not transmit your card details without your consent (Love Money, 2021).

The move away from cash has also contributed to the rise of cryptocurrencies (or digital currencies), particularly bitcoin. In March 2020, each bitcoin cost $6,500, as it was still considered a fringe investment, and dismissed by Warren Buffet, a business tycoon, as having 'no value'. By March 2021, the price of bitcoin rose to nearly $59,000, an elevenfold increase, and has become a hot topic of conversations among big investors and Wall Street firms. The drastic rise in prices was due to the growing adoption of bitcoin as a hedge against the potential currency debasement, caused by the injection of trillion of dollars from central banks and governments around the world to offset the economic effects of the pandemic (Keoun, 2020; Statista, 2021a). However, such development is puzzling. Flight to gold in uncertain times, for example, is common because gold has some real-world uses (industry and jewellery) that may underpin its price to some extent. However, a flight to cryptocurrencies is more difficult to understand, and the argument that bitcoin has a limited supply is not very convincing. However, the outstanding performance of bitcoin relative to other asset classes makes it difficult for institutional investors to ignore it. Led by Blackrock (the world's largest asset mananager), a growing number of institutional investors are allocating a percentage of their portfolios to digital assets. It is estimated that $17 billion institutional capital has been invested in cryptocurrencies between 2020-21, as a portfolio diversification strategy. (Wintermeyer, 2021).

The increasing use of cryptocurrencies is undesirable from an environmental perspective. The energy required to add a transaction to a distributed ledger is huge, making widespread cryptocurrencies in current form unsustainable. One source calculates that one single transaction of bitcoin emits 742 kg of carbon dioxide, equivalent to the carbon footprint of more than 1.6 million VISA transactions or nearly 124,000 hours of watching YouTube. Alongside this massive energy consumption, the other problem is that most bitcoin mining is done in China, which relies heavily on coal-based power. Coal, in other words, is fuelling bitcoin, and so bitcoin mining is indirectly causing environmental damage

(Aratani, 2021; Digiconomist, 2021; Martin and Nauman, 2021). As can be seen in Chapters 10–12, a combination of technological change, pandemic and even environment is presenting new risks to consumers and regulators, as well as financial institutions themselves.

C.3 Customer-centric service

The Target Group, a business services provider in financial services, believes that technological changes will enhance customer experience in two main ways (Target Group). First, virtual platforms will become a more important medium for consumers to access financial products and services. They may be financially oriented, or holistic, offering whole of life solutions, such as Amazon. It is envisaged that the platforms will offer an interconnected network of services, products and solutions. For example, when we buy a house for the first time, we may be able to access all financial and non-financial services on a single platform – from estate agent, surveyor, solicitor, mortgage provider, insurer, removal company and even the retailers for new possessions we may need in our new house. On the one hand, it can be argued that the use of a single platform to access financial and non-financial services and products offers convenience and allows us to save time and avoid stress. On the other hand, this may lead to monopoly/oligopoly.

Secondly, it is believed that the platforms will not only serve as a one-stop shop but also offer us personal solutions. They use their technological power to aggregate data from different sources, permitted by Open Finance, analyse them and then create recommendations tailored to our needs and preferences. For example, the platform will have data on the house we want to buy, our finance and on the things we like. It can then make particular suggestions on room design and furniture. These will be presented to us, with a virtual tour of what our new house could look like with our new possessions in it. This level of personalisation requires a technology infrastructure that captures real-time insights using vast amounts of data from an array of sources. Data and analytics, powered by AI, are believed to hold the key to this personalisation of products and services (Forbes, 2021). However, the increasing use of technology raises fears of risks such as data misuse, cybercrime, mis-selling and ethical issues over data use, as discussed in Chapter 10 (FCA, 2020, p.4).

As the economy and financial system become more digitised, cyber risk is growing in scale. Indeed, the situation is exacerbated by the onset of the pandemic, which has led to a dramatic increase in the number of cyberattacks on the financial sector. Covid-19-related attacks, for example, are estimated to have grown from 5,000 per week in February 2020 to 200,000 per week in late April. The number rose further by around one-third in May and June 2020 compared with March and April (Aldasoro, Frost, Gambacorta and Whyte, 2021, p.6).

Working from home (WFH) is believed to be partly responsible for the rise in cybercrimes. Staff use work devices and access virtual networks from home. But sharing the same internet network with other members of their household exposes their work devices to malware that could then enter their firm's network. In addition, some videoconferencing facilities have also been shown to have suboptimal security standards, and this makes staff and financial institutions vulnerable to cyber risk (Aldasoro, Frost, Gambacorta and Whyte, 2021, p.6).

The use of technology enhances the ability to make near-instantaneous financial decisions, but this may not produce optimal outcomes. Financial decisions are complex and consumers need time for research, reflection, guidance or advice. This is essential because, as Chapter 5 has made clear, our behavioural biases (e.g. overconfidence, loss aversion, herd behaviour) cloud our judgement. Instantaneity in financial decisions, while satisfying our desire for immediate gratification, may not produce the best results. However, behavioural experts such as Thaler and Sunstein argue that, given human beings' cognitive biases, we can deliberately design how information and choices are presented to individuals so that we can 'nudge' them to behave in a certain way to achieve desired outcomes. For example, individuals can be made to save for retirement by being automatically enrolled into a pension scheme, a strategy known as automatic enrolment. In addition, they can be encouraged to save more by employing *Save More Tomorrow* strategies, whereby saving for retirement is set to increase in the future when pay rises. This makes this easier to adopt as it does not happen today and loss-aversion (e.g. pay goes down) is avoided as take-home pay is unaffected (Thaler and Sunstein, Chapter 6).

C.4 Globalisation

Financial services markets are global, interconnected and intertwined, making it prone to systemic risks. This is defined as the risk that 'a large part of the system ceases to function and collapses with potentially dramatic consequences for the system and its constituent parts' (Poledna et al., 2021). This is clearly demonstrated by the Great Financial Crisis of 2008 when the sub-prime mortgage crisis spread from the United States and the ensuing financial crisis engulfed the economy on all five continents (Huwart and Verdier, 2013).

Global economies are connected by inward and outward investments. Billions of pounds of financial investments flow into and out of the UK each year, as a result of a foreign company acquiring a UK company, a fund manager investing in foreign stock markets or someone setting up a savings account with an overseas bank. The value of UK investments abroad was worth around £11 trillion in 2017 (more than five times the value of UK GDP at £2 trillion), with a comparable value of foreign investments in the UK (ONS, 2018). This means that decisions made overseas can have a profound effect on the livelihood of those living in the UK, and vice versa. China is a bigger investor in Africa. In a space of a few years, China has established itself as one of the most active foreign energy players on the African continent, as it searched for more secure oil supplies in the face of static, if not declining, domestic oil production (IDE-JETRO, no date). It is estimated that Chinese foreign indirect investment in Africa was valued at

$110 billion in 2019, contributing to more than 16% of the total foreign direct investment in Africa (Statista, 2021b; Ze Yu, 2021). This means that decisions made in China can profoundly affect the lives of those in Africa.

Reinsurance also ties the fortunes of global economies, as domestic insurers seek to pass on the risks. As the centre for reinsurance, for example, London insures risks beyond its borders. When Christchurch (New Zealand) was devastated by an earthquake in 2011, London paid US$1.2 billion to help rebuild New Zealand's economy, which reinsured over 90% of its risk internationally (UK Parliament, 2021). Many international insurers also provide reinsurance for risks in Japan. The losses resulting from the tsunami in Japan in 2011 caused the share prices of European insurers to fall: Munich Re fell 3.4%, Allianz 2.9%, Aviva fell 3.1% and Axa 3.3% (BBC News, 2011). The interconnection of global economies means that losses caused by natural disasters and financial crises are dispersed through financial systems.

C.5 Global inequality

The wide disparity in global wealth distribution hampers economic growth and development and distorts the provision of financial services. Oxfam paints a gloomy picture of the global wealth distribution: where a tiny group of over 2,000 billionaires had more wealth than they could spend in a thousand lifetimes, where nearly half of humanity was forced to scrape by on less than $5.50 a day, where the richest 1% have earned more than double the income of the bottom half of the global population for the past 40 years. One estimate suggests it would take around 200 years at current rates to lift everyone above the $5.50 poverty line (Oxfam Media Briefing, 2020, p.4).

Inequality is a real concern because, according to Oxfam, it means that more people are sick, fewer are educated and fewer live happy, dignified lives. It also affects politics, as poverty nurtures extremism and racism and leaves many more people living in fear and many fewer in hope (Oxfam Media Briefing, 2021, p.11).

But there is also an environmental dimension to inequality. As people in the West and middle-income countries like China get richer, they spend more money on travel, road and air. Luxury goods, especially sport utility vehicles (SUVs) and private jets, are causing irreparable environmental damage. A recent study found that the richest 10% of households use almost half (45%) of all the energy linked to land transport (car journeys) and three-quarters of all energy linked to aviation (flights) (Oxfam, Sept 2020, pp.7–8). Transportation accounts for a quarter of global emissions, and SUVs were the second biggest driver of global carbon emissions growth between 2010 and 2018 (Milman, 2020).

Each year, SUVs emit 700 megatonnes of CO_2, equivalent to the entire output of the UK and the Netherlands combined. SUVs emit more CO_2 because they require more energy to move around as a result of carrying the weight of 'an adult rhinoceros' and the 'aerodynamics of a refrigerator' (Milman, 2020). In 2019, around 200 million SUVs were in operation worldwide, a near sixfold increase over 2010, when there were about 35 million such vehicles. The annual sales are 27 million units and the bestselling SUV model is Toyota RAV4 (Statista, 2020). There are calls for the government to curb the emissions through taxes and bans on luxury carbon such as SUVs and frequent flights (Oxfam International, 2020).

The demand for private jets is also going up. There are currently 4,600 private jets in operation, and it is expected that 7,600 new private jets will be purchased by multinational companies and the super-rich over the next decade. These are bad for the environment because each of them will burn, according to one estimate, 40 times as much carbon per passenger as regular commercial flights. Bill Gates, the Microsoft founder and world's second-richest man, is one of the identified 'super-emitters'. In 2017, he took 59 flights, travelling more than 200,000 miles. His private jet travel is reported to have emitted about 1,600 tonnes of carbon dioxide, in comparison to a global average of less than five tonnes per person (Neate, 2019).

Global warming has devastating consequences. During 2020, this has fuelled cyclones in India and Bangladesh, caused huge locust swarms that have devastated crops across Africa and resulted in unprecedented heatwaves and wildfires across Australia and the US. While no one is immune, the poorest and the most marginalised people are believed to have been hit the hardest (women are at increased risk of violence and abuse in the aftermath of a disaster) (Oxfam International, 2020). The World Bank has warned that an additional 100 million people may be living in extreme poverty by 2030 if no actions are taken to change the current climate crisis (Georgieva, 2020).

There is a growing global recognition of the need to take actions to tackle climate change. In 2019, for example, the UK government launched the Green Finance Strategy, outlining the role of the finance sector and better climate disclosure from corporate companies in tackling climate change and helping the UK to meet its net-zero emissions target (Davies and Green, 2019). Environmental considerations such as sustainability and low carbon economy are increasingly affecting some consumers' financial decisions, as can be seen in the increase in ESG (environmental, social and governance) investments. As Chapter 5 has shown, global ESG assets are expected to reach $53 trillion by 2025, representing more than a third of the projected $140.5 trillion assets under management (Bloomberg, 2021). As can be seen in Chapters 8 and 12, financial inequality has to be considered not just at a national level but on a global scale. It is also clear that risks which, on the face of it, are generally considered to be socio-scientific are coming to be seen, alongside the more traditional view of risk management, as key risks for the financial services sector.

C.6 Increasing complexity of financial services

Financial services sector has become increasingly more complex in the last decade in several ways. The scope of activities has increased significantly. The number of large banks, which combine commercial banking with investment banking and/ or insurance business, has grown. The scale of their operations has also increased, with banks merging within countries and also across borders (Parliament UK, 2009). In addition, there has been a surge in the number of products on offer. In 2016, for example, there were as many as 17,000 mortgage products on offer, falling during the pandemic to 5,000 by the end of 2020 (Campo, 2021). With increased complexity and choice, it is imperative that consumers have the financial knowledge and skills to enable them to make informed decisions.

C.7 Financial literacy

Claessens (2006) argues that finance is important for the well-being of individuals because it can smooth their income, insure against risks, broaden investment opportunities and reduce poverty and income equality (Claessens, 2006, p.207). However, as demonstrated in Chapter 12, consumers face the risk of vulnerability arising from a lack of financial awareness and capability.

The Standard & Poor's Ratings Services carried out a Global Financial Literacy Survey in 2014, the world's largest, most comprehensive global measurement of financial literacy. It surveyed 150,000 people in more than 140 countries to investigate knowledge of four basic financial concepts: risk diversification, inflation, numeracy and compound interest. The survey showed a great disparity in financial literacy. Developed countries have the highest financial literacy rates, with Sweden, Norway and Denmark having the best score of 71%, followed by Canada (68%), Israel (68%), United Kingdom (67%), the Netherlands (66%), with the US at 57%. At the other end of the spectrum are China scoring 28%, India 24%, but countries with the lowest scores are Albania (14%) and Yemen (13%) (Global Financial Literacy Excellence Center, 2021; Klapper, Lusardi, and van Oudheusden, no date, p.7).

However, the questions used by the Standard and Poor's survey, commonly employed in financial literacy tests, are too generic and unhelpful in identifying weak areas of personal finance. Freetrade, a digital investment app provider, created a *Great British Financial Literacy Test* in 2021, testing 2,000 respondents on 18 questions on savings, investment, ISAs and retirement, topics that most people have to deal with at some point in their lifetime. The result shows that nearly half (48%) were not able to answer questions such as what an ISA (individual savings account) stands for, the difference between fixed rates and variable rates and what annuity providers do (Lane, 2021).

As Figure C.4 shows, consumers' knowledge of retirement is poorest, with only 20% of the respondents able to answer this part of the test correctly. It is worrying that 81% of the over 55 age group, who are approaching retirement, failed to correctly answer the retirement questions. Understanding about investments was better, with only 44% unable to answer the questions correctly, followed by savings (34%) and ISAs (32%) (Lane, 2021).

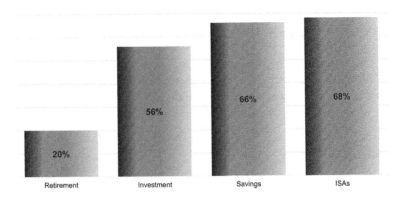

FIGURE C.4 Consumer knowledge of different areas of personal finance.
Source: Lane, 2021.

Low levels of financial literacy are a serious issue because they affect a consumer's ability to manage their personal finances, invest and make the most of their savings and planning for retirement. Low financial literacy affects individuals' financial confidence and well-being, with 88% of those surveyed confessing to lacking confidence, and one in three Brits (32%) admitting its impact on their mental health, as can be seen in Figure C.5 (Lane, 2021).

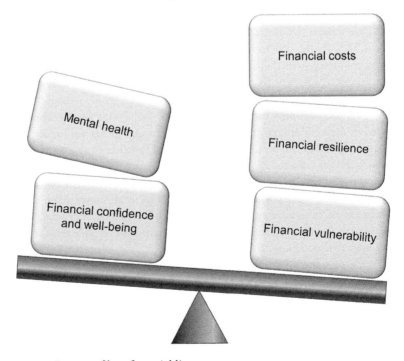

FIGURE C.5 Impact of low financial literacy.

It also affects their financial resilience and ability to deal with the unexpected. The outbreak of the pandemic in March 2020 caused 3.7 million more people to be financially vulnerable in the UK as a result of negative events such as redundancy and reduced working hours. The number of vulnerable adults in the UK, therefore, has reached nearly 28 million adults or 53% of the total adult population by October 2020 (FCA, 2021).

In the US, the Financial Educators Council has calculated the financial costs of low financial literacy. Their calculations show that respondents lost on average $1,634 in 2020 as a result of a lack of knowledge about personal finances. With a population of 254 million adults, a lack of financial literacy is estimated to cost Americans a total of more than $415 billion in 2020 (National Financial Educators Council, 2020).

In short, financial literacy is important, conferring financial and well-being benefits. Indeed, as Robert Kiyosaki, the author of *Rich Dad Poor Dad*, has aptly put it: 'Money is one form of power. But what is more powerful is financial education. Money comes and goes, but if you have the education about how money works, you gain power over it and can begin building wealth' (Kiyosaki, 2002).

As Figure C.6 shows, financial education has an important role in society, because it confers requisite knowledge to enable you to take advantage of financial opportunities and avoid financial exclusion.

This book has shown that financial services is integral to our own individual lives and collective well-being and offers a vast array of products and services to support our financial security. However, it also makes it clear that we face lots of risks, and that while regulation and government can help us in mitigating these, there are also potential challenges that we must tackle as individuals so that we become more capable to meet them ourselves. The size of the challenge is clear given the extent of financial exclusion, vulnerability and inequality that already exist. The inexorable expansion of technology and artificial intelligence may provide ways of addressing these issues, but they also present challenges of their own.

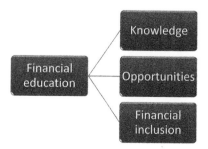

FIGURE C.6 The role of financial education.

We hope that this book has inspired you to develop a greater interest in financial services, helped you become more aware of the challenges facing us, enhanced your financial literacy skills and strengthened your knowledge of key personal finance topics so that you can take advantage of the financial opportunities now and in future.

Self-test questions

1 What are the most important factors driving changes in financial services?
2 How will customer experience be enhanced in the future?
3 What are the environmental concerns of using bitcoin and cryptocurrencies?
4 Discuss five underlying issues in financial services.
5 Briefly discuss five opportunities in financial services.
6 Which areas of personal finance consumers have the least knowledge of? What can be done to enhance financial knowledge?

Further readings

Claessens, S., 2006, 'Access to financial services: A review of the issues and public policy objectives', *The World Bank Research Observer*, Vol.21, no.2. Available at https://openknowledge.worldbank.org/handle/10986/16428.

International Regulatory Strategy Group (IRSG), no date, *Retail Financial Services Bringing Real Benefits to Europe's Customers*. Available at https://www.irsg.co.uk/assets/Retail-Financial-Services-Bringing-real-benefits-to-Europes-customers.pdf.

Klapper, L., Lusardi, A., van Oudheusden, P., no date, *Financial Literacy Around the World: Insights from the Standard and Poor's Ratings Services Global Financial Literacy Survey*. Available at https://gflec.org/wp-content/uploads/2015/11/Finlit_paper_16_F2_singles.pdf.

Target Group, no date, *The Future of the UK Financial Services Ecosystem*, White Paper. Available at https://www.bsa.org.uk/BSA/files/bf/bf62e093-6c20-46b9-b59c-e1adbb9303fa.pdf.

References

Agarwal, R., Jacobson, R., Kline, P., Obeid, M., 2020, 'The future of customer experience: Personalized, white-glove service for all', McKinsey & Company. Available at https://www.mckinsey.com/business-functions/operations/our-insights/the-future-of-customer-experience-personalized-white-glove-service-for-all. [Accessed 8 June 2021]

Akamai, 2021, 'The future of customer experience in financial services: How to fend off new competitors and meet rising customer expectations through web and mobile channels'. Available at https://www.akamai.com/uk/en/resources/our-thinking/for-cios/the-future-of-customer-experience-in-financial-services.jsp. [Accessed 8 June 2021].

Aldasoro, I., Frost, J., Gambacorta, L., Whyte, D., 2021, 'Covid-19 and cyber risk in the financial sector', *BIS Bulletin*, no. 37, 14 January 2021. Available at https://www.bis.org/publ/bisbull37.pdf. [Accessed 30 June 2021].

Aratani, L., 2021, 'Electricity needed to mine bitcoin is more than used by 'entire countries'', *Guardian*. Available at https://www.theguardian.com/technology/2021/feb/27/bitcoin-mining-electricity-use-environmental-impact. [Accessed 9 June 2021].

BBC News, 2011, 'Japan earthquake: Insurers hit by claim fears'. Available at https://www.bbc.co.uk/news/business-12731476. [Accessed 9 June 2021].

Bloomberg, 2021, 'ESG assets may hit $53 trillion by 2025, a third of global AUM'. Available at https://www.bloomberg.com/professional/blog/esg-assets-may-hit-53-trillion-by-2025-a-third-of-global-aum/. [Accessed 7 June 2021].

Campo, R., 2021, 'What to expect in 2021 | Mortgage market update', *Rose Capital Partners*. Available at https://www.rosecp.co.uk/news/mortgage-world-news/what-to-expect-in-2021-mortgage-market-update/. [Accessed 7 June 2021].

Capgemini, 2020, 'Everything will change, starting with consumer behavior and expectations toward FS providers'. Available at https://www.capgemini.com/2020/05/everything-will-change-starting-with-consumer-behavior-and-expectations-toward-fs-providers/. [Accessed 8 June 2021].

Cash Essentials, 2021, 'Despite risks, contactless payments accelerate in the U.K'. Available at https://cashessentials.org/u-k-contactless-payments-accelerate-despite-risks-of-fraud-and-over-spending/. [Accessed 9 June 2021].

Claessens, S., 2006, 'Access to financial services: A review of the issues and public policy objectives', *The World Bank Research Observer*, Vol.21, no.2. Available at https://openknowledge.worldbank.org/handle/10986/16428. [Accessed 5 June 2021].

Davies, P., Green, M.D., 2019, 'UK Government Publishes Green Finance Strategy'. Available at https://www.globalelr.com/2019/07/uk-government-publishes-green-finance-strategy/. [Accessed 7 June 2021].

Digiconomist, 2021, 'Bitcoin energy consumption index'. Available at https://digiconomist.net/bitcoin-energy-consumption. [Accessed 9 June 2021].

FCA, 2020, 'Sector views'. Available at https://www.fca.org.uk/publication/corporate/sector-views-2020.pdf. [Accessed 9 June 2021].

FCA, 2021, *Financial Lives 2020 Survey: The Impact of Coronavirus*. Available at https://www.fca.org.uk/publications/research/financial-lives-2020-survey-impact-coronavirus. [Accessed 7 June 2021].

Forbes, 2021, '6 trends that will shape the financial services industry in 2021'. Available at https://www.forbes.com/sites/googlecloud/2021/02/05/6-trends-that-will-shape-the-financial-services-industry-in-2021/?sh=46c337dd42b6. [Accessed 9 June 2021].

France-Presse, A., 2020, 'Chinese banks disinfect banknotes to stop spread of coronavirus', *Guardian*. Available at https://www.theguardian.com/world/2020/feb/15/chinese-banks-disinfect-banknotes-to-stop-spread-of-coronavirus. [Accessed 8 June 2021].

Georgieva, K., 2020, 'The financial sector in the 2020s: Building a more inclusive system in the new decade'. Available at https://www.imf.org/en/News/Articles/2020/01/17/sp01172019-the-financial-sector-in-the-2020s. [Accessed 7 June 2021].

Global Financial Literacy Excellence Center, 2021, *S&P Global Finlit Survey*. Available at https://gflec.org/initiatives/sp-global-finlit-survey/. [Accessed 10 June 2021].

Huwart, J., Verdier, L., 2013, *Economic Globalisation: Origins and Consequences* (OECD publications). Available at https://www.oecd-ilibrary.org/docserver/9789264111905-en.pdf?expires=1632046124&id=id&accname=guest&checksum=12456081A92EE84998D701A861285B76. [Accessed 8 June 2021].

Institute of Developing Economies Japan External Trade Organization (IDE-JETRO), no date, 'China in Africa'. Available at https://www.ide.go.jp/English/Data/Africa_file/Manualreport/cia_07.html. [Accessed 9 June 2021].

International Regulatory Strategy Group (IRSG), no date, *Retail Financial Services Bringing Real Benefits to Europe's Customers*. Available at https://www.irsg.co.uk/assets/Retail-Financial-Services-Bringing-real-benefits-to-Europes-customers.pdf. [Accessed 8 June 2021].

Keoun, B., 2020, 'Bitcoin prices in 2020: Here's what happened', *Coindesk*. Available at https://www.coindesk.com/bitcoin-prices-in-2020-heres-what-happened. [Accessed 9 June 2021].

Klapper, L., Lusardi, A., van Oudheusden, P., no date, *Financial Literacy Around the World: Insights from the Standard and Poor's Ratings Services Global Financial Literacy Survey*. Available at https://gflec.org/wp-content/uploads/2015/11/Finlit_paper_16_F2_singles.pdf. [Accessed 7 June 2021].

Kiyosaki, R., 2002, *Rich Dad Poor Dad: What The Rich Teach Their Kids About Money - That The Poor and Middle Class Do Not* (London: Time Warner).

Lane, D., 2021, 'How much do Brits understand about their own finances?' *Freetrade*. Available at https://freetrade.io/news/uk-financial-literacy-test. [Accessed 7 June 2021].

Lewis, R., 2021, '5 common behavioral biases and how they lead investors to make bad decisions', *Business Insider*. Available at https://www.businessinsider.com/behavioral-biases?r=US&IR=T. [Accessed 9 June 2021].

Love Money, 2021, 'Contactless payment security, concerns and considerations'. Available at https://www.lovemoney.com/guides/75138/contactless-card-payment-security-concerns-considerations-safety-fraud. [Accessed 9 June 2021].

Marder, T., 2016, 'Fintech for the consumer market: An overview', Consumer compliance outlook: Third issue 2016. Available at https://consumercomplianceoutlook.org/2016/third-issue/fintech-for-the-consumer-market-an-overview. [Accessed 8 June 2021].

Martin, L., Nauman, B., 2021, 'Bitcoin's growing energy problem: 'It's a dirty currency'', *Financial Times*. Available at https://www.ft.com/content/1aecb2db-8f61-427c-a413-3b929291c8ac. [Accessed 9 June 2021].

Milman, O., 2020, 'How SUVs conquered the world – at the expense of its climate'. Available at https://www.theguardian.com/us-news/2020/sep/01/suv-conquered-america-climate-change-emissions. [Accessed 9 June 2021].

National Financial Educators Council, 2020, 'Financial illiteracy cost Americans $1,634 in 2020'. Available at https://www.financialeducatorscouncil.org/financial-illiteracy-costs/. [Accessed 7 June 2021].

Neate, R., 2019, 'Super-rich fuelling growing demand for private jets', *Guardian*. Available at https://www.theguardian.com/environment/2019/oct/27/super-rich-fuelling-growing-demand-for-private-jets-report-finds. [Accessed 7 June 2021].

Nixon, G., 2020, 'Britain was going cashless before coronavirus hit, banking data shows: More than half of payments last year were made by card for the first time', *Thisismoney*. Available at https://www.thisismoney.co.uk/money/saving/article-8383733/Cash-just-23-transactions-2019-contactless-boomed.html. [Accessed 9 June 2021].

Office of National Statistics, 2018, 'Exploring foreign investment: where does the UK invest, and who invests in the UK?'. Available at https://www.ons.gov.uk/economy/nationalaccounts/balanceofpayments/articles/exploringforeigninvestmentwhere-doestheukinvestandwhoinvestsintheuk/2018-11-01. [Accessed 9 June 2021].

Oxfam International, 2020, 'Carbon emissions of richest 1 percent more than double the emissions of the poorest half of humanity'. Available at https://www.oxfam.org/en/

press-releases/carbon-emissions-richest-1-percent-more-double-emissions-poorest-half-humanity. [Accessed 7 June 2021].

Oxfam Media Briefing, September 2020, 'Confronting carbon inequality: Putting climate justice at the heart of the COVID-19 recovery'. Available at https://oxfamilibrary. openrepository.com/bitstream/handle/10546/621052/mb-confronting-carbon-inequality-210920-en.pdf. [Accessed 7 June 2021].

Oxfam Media Briefing, January 2021, 'The inequality virus bringing together a world torn apart by coronavirus through a fair, just and sustainable economy'. Available at https://oxfamilibrary.openrepository.com/bitstream/handle/10546/621149/bp-the-inequality-virus-250121-en.pdf. [Accessed 9 June 2021].

Parliament UK, 2009, 'Complexity in financial services'. Available at https://publications.parliament.uk/pa/ld200809/ldselect/ldeconaf/101/10106.htm. [Accessed 7 June 2021].

Poledna, S., Rovenskaya, E., Dieckmann, U., Hochrainer-Stigler, S., Linkov, I., 2021, 'Systemic risk emerging from interconnections: The case of financial systems', *OECD Library*. Available at https://www.oecd-ilibrary.org/sites/55ade69f-en/index. html?itemId=/content/component/55ade69f-en. [Accessed 2 July 2021].

Statista, 2020, 'SUV market – Statistics & Facts'. Available at https://www.statista. com/topics/6185/suv-market-worldwide/#:~:text=In%202019%2C%20around%20 200%20million, about%2035%20million%20such%20vehicles. [Accessed 7 June 2021].

Statista, 2021a, 'Bitcoin price from October 2013 to June 9, 2021'. Available at https:// www.statista.com/statistics/326707/bitcoin-price-index/. [Accessed 9 June 2021].

Statista, 2021b, 'Leading countries for FDI in Africa 2014–2018, by investor country'. Available at https://www.statista.com/statistics/1122389/leading-countries-for-fdi-in-africa-by-investor-country/. [Accessed 7 June 2021].

Target Group, no date, *The Future of the UK Financial Services Ecosystem*, White Paper. Available at https://www.bsa.org.uk/BSA/files/bf/bf62e093-6c20-46b9-b59c-e1adbb9303fa.pdf. [Accessed 8 June 2021].

Tayeb, Z., 2021, 'More companies, including PayPal and Xbox, are accepting bitcoin and other cryptocurrencies as payment. Others are weighing up their options', *Business Insider*. Available at https://www.businessinsider.com/more-companies-accepting-bitcoin-cryptocurrency-paypal-starbucks-2021-4?r=US&IR=T. [Accessed 9 June 2021].

Thaler, R. H., Sunstein, C.R., 2009, *Nudge: Improving Decisions About Health, Wealth and Happiness* (Penguin, London).

UK Finance, 2021, 'Fraud – The facts 2021: the definitive overview of the payment industry fraud'. Available at https://www.ukfinance.org.uk/system/files/Fraud%20 The%20Facts%202021-%20FINAL.pdf. [Accessed 9 June 2021].

UK Parliament, 2021, 'London market group', https://committees.parliament.uk/writtenevidence/25558/html. [Accessed 9 June 2021].

Vishnoi, L., 2021, '5 ways the financial services industry is adapting to customer expectations and trends in 2021', Acquire. Available at *https://acquire.io/blog/financial-services-industry-customer-expectations/*. [Accessed 8 June 2021].

Wintermeyer, L., 2021, 'Institutional Money Is Pouring Into the Cryto Market And Its Only Going to Grow', *Forbes*. Available at https://www.forbes.com/sites/lawrence-wintermeyer/2021/08/12/institutional-money-is-pouring-into-the-crypto-market-and-its-only-going-to-grow/?sh=329c11f14598. Accessed 19 September 2021.

WNS, 2021, 'Top trends in banking & financial services'. Available at https://www.wns.com/insights/articles/articledetail/547/top-trends-in-banking-and-financial-services. [Accessed 8 June 2021].

Wyman, O., 2020, *The State Of The Financial Services Industry 2020*. Available at https://www.oliverwyman.com/content/dam/oliver-wyman/v2/publications/2020/January/Oliver-Wyman-State-of-the-Financial-Services-Industry-2020.pdf. [Accessed 8 June 2021].

Ze Yu, S., 2021, 'Why substantial Chinese FDI is flowing into Africa'. Available at https://blogs.lse.ac.uk/africaatlse/2021/04/02/why-substantial-chinese-fdi-is-flowing-into-africa-foreign-direct-investment/. [Accessed 9 June 2021].

GLOSSARY

Active management Style of professional fund management where the aim is to beat the performance of a particular benchmark (such as sector performance or a stock market index) by picking which securities to invest in and the timing of purchases and sales.

Adverse selection Situation where, because of asymmetric information, sellers or buyers with the superior information withdraw from a market, causing doubts among remaining buyers or sellers as to whether the market price correctly reflects the risks or quality of item being traded, ultimately causing the market to collapse.

Affinity fraud Practice whereby a fraudster becomes a member of a group in order to persuade individual members to part with their money, typically by investing in a bogus scheme.

Arbitrage Simultaneous trading in two or more markets in order to make a profit from small price anomalies.

Asset price bubble Situation where the price of an asset rises substantially above the intrinsic value of the asset.

Asymmetric information Situation where one party to a contract or one group in a market has relevant information not available to others.

Austerity measures Measures taken by a government to reduce its spending with the aim of either reducing the outstanding amount of government debt or avoiding defaulting on the promised payments to holders of that debt.

Authorised corporate director A company authorised by the UK regulator to operate a particular type of investment fund (called an open-ended investment company or OEIC).

Authorised push payment (APP) fraud Tricking people into making legitimate bank transfers to accounts that are in fact operated by criminals.

Automatic stabilisers Increases in government spending (for example, on unemployment benefits) and falls in tax revenues that happen automatically when economic activity falls, thus offsetting a downturn in the economic growth, and vice versa in an upturn.

Bank rate (also called base rate) Interest rate under a control of the central bank, which it changes in order to influence the level of other interest rates in the economy. Typically, the rate of interest earned by commercial banks on money they must lodge with, or borrow from, the central bank.

Basic bank account Account with a bank that allows transactions to be made (such as receiving earnings and paying bills) but does not enable the holder to go overdrawn.

Boiler room scam Fraudsters posing as investment brokers cold calling people and use high-pressure tactics to persuade them to invest in schemes that are usually bogus.

Bonds An ambiguous term that is often used to mean *fixed income securities*, but may also refer to some types of saving product and some insurance-based investments.

Brexit The act and process of the UK leaving the European Union (a political and economic union of countries that share common trade, industrial, social and security policies).

Bullet payments A lump sum repayment of the whole amount of an outstanding loan - usually at its maturity date. Loans structured in this way, rather than being repaid gradually in instalments, are often referred to as balloon loans.

Business cycle The tendency of an economy to go through periods of buoyant activity and growth, followed by less active periods.

Choice architecture Organising the environment or framing options in such a way that a person is more likely to make an optimal decision.

Collective investment scheme Investment fund where money from many investors is pooled and invested on their behalf by a professional investment manager.

Consumption smoothing The process of balancing the spending and saving from income over the course of one's lifetime in order to maintain balance in one's standard of living. This can be undertaken at individual, household, or nation state level.

Cost-benefit analysis Assessing the viability of a policy or decisions by calculating the money value of the benefits less the costs taking into account that money received or paid today is valued more highly that the same amounts in future.

Council Tax A UK tax on property wealth although adjusted according to the number, and some characteristics of, the people living in the property.

Coupon The amount of income paid periodically by fixed income securities expressed as a set amount relative to the *par value*.

Credit rating agency (CRA) A company whose business is assessing the risk that the issuers of debt securities will not make the promised payments to investors. (Note that 'CRA' can also stand for Credit reference agency.)

Credit crunch A sudden reduction in the general availability of credit or significant restrictions in the conditions upon which credit can be obtained. May also be referred to as a credit squeeze or credit crisis.

Credit record Details of how a person manages their current and past borrowing which is routinely part of the information used to assess how likely they would be to default on a new loan or credit.

Credit union A cooperative organisation where members (who usually have some 'common bond' such as living in the same area or working for the same employer) pool their savings and can borrow from the pool.

Current yield The periodic income (coupons) from a fixed income security expressed as a percentage of the security's market price.

Deflation Reduction in the general level of prices over time (and the opposite of inflation).

Delegated monitoring Simply the delegation of a monitoring role to another. In the case of banking, it refers to role of monitoring borrowers being delegated to a bank by those whose money has been lent.

Demand-side Refers to issues and solutions that relate to the willingness or ability of people to consume good and services.

Dependency ratio The number of dependants in a population expressed as a percentage of the working-age population. Old-age dependency ratio counts the retired population as dependants, while the total dependency ratio includes children as well.

Deposit insurance A scheme, often run by an industry or government, to protect individuals' savings up to a specified amount in the event of a savings institution (such as a bank) going bankrupt.

Derivatives Securities whose value depends on that of some underlying asset (such as shares, mortgage-backed securities, currencies, interest rates, and so on).

Development policy Economic, social and political policies that aim primarily to reduce poverty and increase the economic growth of lower-income countries.

Digital exclusion Lack or reduced access to information and communications technology (ICT), for example, because of low skills, lack of confidence, unaffordability or lack of supply.

Discounted cash flow A flow of future payments where more distant payments are reduced (discounted) by more than nearer payments to reflect the lower desirability of distant payments due to the effects of, for example, inflation and risk of non-payment.

Dividend discount model (DDM) A reduced form of *discounted cash flow* equation that can be used to calculate the present value of the estimated stream of income from a company's *equities*.

Dividends   Income paid to shareholders out of a company's profits.

Duration   A measure of the sensitivity of a *fixed income security*'s price to changes in the general level of interest rates

Duty of care   An ethical or legal obligation to consider the well-being of specified people.

Economies of scope   The economic concept that the cost to produce a unit of any individual product will reduce as the range of products being produced increases.

Environmental Social and Governance (ESG)   Describes a set of criteria, goals or policies that are deemed to be socially desirable, such as combatting climate change, eradicating child labour and promoting gender equality.

Equities   (also called shares) Securities issued by a company that typically give the holder the right to vote at the company's general meetings and the possibility of receiving a share of its profits in the form of *dividends*.

Eurobond   A security issued in a different currency to that of the issuing country and traded in an international financial centre.

Financial deregulation   Removing legal restraints on how financial markets operate and relying instead on free-market forces to determine prices and the amounts supplied and demanded.

Financial exclusion   The inability of economic agents, such as individuals, households and firms, to access and use the financial services they need.

Financial inclusion   Beneficial usage of and smooth access to the formal financial system for all households and firms, in an efficient market environment.

Financial literacy   Having enough knowledge and skills to promote one's own financial wellbeing, including sufficient understanding of basic financial concepts, products and services, basic numerical ability and constructive attitudes towards money.

Fintech   The use of technology to enhance or automate financial services.

Fiscal deficit   A shortfall between the amount a government spends and the amount of income (such as tax revenues) that it receives.

Fiscal policy   Government policies that aim to influence the economy through changes in taxes and government spending.

Fixed income securities   (also called fixed interest securities or sometime *bonds*) Securities that represent loans to companies, government or other entities and typically promise to make regular payments of a fixed amount to the holders.

Floating exchange rate   The rate at which one currency can be exchanged for a different currency, where the rate constantly varies depending on the relative supply and demand for the currencies.

Free rider problem   A form of market failure arising when someone receives the benefit of a good without paying the whole cost e.g. a polluter receives the benefit of a less polluted world as a result of the efforts/costs incurred by other in cleaning the environment.

Front running   Practice whereby market professionals trade to make a profit from information ahead of dealing for their clients.

Futures   Contracts where buyer and seller agree to trade specified assets at an agreed price on a set future date and, in the meantime, the contracts themselves can be traded on an exchange.

G20   A council of nations comprising finance ministers and central bankers from 19 largest national economies and also the European Union, which makes non-binding agreements to promote global economic growth, trade and regulation of financial markets.

Gig economy   System where workers are hired by firms to do short-term tasks and are treated as self-employed rather than employees.

Gilts   (also called gilt-edged securities) Name given to fixed income securities issued by the UK government.

Global Financial Crisis (GFC)   A worldwide event that started in 2007 in which the banking system came close to collapse and which triggered an economic downturn in many countries.

Global South   Broadly used to mean Asia, Africa, Latin America and Oceania, especially lower-income countries in these regions.

Gross domestic product (GDP)   Broadly, a measure of the value of everything an economy produces (which can also be measured as everything it spends or receives as income).

Imputed income   Income that a person is deemed to have when their ownership of an asset means they save on expenditure - for example, the imputed income from home ownership can be measured as the rent that would otherwise have been payable.

Inertia   Behavioural tendency to stay with the current situation rather than go to the effort of making a change.

Inflation   Increase in the general level of prices over time.

Informationand Communication Technology (ICT)   Collective term for devices and related software that enable communication and access to information, such as phones, radio and television, and importantly these days mobile phones and the internet.

Insider dealing   The practice, often illegal, of trading in a securities market to make a profit based on information unavailable to other participants.

Interbank broker   A financial intermediary that specialises in carrying out deals between investment banks and other large financial institutions.

Interest   Income payments from borrowers to lenders or investors.

Intrinsic value   The underlying or genuine value of an asset (often its *present value*) which may differ from the price at which it is traded.

Know-Your-Customer (KYC)   Process which banks and other financial services firms must use to verify the identity of their customers and satisfy themselves that money deposited or invested is not the proceeds of crime.

Laissez faire   Describes a political or economic system where governments do not intervene in the working of free markets.

Leverage   A strategy that involves using credit to magnify the gains (but also losses) from an investment.

Liquidity insurance   Often an issue for banks, it refers to a bank securing the right to access liquid assets from a third party (often a Central Bank) in the event of extreme events creating liquidity problems for that bank. It avoids the need for the bank to hold excessive amount of liquid assets, or to have to quickly sell assets in difficult market conditions if such extreme events arise.

Macroprudential regulation   Financial regulation that aims to reduce risks to the functioning of the entire financial system (in other words to reduce *systemic risk*).

Maturity transformation   A key function of banks, it involves taking short-term sources of finance, such as deposits from savers, and using them to create long-term assets such as mortgages.

Means-tested   Describes welfare payments where eligibility is based on having low income and savings.

Median   A way of measuring an average, whereby the data values are ranked from lowest to highest and the middle value selected.

Merit goods   A good or service, such as education, that society as a whole deems to have greater value than the value placed on it by individual consumers, and so which tends to be under-consumed and under-produced unless the government intervenes.

Microfinance   (also called microcredit) Loans to people who typically do not have access to mainstream credit because their incomes are low or irregular and/or they have no collateral, usually to enable investment in a business and with the ultimate goal of reducing poverty.

Microprudential regulation   Financial regulation that focuses on the sound operation of individual firms.

Monetary policy   Policies (usually administered by a central bank rather than directly by government) that aim to influence the economy through changes in interest rates (via a change to bank rate) or the money supply.

Money laundering   Concealing the origins of the proceeds of crime by transferring them through legitimate financial institutions and businesses.

Money market   Market for fixed income securities with an original term ranging from overnight to less than a year.

Money market fund   Collective investment scheme that pools the money of many investors and invests it in the money markets.

Money purchase scheme   (also called defined-contribution scheme) Type of pension scheme where members, while working, build up their own personalised pot of savings that they can use to provide an income when they retire.

Moral hazard   The concept that, when the risk of an outcome is borne by someone else, this provides an incentive for the decision-maker to alter their behaviour.

Mortgage-backed securities Tradeable security that gives the holder the right to periodic payments derived from a bundle of mortgages bought from the original issuers.

Natural monopoly An industry that works most efficiently when there is one supplier typically because it requires a costly infrastructure and/or costs are substantially reduced when operating at large scale.

Neoliberal Describes a political and economic ideology that favours free-market capitalism, deregulation and low levels of government spending on public services and benefits.

Nominal Describes a variable expressed in money terms that has not been adjusted to take account of inflation.

Non-zero failure regime Regulatory regime that is prepared to allow firms to fail.

Nudge Using *choice architecture* to push someone subconsciously towards making an optimal decision.

Open-ended fund Investment fund that expands and contracts with the amount invested such that the price of units or shares in the fund directly reflects the value of the assets in the fund.

Options Contracts that give the buyer the right but not the obligation to trade specified assets at an agreed price on (or sometimes on or before) a set future date and, in the meantime, the contracts themselves can be traded on an exchange.

Over-the-counter (OTC) Describes trading in securities or other instruments where buyer and seller deal directly with each other rather than through a stock exchange.

Par value (also called nominal value) A unit of account used for describing the main features of fixed income securities.

Passive fund (also called tracker fund) Collective investment scheme that pools the money of many investors and invests it in such a way as to track the performance of a specified market index.

Passive income Income that accrues with minimal or no work, such as rental income from owning property or dividends from owning shares.

Passive management Style of professional fund management where the aim is to track the performance of a particular benchmark (such as a stock market index).

Password manager Computer software that takes over the chore of securely creating, storing and managing multiple passwords.

Payday lender Organisation that makes short-term loans (typically 30 days) to customers usually at very high rates of interest.

Peer-to-peer lending Arrangement whereby investors (lenders) lend money direct to firms and individuals, often through an online platform, with any intermediary (such as a bank) being involved.

Perfect competition   Idealised situation where there are so many buyers and sellers in a market, all with perfect information and equal power, that the market price correctly values their collective wishes.

Phishing   Practice of criminals sending emails that impersonate legitimate organisations and are designed to obtain personal and financial information for use in frauds.

Ponzi scheme   Fraudulent scheme that is promoted as an investment when in fact the so-called returns to earlier investors are financed from the amounts invested by later investors.

Precautionary savings   Money set aside to increase the saver's ability to cope with unexpected future events.

Present bias   Behavioural tendency to give too much weight to income or payments received or incurred today compared with the same amount later.

Present value (PV)   The price or lump sum today that is equivalent to the value of an asset's *discounted cash flow*.

Price walking   Business practice that involves systematically increasing the price charged to loyal customers while offering cheaper deals to new customers.

Progressive   Describes a tax system where the proportion of income taken in tax is higher for people on higher incomes than for those on lower incomes.

Prudential regulation   The legal framework focused on the financial safety and stability of institutions (micro-prudential regulation) and the broader financial system (macro-prudential regulation).

Purchasing power parity   A way of comparing variables expressed in money terms across different countries taking account not only of the exchange rate but also the price of a standard basket of goods and services in the different countries.

Real   Adjusted for inflation by stripping out increases due simply to rising prices.

Regressive   Describes a tax system where the proportion of income taken in tax is higher for people on lower incomes than for those on higher incomes.

Remittances   The transfer of money by a foreign worker in one country to family back in their home country.

Reserve currency   A trusted currency backed by a strong economy favoured for settling international trades and acceptable to central banks as part of their holdings of foreign exchange reserves.

Resolution procedure   Arrangement for the orderly wind-up of a firm that has failed or transfer of its business elsewhere with a view to causing minimal detriment to stakeholders and the system as a whole.

Rotating credit and savings association (ROSCA)   A group of people who informally agree to save regularly and lend to each other.

Salary-related pension scheme   A type of defined-benefit pension scheme, where members are promised a pension when they reach retirement whose level will be calculated by reference to their salary (eg average pay or final pay) while working and the number of years they have belonged to the scheme.

Securities Financial assets, such as equities, corporate bonds and government stocks, that can be traded often on stock exchanges or other markets.

Securitisation Converting one or more assets that have an income stream (for example, mortgage repayments or royalties on artistic work) into a security that can be sold to investors and traded between them.

Solvency 2 A 2016 European directive concerning the regulation of insurance firms with a particular focus on having adequate reserves to survive even extreme expected losses.

Special purpose vehicle (SPV) A company (or other legal entity) that is completely separate from the parent company, but whose activities are controlled by the parent company and typically limited to a narrow area, such as research or selling asset-backed securities.

Spot price The current market price at which an asset, currency or contract can be bought or sold with immediate effect.

Stagflation The combination of stagnant economic growth and high inflation.

Supply-side Refers to issues and solutions that relate to the production or provision of goods and services.

Swaps Contracts where the parties agree to exchange assets, currencies or rights attached to assets (eg the right to receive interest) - for example, exchanging fixed interest for variable payments.

Systemic risk In the context of regulation, the risk that events in a single firm could threaten the functioning of an entire industry or economy. In the context of investment (where it is also called market risk or beta), the risk inherent in the market or sector as a whole that cannot be diversified away by holding different securities in the sector.

Systemic stability Situation where *systemic risks* are low and manageable.

Third party insurance Insurance cover designed to pay out if the insured person injures someone else or damages someone else's property.

Unconventional monetary policy Where a central bank aims to reduce interest rates in the economy through the direct purchase of assets (such as government stocks and corporate bonds) using new money created by the central bank for that purpose.

United Nations (UN) An international organisation founded in 1945 through which 193 member states collaborate with the aim of finding shared solutions to common problems in order to benefit humanity.

Welfare state Provision by the state of services and cash benefits to promote or protect the well-being of the general population, for example health care and unemployment income protection.

Yield to maturity (YTM) (also called redemption yield) The interest rate that sets the *discounted cash flow* of all payments (*coupons* and final payment at maturity) from a fixed income security equal to its market price. It is the return that an investor buying at the current market price would get if they held the security until redemption.

INDEX